SELECTED READINGS IN SUPPLY CHAIN MANAGEMENT

DR PETER HINES
AND
PROFESSOR DAVID JESSOP (EDITORS)

Lean Enterprise Research Centre
Cardiff Business School
Tel: 01222 874544

for

The Chartered Institute of Purchasing and Supply
Easton House
Easton on the Hill
Stamford
Lincolnshire, PE9 3NZ
Tel: 01780 56777

Articles A and B: © Individual Authors, 1996
Articles C: © Institute of Logistics, 1996
Editorial Content: © Chartered Institute of Purchasing and Supply

ISBN No: 1 86124 000 9

Published by

The Chartered Institute of Purchasing and Supply
Easton House
Easton on the Hill
Stamford
Lincolnshire, PE9 3NZ

DISCLAIMER

These articles are for information only and though they are believed to be accurate their accuracy is not guaranteed and neither the copyright holders, nor the editors, the Chartered Institute of Purchasing and Supply or any of its officers or members shall be responsible for any negligent statement whether by error or omission in this information.

All information is provided on an understanding that the purchaser shall use his or her or its corporate skill and judgement in assessing the correctness of the statements made herein.

FOREWORD AND INTRODUCTION

Selected Readings in Supply Chain Management follows on from our **Selected Readings in Purchasing and Supply** published in 1993. The idea was, and continues to be, to bring together a collection of important articles relating to supply chains, already published elsewhere, but collected and collated to form a convenient 'reader' for students of supply related themes. We have found the 1993 publication useful in our teaching work, and have been pleased by the responses from both students and from other tutors, and have felt encouraged to put together a new collection.

The change in title from 'Purchasing and Supply' to 'Supply Chain Management' arises from a wish to differentiate this publication from its predecessor, and to reflect the now more widespread employment of the term 'Supply Chain' to cover all the elements of purchasing, supply and logistics work.

The readings are new, with the exception of two articles carried forward from the 1993 collection which are specifically referred to in a current CIPS study guide, and which, therefore can not be allowed to go out of print with the old edition. The articles in question are identified with an asterisk (*) in the contents pages.

Our publication continues with the aim of assisting the free flow of information to interested readers, and draws its content from the professional journals published by the Chartered Institute of Purchasing and Supply (CIPS) and the Institute of Logistic (IL). The Institute of Logistics is the successor to the Institute of Materials Management who supported the publication of the 1993 readings. The articles have been written by a range of authors from the academic world, consultancy and practice from the manufacturing and service providing sectors of the economy, and have been selected on the grounds of their originality, relevance to recognised study programmes and the extent to which they reflect emerging thinking and practice. The readings should be seen as an accompaniment to the established textbook which tend to cover the substance of their subject area, whilst, naturally, not reflecting the very latest thinking.

The intended readership consists of students pursuing the professional qualifications of the Chartered Institute of Purchasing and Supply and the Institute of Logistics. Students following supply chain themes on HNC, HND and first degree level qualifications will also find the readings to be of value. This should be particularly true of those who are undertaking one of the rapidly growing number of specialised supply qualifications at under and post-graduate level. In view of the fact that many of the articles included are concerned with practical applications, we also expect managers and decision makers to find the collection useful.

The editors would like to draw the attention of readers to the publication 'Case Studies in Logistics' assembled by them and published by the Institute of Logistics. Students and tutors interested in Materials Management and Logistics practice should find this volume helpful.

CONTENTS

Key to publications:

A   Purchasing and Supply Management
B   Logistics
C   Logistics Focus

Matrix of Core Subjects & Specialist Options
Contents
Structure

Chapter 1: Strategy

		Page
1.	Strategic Planning in Purchasing (A, 5/94) Eric Evans	1
2.	Global Purchasing in the Supply Chain (A,1/95) John Stevens	7
3.	Influencing the Strategic Agenda (A, 9/95) Andrew Cox, Jon Hughes and Mark Ralf	13
4.	Developing Purchasing Leadership, Competing on Competence (A,10/95) Andrew Cox, Jon Hughes and Mark Ralf	21
5.	Facilitating Strategic Change-the Key Role for Purchasing Leadership (A, 11/95) Andrew Cox, Jon Hughes and Mark Ralf	29

Chapter 2: Relationships

1.	Carmakers Shed Crocodile Tiers (A, 6/94) Ian Wagstaff	37
2.	Partnerships-What's Really Going On? (A, 7/94) Norman Hosford	40
3.	Implementing a Supply Chain Philosophy (B, 9/94) Keith Smith	45
4.	Capabilities Will Supersede Brands (B, 12/94) Phillip Hastings	49
5.	Supply Tiers, the Purchasing Challenge (A, 7/95) Chris Butterworth	51
6.	Adding Value, the Purchasing Mission (A, 7/95) Chris Butterworth	55
7.	Partnerships-What's Going on in UK SME's? (A, 10/95) Ram Mudambi and Claus Peter Schrunder,	61
8.	The Japanese System of Subcontracting (A,12/95) Howard Barnett, Reg Hibbert and Max Sculthorpe-Pike	65

9	Establishing and Maintaining Buyer-Supplier Relationships (A,) Vas Prabhu and Terry Miskell	*	71
10	Buyer Responsibility and supplier Development (A,) Max Munday	*	79
11	Co-Makership; a Worthwhile Word (A,) Kenneth Deans & Shaun Rejagopal	*	82

Chapter 3: Environment and Ethics

1.	Green Paths Through the Packaging Maze (A, 7/94) David Henderson	88
2.	Waste-A Supply Chain Issue (A, 7/94) Harry Whyte	91
3..	How Green are my Suppliers?-Buying Environmental Risk (A,10/94) Michael Lloyd,	94
5.	Getting Shot of it (A, 9/95) Martin Beauchamp	98
6.	Increasing the Efficiency, Lessening the Impact (C, 10/95) George Hazle	104
7.	Green Supply: Getting a Grip on Whole-Life Costs (A, 11/95) New, Green and Morton,	107
8.	Code or Codswallop, (A, 12/95) Dr. Kenneth Lysons	110

Chapter 4: Non Traditional Acquisition

1.	Contract Hire, Bed of Roses or Bed of Nails? (A, 6/94) Simon Marks	113
2.	Outsourced Everything Else? Why Not Purchasing? (A, 7/94) Martin Beauchamp	116
3.	Outsourcing the Purchasing Function (A, 9/94) Paul Chadwick,	122
4.	Investing in Capital Assets (A, 3/95) Surinder Mahta	123
5.	Global Purchasing and the Rise and Rise of Counter-trade (A, 9/95) John Stevens	126

Chapter 5: Logistics

1.	3C-A Method to Reach Total Customer Service (C, 4/95) Miguel Fernandez-Renada, F. Javier Gurrola-Gal and Enrique Lopez-Tello.	132

2.	Development of Pan-European Distribution Strategy (C, 4/95) Kirsten Tisdale	138
3.	Working as One (C, 9/95) Arthur Vonchek,	142
4.	Benchmarking Warehouse Operations (C, 1/94) Christine Rowat,	144
5.	The Roles of Stock in Logistics (C, 10/94) Anthony H. Lines	147
6.	UK Logistics Excellence (C, 8/95) Douglas Marr	156

Chapter 6: Performance

1.	Adding Value - The Purchasing Mission (A, 7/95) Stephen Cannon	160
2.	Managing Quality and Change-Improving the Purchase Process (A, 11/95) Bob Gilbert	166
3.	The Road to Purchasing Excellence (A, 6/95) Russell Syson	171
4.	Benchmarking for the Purchasing Process (A, 10/94) Eric Evans	176
5.	Electronics Heading for Sunshine State (A, 10/94) Malcolm Wheatley	182
6.	Life Cycle Costing and its Benefits (A, 10/95) Bob Fox	185

Chapter 7: Specification and Quality

1.	Product Change Without Supply Chain Tears (A, 9/95) Brian Davidson	191
2.	Quality: In the Eye of the Beholder, or the Small Print? (A, 5/95) Geoff Tyler	196
3.	Buying Managed Value (A, 12/95) Clive Bone	201

Chapter 8: Contracts and Law

1.	Guarantees Within the Aerospace Business (A, 11/95) Graham Grieve	203
2.	Strict Construction (A, 10/95) Peter Marsh	206
3.	Public Sector Risk and Contract Presentation (A, 3/95) Gareth Jones4. Contractual Management of Risk (A, 11/95)	210

4	Contractual management of risk David Pearson	216
5.	So, Farewell Then, Market Overt (A, 2/95) Professor Geoffrey Woodroffe	220

Chapter 9: Technology and Communications

1.	The Wireless Warehouse-And More (B, 12/94) Martin Hiscox	223
2.	Here's the Medium, What's the Message? (A, 12/94) Marcia Macleod	227
3.	Trading on the Net: Corporate Fears Assuaged (A, 5/95 Anon	230
4.	A Better Way of Extracting the Digits? (A, 12/95) Peter Robson	232

Chapter 10: Staff Development

1.	Purchasing Leadership and Competence Development (A, 5/95) Jon Hughes and Ian Billson	234
2.	Communications and Training Part 1 (A, 1/95) Stephen Cannon	240
3.	Communications and Training Part 2 (A, 2/95) Stephen Cannon	245
4.	Can You Create Your Own World Class Supply Chain? (A, 9/94) Peter Hines	252
5.	Best Practice Around the Supply Chain (B, 7/95) Keith Smith	256

Matrix of CIPS Core Subjects and Specialist Options

CIPS Core Subjects & Specialist Options

Table showing relevance of individual articles.
The table identifies the articles which will be of direct interest to students of the respective subjects. A number of articles appear in more than one row.

PSCM1. Strategy	1.1	1.2	1.3	1.4	1.5	2.5	2.6	3.8			
PSCM2. Tactics	7.1	7.2	7.3	9.1	9.2	9.3	9.4	10.4	10.5		
PSCM3. Legal Aspects	8.1	8.2	8.3	8.4	8.5						
Purchasing	3.3	4.1	4.2	4.3	4.4	4.5	6.1	6.2	6.3	6.4	6.5	6.6
Stores & Inv. Mgt.	5.1	5.3	5.4	5.5	9.1	9.4					
Distribution	3.1	3.2	3.3	3.4	3.5	5.2	5.3	5.6	10.1	10.2	10.3
Relationships	2.1	2.2	2.3	2.4	2.5	2.6	2.7	2.8	2.9	2.10	2.11	4.2

STRUCTURE

The structure of the journal is that articles have been divided into ten chapters covering a range of subjects of interest to those in the field of purchasing and supply. However, it is not easy to draw hard and fast distinctions between the majority of articles as the divisions between these artificial boundaries are increasingly being eroded. This having been said, the following journal layout will aid the interested reader in finding the desired article or articles.

Chapter 1: Strategy

There is nowadays a fairly general recognition that supply related activities involve more than meting operational 'service' needs. Nevertheless, the extent to which the strategic contribution is exploited is still rather limited. This chapter will help the reader to more fully comprehend the transition from service to strategy, and provides useful insights as to how some of the leaders in the field are embodying procurement policies into the corporate strategy.

Chapter 2: Relationships:

The themes in this chapter are related to those in chapter 1: Strategy. A key competitive benefit for many organisations is derived from not just the capabilities within the organisation, but also from the capabilities of its suppliers and of the suppliers' suppliers. The supply chain is increasingly seen as the competitive unit, and the articles in this chapter provide information on supply chains in general, and on 'tiering' in particular.

Chapter 3: Environment and Ethics

This chapter concerns itself with 'responsibility' in the supply chain. Responsibility to society in general, and responsibility in terms of the propriety of supply decisions and activities. Environmental themes of increasing importance such as ';whole life costing', recycling and environmental impact studies are commented upon by authors represented in this chapter, as are ethical codes and other guidance for those involved in making supply decisions.

Chapter 4: Non Traditional Purchasing

This chapter was included to provide a home for papers not readily accommodated in the mainstream of supply issues. Topics such as 'outsourcing', including outsourcing of purchasing; contract hire, 'customer focus', the acquisition of capital assets, barter and countertrade are referred to here.

Chapter 5: Logistics

The logistics chapter is concerned with movement, handling and storage, and with the flows of information necessarily associated with these activities. Whilst we would agree that by many definitions the scope of the word 'logistics' extends beyond these boundaries, we nevertheless could think of no more appropriate title for the chapter. The articles included cover a range of topics, including evolving Materials Management techniques, pan European distribution strategies and warehousing and stock management.

Chapter 6: Performance

The performance of the purchasing function or process is fundamental to company's ability to compete. As such a review of how internal purchasing performance can be measured and improved is of great importance. This chapter addresses this issues as well as reviewing how supplier performance can be improvement through the use of benchmarking, auditing and the use of Life Cycle Costing methods.

Chapter 7: Specification and Quality

The specification of suitable quality is addressed in the seventh chapter. Articles in this section focus on how quality can be built in through the new product development process together with a discussion of the BS 5750/ISO 9000 accreditation scheme. The latter is discussed in terms of why some firms are moving away from specifying this as a minimum supplier quality standard. In addition the extension of ISO 9000 to value management is reviewed.

Chapter 8: Contracts and Law

A sound knowledge of contracts and law has traditionally been a cornerstone of the purchasing profession. This chapter helps to draw attention to some new developments in this area. The articles cover the role of warranties and guarantees in the supply chain, risk taking in the public sector as well as new legislation concerning the construction industry and more generally in the sale of goods.

Chapter 9: Technology and Communications

One of the themes that is taking on greater importance for the purchaser is the role of technology and communications. This chapter summarises some of the newer developments in this area. The articles include the role of wireless communication in warehouse areas together with inter-company or inter-site communication mechanisms such as: Electronic Data Interchange (EDI), the Internet and the Integrated Services Digital Network (ISDN).

Chapter 10: Staff Development

The last chapter takes a look at staff development. This is done in two distinct ways. The first is a review of how internal purchasing staff can be developed along the lines required by their various customers. The three articles addressing this primarily focus on the development of senior purchasing staff. The last two articles take a rather broader based and more novel approach to development in terms of how companies can gain value out of networking with university partners.

CHAPTER 1. STRATEGY

In the first article in this chapter Eric Evans suggests that the benefits of implementing strategic approaches to purchasing are being ignored at Board level. Mr. Evans contends that purchasing should be measured by the extent to which it supports the achievement of corporate objectives, and makes a case for a strategic role for purchasing. A methodology for the development of purchasing strategies is outlined which, instead of following the 'where are we, where do we want to be? How do we get there? cycle, requires that the key strategic issues which purchasing needs to address are first identified, then action plans should be developed which define the core activities which purchasing is involved in.

The article on Global Sourcing by John Stevens makes the crucial point that Global Sourcing is not merely a synonym for international or foreign purchasing. A useful statement is made to the effect that Global Sourcing is the integration and co-ordination of procurement requirements across the world-wide business units (presumably of a Multi-National Corporation). Global Sourcing, we are told, looks at common items, processes, technologies and suppliers. It is clearly strategic in nature and must be implemented as part of the corporate plan. The article goes on to summarise some of the reasons why companies may 'buy foreign', and brings together the key points made by researchers and other writers on international and global themes.

This section of the readings includes three important articles written by Professor Andrew Cox, of Birmingham University, Jon Hughes, who is chairman and director of ADR International Purchasing Consultants, and Mark Ralf, Senior Vice President and Head of Global Purchasing for SmithKline Beecham. In these writings, which we believe will be influential, the authors contend that most organisations and purchasing functions are not leaders but laggards. Convincing arguments are made to this effect, built around six key propositions, some of the salient features of which are that there is insufficient integration of customer needs, business goals and valued purchasing outcomes, organisations sometimes pursue inappropriate types of relationship. Many organisations, it is suggested, are too tactical and short term in their thinking. A continuum is described in supplier relationships, ranging from competitive leverage through to preferred supplier status, then to performance partnership, on to strategic alliance and finally to co-development. The articles propose a methodology for the management of the strategic change which they regard as necessary in the role, contribution and position of purchasing and supplier development.

CONTENTS:

1. Strategic Planning in Purchasing (A, 5/94)
   Eric Evans

2.. Global Purchasing in the Supply Chain (A,1/95)
   John Stevens

3. Influencing the Strategic Agenda (A, 9/95)
   Andrew Cox, Jon Hughes and Mark Ralf

4. Developing Purchasing Leadership, Competing on Competence (A,10/95)
   Andrew Cox, Jon Hughes and Mark Ralf

5. Facilitating Strategic Change-the Key Role for Purchasing Leadership (A, 11/95)
   Andrew Cox, Jon Hughes and Mark Ralf

CHAPTER 2: RELATIONSHIPS

The first article in this chapter is an account by Ian Wagstaff of the movement of the European automotive components industry towards a tiered structure of the kind encountered in Japan. Although strenuous efforts are being made to reduce the number of direct or first tier suppliers, the total number of suppliers may not be significantly affected, the first tier (direct) suppliers managing the second and subsequent tiers on behalf of the vehicle manufacturer. As the author says, 'The days are past when the manufacture of a car was a two level operation, with component manufacturers simply supplying the VM direct. Now the operation has more of a pyramid structure. The first tier suppliers have a raft of second and third tier suppliers.

Norman Hosford in the second article explains the ways in which the formation of partnership sourcing arrangements may depend on a substantial experience of dealing with each other before the full benefits of partnering can be realised. The findings of research into which products and services will be identified by buying organisations as appropriate for partnership arrangements are discussed. A key conclusion is that partners are chosen on the basis of all round ability to provide quality products at a competitive cost and a willingness to become a partner and work towards continuous improvement.

The article on implementing a supply chain philosophy by Keith Smith explains his role as a neutral in chairing a supplier conference for a leading, blue chip UK food retailer. The objectives included, inter alia, encouraging closer links between the company and the invited suppliers, to review the Company's performance from its suppliers point of view and to develop projects for further liaison. The author makes an interesting comparison between the group of companies attending this meeting, and a formal Supplier Association.

The idea that capabilities will take the place of brands as competitive tools is explained by Phillip Hastings in the next article. The author acknowledges the predictions as those of Professor Martin Christopher, made at a seminar organised by Exel Logistics. The presentation made by Prof. Christopher is summarised, and it includes many leading edge ideas relating to supply chains, and a good deal of illustrative case history material.

Supplier Tiering is the theme of the article by Chris Butterworth. The author explains that whilst several major car producers are predicting significant growth in the outsourcing of components while simultaneously reducing the number of direct suppliers, the 'balancing act' may be more apparent than real. A direct consequence of this policy is that first tier suppliers will need to provide complete systems, requiring no pre-assembly before being fitted to the vehicle. It may well be that the first tier suppliers will have to increase their own supplier base to accommodate the new requirements of the system.

The article by Barnett, Hibbert and Sculthorpe-Pike is on the theme of the Japanese system of sub contracting. Insights into Japans organisational structures are given, and the evolution of the *shitauke* relationship is explained. There is further explanation of the idea of 'tiering', and notes are included on the technological and financial advantages and disadvantages of the Japanese approach to both client and sub contractor are given.

The last article in this chapter, written by members of the Business Economics department at the University of Buckingham, summarises a piece of research conducted into the status of buyer-seller relationships in UK small and medium sized enterprises. The conclusion seems to be that SME's may have a long way to go, but that they are moving in what the authors describe as the right direction.

CONTENTS:

1. Carmakers Shed Crocodile Tiers (A, 6/94)
   Ian Wagstaff

2. Partnerships-What's Really Going On? (A, 7/94)
   Norman Hosford

3. Implementing a Supply Chain Philosophy (B, 9/94)
   Keith Smith

4. Capabilities Will Supersede Brands (B, 12/94)
   Phillip Hastings

5. Supply Tiers, the Purchasing Challenge (A, 7/95)
   Chris Butterworth

6. Adding Value, the Purchasing Mission (A, 7/95)
   Chris Butterworth

7. Partnerships-What's Going on in UK SME's? (A, 10/95)
   Ram Mudambi and Claus Peter Schrunder,

8. The Japanese System of Subcontracting (A,12/95)
   Howard Barnett, Reg Hibbert and Max Sculthorpe-Pike

CHAPTER 3: ENVIRONMENT AND ETHICS

There is widespread and increasing recognition that those concerned with decisions relating to the acquisition of goods and services have a duty to consider the environmental and social implications of their actions. Whilst this section is mainly concerned with 'green' issues we have included an article on ethics in purchasing, an issue which we consider to be related.

In the first article David Henderson suggests that being 'green' is no longer a matter of fashion, it is considered by everyone to have an impact on profitability. The article is concerned with the EU packaging directive, and suggests ways in which packaging can be reduced. Recycling, re-use and refillable packaging is discussed.

The second article by Harry White is based on a paper presented in 1993 by Clive Rockingham and Nicola Eury. It is more directly concerned with the management of waste. The legal requirements are discussed, along with ways in which waste can be managed.

Michael Lloyd's article deals with the theme of environmental risk and its management. explaining an appropriate strategic approach, and raising issues relating to information technology and supply chain assessment. Two broad approaches are explained, namely the external certification of suppliers and the development of a company specific approach.

In 'Getting Shot of it' Martin Beauchamp looks at the disposal of surplus equipment, summarising the main approaches to disposal, and paying particular attention to environmental considerations.

New, Green and Morton in their article discuss how the first step towards green supply is whole-life costing. Their article is derived from research into green supply taking place at Manchester School of Management.

The final article in this section is concerned with ethical codes, and in it Dr. Kenneth Lysons looks at the theory and practice of ethical codes in business.

CONTENTS:

1. Green Paths Through the Packaging Maze (A, 7/94)
   David Henderson

2. Waste-A Supply Chain Issue (A, 7/94)
   Harry Whyte

3.. How Green are my Suppliers?-Buying Environmental Risk (A,10/94)
   Michael Lloyd,

5. Getting Shot of it (A, 9/95)
   Martin Beauchamp

6. Increasing the Efficiency, Lessening the Impact (C, 10/95)
   George Hazle

7. Green Supply: Getting a Grip on Whole-Life Costs (A, 11/95)
   New, Green and Morton,

8. Code or Codswallop, (A, 12/95)
   Dr. Kenneth Lysons

CHAPTER 4: NON-TRADITIONAL ACQUISITION

There is no unifying theme for this section which brings together a number of articles which, whilst not closely related in subject to each other, have in common the fact that they are concerned with approaches to acquisition which can be regarded as falling outside the 'mainstream'.

The themes of the articles are all clear from the titles, and provide a good understanding of the various topics addressed.

Each of them includes a different perspective on acquisition, ranging from the pros and cons of contract hire, through the possibility of outsourcing purchasing,, the acquisition of capital items and the practice of countertrade.,

CONTENTS:

1. Contract Hire, Bed of Roses or Bed of Nails? (A, 6/94)
   Simon Marks

2. Outsourced Everything Else? Why Not Purchasing? (A, 7/94)
   Martin Beauchamp

3. Outsourcing the Purchasing Function (A, 9/94)
   Paul Chadwick,

4. Investing in Capital Assets (A, 3/95)
   Surinder Mahta

5. Global Purchasing and the Rise and Rise of Countertrade (A, 9/95)
   John Stevens

CHAPTER 5: LOGISTICS

The first article in this section introduces a new Materials Management approach called '3C'. The 'C's' in question are Capacity, Commonality and Consumption, and the authors, all of whom are associated with AT and T in Spain, explain how 3C has the potential to generate improvements when applied to businesses dealing with unreliable forecasts.

Although labelled as a 'case study', Kirsten Tisdale's article is also a very useful note on the approach that might be taken when determining logistics and service strategies using a pan-European demand model.

Christine Rowat contributes a valuable article on benchmarking warehouse operations. Drawing upon contributions made at a 1995 conference organised by the National Materials Handling Centre, the author makes then point that the generic ideas associated with benchmarking can be usefully applied to specifics of warehouse operations and the identification of reliable performance measures.

The article 'Working as One' describes the formation of a 'think tank' of practitioners and consultants to facilitate debate on current and future supply chain issues.

The penultimate article in this section is another case study, but again is one which provides a valuable note on supply chain concepts, in particular on how established theories are only now finding practical application with the advent of low cost data processing capability.

The chapter is concluded by a piece by Douglas Marr, who explains how UK brewers and retailers, aided by large computer systems have used information which enabled accurate decision making to replace physical effort and inventory.

CONTENTS:

1. 3C-A Method to Reach Total Customer Service (C, 4/95)
   Miguel Fernandez-Renada, F. Javier Gurrola-Gal and Enrique Lopez-Tello.

2. Development of Pan-European Distribution Strategy (C, 4/95)
   Kirsten Tisdale

3. Working as One (C, 9/95)
   Arthur Vonchek,

4. Benchmarking Warehouse Operations (C, ??
   Christine Rowat,

5. The Roles of Stock in Logistics (C, ??
   Anthony H. Lines

6. UK Logistics Excellence (C, 8/95)
   Douglas Marr

CHAPTER 6: PERFORMANCE

This chapter collects a selection of the more important recent articles concerned with the performance of the purchasing process or of suppliers. The first work by Stephen Cannon is a summary of his collection of articles published in Purchasing and Supply Management. The article describes how purchasing offers internal customers three qualities: added value, service and expertise. His focus is thenceforth on added value or "savings generated". In order to maximise this added value Cannon suggests segmenting purchases into those carried out by internal customers with little purchasing involvement, those carried out by purchasing and joint purchasing activities. Bob Gilbert in the second article takes up the theme of improving the purchasing process. Bob shows that existing purchasing performance may not always be valued by internal customers. He analyses the current BT purchasing process and in a spirit of continual improvement suggests how the system can be improved.

Russell Syson in his work "The Road to Purchasing Excellence" reviews how purchasing can play a key role in achieving corporate success. He suggests that measurement is key to the role and future of purchasing. He goes on to provide a useful framework for measuring and understanding purchasing management. One of the tools discussed is benchmarking and the experience of IBM and Motorola is discussed. Picking up the same theme, Eric Evans provides a grounding in what benchmarking is and how it can be used by the purchaser. He discusses various types of benchmarking such as internal benchmarking, industry benchmarking and world class benchmarking.

Malcolm Wheatley, on a similar theme, reviews the use of vendor appraisal and the work that Sun Microsystems have undertaken to employ a simple but effective ways of measuring the performance of their suppliers. He describes the benefits of the system but also some pitfalls....like helping competitors to select your best in class suppliers for themselves.

The last article in this section focuses on the important concept of Life Cycle Costing and how this can be effectively employed in major capital projects. In doing this the important, but often neglected, aspects of ongoing maintenance costs is reviewed. The style of the piece is often list like rather than descriptive. However, this approach does have the benefit of providing a ready reckoning check-list for the reader should they wish to employ Life Cycle Costing.

CONTENTS

1. Adding Value - The Purchasing Mission (A, 7/95)
   Stephen Cannon

2. Managing Quality and Change-Improving the Purchase Process (A, 11/95)
   Bob Gilbert

3. The Road to Purchasing Excellence (A, 6/95)
   Russell Syson

4. Benchmarking for the Purchasing Process (A, 10/94)
   Eric Evans

5. Electronics Heading for Sunshine State (A, 10/94)
   Malcolm Wheatley

6. Life Cycle Costing and its Benefits (A, 10/95)
   Bob Fox

CHAPTER 7: SPECIFICATION and QUALITY

Chapter 7 contains three articles addressing the important areas of specification and quality. The first of these by Brian Davidson reviews the new product development cycle and the involvement of purchasing in this process. The purpose of this article is to identify supply chain issues which arise from the product change process. It reviews some of the problems of new product introduction such as linearity and the lack of supply chain integration. These problems, he shows, can result in long lead times, high inventory and a fire fighting mentality. A useful model is provided that shows better ways to modify existing products.

The articles by Geoff Tyler and Clive Bone discuss the role of the ISO 9000 standard. The first of these is a review of the backlash against "thou shalt have BS 5750/ISO 9000" as part of purchasing conditions. This backlash is being led by smaller firms mainly due to the relatively high cost of implementing often highly bureaucratic quality certification schemes. The theme of the article is refreshingly critical of ISO 9000 and shows evidence that many large purchasers such as BandQ are questioning whether suppliers must have the standard.

The last article in this chapter reviews the introduction of the ISO 9000 quality certification of value management. As Clive Bone explains "value management is the systematic and ongoing use of value analysis or value engineering methods on the supplier's part". Such a move enables purchasers to require suppliers systematically to value analyse their products and their means of production and distribution.

CONTENTS

1. Product Change Without Supply Chain Tears (A, 9/95)
   Brian Davidson

2. Quality: In the Eye of the Beholder, or the Small Print? (A, 5/95)
   Geoff Tyler

3. Buyer Managed Value (A, 12/95)
   Clive Bone

CHAPTER 8: CONTRACTS AND LAW

Graham Grieve, in the first article in this chapter, reviews how warranties and guarantees are passed up the supply chain in the aerospace industry. He suggests that these warranties are often after thoughts added by purchases to contracts. He goes on to explain the different types of warranties and guarantees used together with the role that purchasing plays in enlisting supplier commitment to them. He concludes by suggesting that these warranties are both important and need continuous enhancement. Peter Marsh, in the second piece discusses the importance of the Latham report in terms of liability in the construction industry. In essence the report suggests moving from joint liability to concurrent or 'fair proportion' liability. Lessons for other industries are also suggested.

The next two articles by Gareth Jones and David Pearson respectively review public sector risk exposure. The first of these looks at the conflict between safety and value which requires new tools for the public sector to manage effectively. Data presented shows the risk aversion of the public sector buyer; but often at the expense of costly fixed term contracts. This finding is associated with highly centralised purchasing with little use of incentive contracts. Following from this article are additional comments on how the public sector may manage risk by David Pearson. This latter article reviews the use of fixed pricing, contract price management, general contract management and performance measurement.

The last article in this chapter written by Geoffrey Woodroffe takes a look at the Sale of Goods Act and reviews its evolution after its 1994 amendment. Whilst far from entertaining in style, the short piece does highlight some important changes of which every purchaser should be aware..

CONTENTS

1. Guarantees Within the Aerospace Business (A, 11/95)
   Graham Grieve

2. Strict Construction (A, 10/95)
   Peter Marsh

3. Public Sector Risk and Contract Presentation (A, 3/95)
   Gareth Jones

4. Contractual Management of Risk (A, 11/95)
   David Pearson

5. So, Farewell Then, Market Overt (A, 2/95)
   Geoffrey Woodroffe

CHAPTER 9: TECHNOLOGY AND COMMUNICATIONS

The use of technology and communications in purchasing and supply is increasingly being seen as important by practitioners. This short chapter collects four aspects of this movement. The first by Martin Hiscox looks at the use of radio frequency communication in a logistics operation. This technology is being used in putaway, picking and shipping in industrial and retail warehousing, parts stores control and line feed in manufacturing as well as the control of containers and vehicles in docks and ports.

Marcia Macleod, in the second article, takes a look at Electronic Data Interchange (EDI) and in particular what is holding back its widespread take-off. However, her estimate of 1,000 UK users seems to be something of an underestimate as one single company such as Tesco may have more suppliers linked to it electronically than this number. However, her point is still well made. She finds that the largest barrier is the investment of time and money in the implementation stage. However, she discusses other major barriers such as standards and lack of company awareness.

In a similar vein, the third article discusses the use of the Internet by companies and by purchasing in particular. It again warns of potential problems such as corporate security. The article focuses on Digital's World Wide Web and how the server provider minimises such problems in their system. The last article by Peter Robson looks at the use of the Integrated Services Digital Network or ISDN. He reports that it now accounts for 20% of BT's new business exchange lines and is growing at an astonishing rate. The benefits of the system are reviewed and include speed, cost, flexibility, productivity enhancement and better customer service. The article concludes with a series of case studies of successful use.

CONTENTS

1. The Wireless Warehouse-And More (B, 12/94)
   Martin Hiscox

2. Here's the Medium, What's the Message? (A, 12/94)
   Marcia Macleod

3. Trading on the Net: Corporate Fears Assuaged (A, 5/95)
   Anon

4. A Better Way of Extracting the Digits? (A, 12/95)
   Peter Robson

CHAPTER 10: STAFF DEVELOPMENT

The last chapter deals with the development of staff in the purchasing and supply area. The first three articles address more traditional approaches to this task with the last two pieces suggesting a newer more novel approach.

The first article by Jon Hughes and Ian Billson outlines the application of competence analysis as a strategic tool for the development of staff. As noted in this work "purchasing leadership is characterised by the building of fundamentally different ways of working with suppliers, developing a strong external focus on sourcing strategies that support business needs, creating internal platforms for change through the development and application of reliable purchasing processes and ensuring appropriate collaboration with internal customers, clients and cross-functional groups". The article provides a useful example of the integration of business requirements and staff development needs in Figure 2 together with a competency profiling and purchasing planning two-by-two matrix (Figure 3).

The next two articles, both by Stephen Cannon, carry on this theme and review the role of communications and training. The first of these focuses broadly on this vital but often neglected part of the purchasing manager's role whilst the second looks more at marketing the function. Both articles make good use of simple diagrams. The first looks at perceptions of purchasing and suggests an appropriate communication and training approach to address any problem areas. The second article reviews where communications needs are at their greatest. It then suggests how teambuilding, training and staff development can lead to better performance and quality of service.

The last two articles in this chapter focus on how companies can gain insights, knowledge and experience of world class practice in the supply chain by joining inter-company networking groups facilitated by academic partners. The first of these by Peter Hines takes a look at the Supply Chain Development Programme run by Cardiff Business School and the University of Bath. This work focuses particularly on the retail, FMCG, automotive and electronics industries. The article shows how this programme involves: an assessment of the areas for improvement within member firms (and their supply chains), a focused programme of research activities, subsequent analysis, synthesis and piloting together with significant dissemination and piloting.

The last article by Keith Smith takes a look at a similar initiative at the University of Northumbria where a Logistics Best Practice Club has been formed. The focus of the article is on how this group was formed and what activities the ten members undertake. The early results of this work are reported together with "a real sense of excitement in company to company learning which rubs off on everyone involved".

CONTENTS

1. Purchasing Leadership and Competence Development (A, 5/95)
   Jon Hughes and Ian Billson

2. Communications and Training Part 1 (A, 1/95)
   Stephen Cannon

3. Communications and Training Part 2 (A, 2/95)
   Stephen Cannon

4. Can You Create Your Own World Class Supply Chain? (A, 9/94)
   Peter Hines

5. Best Practice Around the Supply Chain (B, 7/95)
   Keith Smith

Chapter 1 Strategy

Strategic Planning in Purchasing

Eric Evans suggests that the benefits of implementing strategic approaches to purchasing are being ignored at Board level

In recent years the demands placed upon purchasing have both increased and changed. Short-term competitive demands have continued to define cost pressures, and these have been supplemented by lead time, quality and time-to-market tensions. There is now a well documented assortment of purchasing tools, techniques and approaches to these issues.

But purchasing has also been thrust into a more strategic role as the business world has become increasingly dynamic and change seeking. In this environment, purchasing is more than ever required to contribute to and support corporate strategy rather than simply obtain requirements cost-effectively against a materials schedule.

In addition to support for corporate strategy there are many other strategic issues now facing purchasing. The supply markets and economic and legislative changes which have always provided a backdrop for purchasing are now increasingly coming to the fore and purchasing management needs to take a strategic view of the supply issues facing the business today and a pre-emptive view of the issues likely to face the business in years to come. Supply sources in eastern Europe, mergers and joint ventures amongst multi-nationals in many industries, EAN coding and the increasing 'threat' of legislation and control over purchasing activities from Brussels are typical of the issues facing many purchasing managers which need to be addressed in a coherent way.

Organisational culture is also changing in the 1990s, and this provides a third reason why purchasing management needs to be more strategic in its thinking. Management styles based upon empowerment and devolved authority have a significant impact upon purchasing, and it is no longer sufficient for purchasing management simply to insist that its 'internal customers' follow contracts and procedures laid down with the intention of harnessing spend. Public sector agencies have experienced the difficulties which untying customers from centrally negotiated agreements have caused. The NHS Supplies Authority is beginning to feel the impact and the private sector will increasingly experience the effects if the trend towards empowerment and devolved authority continues.

Over the last few years, it has increasingly become standard practice to define and publish a purchasing strategy which has the endorsement of the Board of Directors. This strategy is expected to cover support for corporate objectives, plans to deal with key supply issues which will hit the business and approaches to internal customers which recognise that purchasing is a business process in which other business functions have a legitimate interest. There are a number of reasons why purchasing directors and managers have found this a positive move:

- *a unifying sense of purpose and direction*

At operational level in purchasing there is often a failure to differentiate between means and ends. It is not uncommon to find staff who have lost sight of the true objectives which they should be pursuing. The buyers at one client were intent upon reducing the size of the supplier base without any consideration of the criteria which should be used for deleting or retaining suppliers. The decision was made on price, and some of the buyers were successful in removing key suppliers from their portfolio without consideration of wider issues.

The development of a purchasing strategy allows those involved in purchasing to understand why things are being done in a particular way so that dogma and ill-considered actions are replaced by a unifying sense of purpose and direction.

- *Synergy with the corporate plan*

Purchasing should be measured by the extent to which it supports the achievement of corporate objectives. If purchasing staff do not have a clear appreciation of exactly how they can support the organisation, they are unlikely to be making the maximum contribution possible.

One food industry client had decided that its corporate strategy was to emphasise the quality of its products. This it saw as means of differentiating itself from its competitors and allowing a premium price for its products, something which was necessary if it was to survive. The buyers continued to buy as they had always bought - on price. Specifications were reduced, price was the key criterion, and to achieve it suppliers were taken on and discarded without a thought. It was almost as though the buyers were doing everything possible to undermine the corporate strategy.

Defining the purchasing strategy and the extent to which it supports the corporate strategy helps to make sure that this cannot happen.

- *A long-term framework for short-term decisions*

A number of management decisions have long-term consequences. The specification of a computer system, the decision to insist upon BS5750 for approved suppliers, even the man-specification for the post of buyer are all examples. No manager should take such decisions without considering the implications and consequences of his actions, yet frequently decisions are taken which have long-term implications but which are viewed as short-term only.

Supplier selection criteria, allocation of work responsibilities, choice of training programmes, all fall into this category. There are also instances where no decision is made, but rather the previous decision is merely repeated.

The development of a purchasing strategy helps to ensure that short-term decisions are made within a long-term framework.

- *Optimisation of resources*

Time is a finite resource and few purchasing managers have sufficient resources to do all that they wish. Choice has to be made, therefore, and resources have to be allocated on a prioritised basis.

Developing a purchasing strategy helps management to think through the issues, determine the priorities and therefore optimise the use of resources.

- *The increase in supply market complexity*

Technology is changing at a faster rate than ever before. Products are hitting markets with shorter development times. Suppliers are ceasing to trade at unheard of rates. Mergers and acquisitions reduce effective competition and lead to changes in the balance of power within supply markets, and economic and legislative change adds to the complexity of life.

A strategy helps to identify the critical issues and to define interventions in markets which will have a significant and beneficial effect. It helps to identify pre-emptive measures which can make the difference between wasted effort and success and which can lead to the development of a competitive edge.

- *Defining a new role for purchasing*

Developing a purchasing strategy can also raise the profile of the purchasing function, secure corporate commitment and backing for initiatives which cross functional boundaries, and lead to the development of a more pro-active role for the purchasing function.

Without this backing there is little chance of securing the unambiguous corporate commitment which is needed to implement approaches such as Business Process Re-design.

Those organisations which have developed Board-endorsed purchasing strategies tend to have reached the stage where they are managing supply markets, have identified the strategic initiatives which will provide competitive advantage, have a sense of purpose which pervades the organisation and emphasise added-value activities which provide a return for the organisation.

So how are such strategies developed?

The core strategic issues

There are a number of approaches to developing purchasing strategies, and most follow a standard approach which takes in:
- where are we now?
- where do we want to be?
- how do we get from A to B?

This is an eminently sensible approach, but one which can be tortuous and with the wrong initial emphasis. A shorter and more direct approach has proved itself on consulting assignments in a variety of industries. The approach involves two distinct elements.

First of all, it is necessary to define the key strategic issues which purchasing needs to address. Secondly action plans need to be developed which define the core activities in which purchasing is involved.

In defining key strategic issues, it is important to break down the corporate goals and objectives in such a way that the purchasing contribution to each objective can be identified. From previous consulting assignments these goals and objectives have included the obvious and obscure such as:
- taking out cost quickly and substantially
- improving supplier quality
- reducing stock levels, and keeping them down
- shortening the 'time to market' cycle
- eliminating unproductive activity and thereby reducing staffing levels and overheads
- protecting or guaranteeing sources of supply
- outsourcing or market testing key activities
- avoiding Government enquiries into methods of operation.

Having broken down the corporate plan there is a need for some form of stakeholder analysis. This involves identifying all of those with an interest in the way that the purchasing process is carried out and reaching an understanding of their needs and interests. The intention is to make sure that purchasing is focused on providing what is required. Figure 1 lists some typical stakeholders and their possible interests. In developing a strategy, stakeholder analysis must involve discussions with key stakeholders. It is not enough to assume that their requirements are obvious. No salesman or market research organisation would assume an understanding of their customer's needs, and we have no right to assume that we understand the needs of our 'internal customers' and other stakeholders. It is not surprising that the organisations which have achieved a high level of co-operation with internal customers have done so with discussions on how purchasing can best satisfy explicitly stated customer needs.

Having identified the ways in which purchasing can contribute to corporate success, and selected the key stakeholders and developed an explicit understanding of their requirements it is necessary to be forward looking.

Anticipating other issues

One of the tools most frequently used in developing strategies is SWOT analysis where strengths, weaknesses, opportunities and threats are identified. This can be a useful tool, but frequently produces no more than a lot of debate as to whether something is a strength or a weakness, an opportunity or a threat. It may also produce four lists, and the question then is 'What do we do with this?' A variation on SWOT analysis is perhaps more helpful to determine the strategic issues which purchasing will face in the future.

First of all, a brainstorming session is needed to identify the issues (not opportunities and threats) which the purchasing function is going to face in the future. These might include, for example:
- difficulty in recruiting staff of the right calibre
- suppliers going out of business
- increasing use of technology
- patents leading to monopoly supply sources
- exchange rate fluctuations.

For each of these issues it is then necessary to identify relevant strengths and weaknesses which exist. It should be noted that something should only be regarded as a strength or weakness if it relates to one of these issues. The table illustrates how this might look.

FIGURE 1 Stakeholder analysis

Stakeholder	Possible Interest
Senior Management	Cost containment No purchasing difficulties Confidence that things are done well
Internal customers	Promises kept Certainly Minimal bureaucracy Advice Freedom to be unconstrianed by approaches to purchasing which are not considered appropriate
Purchasing Staff	Recognition An opportunity to achieve Management support The tools and training to do the job
Suppliers	Consistency of approach Early warning of changes To know where you stand Payment on time

By linking strengths and weaknesses to issues, we develop an understanding of the strengths we need to build upon, and the weaknesses which require urgent action.

Developing a vision
The stakeholder analysis and the contribution needed to support corporate objectives then needs to be distilled into a series of critical success factors. These are the factors which provide direction for the development of the strategy. Many organisations now have corporate visions or mission statements which succinctly summarise the critical success factors. Some have produced mission statements or visions for the purchasing function.

The vision needs to be more than motherhood and apple pie. It needs to be built from the critical success factors and focus attention of those things which are important. The best mission statements have a tangible quality which can be brought to life.

The critical success factors are, generally speaking, not capable of quantification, but they can in turn be broken down into a number of quantifiable business objectives. Once quantifiable business objectives have been set, the cascade process continues and a series of strategic initiatives are developed which will lead to the achievement of the objectives, which in turn, will make the critical success factors live, and in turn, make the vision a reality.

The beauty of this approach to developing a purchasing strategy is that it has a number of by-products including a performance measurement system for the purchasing department, and a series of strategic initiatives which can then be incorporated in the performance appraisal system as individual objectives.

Supplier strategies - supplier engineering
In addition to an overall purchasing strategy, there is often the need for a strategic approach at supplier level. Most purchasing managers are well versed in the techniques of pareto analysis, and will be aware of their pareto 'A' class suppliers. Most will also have identified their vulnerable or weak suppliers and their preferred or 'partnership' candidate suppliers.

Some have progressed with the principles of supplier assessment to the point where they are practising supplier engineering. This idea is based upon the principle that rather than simply select suppliers, purchasing managers should be seeking to develop their suppliers.

A simple matrix is first developed in which the vertical axis shows Tomorrow's (preferred) suppliers, Today's (average) suppliers and Yesterday's (unsatisfactory) suppliers. The criteria on which the suppliers are to be assessed are represented on the horizontal axis. In the example shown below, it has been decided that the most important criteria are manufacturing capability, quality, information, and 'actions'. In developing a strategy, management will need to define the most appropriate criteria for themselves.

It is then necessary to define the characteristics of Tomorrow's suppliers etc against these criteria. Figure 2 is meant to illustrate the basis upon which this can be done.

Each supplier will have a particular profile. Supplier A in Figure 3 is highly regarded, but with weaknesses in manufacturing. It would be in the buyer's interests to improve his performance in this area, and supplier engineering involves sitting down with the supplier, giving feedback on his performance, and working with him to determine how he is going to improve his performance in this area.

FIGURE 2 Basis for Supplier Engineering

Tomorrow's Suppliers	FMS JIT	TQM Zero defects	EDI Bar coding	"Star Trek"
Today's Suppliers	EBQ	AQL	Direct Access	Follow change
Yesterday's Suppliers	Poor	Poor	Sales driven	Resist change
	Manufacturing	**Quality**	**Information**	**Action**

FIGURE 3 Supplier A

Tomorrow's Suppliers	FMS JIT	TQM Zero defects	EDI Bar coding	"Star Trek"
Today's Suppliers	EBQ	AQL	Direct Access	Follow change
Yesterday's Suppliers	Poor	Poor	Sales driven	Resist change
	Manufacturing	**Quality**	**Information**	**Action**

Commodity strategies

The strategic approach may also extend to particular commodities. There is a distinction between being sold to, buying and managing the marketplace. If buying organisations are to get close to the stage where they are managing supply markets, they will need to have developed strategies for each of their commodity groups.

The starting point should be an assessment of the risk inherent in each of the major commodity groups. By identifying the risks involved in each commodity group, it is possible to pre-empt high risk and high impact supply problems. This is best carried out by a form of Failure Mode and Effects Analysis. This involves a simple three column analysis, usually produced on a spreadsheet. The starting point is the identification of the risk associated with each commodity group. These risks may include:

- supply industry or supplier weakness
- long supply chains
- political instability in the country of origin
- risks inherent in the manufacturing process or product itself
- possible supply and demand imbalances
- quality problems.

An attempt is then made to quantify the risk of each of these failure modes occurring, usually by attaching a probability figure.

Against each of these failure modes, the seriousness of the failure in terms of the implications for the buying organisation is then quantified.

The third column identifies and quantifies the predictability and ease of avoidance of such problems occuring, which is again quantified.

Each row on the spreadsheet is then totalled by multiplying the risk probability by the impact factor by the predictability/avoidance score to produce a vulnerability score. Management now has a basis for prioritising risk and determining action plans in advance of a problem. Figure 4 shows a simple example, suggesting that the quality problems at supplier Y are the most pressing management priority.

FIGURE 4 Example

	Probability 1 = low 9 = high	Seriousness 1 = low 9 = high	Predictability 1 = high 9 = low	Risk Priority Number
Supplier X ceasing to trade	3	8	4	96
Quality problems at supplier Y	2	8	8	128
Difficulties in relation supplier from Bosnia	8	2	2	32

Matrix analysis has also become a fashionable business tool for purchasing managers. The ease of use of the tool and the flexibility it brings to commodity analysis are the source of its power. It has a number of different uses. Matrices can, for example, chart:
- spend against risk of non-supply
- spend against implications of non-supply
- risk of non-supply against implications of non-supply
- strength of buyer against strength of supplier
- supplier profitability against industry profitability

One of the benefits of this analysis is the resulting though process which identifies options for each quadrant of the matrix. Figure 5 illustrates this.

Supplier and commodity strategies cannot, of course, be viewed in isolation. As part of the commodity strategy there needs to be a justification for the sourcing strategy. This should include consideration of issues such as:
- the benefits and potential problems associated with partnership
- the need to develop new sources of supply
- the opportunities to reduce the size of the supplier base
- the size of supplier to be used.

FIGURE 5 Possible supply strategies

	Low value spend	High value spend
High consequences of non supply	Change spec Stock Dual purpose	Partnership
Low consequences	Wholesaler Delegate Imprest	Opportunistic

Conclusion

Marketing strategies have been accepted as key business tools since the 1950s and manufacturing strategies and logistics strategies have been part of business planning since the late 70s. To date, written and articulated purchasing strategies approved by a Board of Directors are the exception rather than the rule.

The rigour of developing a written strategy document for discussion at Board level is helpful in ensuring that purchasing plans have been well thought through and flaws in logic have been identified and appropriate action taken. The process is not necessarily time consuming, but can lead to the focused and shared sense of purpose which so frequently accompanies success.

Global purchasing in the supply chain

There is more to a global purchasing strategy than simply 'buying foreign' writes John Stevens

Global purchasing should be seen as distinct from international or foreign purchasing. International purchasing suggests that firms are buying from foreign suppliers. Typically there is a lack of co-ordination of requirements between business units. Global sourcing, however, is the *integration* and *co-ordination* of procurement requirements across the worldwide business units, looking at common items, processes, technologies and suppliers. It is clearly strategic in nature and must be implemented as part of the corporate plan. There are several reasons why a company may adopt a 'buy foreign' policy in the procurement of materials. Some of these include:

Materials not available domestically
Home-based manufacturers may be unable to supply specific goods. They may be unable to meet the required delivery dates, or the supply of these materials is beyond their technical capabilities.

Unsatisfactory quality of goods from the home market
The quality of components available from the home market may not be satisfactory. The quality available from domestic suppliers may not be sufficient for the company to sell its product to international markets that demand high standards. The supplier perhaps may be offering unsatisfactory warranties, or after-sales service.

Price
The price of materials supplied by domestic suppliers may be too high and cheaper elsewhere around the world.

Technology
A company may have no choice but to source internationally in order to acquire world-class levels of technology.

Compensation and counter-trading
Compensation trading or counter-trade is defined as any sales in which payment is made at least partially with goods rather than money. World reciprocal trading is estimated to be running at about $150,000,000,000 per year. Many developing countries require their non-domestic suppliers to purchase materials in their country, their reserves are so low that unless special arrangements are made they will be unable to pay for imports.

A study by *Purchasing* (USA) in June 1987 identified lower price as the biggest reason (74 per cent) for companies adopting a foreign sourcing policy; better quality came second; and 'only source available' third. The full results are shown in Figure 1

FIGURE 1 Why buyers buy foreign

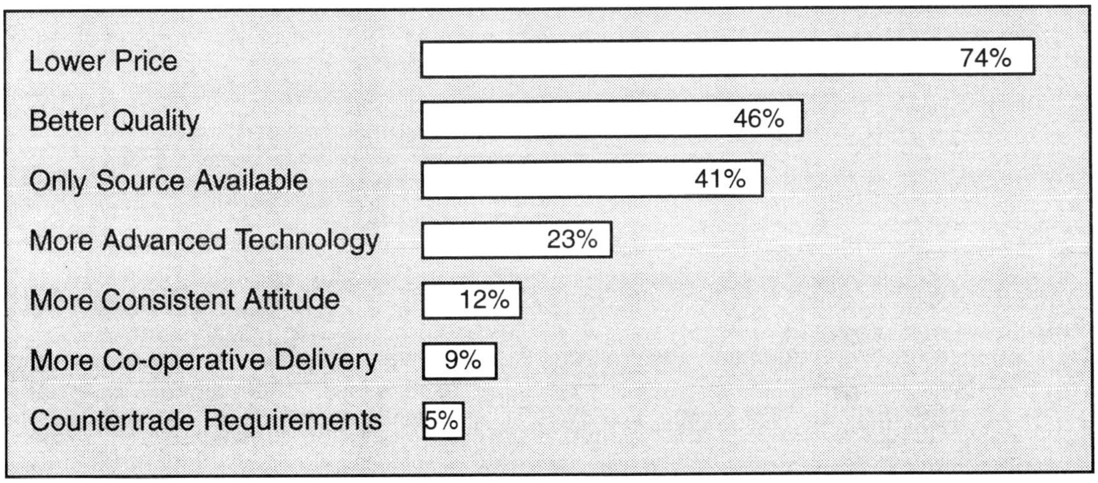

Lower Price	74%
Better Quality	46%
Only Source Available	41%
More Advanced Technology	23%
More Consistent Attitude	12%
More Co-operative Delivery	9%
Countertrade Requirements	5%

In 'Patriotism is not enough' (*Purchasing & Supply Management* January 1993), Unger identified lack of availability as the reason for American companies increasingly sourcing away from traditional home markets. A startling example was the Boeing Aircraft Company, which once imported fewer than 4 per cent of its parts from overseas, but will import approximately 20 per cent of the airframe for its new 777. US-based suppliers neither have the technologies nor are competitively priced for the company to continue to source key components within the country.

Current thinking, however, suggests that merely 'buying foreign' is not able to produce optimum solutions. A two-year study by Michigan State University, published as 'Competitive Strategies for the 1990s' identified four factors which firms felt would determine their future success. These were:
- Achieving a position near to being the lowest cost producer
- World class quality levels
- Development of innovative product technology
- Ability to move from concept to market in reduced time.

British writers have begun to consider the importance of a global purchasing strategy. MJ Saunders in *Strategic Purchasing and Supply Chain Management* (Pitman 1994 Page 81), refers to International and Global operations as meaning the same, but he does suggest that with the existence of three big trading blocs, Europe, North America and the Pacific Rim countries, changes to trading policies may be required. Moving forward from mere exporting and importing between these theatres might take the following developments, Saunders suggests:

(1) The development of value chains throughout the world, as operations to make and supply products or services become distributed on a global scale.'

(2) 'An intermediate choice may be related to the choice of one or more of the key regional blocs as the focus for the main activities.'

Indeed this was put forward by Richard Lamming at the International Communications for Management Conference in January 1991 in a paper entitled 'Global Sourcing and Lean Purchasing' which was aimed at bringing together these two seemingly disparate strategies.

In essence the argument made was that say, a European manufacturer might use one of a number of strategies:

(1) Source with a European 'local' supplier who is part of a global network.

(2) Source with a foreign supplier who supplies to a foreign part of your global network

(3) Source with a foreign supplier who has European support eg R&D intelligence.

(4) Maintain your own support (R&D intelligence) in a foreign country and source there

Global sourcing then might start with a regional focus eg in the Americas, or Europe or the Pacific Rim. From here the approach might be developed as follows:-

(1) To select global locations for manufacturing/support operations.

(2) To develop a supply base with a corresponding global network.

(3) To develop a local supply arrangement in each location with the ability to cross-trade to supply niche requirements.

Lamming summarised the 'squaring' of lean purchasing and global sourcing in a typical matrix model (Figure 2).

Global sourcing involves integration and co-ordination in two respects - the internationalisation of purchasing activities and the adoption of a strategic orientation for all resource management. The goal of global sourcing is to use purchasing potential on the worldwide level.

Figure 2 Lean purchasing and global sourcing

	SUPPLIER LOCAL	SUPPLIER GLOBAL
LOCAL SUPPLIER	NO GLOBAL BENEFIT	CUSTOMER PROVIDES GLOBAL BENEFIT TO CUSTOMER
GLOBAL SUPPLIER	CUSTOMER PROVIDES BENEFIT TO SUPPLIER	FULL GLOBAL BENEFIT

In *Global Sourcing - An Indispensable Element in Worldwide Competition,* Ulli Arnold identified global sourcing as being a critical factor in a variety of competitive strategies which included:-

(1) Supporting a global strategy by realizing economies of scale through material inputs

(2) Supporting a multinational strategy by developing potentials for differentiation, and by having an active influence on quality standards.

(3) Supporting a strategy concerning the general improvement of input-output relations.

Given the performance requirements to sustain global competitiveness, global sourcing has a very clear role to play in the future success of manufacturers.

In *Global Sourcing: A Development Approach* Monczka & Trent identified four stages that firms went through as they moved from domestic purchasing to a global procurement strategy. Whilst stage 1 represented the least sophisticated level of purchasing, stage 4 was the most advanced level, and saw the development of full global procurement strategy. Their model is shown in Figure 3.

FIGURE 3 Internationalisation of the procurement process

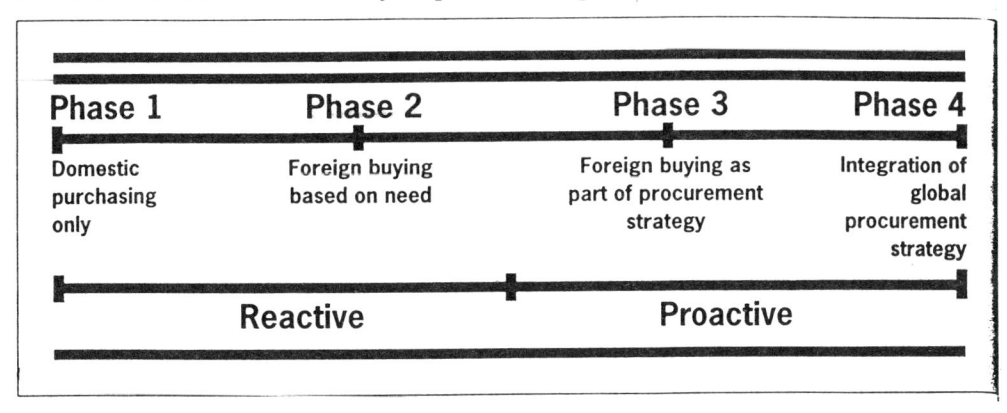

Phase 1	Phase 2	Phase 3	Phase 4
Domestic purchasing only	Foreign buying based on need	Foreign buying as part of procurement strategy	Integration of global procurement strategy

Reactive — Proactive

They went on to identify 5 strategies firms went through in the development of a global strategy:

STRATEGY 1: *Domestic buyers designated by the business unit for international purchasing*

The initial strategy employed by firms pursuing proactive international purchasing is the designation of a buyer with responsibilities for international purchasing.

STRATEGY 2: *Business units use subsidiaries or other corporate units for international sourcing assistance*

The next stage in the strategy progression is the expanded use of external sources of information and expertise. They include the use of subsidiaries and other corporate strategic business units.

A foreign-based subsidiary can perform a variety of functions for the domestic firm. Some of their advantages to the parent company include:

- Knowledge of local suppliers by foreign unit
- Proximity to foreign suppliers
- Knowledge of foreign business practices
- Better communication skills with non-English speaking suppliers.

STRATEGY 3: *International purchasing offices established throughout the world*

The needs of domestic buying units are not always provided by the support of foreign corporate units or local affiliates. The response has been the establishment of international purchasing offices (IPOs).

Foreign buying offices typically are staffed almost exclusively with foreign nationals who usually report to a corporate procurement office. The IPO tasks often include:

- Identification of foreign suppliers for company operations
- Expediting and tracing shipments
- Negotiating supply contracts
- Ensuring that the buyer and seller understand all communications
- Obtaining samples
- Managing technical samples
- Acting as the sole representative of the firm to the supplier
- Managing counter trade
- Obtaining design and engineering support
- providing quality focus.

STRATEGY 4: *Assign design, build and sourcing responsibility to a specific business unit somewhere in the world.*

This strategy recognises that within a firm, one unit may have comparative advantage in technology, manufacturing or distribution. By exploiting such advantages, the firm can attain results superior to normal expectations.

For example, the Ford Motor Company procurement strategy involved centralising the development of a car or a component wherever Ford has the greatest world-wide experience. Ford of Europe is recognised as having a comparative advantage over the rest of the firm in the small car market. Because of this advantage it developed a common suspension and floor pan for compact cars sold in Europe and the US.

STRATEGY 5: *Integration and co-ordination of worldwide global sourcing strategy.*

This involves integration and co-ordination of a firm's procurement requirements. Its main objective is to maximise the buying leverage of the firm on a global basis. Business units must be committed to using common worldwide sources of supply to achieve maximum procurement benefits.

Figure 4 shows the relationship between the five strategies. Firms that employ strategies 4 & 5 will get the maximum benefits, but must be prepared to commit resources to achieve this.

FIGURE 4 International versus Global Sourcing: the performance gap

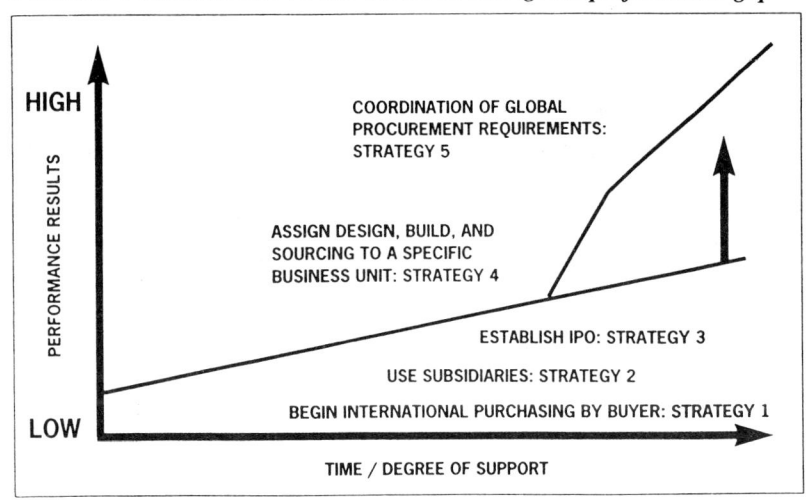

Perhaps the most interesting example of a company at stage 5 is the Xerox organisation. In 1982 Xerox, in conjunction with its Japanese subsidiary Fuji, discovered a 30-40 per cent disparity between copier manufacturing costs for Xerox and its Japanese competition. The purchased material costs in machine manufacturing were running at approximately 80 per cent of total manufacturing costs. The company's study concluded that costs had to be reduced worldwide whilst quality improved if the company was to sustain a competitive position in the marketplace.

The company's answer was to introduce Centralised Commodity Management. The company identified geographical areas of excellence where groups of products would be competitively priced at world class quality levels. These groups or 'commodities' were allocated to commodity managers who would be based within these geographical areas. Each commodity manager was made responsible for the co-ordination of the company's material requirements, and buys for the plants no matter where he or she is situated in relation to them. The company found that by and large commodity classes tended to be clustered in large geographical areas. For example, the company sourced motors, machining, air moving devices and transformers from Europe, recognising that area's technical lead in the manufacture of these products, whilst the company purchased electrical and mechanical parts from the Far East.

To adopt a global procurement policy, the company also developed its procurement organisation to reflect these commodity groups and their location around the world. The company's organisation structure is shown in Figure 5.

FIGURE 5 Xerox worldwide procurement group

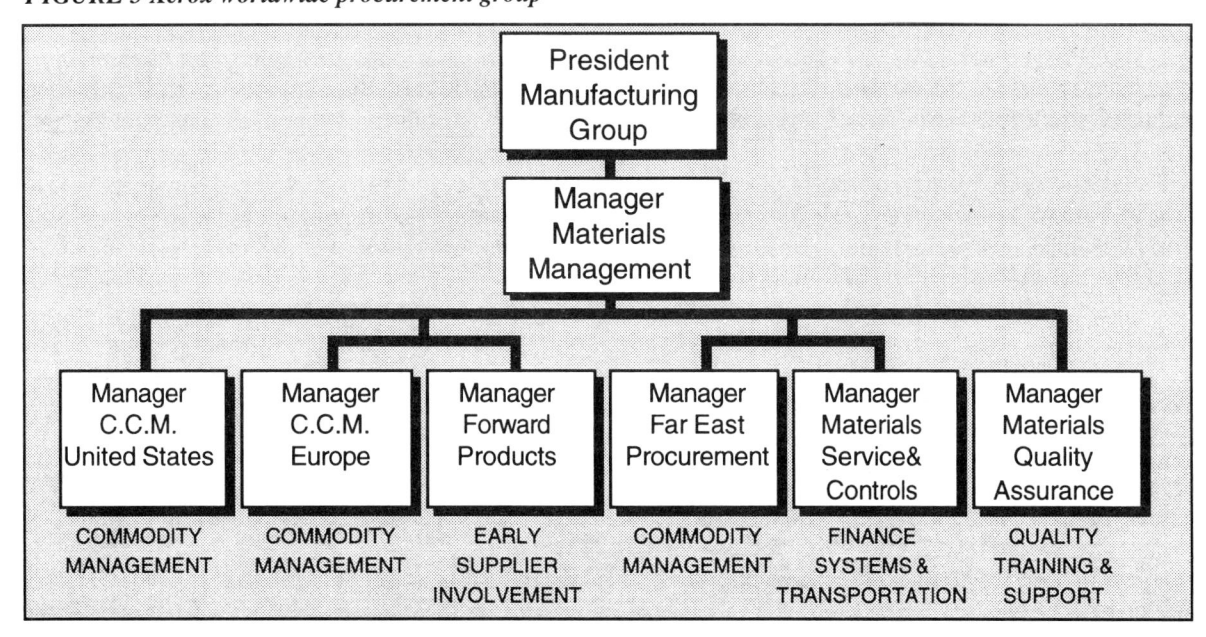

The company believes that global sourcing will enable it to sustain a competitive advantage. Clearly then Xerox is at stage 5, as identified by Monczka & Trent.

Another company which is moving from international to global procurement is Chrysler. The company has set up regional purchasing offices in the Far East and Latin America as a prelude to setting up manufacturing facilities which exploit the purchasing opportunities available in these countries. The recently introduced Chrysler International Procurement structure is shown in Figure 6.

FIGURE 6 - Chrysler's international procurement structure

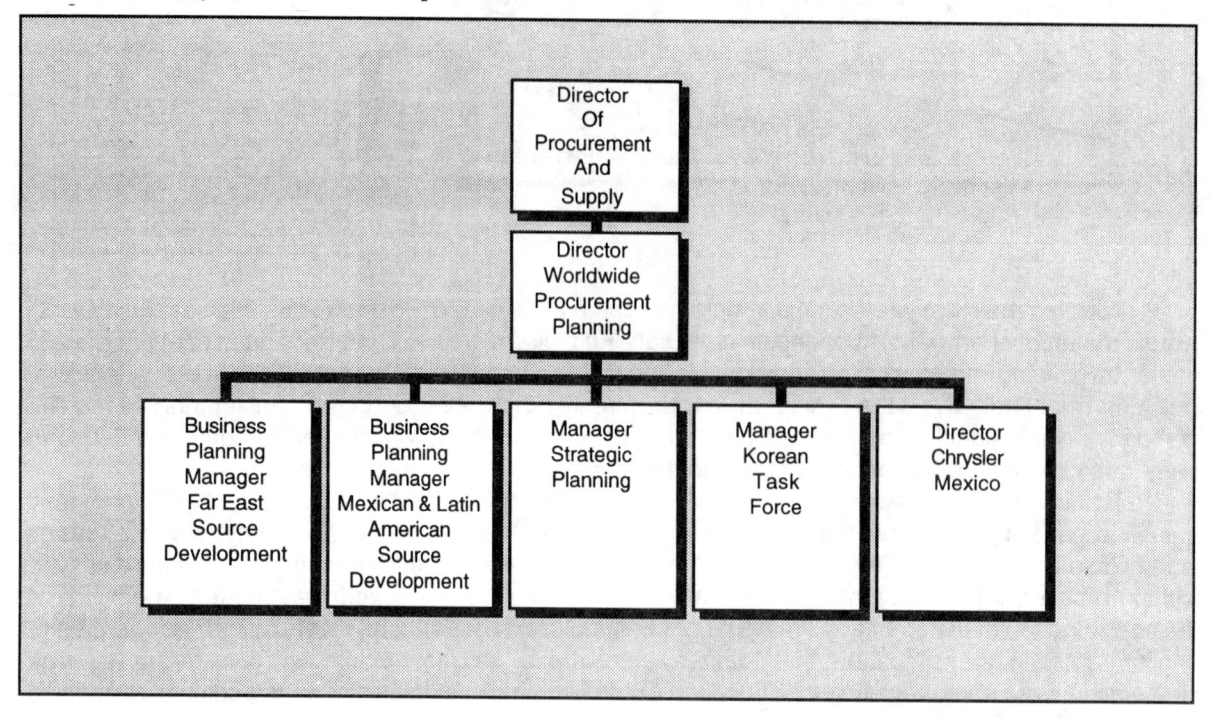

```
                    Director
                       Of
                   Procurement
                      And
                     Supply
                        |
                    Director
                   Worldwide
                   Procurement
                    Planning
                        |
    ┌───────────┬───────────┬───────────┬───────────┐
  Business    Business    Manager     Manager     Director
  Planning    Planning   Strategic    Korean      Chrysler
  Manager     Manager    Planning      Task        Mexico
  Far East   Mexican &                 Force
   Source      Latin
 Development  American
              Source
            Development
```

Black & Decker operate global purchasing similarly (see *Purchasing* USA, September 1988 *A Model of Modern Purchasing with a Global Perspective,* Ernest Ria, Editor). Black & Decker operated a multi-tier purchasing function, with a corporate activity in the USA, then divided the world at hemisphere level - Far East/USA and Europe; a continental level ie Europe only; a country level; and finally at manufacturing plant level, eg Black & Decker, Spennymoor, England.

The origin of sources reflected the global approach, 21 per cent of value brought in the Far East, 44 per cent in North America and 35 per cent in Europe.

However, if the study by Frear, Metcalf and Alguire, *Offshore sourcing: its nature and scope,* is to be believed most companies are still far away from delegating procurement responsibility to subsidiaries abroad. Company are still likely to conduct purchasing through user organisations with little co-ordination across national boundaries.

Global sourcing is becoming a pre-requisite to competing in today's marketplace. Lower costs are no longer the only benefit of global sourcing. Many firms are finding that the pay-off increasingly comes from availability, uniqueness and quality. Global sourcing offers the potential for a lasting advantage in supremacy, penetration of growth markets and high speed.

If a firm is to achieve maximum benefits from the global co-ordination of procurement requirements, it must have the proper organisational structure and the commitment by management to overcome entrenched attitudes within the firm. A firm must continuously develop its organisational structure, information systems and global sourcing expertise to facilitate maximum global performance in the way that companies such as Xerox and Black & Decker have demonstrated.

Influencing the strategic agenda
The challenge for purchasing leadership

Andrew Cox, Jon Hughes and Mark Ralf present their arguments in favour of six key business propositions

We begin this series of articles with a number of linked questions; why is purchasing and supplier management becoming so much more important; how well integrated is it with business strategy; and how effectively are we delivering outcomes that truly impact and support our organisations, rather than merely addressing a more narrowly defined functional agenda? We see this as the prime challenge for purchasing leadership.

In many ways the past few years have provided a natural platform for the purchasing professional. Manufacturing, financial and public service organisations are facing relentless pressure for improvement to bottom-line profitability. All of us, as customers, have higher expectations of value for money. As consumers of goods and services, we want convenience, on-time delivery, quality and high levels of innovation, but all at the lowest possible price. The result in the manufacturing sector of business is that branded and consumer products companies worldwide are experiencing the growing pressures of what has been termed 'value retailing'. Trading environments are becoming tougher and more competitive, while at the same time there is much greater price sensitivity from retail customers and end consumers.

Public sector bodies, the health service and government departments, both in the UK and worldwide, are struggling to come to terms with significant changes in organisation and business practice. We have all become aware of the commercial pressures associated with compulsory competitive tendering, market testing, outsourcing, privatisation and similar value-for-money initiatives. Certainly, we are seeing much greater cost control pressure from hospitals, schools, utilities and government agencies.

Such pressures are forcing these private and public sector bodies to look for new areas of strategic, operational, process and staff development. Executive management, internal and external customers are demanding continuous improvements day by day, month by month and year by year, in quality, value, pricing, innovation and customer service.

Purchasing leaders and laggards

The purchased content of goods and services provided to these customers continues to climb; in many instances, to well over 60% of total business costs. Worldwide, we are seeing an increase in manufacturing organisations focusing onto their strategic core competencies and accelerating the divestment of the less important parts of their business. (The work of Gary Hamel and CK Prahalad is of particular interest in this area.) As a direct consequence, the importance of external sourcing is increasing rapidly. Furthermore in the public sector, with the development of policies for private finance, marketing, contracting out and internal markets, government departments are doing more of their business than ever before through external procurement as opposed to direct internal provision. This is a trend that will continue and, indeed, accelerate.

Not surprisingly, therefore, this is triggering an increased focus on the ways in which the external expenditure, on purchased materials, goods and services, should be managed. Encouragingly, many progressive organisations have begun to realise that strengthening the processes of purchasing and the supply chain can have a significant impact on their performance in meeting their customer and stakeholder demands. Equally, the bottom line is concerned not just with immediate financial impact, although that is still very important. It also has to do with improvements in quality, speed of response, design input, new product development, appropriate supplier relationships, and the overall value that can be received from suppliers. Furthermore, for those organisations which are able to respond to this challenge, additional benefits accrue through improved business and working relationships and less complex ways of working.

Against such scenarios, therefore, it is apparently self-evident that purchasing has the potential to become one of the prime sources of substantial process and cost improvement. In turn, it is a key area for executive management attention, and has attained a leadership status in a few exemplar organisations.

Six key propositions

Unfortunately, despite all of the company case studies that many of us read about or listen to on the conference circuit, the truth is far from the reality. Most organisations and purchasing functions are not leaders but laggards. Furthermore, in this article, we intend to develop our arguments in support of that statement around six key propositions:

1 There is insufficient integration of customer needs, business goals and valued purchasing outcomes. As a result, many purchasing staff are pursuing an agenda that is at best sub-optimal, and at worst, almost irrelevant for their organisations.

2 The purchasing function has focused inappropriately on the pursuit of certain types of supplier relationships, such as partnerships, and has little sense of the linkages between different relationship types and core business requirements.

3 Substantial additional value could be secured by a greater focus on the supply chain. This involves an integrated approach to value acquisition (from suppliers), value added (from manufacturing) and value delivery (to customers). Few organisations have achieved such a focus.

4 The purchasing heartland has tended to be the on-time supply of goods and raw materials. This neglects the substantial opportunity of creative, technical land intellectual services. Most purchasers are actually impacting the minority of their prime categories of expenditure.

5. Too many purchasing department are only concentrating on 'doing the deal.' Tactical negotiation and short-termism preclude a more balanced approach to attaining agreed business deliverables across the full range of value, risk, cost and cash management.

There is little insight in the purchasing community into the ways and means of bringing about change that can facilitate an appropriate realignment in effort and expertise. It is not surprising, therefore, that propositions one to five above are so detectable in most organisations.

FIGURE 1 - Proposition 1: **Customer, business and supplier integration**

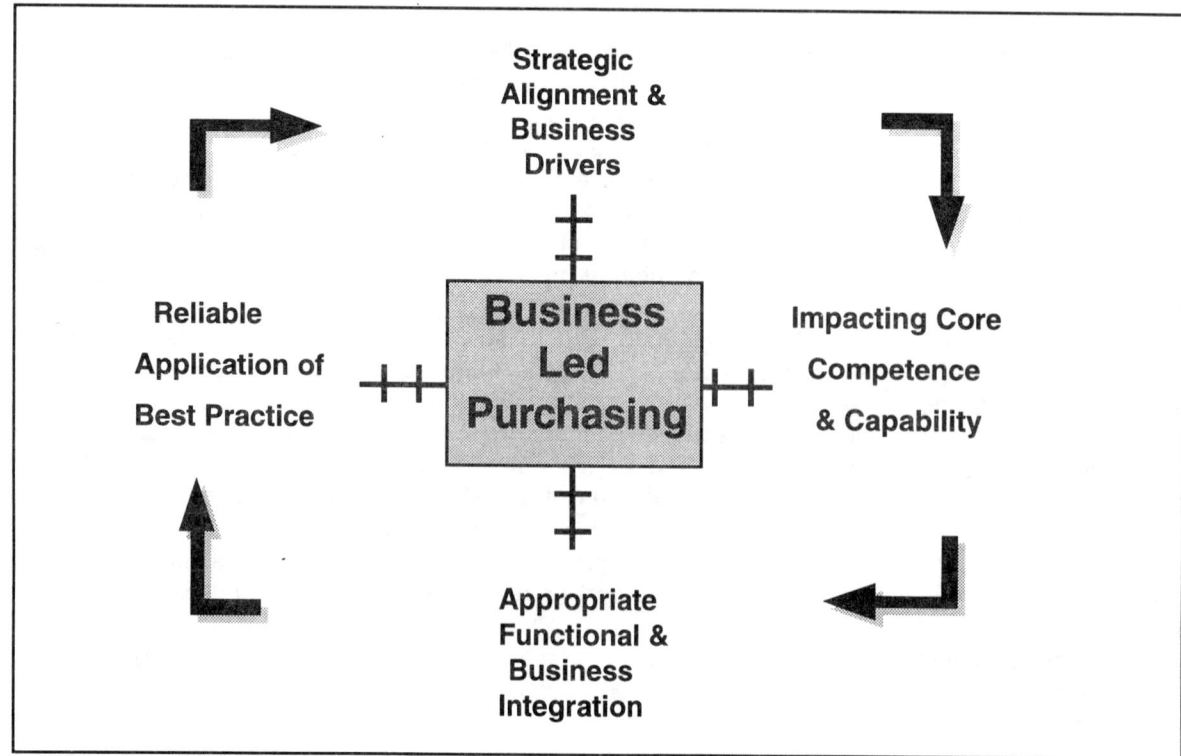

From our experience, not many companies have yet put sufficient emphasis on stating explicitly the connections between customer needs, business goals and the ways in which they should be managing suppliers; the most effective means of purchasing major categories of expenditure; and the most appropriate organisational configuration to achieve this. We argue that there should be such clear linkages, and that these should be the main drivers of the processes and practices by which we are purchasing from suppliers. In most organisations, purchasing still remains essentially tactical. It is focused onto doing deals, rather than securing agreement from suppliers to supporting the customer fully through top class performance. This cannot be achieved without a fundamental reappraisal of the purchasing role. This is illustrated in Figure 1.

Strategic alignment and business drivers
What mechanisms are used within your organisation to map out the strategic intent and required ways forward on a medium to longer term horizon? As you can see from the two case studies in this article, from Government and SmithKline Beecham, such mapping produces the necessary connections between strategy and operational practice.

Impacting core competence and capability. These are the bundles of skills and technologies that enable a company to provide a particular benefit to customers. Increasingly, we believe, both public and private sector organisations will be regarded as a collection of such competencies rather than purely producing and delivering products or services. Locating, assessing, acquiring and protecting such competencies will become a vital part of strategic procurement.

Appropriate functional and business integration. A growing number of organisations are recognising that their success depends on the strength of their internal, cross-functional staff partnerships. Rather than purchasing endeavouring to be the custodian of commercial practice, and seeking to control and own supplier contact and relationships, there is a much more productive and profitable alternative available, provided that facilitative and process skills have been well developed.

Reliable application of best practice. This calls for a standardised and systematised approach whereby relevant practices, those which meet and support business needs, are properly embedded and applied at all appropriate purchasing points.

Unfortunately, this cycle of activity all too frequently works the other way round and is driven by purchasing functionalism. Poorly thought-through benchmarking encourages organisations to assess best practice and then assume that it should be applied to their own business. This is a fallacy and one that can lead to the pursuit of professional approaches that are neither required nor valued because they are inadequately connected to business drivers, organisational cultures and ways of operating. This is why lean production and the motor sector model of purchasing should not necessarily be regarded as the only model of procurement. Indeed, in some sectors they can be positively damaging.

Proposition 2: Development of strategic supplier relationships
During a recent consulting assignment, an opportunity was provided to meet with a wide range of exemplar companies which would be recognised under the banner of 'best in class' purchasing. During the course of a series of video interviews, it became very apparent that while they were all aware of the potential of partnerships, they equally felt that this was only one of a wide array of relationship options. Subsequent research has confirmed this viewpoint.

We advocate an approach that assesses the most suitable relationship with suppliers within a business supported sourcing strategy. In turn, this strategy is driven by the defined business drivers as referred to earlier in the article.

In Figure 2, a number of relationship options are mapped out in a way that reflects the balance of competition and collaboration appropriate to the type and nature of competencies that are required. This is an exciting and innovative approach to purchasing, and one that will be the focus of our next article. It will build directly on concepts presented by the authors earlier in the year at the First Worldwide Research Symposium on Purchasing and Supply Chain Management at Arizona State University, and the 80th Annual International Purchasing Conference of the National Association of Purchasing Management at Anaheim, California. This reflects pioneering work done over the past few years in SmithKline Beecham.

Proposition 3: Planned improvement across the supply chain

This is another neglected purchasing opportunity. Most purchasing professionals are aware that it refers to the number of stages or links that can exist in the supply process from primary manufacture or creation of a service, through to its delivery to a purchaser and then on to the end-customer or consumer. It is primarily about examining in detail the number of stages or elements within that chain. The rationale behind the approach is that since the price we pay, and the quality of the product or service we obtain are determined by the number of previous transactions there have been in the chain, then the scope for significant cost and value improvement at each stage can be considerable.

One of the differences between the purchasing leaders and laggards is the amount of emphasis given to the complete supply chain and the connection of suppliers to the business needs as a whole. Indeed, we believe that the supply chain is a process at the very heart of both manufacturing and service organisations. It is driven by two prime requirements: firstly, the need for all operations to focus on to the customer; and secondly, the need to enhance the contribution of suppliers across this chain, in a way that more effectively meets the business needs. Many leading companies worldwide are increasingly focusing on the requirement for managing such chains more productively.

Unfortunately, though, an insufficient number of organisations have influenced their business colleagues to conduct the necessary searching review that assesses:
- What are the number of stages or transactions in a particular supply chain?
- To what extent do you possess the detailed information that highlights the points where cost, value and vulnerability are added?
- How would you obtain such information?
- What opportunities are there for reducing, simplifying or containing the costs at each stage?
- Can you reduce the number of stages in the chain, thereby reducing costs, as well as the probability of delay or damage to goods and services?
- At which points in the supply chain can improvement initiatives be launched to secure better quality, improved delivery or lower stock holding?
- And finally, at what point in the chain do risk and vulnerability occur, and what steps can be put in place, jointly with suppliers, to reduce or remove them?

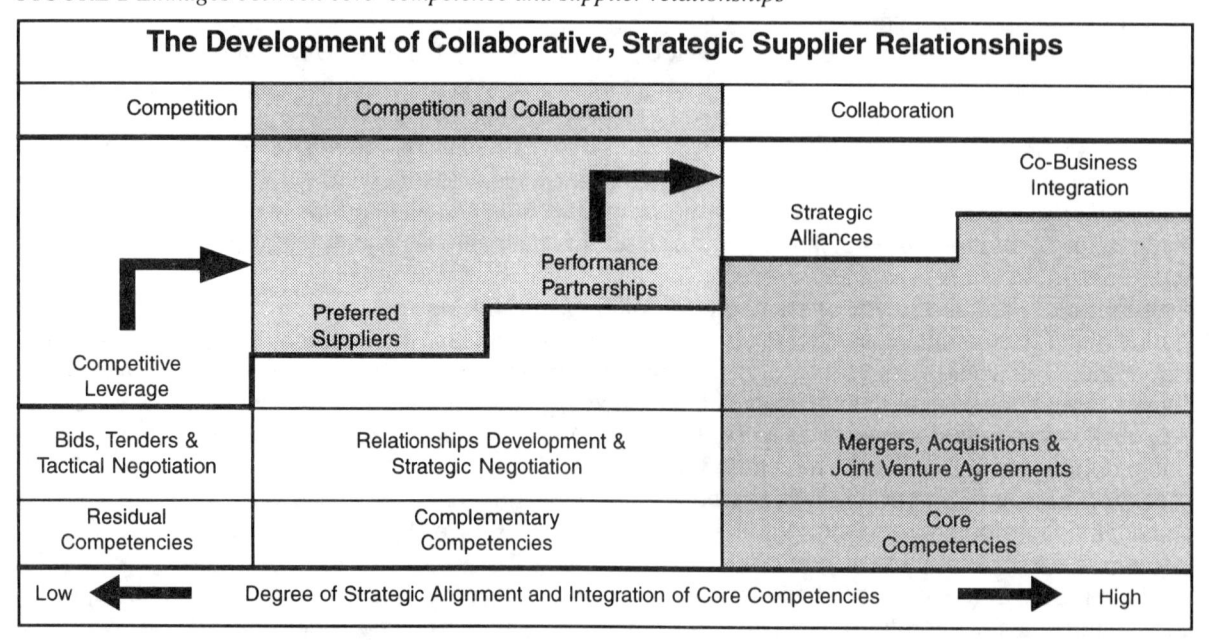

FIGURE 2 Linkages between core competence and supplier relationships

Competition	Competition and Collaboration	Collaboration
Competitive Leverage	Preferred Suppliers → Performance Partnerships	Strategic Alliances → Co-Business Integration
Bids, Tenders & Tactical Negotiation	Relationships Development & Strategic Negotiation	Mergers, Acquisitions & Joint Venture Agreements
Residual Competencies	Complementary Competencies	Core Competencies

Low ← Degree of Strategic Alignment and Integration of Core Competencies → High

The Development of Collaborative, Strategic Supplier Relationships

Proposition 4: Impacting all of the purchasing portfolio

Even where organisations have properly addressed the supply chain, they have invariably perceived it as only being relevant for manufacturing assembly. Nothing could be further from the truth. For example, in many fast moving consumer goods companies, purchasing and marketing services are often the biggest single category of expenditure. Advertising and media represent a most interesting supply chain, with many subcontractors and agencies being involved. By majoring on the different roles and added value in that chain, in terms of creative input, project management and associated technology, it is possible to pinpoint significant scope for value improvement and cost reduction in media campaigns.

Unfortunately, commercial development of staff is invariably targeted only at the purchasing community rather than with other staff in functions such as marketing, engineering, research and development and information resources. It is not being recognised at an early enough stage that more expenditure is often controlled by these groups than by the full-time purchasing department. We need to be truly impacting the full purchasing portfolio.

Proposition 5: A balanced approach to business deliverables

As we emphasised earlier in this article, traditionally in purchasing there has been far too great an emphasis on 'doing the deal', and not enough on the actual delivery of top class performance back into the company. We argue for purchasing meeting defined and balanced goals in terms of the deliverables of value, risk, cost and cash management. Let us illustrate that from value management.

There is huge scope for improvement in this area. Unfortunately, most organisations just do not have appropriate supplier management processes and mechanisms in place to involve and influence suppliers in a manageable and proactive fashion. Rarely is there an effective and well structured agenda for supplier management across a complete organisation and business. All too frequently, we find purchasing staff defining their roles in terms of annual cost savings or the most tactical application of supplier ratings and appraisal schemes that are decades out of date.

Value management is all about securing maximum value for the money spent with suppliers. There are many definitions and illustrations of this term. Ten prime areas are summarised below:
- cutting lead times to give increased flexibility and high market responsiveness;
- integrating purchaser/supplier information systems to reduce administration costs dramatically;
- early involvement on product design and exclusive access to a supplier's design capabilities;
- reducing inventory through the meshing-in of production planning and logistics systems;
- majoring on service improvement, delivery performance and overall product quality;
- emphasising right first time and zero defect programmes rather than inbound quality assurance;
- securing access to suppliers' centres of excellence for creativity and innovation;
- strengthening working relationships and developing appropriate forums for continuous improvement;
- challenging operational practices and encouraging best manufacturing and service practice;
- building common understanding of, and commitment to, each other's values and ways of working.

FIGURE 3 Value Management

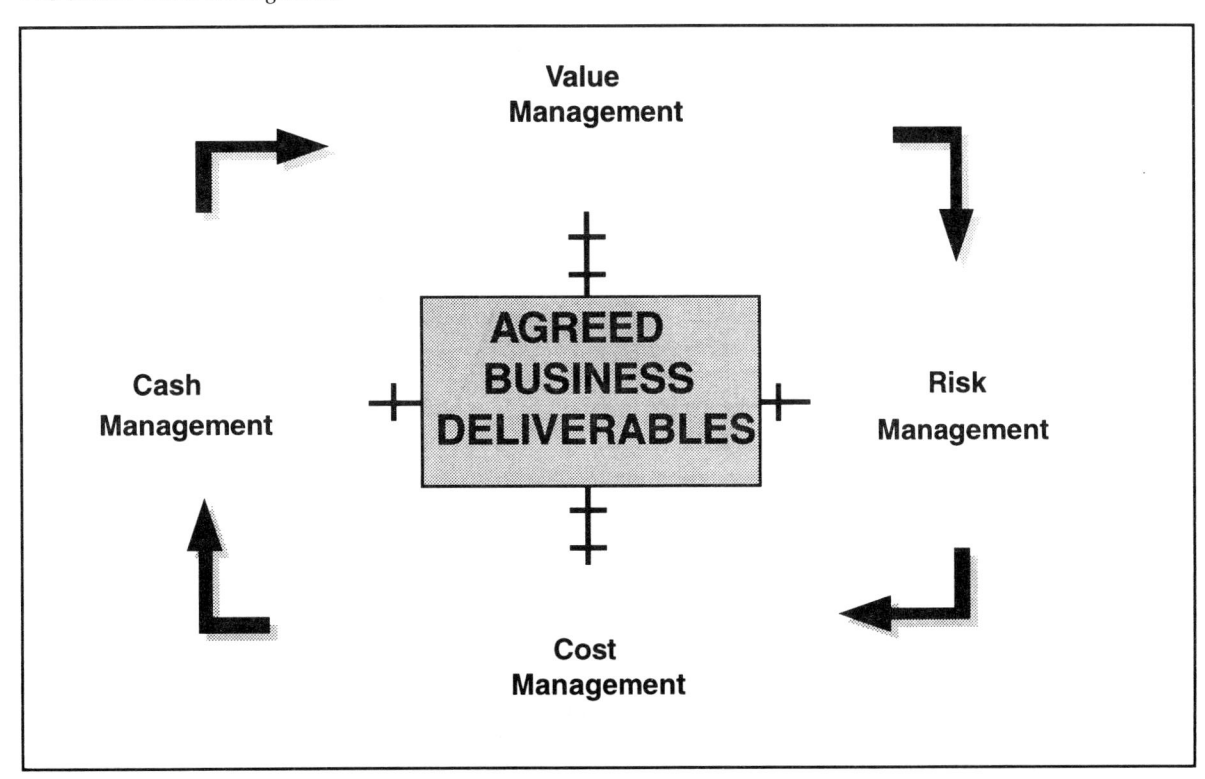

We have seen much pioneering work done by companies such as Xerox, Black & Decker, Nissan, Millican, Hewlett Packard, Rover and Motorola. Unfortunately, European organisations still lag behind the USA in this area; and the USA in turn lags behind Japan. It is interesting to note that many Japanese companies have been focusing onto such value improvement for the last 30 years or so. Indeed, the Deming prize, Japan's highly influential quality award, was introduced in 1951. However, there is still lip service paid on the part of many organisations to Philip Crosby's famous dictum that 'quality is free'. Many unimproved companies are still staggeringly inefficient, spending a huge amount of money on rectifying products to meet specification, paying tangibly in the form of scrap, rework or defective items, repeated quality inspections, warranty repairs, and discounts to aggrieved customers; but also, less obviously, in cluttered factories, ineffective working processes, needless delay, reduced speed to market, and blizzards of paperwork.

Proposition 6: Realignment, strategic learning and change management
From our experience in many countries, business sectors and companies, there is usually only patchy evidence of well managed and professionally focused purchasing and cross-functional teams capable of implementing best practice in cost management, sourcing strategy and supplier management. Purchasing invariably lacks identity; it is positioned at a lower level than other key functions; staff have received relatively little or no training and development; there is inappropriate visibility to professional practice; there are few measurement systems in place; and there is often scant evidence of collaboration, either across the function or with teams in other service areas.

The authors of this article are united in their conviction that there has to be a significant commitment to strengthening the competence of individuals and the associated organisation capabilities of teamwork and effective purchasing practice. Equally, it cannot just be imposed, either on employees or on suppliers. It depends on empowerment, a closer involvement of the main stakeholders, and full involvement of executive management. Quality oriented companies have to practice what they preach, right across the supply chain. But the benefits are considerable. Indeed, a recent university survey found that of those companies that have concentrated on strengthening their quality, value and supplier management practices, a substantial proportion out-performed industry norms on profit per employee, average remuneration, assets and sales turnover per employee, investment in fixed assets and overall profit margins.

Such a focus on development needs to be congruent with the prime business and organisational drivers. This is why we use the term 'strategic learning'. Furthermore, particularly in the larger or multinational companies there can be a significant requirement for reorganisation, realignment and change management. Purchasing improvement is invariably as much to do with organisational design and development as it is to do with purchasing tools and techniques. This will be the subject of our third and final article.

CASE EXAMPLE 1

'Setting new standards', a strategy for Government procurement

The Government's strategy for procurement is to achieve continuing improvement in value for money, based on whole life cost and quality, and to enhance the competitiveness of suppliers, through the development of world class professional procurement systems and practices. The strategy forms part of the Government's continuing quest for efficiency and effectiveness set out in the White Paper, The Civil Service - Continuity and Change. Top management in Departments will be responsible for its delivery.

Key elements in the strategy are:
● Best practice procurement will be a central element in Departments' businesses at all management levels. Departments will seek to match the cost savings achieved by best practice private and public sector organisations and will collaborate to achieve best value for money.
● Best value for money will continue to be sought through a range of techniques involving procurement, including private finance, market testing and contracting out.
● Departments will be intelligent customers with well defined objectives and requirements.
● The emphasis will be on integrated procurement processes, covering the whole cycle of acquisition and use from start to finish, to ensure quality and economy over time, not short term lowest price.

- Business cases, risks and contracts will be carefully drawn, assessed and managed.
- For each contract there will be a contract manager and for each capital project a project sponsor. | | Cross-functional teams will help to identify and deliver value for money solutions.
- Training and skill development will be enhanced to produce world class professional procurement staff.
- Benchmarking to world standards and systematic measurement of effectiveness will be developed to support continuous improvement.
- With the help of user-friendly information systems, departments will collaborate on procurement decisions and share appropriate information both with each other and with suppliers.
- Relationships with suppliers will combine competition with co-operation. Contracts with suppliers will be designed wherever practicable to promote continuous improvement and benefit sharing.
- In all dealings with suppliers and potential suppliers, Government departments will seek to preserve the highest standards of integrity, objectivity, fairness, efficiency, courtesy and professionalism, as set out in a new statement of good practice, and will look to suppliers to set similar standards.

Source: British Government White Paper, CM2840, HMSO, May 1995.

Shifting the focus

Although we are critical of the point attained by many organisations, significant changes in purchasing and supplier management are certainly under way. Many long-established beliefs, practices, processes and outcomes are being challenged and questioned.

Leading organisations across Europe, North America and the Asia Pacific Region are becoming increasingly aware of the potential to improve organisation and business performance dramatically by turning the spotlight onto purchasing and supplier management.

Influencing the strategic agenda is a real challenge for purchasing leaders. We will revisit that theme in our subsequent articles

CASE EXAMPLE 2

'Provoking the change in purchasing '- business development in SB

SB, in common with many leading worldwide pharmaceuticals and healthcare businesses, is increasingly focusing on the need to manage its supply chain much more effectively. This focus is one of a number of initiatives designed to strengthen core capabilities, improve operating efficiencies and deliver superior value to the customer.

Achieving the SB strategic intent requires the company to:
- establish itself as a world-class, customer-driven competitor;
- produce pioneer products and services;
- achieve critical mass geographically and through the product portfolio;
- achieve leadership in operational performance;
- adapt its cost structure and infrastructure to a new competitive and regulatory environment;
- develop cross-sector and cross-country initiatives;

and, in turn, become one of the world's best managed companies.

In purchasing, therefore, the goal is to support fully the needs of both the internal and external customer by maximising value, controlling costs and reducing complexity right across the supply chain. This covers not just raw materials, but all the company's goods and services.

We are ensuring that purchasing's potential for impacting business needs is maximised in terms of:
- Short-term profitability;
- longer-term competitiveness;
- achieving preferred customer status.

In essence; it is about:
- responding to the impact of major structure changes in the wider business environment;
- integrating acquired businesses and supporting strategic alliances at the most appropriate geographical level;
- driving purchasing practice to deliver valued business outcomes rather than functional agendas;
- harnessing the potential for enhancing internal cross-functional and cross-country/area team part-

nerships;
- developing reliable purchasing processes that impact all of the $3.6bn annual expenditure, both manufacturing and non-production services;
- standardising approaches to sourcing strategy that are capable of being delivered locally, regionally and globally;
- ensuring complexity reduction and business simplification through supplier rationalisation, preferred supplier programmes and transaction processing centres;
- emphasising individual competence and team development as part of a robust commitment to continuous improvement.

References:
1 Hamel, G & Parahalad, CK *Competing for the future*; Boston: Harvard University Press 1994.
2 Cox, A *Relational competence and strategic procurement management.* Paper presented to the First Worldwide Research Symposium on Purchasing and Supply Chain Management, Arizona State University, March 1995.
3. Hughes, J & Michels W. *The reality of strategic relationships: ten keys to success'.* Paper presented to the 80th Annual International Purchasing Conference of the National Association of Purchasing Management, Anaheim, California, May 1995.
4 Ralf, M, & Hughes J. *Re-engineering through training: transforming the purchasing process,* Purchasing & Supply Management, March 1994.

Developing purchasing leadership: competing on competence

Mark Ralf, Jon Hughes and Andrew Cox apply the frameworks of competence analysis to strategic supplier development

The aim of this article is to guide the reader through a number of important features of purchasing leadership in the context of the development of strategic supplier relationships. It will enable you to assess, profile and challenge your purchasing approaches with key suppliers in this area.

However, this is a subject which cannot be disengaged from the broader field of systematic source management. It is where commercial relationships, negotiating skill and long-term business needs overlap. It is about challenging the traditional thinking that often dominates the purchasing area. Developing strategic relationships is characterised by the building of fundamentally different ways of working with suppliers, creating breakthrough change, and structuring agreements that truly reflect the longer term goals of both sides. We argue that this reflects the full utilisation of the purchasing resource, achieving a business, competitive or collaborative advantage through the application of the processes and tools of core competence and capability development. This builds on, and is in reaction to, the six key propositions that were put forward in the first article in this series. The missing element, concepts and practice in change management, will be explored in our final article.

Rising to the challenge

It is true to say that significant changes have occurred worldwide in strategic supplier development. Many long-established practices, beliefs, tools and techniques are being challenged and questioned. Major organisations across Europe, North America and the Asia Pacific region are becoming increasingly aware of the potential to improve organisational and business performance dramatically, by turning the spotlight on to the purchasing and supplier management process. In turn this calls for a systematic review of the different types and possibilities of supplier relationship that are available to the purchasing professional.

Leading organisations, such as SmithKline Beecham, have demonstrated that whenever senior executives pay real attention to sourcing, the supply market and supplier management, then it leads to fundamental changes in the way in which they operate. However, these drives have to be planned and managed carefully, with structured and reliable implementation of proven world-class methods and tools. And they need to be fully supported by just-in-time training and development, for the considerable numbers of staff who can influence suppliers.

However, a lot of purchasing thinking and practice in developing effective supplier relationships has pursued a simplistic approach. It has tended to focus on skills and behaviour in isolation from the business context in which those relationships are operating. If an organisation is going to derive maximum benefit from its suppliers, real added value, then there has to be a systematic framework for developing and taking forward clearly defined sourcing strategies.

Indeed, developing strategic relationships, almost by definition, is not so much about a deal being negotiated; it is about the way in which two or more parties intend to work together over the longer term. In essence, it is about developing a robust and rigorous business relationship that is capable of being tested against specified deliverables. Indeed, the crucial outcome of the process can often best be gauged in the quality of the relationship, and the commitment to the deliverables, by both the purchaser and the supplier. And that is something which has to make sound and significant business sense for both sides; it ensures purchasing leadership. So, let's look at the nature of supplier relationships in more detail.

Supplier relationships

As we described in our first article, there is a continuum in supplier relationships from competitive leverage, through to preferred supplier status, then to performance partnership, on to strategic alliance and finally to co-development. This is graphically summarised in Figure 1.

Competitive leverage

Traditionally, competitive leverage is the heartland of tactical negotiation. Such leverage is characterised by an easy marketplace, where there are many suppliers to choose from, and where the purchaser is spending significant amounts of money. Therefore, the prime purchasing practices tend to be multiple sourcing, frequent and tough negotiation and lots of positioning and bargaining. Full use of competition is one of the main persuaders adopted by purchasers in this marketplace. It is an area where we find lots of competitive bids and full use of enquiries.

However, this traditional competitive purchasing approach is appropriate in many situations. Furthermore, there have been striking examples of competitive leverage purchasing in recent years, such as the major initiatives launched by automotive companies such as General Motors and their PICOS teams - their programme for improvement and cost optimisation of suppliers. Despite the howls of anguish from Detroit, we believe that a radical shake-up of the way in which General Motors was organising its automotive parts purchasing across North America was long overdue. Many suppliers had become substantially less competitive than those in Europe, Japan and the rest of the world. So-called partnerships had become cosy, inward focused and out of touch. There was a need to drive huge productivity improvements, and fully implement global benchmarking of price, performance and supplier capability. To achieve the rapid breakthroughs that were required, competition and fierce re-bidding of suppliers were justified in the context of global competition to determine which ones were prepared to put the customer first in terms of quality, service, and very importantly, price.

Having achieved a considerable shake-up in the supply market, the next phase at General Motors has been to re-consolidate the purchasing operations, strengthen supplier relationships again and begin the process of closer integration with the more committed suppliers - those determined and prepared to embrace the requirements of a much more demanding customer base. As can be seen in this case study, planned competitive leverage still has an important part to play in modern purchasing. But let's look at some alternative approaches, which move us into a more strategic focus on the supply market.

Preferred suppliers

Even in the competitive leverage area, it may make sense to concentrate on a smaller number of preferred suppliers, particularly where companies have systematically tested the performance of suppliers through structured appraisal, evaluation and regular benchmarking on costs. As a result of this appraisal process, the decision can be taken to select a smaller number of suppliers for preferred supplier status. Although they may have different names for their programmes, organisations such as Toyota, BMW and SmithKline Beecham have been pursuing this type of process with significant success. For example, when Toyota made a strategic decision to invest heavily in motor manufacture in the UK, it focused on its potential supplier network several years ahead of components actually being required for volume car production. In line with best practice, it majored on very structured supplier evaluation of quality, cost, technological expertise and, most interestingly, its suppliers' management styles, commitment and capability. Furthermore, it found through the joint investment with their preferred suppliers, that it had improved supplier relationships, significantly reduced defects and cycle times, and stimulated faster new product introduction times.

Performance partnerships

Having decided to concentrate on preferred suppliers, and having tested the quality and price performance in comparison with the best companies in the marketplace, it is a relatively straightforward step for an organisation to select an even smaller group of suppliers for co-development through performance partnership agreements. Excellent examples can be seen in companies such as Motorola, Intel, Digital and Texas Instruments, in a sector where there has been major transformation in relationships between the semi-conductor suppliers and their customers. Such companies have pursued similar routes, in terms of supplier rationalisation, joint definition of improvement plans and priorities, the creation of joint purchaser-supplier fusion teams with specific improvement objectives, and a focus onto maximising strategic value within the context of total cost of acquisition. Significantly, in such companies, the direction and leadership have come from the top. Joint business steering tams are in place, with representatives being drawn from both companies and their suppliers.

However, it is worthwhile correcting a serious misunderstanding on such partnerships. As we have seen, they are only one of a number of approaches towards the management of the supply market. Furthermore, there needs to be a number of important preconditions and tests which are applied to suppliers, and also the purchasing organisation, if they are to succeed. There has to be a commitment to openness on both sides, particularly on pricing, target costs, future business plans and investment. All of this must be benchmarked against developments elsewhere within increasingly competitive market places.

Our approaching this area is to advocate 'performance partnerships', which explicitly map out the required performance, establish principles on continuous improvement, and which define an agreed process for evaluating the success of the agreement and the deliverables from both sides over a designated period of time.

In summary, with such partnership relationships, we are invariably talking about single or reduced sourcing, a joint focus on quality and value, technology sharing and dedicated resources, from top management down.

Strategic alliances and business integration

Finally, companies may get into a full strategic alliance. At this stage, there is likely to be cross share ownership, single sourcing, joint investment strategies, and even co-location and co-manufacturing. Not surprisingly, inmost organisations there is limited scope for this approach. However, putting in place a successful strategic alliance is one of the most demanding, satisfying, features of strategic purchasing.

Leadership through relational competence

Within our model of the development of collaborative, strategic supplier relationships we have incorporated the very important concept of 'relational competence'. Why do we believe that this is a significant step forward in the application of a more business-led approach to procurement?

Clearly, most private sector organisations are attempting to achieve and sustain competitive advantage. Equally, public bodies are experiencing the accelerating regulatory pressures for improved value and quality, at lower costs. This is often being achieved through the creation of pseudo-competition and internal markets.

Conventionally, and particularly through the influence of Michael Porter's value chain model, it has been held that organisations will be most successful if they develop a rational approach to the sourcing of products and services in a way that acquires maximum value from suppliers, and delivers appropriate value to end customers and consumers. Invariably, this leads to a very logical approach to the development, marketing and positioning of such products and services.

FIGURE 1 Core competence and supplier relationships

Competition	Competition and Collaboration	Collaboration
Competitive Leverage	Preferred Suppliers → Performance Partnerships	Strategic Alliances → Co-Business Integration
Bids, Tenders & Tactical Negotiation	Relationships Development & Strategic Negotiation	Mergers, Acquisitions & Joint Venture Agreements
Residual Competencies	Complementary Competencies	Core Competencies

Low ← Degree of Strategic Alignment and Integration of Core Competencies → High

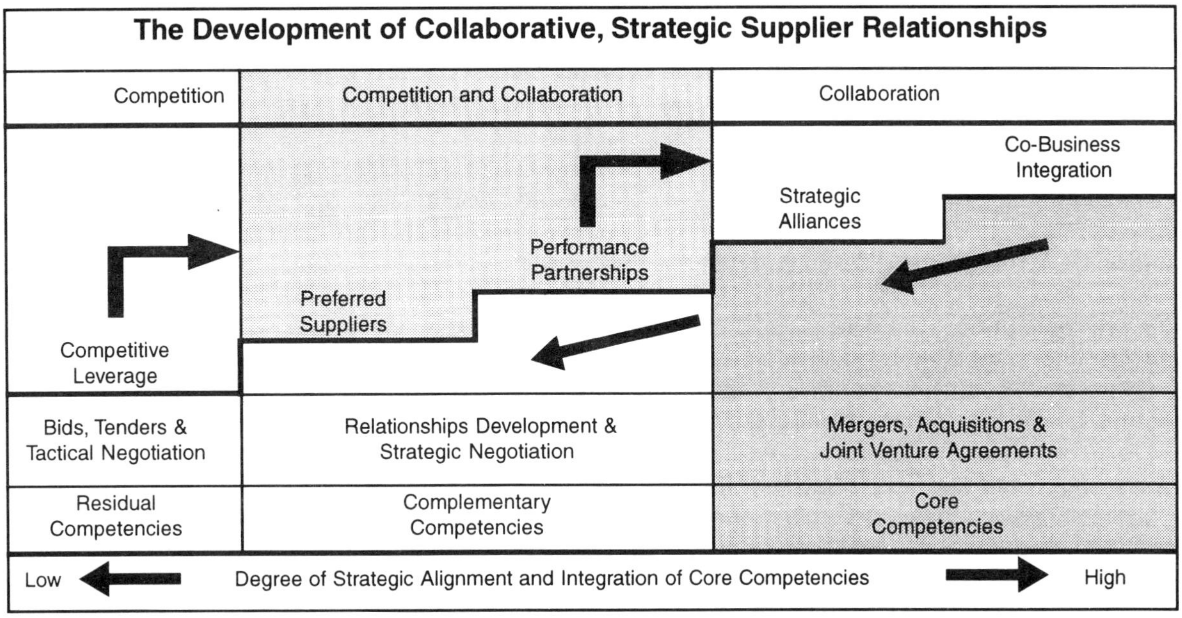

We believe, in line with some of the pioneering work done by Prahalad and Hamel, that this maybe a somewhat restrictive view of the potential of our more strategic suppliers. Organisations are not just competing over products; they also compete over access to, and the development of, bundles of human skills, knowledge sets and capabilities which enable organisations to co-ordinate and integrate complex technologies and processes across a wide diversity of business activities and markets. These skills and capabilities are not product or function-specific, and, unlike products, they cannot easily be replaced or duplicated. This is the essence of the relational competence approach.

Competing on competence

Increasingly, we believe, both public and private-sector organisations will be regarded as a collection of core comptences rather than just a mans of producing and delivering products or services. Locating, assessing, acquiring and protecting such competences should become as much a part of strategic procurement as more conventional, commodity-led sourcing strategies. As you can see from the case study on SmithKline Beecham's collaborative work in genetic medicine, this becomes a prime way of achieving competitive advantage through access to such competencies.

Clearly, if companies can achieve competitive advantage in this way, then it follows that they should concentrate on their identification and development as well as the more traditional product and functional specialisms. This is a central feature of relational competence analysis. Once an organisation has defined its core competences, it is possible to appraise, in a structured way, those activities which are deemed to be non-core or residual competences. Such activities can usually be safely outsourced.

It is often at this stage that purchasing becomes involved. A strategic, competence-led implementation plan can be developed, utilising the important distinction between core and non-core activities. This should draw on a well-defined analysis of make/buy, but across competences and capabilities as well as products and services. Unfortunately, not enough organisations are able to do this with sufficient objectivity and it is an area where external input can add significant value.

Fit for purpose relationships

Having undertaken the detailed analysis of required competences and potential targets for in-sourcing and out-sourcing, the next step is to align this approach to a similarly objective analysis of the appropriate or 'fit for purpose' relationship with potential suppliers. This is undertaken using relational competence analysis:

● Residual competences normally refer to those products and services which by their very nature are freely available and relatively interchangeable in supply market terms. Such competences can safely be handled by shorter-term contracts and relatively arm's length or leveraged relationships.

● Complimentary competences are those of greater value to the purchaser and should normally be managed through more collaborative forms of contracts and relationships, and over a longer period than the less important or residual competences. They are prime targets for the purchasing practices associated with preferred suppliers and performance partnerships.

● Core competences are normally associated with the more sophisticated contractual arrangements of joint venture agreements and even cross-shareholding. The arrangement between purchaser and supplier has to b a seamless one, calling for a fundamental meshing-in of business systems and processes. Indeed, there may be pressure for a merger or acquisition to protect the nature of the competence.

The evolution of strategic relationships

A very important perspective on the range of potential strategic relationships available to companies is that they should not necessarily be regarded as fixed. They can change over time. They can become closer, and they can also become more arm's length. After all, you may, or may not, have full control over them, depending on changes in the marketplace, changes at senior management level, changes in your own products or product technologies. Furthermore, there are usually only a small number of suppliers who actually have the capability and the management commitment for you to enter into a full performance partnership or strategic alliance with them.

Indeed, a theme that has been running through this analysis of the continuum from competitive leverage to co-business integration is the need for clear and strong guidelines on how a public or private sector organisation should be analysing and mapping relationships with its suppliers. We believe that

CHART OF KEY FACTORS

Case Example: Competitive advantage through capability development in SmithKline Beecham

The Promise
At SmithKline Beecham, healthcare - prevention, diagnosis, treatment and cure - is our purpose. Through scientific excellence and commercial expertise, we provide products and services throughout the world that promote health and wellbeing.

The source of our competitive advantage is the energy and ideas of our people; our strength lies in what we value: customers, innovation, integrity, people and performance.

At SmithKline Beecham, we are people with purpose, working together to make the lives of people everywhere better, striving in everything we do to become The 'Simply Better' Healthcare Company, as judged by all those we serve: customers, shareholders, employees and the global community.

Core Capabilities
SB's key skills, together with reliable processes that drive the business, form the core capabilities that are the source of SB's competitive advantage. Building and strengthening these capabilities will enable the company to achieve its goal of leadership in the healthcare industry in the 21st century. The six core capabilities that increasingly set SB apart are its abilities to:

- generate pioneer discoveries through scientific excellence;
- bring new products to market more quickly through efficient power development;
- develop value added products and services that exceed customer expectations;
- effectively manage manufacturing processes and the supply chain to be a low cost producer;
- build external alliances to gain access to leading edge technology and discovery;
- and, at all times, engage in continuous improvement.

Change as opportunity
Through a series of strategic acquisitions and disposals, such as the £927M sale of its Animal Health business to Pfizer, SB made progress during 1994 in its transformation from a company made up of four successful, but separate businesses, into a unified organisation focused on human healthcare.

SB's core businesses, pharmaceuticals (including vaccines), consumer healthcare and clinical laboratories, provide the keys to building leadership in the four corner stones of human healthcare: prevention, diagnosis, treatment and cure. Together with the company's added proficiencies in genetics and pharmaceutical benefit management, a unique capability has been developed to provide the pioneer products and services, offered in the cost effective, efficient packages, that customers trying to manage healthcare costs now demand.

Pioneer Research and Capability Access
A major step in the transformation of SB through science based innovation took place in May 1993, with the $125M alliance with Human Genome Sciences (HGS). The collaboration has produced the world's largest data base of human gene sequences, which has been thoroughly integrated into SB's discovery programmes. The company is now much better positioned than any competitor to take advantage of the revolutionary technology in genetic medicine.

SB's affiliation with HGS, in collaboration with the Institute for Genomic Research, is the largest among a growing number of scientific alliances which now complement SB's internal research capabilities. SB has established itself as 'partner of choice' in biotechnology, securing access to emerging technologies and products. Over the last three years, SB has entered into over 130 collaborations and agreements, including over 30 equity investments. In addition, more than 40 agreements with academia and biotechnology companies have strengthened leadership in the vaccine business.

This high level of activity illustrates SB's 'open door' policy to partnering - a prime way of achieving competitive advantage through capability access and development.

such mapping tools really can facilitate more appropriate business thinking and help address the confusion that has been endemic in this area. In Figure 2, an extract from an ADR methodology for analysing supplier relationships is provided to illustrate this approach.

Linking strategic relationships to the business plan
One of the starting points for developing more effective supplier relationships is the definition and linking of business needs to the purchasing and supply chain, through an explicit source plan.

This provides a very sharp focus on what you are trying to achieve. Let's look at some examples. It could be:
- cutting lead times to give increased flexibility and high market responsiveness
- close meshing-in of systems and information flows to reduce administration costs dramatically
- early involvement on product design and with full access to a supplier's design capabilities
- reducing inventory through the meshing-in of production planning and logistics
- majoring on service improvement, delivery performance and overall product quality
- emphasising 'right first time' and ' zero defect' programmes, rather than inbound quality assurance.

However, it is very important to develop some clear rules of engagement. One approach can be the framing of broad guiding principles into a detailed relationships agreement that states how both sides should be working together. We have found that particularly in strategic relationships, the framing of such principles and criteria can be used to resist the parties' slipping back into positional bargaining and very tactical responses. The development of such principles provides a very robust and rigorous process. Let's look at a number of examples in more detail.

i) Best in Market Pricing
One example would be to agree 'best in market pricing'. If that principle were being negotiated, then for the duration of the strategic agreement, the supplier would be committing to remain commercially competitive and using his best endeavours to bring about ongoing cost reduction.

ii) Value for Money
A second, and linked, principle could be to do with 'value for money'. The supplier is agreeing to be benchmarked against external indicators of lowest base cost, rather than merely market pricing.

iii) Continuous Improvement
A third principle could relate to an agreement on 'continuous improvements in quality and service levels.' Again, quality could be benchmarked at or beyond the best in class level, and be fully backed up by an itemised statement of deliverables.

iv) Business Development
A fourth example could be to do with 'jointly growing volumes of business'. In this instance, the parties would be collaborating together to use their combined expertise to provide designated customers with superior products or services. Having accepted that principle, then both sides would jointly focus on to the value delivery required to achieve that end result, and the strategic relationships necessary to sustain it.

Similar principles can be developed to cover speed to market, access to a supplier's technology, transfer of expertise, joint collaboration on new product development and design, improved speed of response times, or labour productivity and efficiency. They are then integrated into the sourcing plan for that supplier.

The keys to business advantage
By using the approaches described within this article, organisations such as SmithKline Beecham are able to achieve three major advantages. Firstly, core competence and capability tools encourage businesses to focus in a robust and systematic way on the keys to competitive advantage. Secondly, they encourage senior purchasing professionals to play a more strategic role in the development of corporate decision making through the application of systematic supplier relationship assessment and management. Thirdly, by understanding more thoroughly the linkages between core, complementary and residual competences and such supplier relationships, significant improvements in cost, quality and innovation can be secured.

Pursuit of such goals, however, is a real challenge to purchasing leadership and requires insight, expertise and skill in change management. This will be pursued in the next chapter.

Mark Ralfis Senior Vice President and Head of Global Purchasing for SmithKline Beecham.
John Hughes is Chairman and Director of ADR International Purchasing Consultants
Andrew Cox is Professor of Strategic Procurement at Birmingham University.

References:
1 Cox, A Hughes, J & Ralf, M, *Influencing the Strategic Agenda: The Challenge for Purchasing Leadership* Purchasing & Supply Management, September 1995
2 Porter, ME *Competitive Advantage*, New York Free Press 1987
3 Hughes, J, & Billson, I, *Purchasing Leadership and Competence Development,* Purchasing & Supply Management, May 1995
4 Prahalad, CK & Hame, G, *The Core Competence of the Corporation*, Harvard Business Review, 82, May-June 2990; and Hamel, G & Heene, A (eds), *Competence Based Competition*, Chichester, J Wiley, 1994
5 Hughes, J, & Michels, W. *The Reality of Strategic Relationships*. Paper presented to the 80th Annual International Purchasing Conference of the National Association of Purchasing Management, Anaheim, California, May 1995
6 Cox, A. *Relational Competence Analysis and Strategic Procurement Management*, European Journal of Purchasing & Supply Management (Vol 2, No 2, 1996) (forthcoming).

Case Example:

Competitive advantage through capability development in SmithKline Beecham

The Promise
At SmithKline Beecham, healthcare - prevention, diagnosis, treatment and cure - is our purpose. Through scientific excellence and commercial expertise, we provide products and services throughout the world that promote health and wellbeing.

The source of our competitive advantage is the energy and ideas of our people; our strength lies in what we value: customers, innovation, integrity, people and performance.

At SmithKline Beecham, we are people with purpose, working together to make the lives of people everywhere better, striving in everything we do to become The 'Simply Better' Healthcare Company, as judged by all those we serve: customers, shareholders, employees and the global community.

Core Capabilities
SB's key skills, together with reliable processes that drive the business, form the core capabilities that are the source of SB's competitive advantage. Building and strengthening these capabilities will enable the company to achieve its goal of leadership in the healthcare industry in the 21st century. The six core capabilities that increasingly set SB apart are its abilities to:
- generate pioneer discoveries through scientific excellence;
- bring new products to market more quickly through efficient power development;
- develop value added products and services that exceed customer expectations;
- effectively manage manufacturing processes and the supply chain to be a low cost producer;
- build external alliances to gain access to leading edge technology and discovery;
- and, at all times, engage in continuous improvement

Change as opportunity
Though a series of strategic acquisitions and disposals, such as the #92M sale of its Animal Health business to Pfizer, SB made progress during 1994 in its transformation from a company made up of four successful, but separate businesses, into a unified organisation focused on human healthcare.

SB's core businesses, pharmaceuticals (including vaccines), consumer healthcare and clinical laboratories, provide the keys to building leadership in the four cornerstones of human healthcare: prevention, diagnosis, treatment and cure. Together with the company's added proficiencies in genetics and pharmaceutical benefit management, a unique capability has been developed to provide the pioneer products and services offered in the cost-effective, efficient packages, that customers trying to manage healthcare costs now demand.

Pioneer Research and Capability Access
A major step in the transformation of SB through science based innovation took place in May 1993, with the $125M alliance with Human Genome Sciences (HGS). The collaboration has produced the world's largest database of human gene sequences, which has been thoroughly integrated into SB's discovery programmes. The company is now much better positioned than any competitor to take advantage of the revolutionary technology in genetic medicine.

SB's affiliation with HGS, in collaboration with the Institute for Genomic Research, is the largest among a growing number of scientific alliances which now complement SB's internal research capabilities. SB has established itself as 'partner of choice' in biotechnology, securing access to emerging technologies and products. Over the last three years, SB has entered into over 130 collaborations and agreements, including over 30 equity investments. In addition, more than 40 agreements with academia and biotechnology companies have strengthened leadership in the vaccine business.

this high level of activity illustrates SB's 'open door' policy to partnering - a prime way of achieving competitive advantage through capability access and development.

Facilitating strategic change - the key role for purchasing leadership

Jon Hughes, Andrew Cox and Mark Ralf address five key themes

Ask almost any organisation, from the public or private sector, to identify the issues which are at the top of their priority action list for the next five years and the chances are they will declare that amongst the highest are significant changes in corporate culture, organisational structure, strategic processes and new ways of working. These requirements are often described under the banners of such terms as 'transformation,' 'business process re-engineering' and 'total quality management'.

However, it often seems that companies are being bombarded with what can easily appear to be mere fads and fashions. Indeed, the readers of *Purchasing & Supply Management* may feel that never before has there been such sheer volume of new approaches. Furthermore, this can easily lead senior purchasing executives, who are famed for their wariness and scepticism of many business innovations, to reach one of three incorrect conclusions: firstly, that these new approaches are all hype with no substance and can be dismissed as such; secondly, that they can be ignored as being impractical conceptual and overly theoretical; and thirdly, that they will not impact the often neglected area of purchasing and supplier management. Nothing could be further from the truth. Many of the comfortable and predictable approaches to the function are changing rapidly as top management increasingly focus on to the supply chain as a source of relatively untapped profit improvement and competitive advantage.

As a consequence, it is inevitable that many readers will be drawn into the issues associated with designing, managing or supporting significant change programmes. It is our goal in this final article on facilitating change to highlight a number of the key themes connected with this area; to illustrate it with proven maps through the change management minefield; ;and to reinforce the need for a proactive, considered and analytical assessment of the strategic options available for purchasing leadership.

So, please detach some of your scepticism as we guide you through the jargon! Indeed, it can be helpful to consider the business and performance improvement potential of applying the approaches that we will be describing. Finally, you may wish to link our key themes on change management to the propositions developed in the earlier articles in this series.

Theme 1: The power of management by process

In all but the smallest organisations, operational processes have always been carried out, somewhat laboriously, across a range of fragmented 'functions' or departments such as production, design, engineering, marketing, accounts and, of course, purchasing. Each had its own hierarchy, up and down which communication would pass before being transferred down the line to the next department.

Throughout the 1980s, many western organisations came to similar conclusions about the inefficiencies and rigidities associated with the structural weaknesses of this way of operating and began to experiment with means of bridging such vertical structures, either through matrix type arrangements or via (semi-permanent) project teams, task forces and cross-functional workgroups.

This approach accelerated in the early 19990s as thousands of organisations all over the world were launched on to the business process re-engineering path by Hammer and Champy's important and influential book, *Re-engineering the Corporation*. As a management concept, re-engineering, often known by the equally awkward term 'core process redesign', applies a very straightforward principle: 'a fundamental re-thinking and radical redesign of business processes to achieve dramatic improvements in critical measures of performance such as cost, quality, service and speed.' Not surprisingly, it's easy to see the relevance of these goals to the many processes of purchasing and supplier management.

The key word in the approach is 'radical'. While readers may be aware that re-engineering has many parallels with the old disciplines of work study and time and motion analysis, unlike them, in theory at least, it does not just focus on to the simplification and improvement of existing processes. Instead it involves transforming an organisation from one based on separate 'functions' or specialist departments to one based on the core processes which span most or all of these functional activities. These might include such operational processes as product development, order generation and fulfilment, and the supply chain. At a higher level they increasingly impact the overall strategic approach and 'architecture' of business change, as the SmithKline Beecham case study later in this article demonstrates.

In essence, therefore, there are two types of re-engineering programme. Firstly, there is the reconfiguring and realignment of entire business processes that alter fundamentally the strategic and competitive capabilities of an organisation. Examples might include:
- radically cutting back on internal manufacturing via substantial programmes of in-sourcing or out-sourcing
- creating networks of strategic alliances with external trading partners
- using joint ventures and co-business ownership to pioneer new fields of research and development
- focusing on suppliers as the prime source of product innovation
- completely reorganising local, regional and global sourcing responsibilities.

Secondly, there are many sub-processes of purchasing and supplier management that can be redesigned, albeit at an operational rather than a strategic level:
- transactional simplification of requisitioning and order processing
- closer integration of accounts payable, sales order processing and purchasing systems
- strengthening of purchaser-support interfaces via autofax and electronic data integration (EDI)
- reorganising sourcing teams into cross-functional groups
- sharing and transferring of best practice across sites and between business sectors or divisions.

Taking such processes and assessing the scope for making radical improvements in performance is the essence of redesign of core purchasing processes. It involves a rethink and searching challenge of how an organisation develops, sources and delivers its products or service to either an internal or an external customer. Not surprisingly the approach has been taken up with a vengeance, particularly within the larger corporations and across major public sector bodies in government, the civil service, recently privatised utilities and the health service. Interestingly, the approach is prompting a reconsideration of many of the ways in which organisations are structured, particularly those where decentralisation and autonomy of operation have been strong features. This leads into the second key theme in change management.

Theme 2: The downside of decentralisation
One of the most powerful models of business management over the last 25 years has been that of 'small is beautiful'. Manufacturing companies have pursued this organisational and structural goal by splitting themselves into sectors, divisions, areas, countries and strategic business units focused on to particular product markets and customer groups. Even when large organisations grew outwardly bigger and broader in the diversification minded 1970s, internally they tended to break themselves down into smaller and increasingly decentralised entities. Public sector bodies have adopted similar routes with the emergence of agencies in government and trusts within the healthcare sector.

This is very apparent which purchasing and supplier management organisations are examined in many manufacturing and service companies, particularly those with global or pan-European geographical reach. While there may be an apparent structural overlay of an above-country or cross-business purchasing organisation, the reality is often that purchasing staff are locally focused on to meeting the pressing, operational needs of their sites and factories.

When such an approach is well deigned and competently managed it can lead to efficient purchasing, identification with the needs of the local market, development and support of a network of country-specific preferred suppliers and high levels of staff motivation.

However, such a process has frequently been accompanied by either a hands-off attitude on the part of head office and corporate staffs, or an endorsement for loose networking arrangements to try and capture the synergies across the various locations. Unfortunately, such collaboration processes often lack the necessary authority to act, while accountability for action is often indistinct. Local divisions and country-specific businesses generally hold the power and narrow, parochial perspectives can easily prevail. The authors of this article believe that a reliance on such loose, network driven approach is inappropriate and needs to be significantly strengthened. This is also the conclusion being drawn by many companies which have experienced the failures of the collaboration process. Indeed, as a senior executive emphasised to one of the authors of this article, 'the main problem with purchasing staff is that they over-promise but under-perform'.

The need to strengthen and integrate cross-business processes was certainly the case in SmithKline Beecham, as Jan Leschly, the Chief Executive, confirmed in a recent discussion forum: 'SB was always a physician-driven business; now we're payer-driven. In the United States today, employers and insurance companies pay our bills; in Europe, the government pays. So we figured, we'd better find out how to satisfy these new customers, and that led us to a powerful realisation; the way we do business had to change completely. For a long time, we had four separate businesses: pharmaceuticals, consumer healthcare, animal health and clinical laboratories - each working in silos independent of the others, developing strategies of their own. But when we looked t the healthcare system as a whole and tried to understand how it was changing, we had trouble fitting these businesses into the new world.'

SB is not untypical. Indeed, there is a groundswell of opinion that local business units and even operating divisions in many companies may provide too narrow a set of perspectives from which to make appropriate purchasing decisions. In facilitating strategic change in this area it is important that a number of issues are properly and systematically addressed.

Let us examine a typical problem from a European fast-moving consumer goods (EFMCG) company. They evaluated their purchasing processes through framing a number of key questions:

- To what extent is the company purchasing structure organised primarily by site rather than on a country, country cluster or regional basis, and how well is it functioning?
- Is the purchasing focus of effort and expertise concentrated purely on manufacturing support rather than maximising total business profitability and supporting product and business development?
- What strategic realignment and consolidation is taking place across the supply base, and how will this impact pan-European sourcing?
- Are there multiple contact points with suppliers rather than single, high quality account and category management?
- What processes may need to be strengthened to ensure that knowledge, expertise and best practice are successfully transferred from one part of the company to another?
- What business realignment of purchasing operations may be needed to utilise business leverage with pan-European suppliers?
- Is there a purchasing process plan in place that addressesthe internal business issues that inhibit pan-regional purchasing?

In-country research confirmed the need for a radical shift in purchasing's role across Europe. In particular, it prompted a much stronger external focus around a number of 'themes for change'. This is illustrated in Figure 1, and demonstrates the linkages between such themes and both keys to success and requirement improvements in purchasing performance. In addition, there was also a need for much closer integration of purchasing initiatives with business-led supplier management. This is illustrated in Figure 2.

FIGURE 1 A case example of purchasing's role in change - the external focus

Goal: Influencing the Future in the Company's Favour; Securing a Sustainable Competitive Advantage

Themes for Change	Keys to Success	Required Purchasing Performance
1. All business segments contributing substantially to profitability	● Obtaining a cost advantage over competitors. ● Generating the cash flow to fund business growth.	● To what extent is there an aggressive pursuit of cost control, cost reduction and cost improvement opportunities? ● Do these programmes cover all expenditure and deliver significant negative net inflation on the price of goods and services?
2. Supporting brands within a framework of value delivery.	● Managing the supply chain to acquire and deliver superior value. ● Integrating value acquisition (from suppliers) with value delivery (through superior marketing and customer service).	● Are suppliers actively supporting brand performance by complying with best manufacturing practice? ● Is the company obtaining and securing flexibility exclusivity and innovation from suppliers ahead of its competitors?
3. Fully utilising global and regional strength.	● Acting as a global competitor in the supply market. Retaining divisional flexibility to act, while operating together.	● To what extent is a plan of purchase in place to capture the opportunities that exist for global and area purchasing collaboration? ● Is there a purchasing process plan in place that addresses the internal business issues that inhibit pan-regional purchasing?

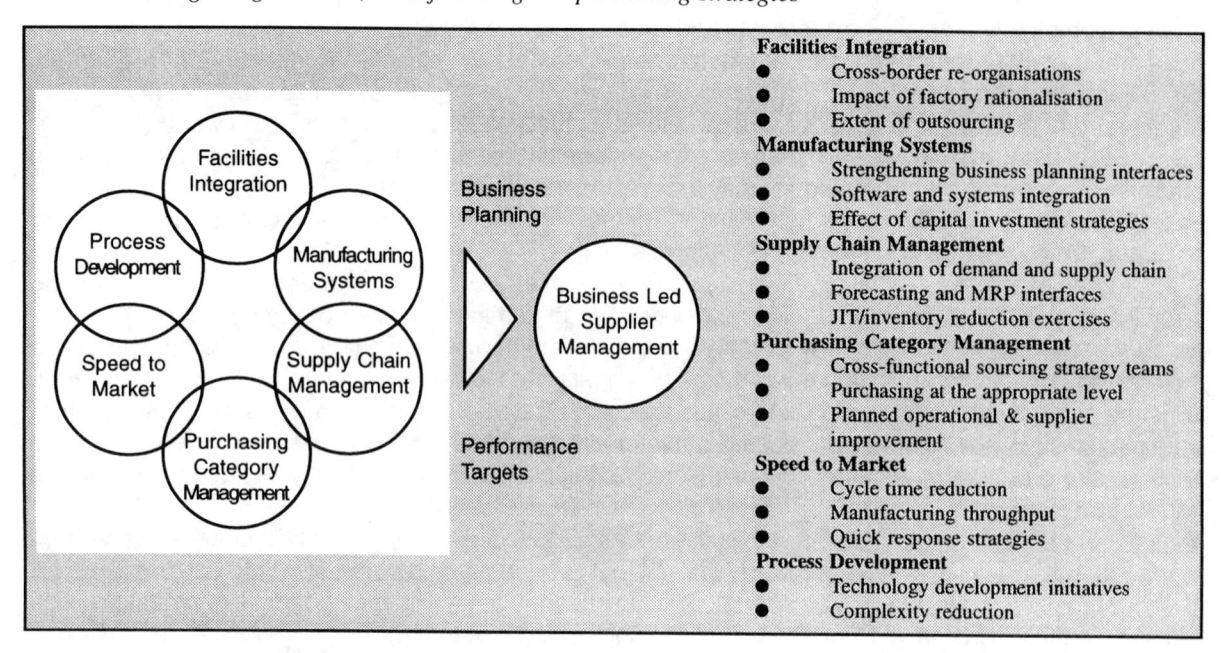

FIGURE 2 *Integrating business, manufacturing and purchasing strategies*

Facilities Integration
- Cross-border re-organisations
- Impact of factory rationalisation
- Extent of outsourcing

Manufacturing Systems
- Strengthening business planning interfaces
- Software and systems integration
- Effect of capital investment strategies

Supply Chain Management
- Integration of demand and supply chain
- Forecasting and MRP interfaces
- JIT/inventory reduction exercises

Purchasing Category Management
- Cross-functional sourcing strategy teams
- Purchasing at the appropriate level
- Planned operational & supplier improvement

Speed to Market
- Cycle time reduction
- Manufacturing throughput
- Quick response strategies

Process Development
- Technology development initiatives
- Complexity reduction

Theme 3: Developing a change architecture

Throughout this series of articles, the authors have tried to illustrate their arguments and propositions on strategic change through reference to 'live' case examples, particularly drawn from SmithKline Beecham. Clearly, much of the detail and insight into operational practice cannot be disclosed for reasons of business confidentiality, but it is possible to share a number of the architectural features of the blueprint that is guiding change management and strategic integration across the corporation. For those who wish to pursue this subject further, and also tune into similar cases on Xerox and Pepsi, these have been written up by David Garvin in the most recent issue of the Harvard Business Review. In particular, this review emphasises the need to 'leverage strategic processes'.

Our goal in writing this series of articles has been to illustrate the need for explicit linkages between strategic drivers, business goals and improvement themes. In addition, we would argue that it is a prime role of purchasing leadership to establish the required organisational actions to deliver substantial change and added value benefits in support of company-wide programmes of change. Let us illustrate that approach from SB.

SmithKline Beecham's blueprint for future success is the 'Simply Better' way, a well-defined process management approach built on SB's core capabilities and a systematically developed corporate culture that aims to create a sustainable competitive advantage through the skills, compete competencies and endeavour of its 50,000 employees worldwide. The strategic intent is 'to be the world's best healthcare company'. This is intended to be SB's aspirational, long-term business goal; far-reaching, yet attainable in ten years. Strategic intent consists of three components: the aspirational statement; the 10-year objectives; and core capabilities - defined s the management and business processes that, when uniquely combined with technical skills and targeted to satisfy customer needs, create the required position of sustainable competitive advantage.

Strategic intent is established at the corporate level and defined by each business sector, area, country and function. The aim is to stretch the organisation to strive for and attain challenging targets that are common and which remain stable over time. This provides alignment throughout the organisation by focusing everyone on one clear goal.

SB sets demanding goals for every part of the organisation. Clearly, significant gaps in potential and performance can be detected and are mapped for systematic action. These gaps are managed through:

Improvement themes: a focused and relentless pursuit by every employee of continuous productivity improvement
Breakthrough projects: the fundamental redesign of key processes
Strategic initiatives: major actions such as mergers, acquisitions and alliances.

This approach has been termed the 'change architecture' for the corporation and is being applied across the total business worldwide. As can be seen from the case study, purchasing is fully integrated into the approach and, indeed, is central to a number of major interventions in business process change at regional land global level.

Theme 4: Competing on capabilities

Achieving the SB goal of healthcare leadership calls for the building and strengthening of key skills, together with reliable processes that drive the business and form the core capabilities that are at the heart of the company's current and future success. Six core capabilities have been carefully and systematically defined. They re the ability to:
- generate pioneer discoveries through scientific excellence
- bring new products to market more quickly through efficient power development
- develop value added products and services that exceed customer expectations
- effectively manage manufacturing processes and the supply chain to be a low cost producer
- build external alliances to gain access to lading edge technology and discovery
- and, at all times, engage in continuous improvement.

A case study on competitive advantage through such capability development was described in the second article of this series. We believe that the definition of prime business and organisational capabilities, the assessment of the gap between current practice and required future positioning and then the design of a structured approach and migration plan to close the gap is the essence of effective change management. This leads to focused change that is driven by and embedded within business needs.

Clearly, as can be seen in Figure 3, it may have many strands and activities to be successful in roll-out. But such an approach produces change that endures, and which can be sustained, rather than its being a temporary and ultimately unsuccessful initiative.

FIGURE 3 Structured approach to purchasing change management

1. Developing the Change Process	2. Linkages to Business Needs	3. Securing Commitment to Action	4. Baselining and Benchmarking
• High Level Steering Group • Design of the Architecture • Mapping the Way Forward	• Executive/Customer Involvement • Specification of Needs • Statement of Deliverables	• Senior Management Support • Site and Functional Sponsors • Executive Briefing Sessions	• Developing the Audit Tools • Profiling for Purchasing Improvement • Systematic Opportunity Analysis

Figure 3: Structured approach to purchasing change management →

• Allocation of Roles • Determining Priorities of Attack • Supported by Policies Guidelines & Frameworks	• Structured "Cost Down" Campaigns • Targeted Value Improvement • Introduction of Performance Measurement	• Application of Standardised Approach • Use of Development Guides • Best Practice Tools and Techniques	• Assessment of Competence Gaps • Development of Team Leaders • Just-in-Time Training
5. Defining Roles and Accountabilities	**6. Securing Appropriate Outcomes**	**7. Refocusing Effort and Expertise**	**8. Strengthening Team Competence**

"Facilitating Strategic Change: The Key Role for Purchasing Leadership", Purchasing & Supply Management, November 1995

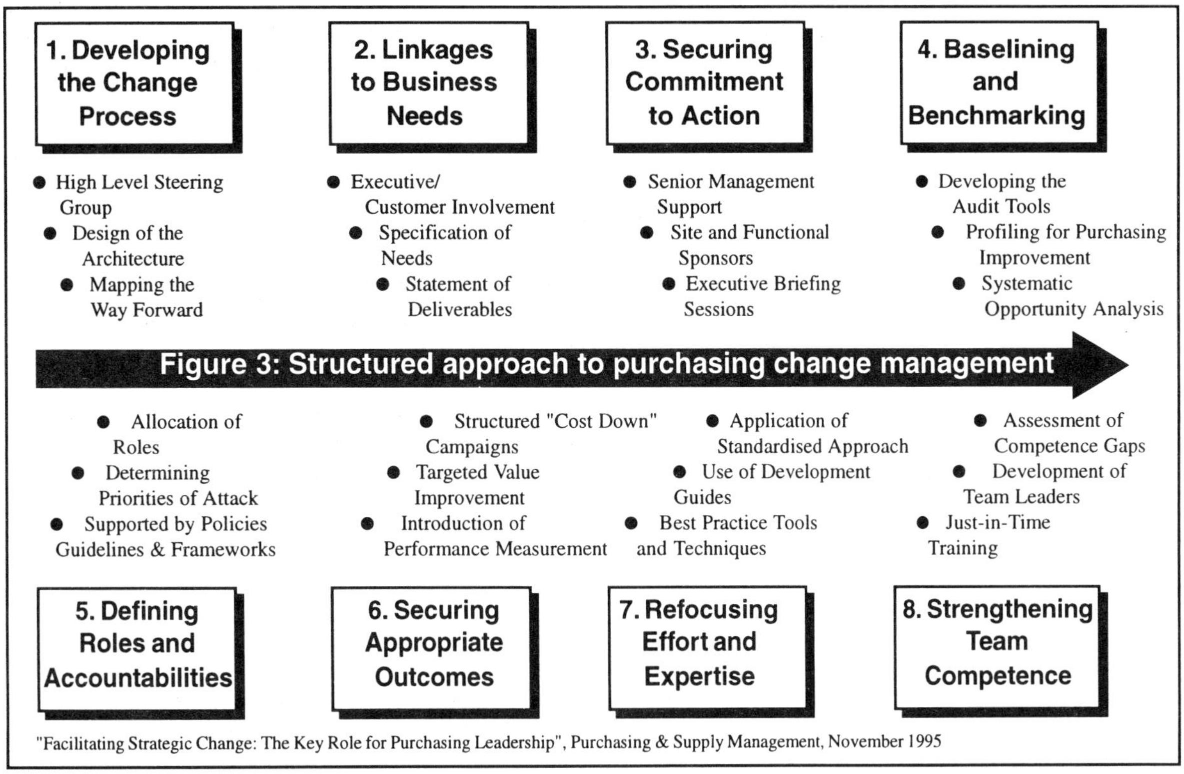

Theme 5: Applying the critical success factors

Obviously, for any change management programme to succeed, a number of critical success factors have to be present. Research evidence and practical exposure to many different types of change programmes convince us that even apparently complex change can be structured, facilitated and implemented successfully and more quickly than has sometimes been advocated. Indeed, our experience from working in many companies and sectors is that most purchasing change programmes do not fail due to an inherent flaw in the concept, vision or strategic intent but simply because of inadequacies and shortcomings of implementation. While there is no 'one right way' of bringing about change, it is possible to establish a number of the critical success factors - and these should be ignored at your peril.

1 Secure active sponsorship and involvement of senior management: for any change programme to be successful, senior managers will need to be committed and be prepared to devote considerable time to it. But once they are involved and supportive, be wary of overdoing top-down change and trying to mandate the required improvements and process changes. Their role is to create the climate for change rather than forcing it through themselves; that is the role for change drivers and facilitators.

2 Form a team of change drivers: working with a committed group of like-minded individuals is an essential feature of most successful programmes - particularly early on in the exercise. Such teams will have a strong action orientation on requirements, tasks, processes, practices, outputs and deliverables. On many occasions they will need to use concentrated effort and keenly developed influencing skills to facilitate and drive change through. At the start of any programme, change rarely happens purely from consensus, although developing and building a common vision of what is attainable is essential. Consensus becomes much more important once momentum for change has been established.

3 Early wins are crucial: they are vital in building credibility, fostering management support and building or sustaining momentum. Significant performance improvement needs to be delivered in the first 12 months of implementation, even though the full impact of a change programme may not be fully experienced inside three to five years.

4 Be realistic in your timescales: although this may seem at odds with the previous point, change takes considerable time unless you are merely impacting a single operational process, such as transactional simplification or the introduction of procurement cards. A broad programme of purchasing improvement across an entire organisation calls for a measured, planned delivery path and top class project management skills. Such competencies are invariably more important than purchasing functional expertise. Unfortunately the profile of many individuals attempting to influence strategic change in purchasing is exactly the opposite way round to that which is required.

5 Concentrate on restructuring roles and responsibilities: many organisations and senior managers involved in change tend to follow a misguided theory of the ways of bringing it about. Either they have a misplaced faith in the power of training or they attempt to change behaviour by programmes of communication, consultation and other knowledge sharing activities. While these are necessary building blocks, the most powerful ways of changing behaviour are associated with placing staff into new roles, responsibilities and relationships within a different organisational context. Creating such situations forces new behaviours on people, thereby changing their attitudes.

6 Recognise the interdependencies: substantial strategic and operational change cannot be achieved without also influencing the deep-seated values, assumptions and beliefs which managers and staff in any organisation share about the way they do things. It is therefore essential that purchasing change drivers recognise that they are invariably influencing culture as much as they are improving purchasing practice. It can be of real benefit to consider ways of utilising all the levers of change, particularly those linked to reward, remuneration, performance assessment, selection criteria, career development and teamwork.

7 Measure and monitor progress: for change to work, a series of specific goals should be set covering not only the prime financial benefits of cost reduction and cash release, but also the added value deliverables of performance improvement. These goals should be careful enumerated and linked to measurement systems that track both the quantum and the process of attainment.

Capturing the full benefits

Due to many organisations either not being aware of, or not paying sufficient attention to, the critical success factors associated with business change and purchasing improvement, it is hardly surprising that their programmes have not effectively realised the anticipated benefits in quite a large number of cases. Clearly, there is considerable work still to be done in learning from effective models of change and applying such insights within carefully structured and well thought through programmes.

In this series of articles the authors have been advocating the need for strategic change and the application of a number of pioneering approaches in purchasing and supplier management. One hopes that these will be of value to the senior practitioner as some of the keys to attaining success in their efforts to enhance and strengthen purchasing's contribution to business needs. We would welcome feedback on their application.

FIGURE 4 Strategic intent at SmithKline Beecham

SUPPORTING STRATEGIC INTENT AT SMITHKLINE BEECHAM

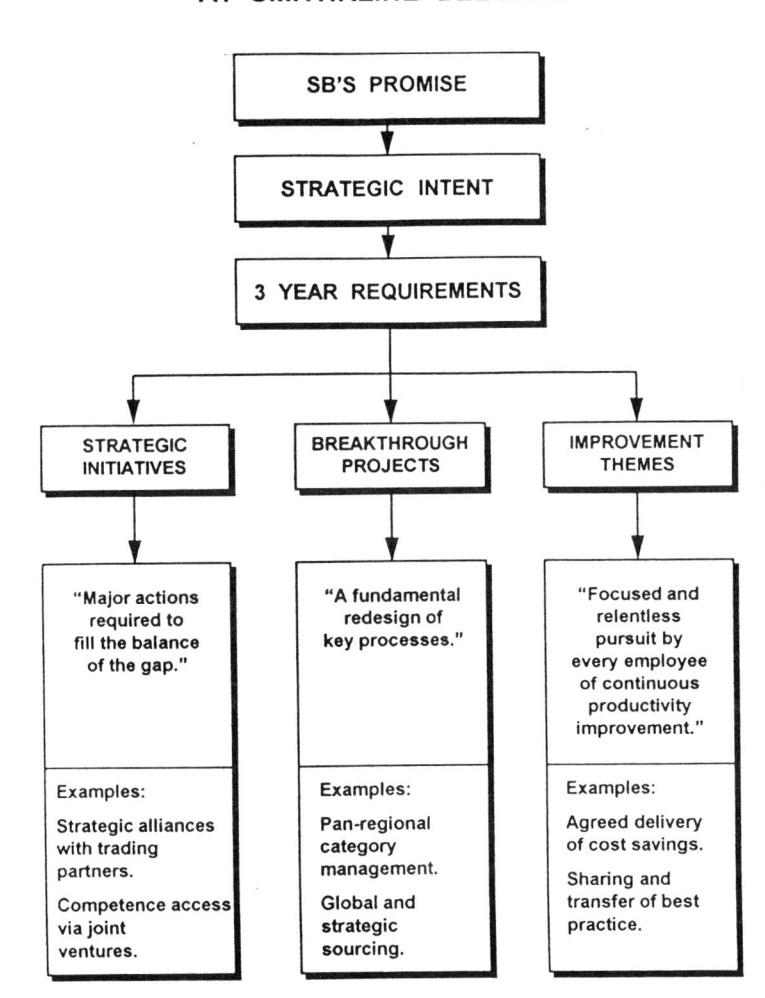

SB'S PROMISE
↓
STRATEGIC INTENT
↓
3 YEAR REQUIREMENTS
↓
- STRATEGIC INITIATIVES
- BREAKTHROUGH PROJECTS
- IMPROVEMENT THEMES

STRATEGIC INITIATIVES: "Major actions required to fill the balance of the gap."
Examples:
Strategic alliances with trading partners.
Competence access via joint ventures.

BREAKTHROUGH PROJECTS: "A fundamental redesign of key processes."
Examples:
Pan-regional category management.
Global and strategic sourcing.

IMPROVEMENT THEMES: "Focused and relentless pursuit by every employee of continuous productivity improvement."
Examples:
Agreed delivery of cost savings.
Sharing and transfer of best practice.

References:

Cox A, Hughes, J & Ralf, M, *Influencing the Strategic Agenda: The Challenge for Purchasing Leadership*, Purchasing & Supply Management, September, 1995

Ralf, M, Hughes, J & Cox, A *Developing Purchasing Leadership: Competing on Competence and Capability*, Purchasing & Supply Management, October 1995

Hughes, J & Billson, I *Purchasing Leadership and Competence Development*, Purchasing & Supply Management, May 1995

Hammer, M *Re-engineering Work: Don't Automate, Obliterate*, Harvard Business Review, July/August 1990

Hammer, M & Champy, J *Re-engineering the Corporation*, Nicholas Brealey Publishing, 1992

Garvin, DA, *Leveraging Processes for Strategic Advantage*, Harvard Business Review, September/October 1995

Schaffer, R & Thomson, HA *Successful Change Progams Begin with Results*, Harvard Business Review, January/February 1992

Chapter 2 Relationships

Carmakers shed crocodile tiers

Reduction in first-tier suppliers may not reduce the total number of firms in the supply chain

The many companies supplying original equipment (OE) components for Europe's vehicle manufacturers (VMs) are under threat on two fronts. They are being squeezed on price in what is a rapidly shrinking market.

Most of the European VMs have had to reduce production sharply with firms such ass Fiat, Ford, PSA (Peugeot and Citroen) and the Volkswagen Group suffering losses in 1993. The only significant VM to increase its sales volume during 1993 was the now BMW-controlled, but UK-based and then British Aerospace-owned, Rover Group.

As components bought in from outside suppliers make up as much as 60 to 70 per cent of a car's final cost, the above has had a notable effect on the auto component industry.

To this can be added the squeeze on price. This was highlighted by the much publicised move of the controversial director Jose Ignacio Lopez de Arriortua from General Motors to the Volkswagen Group. While at the former, he had insisted that suppliers cut their prices by as much as 20 per cent. He drastically changed GM's relations with its European suppliers prior to moving with the company to the USA. GM was able to claim one of the lowest cost bases of any European VM.

Even before Dr Lopez's return to Europe, the Volkswagen Group had been applying pressure on its suppliers to cut prices, Volkswagen talking of reductions of 25 to 30 per cent over three years; Audi and the Spanish division, Seat, demanding immediate cuts of five per cent.

Another recent development, and one which is again benefiting the UK, has been the increase in component purchasing from this country by the major European VMs, Volkswagen announced that it was to double its spend here - to DM1bn - during 1993. Another German manufacturer, Mercedes-Benz, is also spending more in the UK, while Ford has, during the lax six years, switched a higher proportion of its total European purchasing of components to the UK. Lucas Industries, for example, has reported significant contacts which include the electronic management system for the Mercedes-Benz C class, the electronic unit injector system for the Volvo FH12 and an innovative supply contract for the rear axle module on the Volkswagen Group's Skoda Favorit.

During a speech made at the biennial Paris automotive trade show, Equip'Auto in late 1993, Nissan Europe's general manager, Bob Hampson, said that component suppliers in the north-east of England now represent 'the best practice for their products in Europe'. Rover's group purchasing director, Ian Robertson, points out that due to relatively inexpensive labour costs, the present currency position, the adoption of best practice and the recognition of the gap to world class, British component makers are building a firm base for future progress.

In addition to this, the Japanese transplants in the UK, Nissan, Honda and Toyota, have made a difference to the way Britain is viewed by the components industry. In some cases the Japanese have formed their own operations. For example, in 1989, Calsonic, which is 34.5 per cent owned by the Nissan Motor Company Ltd, acquired Llanelli Radiators. Although the headquarters of this former Rover Group division are in Wales, it now has manufacturing plants close to Nissan UK's Washington, Tyne & Wear, factory in order to cope with the increasing demands of Just In Time.

Another, and very different example, is the German giant, Robert Bosch, which chose a site in Miskin, South Wales, to build a new compact alternator plant in 1992. This represented Bosch's largest-ever investment outside its own country. To prove that it is almost impossible to think of the UK component industry as a specific entity any more, 1993 saw the establishment of NMD Manufacturing, said to be one of the largest foreign investments ever made in n the West Midlands. This automotive air conditioning and heating systems manufacturer is a $97.5M joint investment between the major Italian concern Magneti Marelli and Nippondenso of Japan. The latter, according to a report published in April 1994 by The Economist Intelligence Unit, is now the third largest automotive component supplier in Europe, ahead of Bosch and behind only ACG, the components arm of General Motors, and the French tyre manufacturer, Michelin. The latter has two plants in the UK, Stoke-on-Trent and Dundee.

It is not just the UK that has become attractive to the Japanese, the EC ensuring that the term 'local content' applies to anything manufactured in Europe. NGK, second only to Champion among the world's sparking plug manufacturers, now has a plant at Meung-sur-Loire in France.

The above must, though, be viewed against a background where the VMs are making strenuous efforts to cut down on the number of first-tier suppliers. Ford intends cutting its 900 suppliers to 600 over the next five years, Audi want to reduce its 950 to between 300 and 400 over a similar period. Peugeot and Citroen hope to cut their 900 by half by the end of the century. Ten years ago the number stood at 2,800.

The use of second-tier suppliers means that this is not as drastic as it first sounds. According to a report prepared for the European Commission by the Boston Consultancy Group and presented in November last year, the European automotive components industry is likely to change to a tiered structure similar to that of the Japanese. It sees a concentration of around 500 first-tier suppliers with two to six competitors for most key sub-systems.

The VMs will point out that they understand the problems such drastic changes bring, and are at pains to preserve the health of their supplier base for the good of all parties.

Nissan UK, for example, states that it looks upon its suppliers as a 'family'. It operates a supplier development team (SDT) which initially worked with a pilot group of 12 suppliers, but now with between 59 and 60 per cent of just under 200-company supplier base. Indeed, any company 'doing significant business' with Nissan is likely to be involved with the SDT team.

TABLE 1 Europe's top component companies by automotive turnover, 1993 (Ecu million)

Table 1 Europe's top component companies by automotive turnover, 1993
(Ecu million)

1 ACG (various)	19,250
2 Michelin (tyres)	9,616
3 Nippondenso (various including electrics & electronics)	9,016
4 Bosch ((electrics & electronics)	8,600
5 Goodyear (tyres)	7,777
6 Motorola (electrics & electronics)	6,160
7 Continental (tyres)	4,201
8 Philips (electrics & electronics)	3,608
9 TRW (restraints, steering, suspension & engine valves)	3,554
10 AlliedSignal (various, including brakes, plugs, turbochargers and filters)	3,465

Source: The Economist Intelligence Unit

TABLE 2 Automotive components production in the EC by country, 1992

Table 2 Automotive components production in the EC by country, 1992

	Ecu bn	%
1 Germany	43.6	47
2 France	18.0	19
3 UK	10.8	12
4 Italy	10.2	11
5 Spain	6.9	7
6 Rest of EC	3.2	4
Total	92.7	100

Source: Boston Consultancy Group

Rover is another which points out that it has moved away from the debilitating, adversarial relationships of the past and has developed interdependent partnerships. A 1991 purchasing mission statement said: 'Suppliers have a choice. Our ability to purchase the best goods and services depends on their ability to supply. They need to have confidence in our commitment to them in order to invest in the sort of future products that we will need for the benefit of both parties. We depend on the co-operation of the other. We must strive to act as a preferred customer in these relationships.'

It is not just its first-tier suppliers with which Rover is concerned. While VMs are cutting down drastically on the number of these, relying more on sub assemblies, the health of the second and third-tier suppliers remains of vital importance to the whole. Ian Robertson wants his direct suppliers to pass on what they are learning down the value chain to their own suppliers. This, he believes, is an area in which European manufacturers have the edge over their competitors in Japan, where standards deteriorate further down the chain.

Assistance is given to Rover's suppliers through the VM's Supplier Development Team and Suppliers Associations. An example of the latter is the 25-strong Welsh Suppliers Organisation which was wet up in 1993 sharing such a bet practice.

As part of the interdependence between VM and component manufacturers, Rover Group has taken steps to assist its traditional supplier base in achieving even better levels of quality control. ('There is no point in taking initiative if our supplier base is not prepared to come with us,' Rover International managing director, John Russell told this year's *Financial Times* London Motor Conference.) One of the most visible examples of support was the introduction last year of a new Supplier Excellence award.

Such awards are perhaps the most visible way in which the VMs support their suppliers. Arguably the best known is the Ford Q1 programme. Such schemes are not just a reward. Speaking in 1991 in 1991, Ford Europe's vice president of supply Alan Spencer said 'From 1 January 1992 we will not give any new business to anyone who is not Q1 and by the end of 1993 we will be looking to take business away, if we have to, from people who are not Q1.'

The French-owned PSA (which operates the Peugeot factory in the UK) rates suppliers as A, B and C. It stated that all of them must be A-rated by the end of 1993 or they would be removed from its approved list.

Quality supply awards, given by VMs to their first-tier suppliers, have become almost commonplace. In the USA those suppliers themselves are now starting their own such schemes. One such is Hitachi Automotive Products (USA) Inc, of Harrodsburg, Kentucky, a manufacturer of automotive electric and electronic components, which has just handed out its third annual set of top supplier awards.

this is a logical step. The days are past when the manufacture of a car was a two-level operation, with component manufacturer simply supplying VM direct. Now the operation has more of a pyramid structure. The first-tier suppliers have a raft of second and third-tier suppliers, all of which must come up to the high standards expected by the VMs. It is up to the first tier companies to ensure that they are dealing with the right manufacturers if they, in their turn, wish to retain the VMs' business and to win for themselves the coveted VMs' quality supply awards.

According to Ian Robertson, Rover's new Supplier Excellence awards were not introduced to celebrate any achievements that may have been made by the component companies, but to encourage them to improve even further and ultimately achieve world class quality. Interestingly, Robertson observes that the companies most likely to achieve the higher scores in the wards come from the electrical electronic and trim fields. Those achieving awards, but with lower scores, are more likely to supply items such ass forgings and castings.

The 'highly objective' scheme is driven by Rover's supplier initiative RG 2000 which itself was launched in October 1991. This replaced the traditional ARG 100 programme. (Rover's previous awards scheme, the Sterling Awards, have been based strongly on on-site service as well as product quality.) RG 2000 was designed to consider all the elements of a supplier's performance, including its management culture, in order to construct a joint development plan based on best practice and Just In Time production. It uses BS5750 as a base quality benchmark. Rover's opinion was that there was too much waste in other VMs' supplier assessment programmes and that an external, international standard like BS5750/ISO9000 should be accepted.

The reduction in the number of suppliers mentioned above has naturally been accompanied by a move away from dual sourcing. For the VMs this places an increased dependence on their chosen suppliers.

Rover expects to be involved in the design process enabling components to be manufactured in the most cost-effective way for both parties. A benefit of this has been that the company has been able to reduce its new model development from the traditional Western norm of bout 50 months to 39, not much more than the Japanese norm of approximately 36 months.

Ian Robertson places suppliers into four distinct groups. He describes those suppliers who have achieved World Class as 'mature'. The second category consists of those learning what has to be done to move up a division. The third group are those who have come to realise that something has to be done and, probably, what that is, but have yet to progress further. The fourth category he dismisses as 'the total what?' - those who have no idea that they need to improve, let alone what has to be done.

It is his contention that most of his company's suppliers are currently in the second and third categories, a state of affairs that he hopes the new awards will alter. As an incentive, Rover broadcast the results in paid space placed in the *Financial Time.* Robertson hoped that sight of such an advertisement

Partnerships - what's really going on?

During 1993, Norman Hosford was assigned from the Purchasing Department of British Airways to become Deputy Director of Partnership Sourcing Ltd. Part of his task was to research the development of partnership sourcing as a strategic approach to purchasing by companies of all sectors and sizes, spanning those engaged both in manufacturing and in services.

The research carried out was a mix of desk research, mainly of British and American writings, and personal interviews with purchasing executives. 28 companies in the UK were visited, along with 4 in the USA and 4 in Europe. As a form of triangulation, discussions took place with purchasing academics in England, Scotland, Wales, the Netherlands, France and the USA. The research endeavoured to be qualitative rather than quantitative, to provide a richness of case histories.

One aspect of the research was to ascertain how companies chose a partner, how they implement a programme and what the implications for their supply base might be.

This article looks at whether companies consciously choose a partner in a considered and scientific way, or whether they wake up one morning and find this partner alongside them. Do deliberate partnerships work better than accidental ones? Do companies implement partnering programmes in a 'big bang' way, or do they implement incrementally?

Ian Robinson (1992) Chairman of the Engineering division of John Brown, says: 'Partnerships are only possible with clients and contractors who have worked together for some time - perhaps five years as a minimum.'

This is more than substantiated by Hendricks and Ellram (1993) who report that companies form full partnering relations after doing business together for a mean of 14 years.

In my research, all companies said that their preference was to form partnering relations with companies they had been dealing with for some time. Unlike in the Hendrick and Ellram survey (1993) buyers were not specific in how long they had been dealing with those companies.

Several companies used the same analogy for the progression of their business relationships; courtship, engagement and eventually marriage.

The exception to this progression is one company's use of new suppliers to break cartel supply situations, where they deliberately seek out new suppliers, and two other companies where both said they look to new suppliers where different and advanced technologies were required.

Another company is very specific in its requirements for partnering. They believe it needs to be a company with whom they have had good dealings in the past, who they can understand and who are culturally acceptable. They need to open their books to the extent that their financial viability and stability can be assessed, and they need to provide a financial plan for the future. Moreover, they need to be willing to co-cost their products and they need to work with their customer to value engineer cost out. This need for cost development is echoed by one motor manufacturer which said that each of its partners has to be willing to accept the principles of continuous step by step improvement, and by another which looks for companies willing to adopt continuous improvement processes.

As well as this requirement for continuous improvement, other attributes sought by companies in a partner are:

- sustainable quality - the elimination of defects
- good delivery performance - for security of supply, and on time
- clear communication channels - sharing of views, plans etc.
- competitive pricing - in world markets
- production flexibility - the ability to gear volume up or down and to modify the product if required.

How companies implement

This part will review two aspects, the first being whether companies implement their programme in an incremental way, or whether they implement with all their partners at once. The second is the length of time they have been operating partnerships, and the third aspect is a review of which products and services they choose to cover with partnering arrangements.

Incrementally or at once?

There is nothing in the literature reviewed that discusses this aspect, and I believe no previous research has addressed this.

FIGURE 1 - PIE CHART: *Implementation*

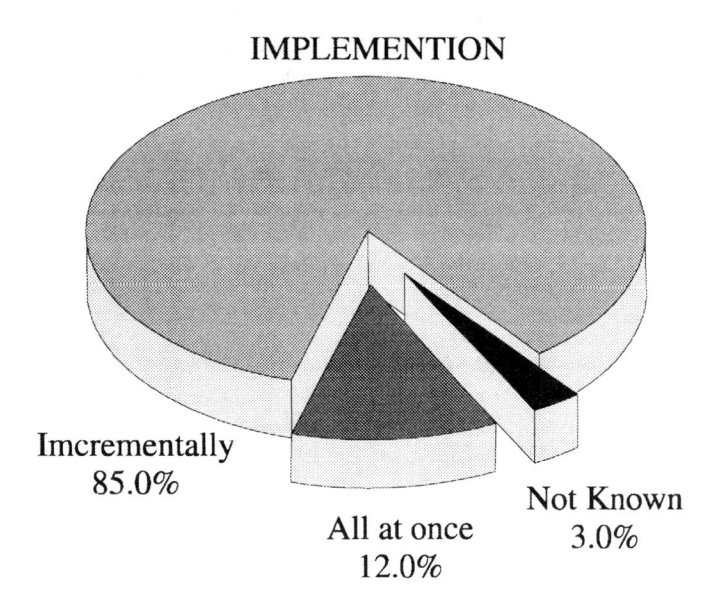

IMPLEMENTION

Imcrementally 85.0%

All at once 12.0%

Not Known 3.0%

Of the companies I researched, 85 per cent say that they implemented partnering incrementally (see Figure 1). That is, gradually and over time, partnering with a chosen few and then expanding as required.

Twelve per cent of companies said they implemented their programme all at once, but of these half said it caused some problems. One company in the UK in fact said that the whole programme went wrong as it had not communicated fully to its suppliers the philosophy behind the change in approach, and neither did it have the staff resource to manage the implementation. One American company also introduced partnering in a 'big bang' way, but admitted that it is still tuning the process. One particular company said that it had implemented partnering so long ago and it was such a part of the culture it had forgotten how it did it.

Length of time companies have been operating partnering

It is relevant to know this to put into context the claimed benefits and to be able to make judgements about how valid the learning experiences are. Most relationships do not come to partnering in a 'big bang' way, but evolve and develop over time. Nevertheless, there is a point where, according to the judgement of those involved, partnering exists.

There is little in the literature regarding the length of time UK companies have been operating in a partnering way, except the Cousins (1993) survey report.

In this he finds it surprising that the majority of respondents have been operating partnership for between one an three years only, even though this substantiates current literature. However, also surprisingly, some 11 per cent of the respondents have been operating partnering relationships for more than five years. He views this as a higher number than expected and, assuming that the definition of partnership was understood, is an encouraging result.

In their survey, Hendrick and Ellram (1993), report that the mean number of years buyers have been operating partnering relations is 4.31 years.

Of the UK companies I interviewed, there was a range of duration of partnering relationships. The minimum period was one year, with a mode of two years. However, one company had been operating for 35 years, another for 15 years and one for 10 years. So, with these latter exceptions, strategic purchasing partnering has been in operation for a relatively short period of time, which bears out Cousins' findings.

The US companies I researched had been operating for longer periods; the average is 7 years, somewhat longer than that in the Hendrick and Ellram survey.

Which products and services?

Companies select their approach to this aspect according to their motivation for partnering. This is manifested in two ways. If the company is an assembler of bought-in assemblies and believes that to have a quality product for the market it needs all of its bought-in products to be perfect in every sense, it will partner with all of its suppliers. The most common examples are in the motor vehicle and computer industries.

The second practice occurs where a company purchases a wide range of goods and services that require varying degrees of attention. Companies usually select these for partnering through a three-stage process:
i) pareto on spend
ii) risk items
iii) routine

i) The company analyses all goods and services an selects those that are the highest spend. Typically they find 20 per cent of suppliers account for 80 per cent of the spend. Therefore, it is possible to form partnering relations with relatively few suppliers, but at the same time to cover the majority of spend with strategic partnering relations.

ii) Purchases are then analysed for risk. If they are absolutely critical to the company's operation, whilst being of low value, then these too are added to the partnering portfolio to secure supply and non-interrupted deliveries. Fairly obviously any item which is high spend and also jeopardises the operation will attract a greater degree of attention.

iii) Almost a paradox, some companies find worth in partnering for low value, low risk items. An example is stationery, which today many companies obtain from one partner supplier under a blanket contract and have delivered to the desk of the user, bypassing the traditional store. This reduces the amount of purchasing time spent on a low value activity, releasing staff for higher value adding projects and eliminating the cost of operating the store.

There is a general belief that the only purchase area unsuited to partnering is for commodity goods. By definition the specification and quality are equal wherever the purchase is made. As there is no differentiation, the purchase decision is based on price alone and there is no benefit in staying with the incumbent supplier.

I consider that partnering is applicable in commodity purchases for two reasons. The first and most obvious is to avoid switching costs. The second is that although the product may be solely price driven, certain service features can be implemented by the vendor to provide differentiation and enhancement.

Supplier reduction

The research showed that only 16 per cent of companies had supplier reduction as a motivating factor for partnering.

However, there is a reality for many companies who approach partnering from another motivational point that, as a result of the introduction of partnering, they reduce their supplier base.

this move is complemented by organisations reducing the levels of management, resulting in managers no longer having the time to manage a large supplier base.

Lamming (1992) says: 'Industrial companies frequently speak in terms of working with fewer, closer suppliers with whom partnerships can be built. Evidence shows supply bases shrinking as attempts are made to emulate Japanese business relationships.'

These observations are in line with those of Deming (1982) and Mangelsdorf (1991). AT Kearney (1993) reports that a sample of buyers said that they aim to reduce the number of suppliers by 20 per cent per annum, although they do not state for how many years the activity will be effected.

However, Porter (1985, p106) takes a very different view. He proposes that firms can take a number of specific actions to enhance their bargaining power with suppliers:

- Keep the number of sources sufficient to ensure competition, but small enough to be an important buyer to each source.
- Select suppliers who are especially competitive with each other, and divide purchases amongst them.
- Vary the proportion of business awarded to suppliers over time to ensure that they do not view it as an entitlement.

Whereas I did not ask the specific question, as I was not initially aware of the significance, companies volunteered the information on supplier reduction, shown below

Company	Originally	Now
A	10,000	3,000
B	10,000	3,000
C	265	117
D	6,000	1,000
E	2,000	750
F	900	332
G	450	300
H	2,000	500
I	2,300	500
J	3,300	979

this has been achieved in two significant ways, first, by reducing the degree of multiple sourcing carried out. Although not always the case, most buyers are tending towards single sourcing to reduce the waste inherent in multiple sourcing situations. They reduce the cost of duplication in R&D, design, tooling, plant and equipment, as well as internal costs. This desire to reduce suppliers is coupled to the partnering strategy as a way to reduce risk by exposure to a reduced supply base.

Secondly, they are purchasing assemblies rather than individual components. I was given this example, which may be apocryphal, but serves very well to illustrate the point. A motor vehicle manufacturer used to buy nuts, bolts, vinyl, foam, runners and a host of other materials from a total of 57 companies to manufacture seats. Now it purchases seats complete from one specialist manufacturer.

Implications

The movement toward reducing supplier numbers must have a significant, if not yet researched, effect on manufacturing companies. Those who are chosen suppliers in single sourcing will do very well as their production levels increase and reduce unit cost. In his study commissioned by 3i, Robinson (1992) describes the benefit to a company which had been chosen as a single source supplier as an increase to production of 70,000 pieces a year, rather than the original 100,000. Those which were de-listed and lost the business will suffer accordingly. There ought to be, however, a situation where other OEMs deal with these companies, balancing the effect of the original loss of business. This suggests that in time supply chains will become more discrete.

The other phenomenon is the one of assembly buying which creates a tiering of suppliers. In the example used above, the assemblers of the seat will still have to purchase the majority of his components from the original suppliers of their competitors. Thus the end-purchaser of the components produced is still the same, but another link in the supply chain has been introduced to allow the OEM to concentrate on his core manufacturing activity.

This does not suggest an abrogation of control of quality, delivery, service or cost. Gray (1992) describes Nissan training some of its suppliers' purchasing staff in 'partnership philosophy' so they can help their production costs. This initiative has led to Nissan personnel visiting more than 30 second-tier suppliers, to work with them on eliminating waste and improving assembly-line organisation. In some cases this has produced reductions in cost, which are being passed along the chain to Nissan.

Summary

Although companies may have different motivating factors for entering into partnering relationships, there is no evidence to suggest a correlation between motivation and choice of partner. Partners are chosen on the basis of all-round excellent ability to provide quality products at a competitive cost and willingness to become a partner and work toward continuous improvement.

It is important to understand that partnership relations grow over time as mutual respect and trust develops. It takes commitment and attention to create a partnership which will succeed in the medium and long terms.

Consistently, all recent research shows that companies in America have been partnering for longer than those in the UK.

One of the most significant products of this research is that since Michael Porter put his views on leverage in 1985, strongly proposing the advantage of a fragmented supply base, the large majority of companies which view purchasing as a strategic function have radically reduced their supply base or are in the process of doing so.

The implication of partnering programmes consistently reduces supplier bases, whether or not this was an original motivation. Consequently, the structure of supply chains and of industry itself is changing.

References:

Cousins, P, UK Partnership Sourcing Survey, University of Bath, 1993

Deming, WE Improvement of quality and productivity through action by management, National productivity Review, Winter 1982 pp 12-22

Gray, R, Nissan links up ;with suppliers, *Financial Times*, 14 December 1992

Hendrick, T, and Ellram, I, Strategic supplier partnering: an international study, Center for Advanced Purchasing Studies, University of Arizona, Phoenix, 1993

Kearney, AT, *Leaders and Laggers in Logistics '92*, February 1993, pp14

Lamming, R, ACME Research Project: Relationship Assessment, 15 July 1992,

Case for support; new research project

Mangelsdorf, ME, Broken promises INC, July 1991, pp25-27

Porter, ME, Competitive advantage, Collier MacMillan, London, 1985 pp106

Robinson, T Partners in providing the goods, A study commissioned by 3i, 1992

Robinson, I Partnering secures plans for the future, *Trafalgar House News*, September 1992 p9.

Implementing a supply chain philosophy

Seeing fair play at a supplier conference for a major food retailer

Questions:

What does being unknown, an academic, having o previous experience in the role, and unpaid, qualify you to do? Answer: Chair a supplier conference for a leading, blue-chip UK food retailer. This was the eagerly awaited task which befell me recently because I had precisely those qualities which the company was looking for. In other words, I was in the neutral corner! More seriously, the food company's Supply Chain Director, having realised many of his ambitions internally in terms of creating a supply chain philosophy, was now intent on developing the necessary external links and partnerships which would self-evidently be the next step. He therefore drew up a shortlist of those of his suppliers and distribution contractors who were likely to respond most positively to his initiative and invited them to a half-day Supply Chain Conference at the company's head office. Eleven companies were on the list ranging from medium to large UK-based food manufacturers and processors. There was also one small to medium sized transport contractor and a large national distribution company which was a significant operator of the firm's infrastructure.

The chairman's role

The Supply Chain Director was anxious that the discussions be as free-flowing and open as possible. In no way did he want to inhibit or intimidate the participants. This however was obviously a strong possibility since the talks were taking place in the inner sanctum of the company's operations. Also, not only would he himself be present and take a leading role (and he was a strong and forceful character with well-known views and, of course, a Board member), but also there would be several of his team there. The chances of raw nerves being touched, or defensive attitudes being struck were evidently high. He therefore decided to introduce a neutral chairman whose job would be threefold:

- To keep the event free-flowing, ensure fair play, encourage everyone to participate, and ensure that the host learned from, rather than dominated, the proceedings
- Develop and maintain a momentum to the meeting
- To come up with a series of joint action plans which would represent positive outcomes of the conference.

The job could be intimidating or easy. Like all these things it depended on whether there was a willingness to participate, and a meeting of minds.

The participants

A basic philosophy underlying the organising of the conference had been that Buyers and National Accounts Managers, as traditional antagonists or, at the least, cast in a negotiating role should be *persona non grata*. Therefore the participants were, on the suppliers' side, mainly operations or logistics directors and managers, and on the company's side, stock re-ordering, distribution and logistics personnel. It was interesting to note, however, that some companies just could not envisage a meeting taking place with an important customer without a certain amount of hand-holding by the senior sales staff, who therefore tagged along! All those invited turned up on the day. In all, there were 17 supplier representatives, half a dozen representatives of the company and myself. A sufficiently small number to be manageable and, one hoped, to allow everyone's views to be heard. There had been some attempt to spread participation across the product groups and make sure that out-and-out rivals were not forced to endure each other's company although in the event direct competitors did sit down together, and on the day this was no problem.

Format

A regular conference room was used, a round table seating arrangement and dualled video equipment for ease of viewing. Flipboards were set up at each end of the room so that anyone who wanted to demonstrate a point could easily do so. The running of the meeting and the atmosphere were kept as informal as possible to encourage people to relax and be forthcoming. A particular point was made of the fact that no minutes were taken. The only written output was the list of problems, issues, opportunities, listed on the flip chart by the chairman.

The conference opened with two brief slide /video presentations which outlined the company's position and its objectives, plus a survey of recent developments.

The next two sessions were allowed to run into each other. Basically the flip chart was used to note the company's strengths and weaknesses under five main headings:

1   Putting on promotions
2   Forecasting
3   Ordering systems
4   Warehouse operations
5   Payment methods

Any examples where other companies were doing things better, or examples of Best Practice, were noted in a different coloured marker pen.

The last session before lunch was an opportunity for everyone around the table to predict, Delphi-like, their views of the future.

A shortened lunch break was followed by the formulation of a series of short-term projects between the company and individual suppliers, and the meeting closed one hour early without moving onto the development of a long term plan which, it was generally felt, would arise out of reports to the follow-up meeting.

How did it go?

The conference was, in fact, wonderfully easy to chair. The level of participation was high, the agenda was covered, and the company's original objectives achieved. The chairman's role was virtually that of wielding a marker-pen! What then were these objectives?
1   To encourage closer links between the company an the invited suppliers
2   To review the company's performance from its suppliers' point of view
3   To develop a short-term plan to improve upon some of the weaknesses identified
4   To come up with defined projects with a number of individual suppliers which could be reviewed at a further meeting
5   To develop long-term projects with individual suppliers
6   To develop sufficient enthusiasm for a further meeting.
All the objectives, with the exception of No 5 as already mentioned, were, I feel achieved.

After the initial back ground presentation, it was decided to do a quick first-pass on the five headings listed for discussion, noting strengths and weaknesses. This went well, but of course the emphasis was on the weaknesses rather than the strengths. The only issue which was not discussed was the last one - payment methods. This had, in fact, been added almost as an afterthought, but in any case there was a great reluctance amongst those present to say anything about it at all. As the issue was therefore apparently taboo, it was left on one side to avoid interrupting the very free flow of ideas an give-and-take which was otherwise evident.

The discussion was not led at all, and the emphasis given to topics was decided by the group as a whole. The only constraint imposed was a time limit which ensured that all the issues were covered.

In examining the outcomes, I think it is important to stress that having visited the company on several occasions (indeed having had two of my students on placement there for a year), I found it to be vibrant, positive and alive with the ethos of tea,-working. Staff were on the whole young, friendly and professional. And this is how the suppliers found the company - internally. Externally, in terms of the quality and depth of the relationship it had with its suppliers, and in terms of the amount and quality of information provided and the level of communication, it was perceived to be poor - one of the worst of the blue-chip customers in fact. This came, I think, as something of a shock to the management.

The main issues

What then were some of the main issues raised? First of all forecasting. The company's forecasts were not deemed worth the paper they were printed on. Despite all the money invested in improving systems, revamping technology, installing DALLAS, EDI links and EPOS (with which all stores would be equipped by the middle of next year), and its developments towards a sales-based ordering system, the company in general terms failed its suppliers in predicting what demand would be on a disaggregated bias. Overall monthly figures might be reasonably accurate, but when it came down to daily or weekly figures, weaknesses were quite apparent. Not only was the forecasting not robust enough, but the phasing of take-off of product was continually being changed.

In part, and this raises the second main issue, this was due to changes in promotional activity. Promotional dates and volumes were totally unreliable. The fact that the company was promotion-led (promotion accounting for up to 30 per cent of total volumes sold) obviously did not help, but it was clear that there were some fundamental problems here. The ramifications along the supply chain were significant - lack of an ability to plan effective use of resources, excess stocks, extra transport having to be laid on at short notice, or deliveries being refused because they were not wanted. Often only deliveries which were needed urgently because of a backlog of demand were accepted. Written like this in the cold light of day, this situation for a blue-chip company in 1994 seems perhaps surprising. But is it so very different from what happens in other companies? My own experience would suggest not. We read a lot in both professional and academic journals about leading-edge technologies, systems and operations, yet the reality is often starkly different.

The third main issue raised was lack of co-ordination in warehouse operations. There was no effective booking-slot system, lorries were delayed unreasonably or, as noted before, turned away altogether - the typical reason given was that the warehouse was full.

Fourthly, on the question of ordering systems, lead-times and related issues, the company currently worked on a one week lead-time. But it became evident at the conference that far from having difficulty in meeting the 72 hour call-off which was mooted, some companies were offering a 48 hour turn-around. This had always been available but never been requested or discussed!

Fifthly, it became apparent throughout the talks that the retailer had not implemented any effective measurements of operations in the supply chain, or if it had it was keeping them to itself. The suppliers wanted to be involved in measurement of their service level and indeed measurement of the customers' activities - accuracy of forecasts, unloading times etc.

Last, but most important, and the thread that ran throughout the day, communications. It would be unfair to say that there were no communications between the company an its suppliers but at times, listening to the comments they made, it certainly seemed that way. The company's personnel each presumably thought that communications were adequate enough, but virtually every weakness identified at the meeting revolved around poor communications in one way or another. Is it not often the case that 'get the communications right and any other problems will fall away?'

The outcomes

So, plenty to think about. What could be done to improve the situation? As per the agenda, the session after lunch was given over to considering all the points raised and putting together a short-term plan. In the context of the meeting this was done by suggesting a course of action, a project, for each of the issues, and then asking for a volunteer supplier to work with the company to devise an action plan. The results were to be reported at a future meeting. In all, seven projects were agreed, and there was no shortage of volunteers. The objectives of each project were outlined, and a careful note made of those responsible within the company for its planning and implementation.

As examples of the projects, one was set up to put into practice fixed time-slot delivery bookings and improved turnaround procedures. The benefits of this were to be measured in as much detail as possible. Another was devised to try to crack the problem of alternations in the promotional programmes by ensuring an overkill in communications. However, one thing which became quite clear was that the definitions of the issues involved in each project blurred imperceptibly into each other. All the projects demanded measurement and improved communications, and all depended to some extent on accuracy of orders and therefore demand. Having said that, there was a different *emphasis* to each, and the different parties taking part would obviously ensure that different directions were taken in each project. Finally, it was agreed that the group would be kept in being and would met again six months hence to review progress, learn whatever lessons there were to be learned and make longer term plans.

Was the conference successful? On almost every count, yes. The Supply Chain Director had made a bold decision to convene the conference in the first place, subjecting himself and his staff to the possibility of some strong criticism. However, the decision to base the format essentially on a review of the company's weaknesses proved to be a wise one. It cleared the air and enabled the group to enter a problem-solving mode. As one participant said, what was being done was essential. Without a move towards co-operation along the supply chain, companies would simply not survive.

It was interesting that the suppliers all saw the implementation of a supply chain philosophy as a series of practical measures rather than some airy-fairy, academic paradigm. They saw the results in the hands of those present, and were reluctant to see the benefits of analysing leading-edge and Best Practice techniques in other industries - the car industry for example.

Also, the least suggestion of any exploratory work being done which was not specifically related to a particular problem or issue was viewed in a very negative way. At one point, for instance, I raised the possibility of a project which would concentrate on supply chain mapping, but quickly moved the discussion onto other areas when the reaction suggested there was no interest. This was - I feel, a pity - for Supply Chain Mapping is aimed at identifying both stocks and processes in the supply chain and therefore facilitating a problem-solving approach - highlighting pinch-points and duplication of resources for example.

Perhaps this short-term outlook was inevitable. After all, we deliberately omitted the session which would look at developing a long-term plan. But it does contrast rather strangely with the suppliers' request that the company articulate a clear vision for the future which all could understand and work towards.

It could be argued that the tenor and level of the conference was pitched exactly right. There was no discussion of finance, or division of the costs and benefits which might arise. This was rightly left for a future occasion although it could just as well have been tackled by agreeing to share costs and benefits 50/50 (a lesson from the United States which in my experience, probably goes right over the tops of the heads of most UK companies!).

It could be argued that six months is too long a gap before holding the next meeting, but it does enable sound analysis of the problems to take place and, one hopes, effective solutions to be developed which can then be shared. If the group gels, if there are positive outcomes and if there is a willingness to continue working in a co-ordinated way, then it may be appropriate to set up more regular meetings.

Comparison with the Kyoryoku Kai mechanism

One of the latest flavours of the month to come out of Japan is the forming of supplier associations or Kyoryoku Kai. Peter Hines was instrumental in setting up an early pilot trial with Calsonic Llanelli Radiators which has since blossomed into nine fully operational suppliers associations, most clustered in Wales*

However, the UK type or model of suppliers association which he describes seems to be a long way from the Japanese closed society or club on which he bases his comparison. But it is very close, I feel, to what I have been describing here. In fact, without any formal framework at all, a much softer, informal UK-style approach has created a vibrancy, a momentum which has the potential to bring very substantial benefits, and will, I am sure, lead to true supply chain partnership. This does not owe anything in principle to Japanese teaching and, personally, I think it is the stronger for that.

This is not to say that there are not certain features of the supplier associations which could be taken and developed by the food retailer. There are. Risk-sharing between customer and supplier, for example, a high degree of R&D interlock, supplier self-certification, customer development of suppliers close, long-term relations between 'club' members.

Creating World Class Suppliers: unlocking mutual competitive advantage, P Hines, Pitman, available through the CIPS Bookshop, telephone 01780 56777 for order details.

Capabilities will supersede brands

Supply chain management will increasingly be the key area of competition for manufacturing and retail companies as competitive tools. Instead, the emphasis will be on a company's overall capabilities and partnership relationships between buying organisations and their suppliers will become an accepted feature of business life.

Those were some of the predictions made by the professor of marketing and logistics systems at the UK's Cranfield School of Management, Martin Christopher, during a recent seminar organised by logistics service company Exel Logistics in London.

Speaking on the subject of 'Strategic Partnering in the Supply Chain', he said that in marketing terms, companies had traditionally competed through the development of strong brands, projection of a corporate image and by focusing on the benefits their products could give customers.

'Now obviously that is still there - I am not trying in any way to diminish the importance of strong brands, of strong corporate images and so forth', he said, 'but classic marketing really is having to change to take on board the fact that the way companies today are winning is not so much through their brands but through what we call their capabilities.'

Elaborating on that point he said that by 'capabilities', he basically meant the way things were done.

For instance, one of the factors in the success of North American retailer Wal-Mart over recent years - getting double the margins of most retailers in that market - was not that it sold a vastly different range of products at vastly different prices to its competitors but the efficiency of the company's inbound logistics. That operation enabled the company to get products onto shelves in an incredible - by North American standards - timescale with superior stockturns with resultant benefits for the bottom line.

In the UK, continued Professor Christopher, one of the reasons why 3M has developed its leadership position in many markets was its prowess in getting new products to market quickly. The company was able to do that because it had developed extremely fast ways of getting products from the drawing board into the market.

'Increasingly, capabilities will be where the action is. In logistics terms, that essentially means we are going to start putting that process under a lot more scrutiny - the process of how we manage the flow from whatever part of the chain we are looking at', he said.

He cited the case of UK automotive industry manufacturer Rover. That company, he said, had put a 'quite dramatic' focus on developing upstream partnerships. A few years ago, the company had 2000 suppliers - now that was down to 500 and the immediate target was a further reduction to 300.

Rover and its suppliers were now working in what they called the 'extended enterprise'. The manufacturer was seeking to break down any remaining barriers with that much smaller supplier base, to see them as part of the same business. The benefits emerging from that approach had been dramatic in terms of taking costs out, claimed Professor Christopher.

In many supply chains, costs were simply transferred to someone else rather than actually taken out altogether. 'Several studies have shown that the advantages companies have gained from going over to JIT manufacturing have in many cases been bought t the expense of their upstream suppliers. In other words, all they have done is pushed the inventory onto someone else's shelf,' he said.

'The same is true if we look outside the manufacturing sector - many of the leaps forward taken by retailers in improving their stockturns have been gained at the expense of upstream suppliers.'

Now, companies were coming to realise that all costs ultimately ended up in the finished products, and those costs had got to be covered by price at some point. So in looking at ways of taking costs out, companies were focusing on the way they did things - in other words, their capabilities.

Another important trend in purchasing habits, continued Prof Christopher, was that even though people still looked for strong brands, customers were making more and more buying decisions on the basis of commodity purchases. That trend was highlighted, for example, by the rise of own-label brands.

'There are some fundamental changes going on in the market place. Recession may have accelerated that process but it is a lot to do with consumer choice and sophistication and the growing experience of buyers whether it be in manufacturing, or as individual consumers', said Prof Christopher.

Customers were getting much more demanding in terms of looking for value - and not just value money. Increasingly, the focus was on ways they could add more value to their customer's business or, in the case of sales to consumers, how they could add more value to the purchaser's lifestyle.

The successful companies were those which were able to work more successfully with their downstream customers, seeking to impact their value chain, continued Prof Christopher.

'By that, I mean they are trying to find better ways in which they can service their customers so they take costs out of their value chain - for example, taking out inventory, reducing the need for inbound inspection and re-working because the supplier has got total quality, and cutting the costs of paperwork, re-ordering and invoice checking through the use of EDI (electronic data interchange) linkages and so on,' he said.

'Interestingly, when you bring all this together, you are in fact creating one of the strongest barriers to entry for competitors that you are ever going to find, because when you have established these multiple linkages with customers in this way, it gets increasingly more difficult for competitors to break them apart.'

Explaining that argument, he claimed the traditional relationship between a buyer and a supplier was a pretty tenuous one. It was an argument, basically, between a sales person and a buyer.

The sales person would be focused on volume, because that was how he or she was remunerated, and the buyers would be focused on margin because that was how they were judged.

In that situation it was easy for a competitor to move in and break up the supplier-buyer relationship. Basically, all the newcomer had to do was offer a better deal.

With the new style partnership relationships though, suppliers were beginning to think in terms of teams - for example a customer focus team. Those groups would front up against the customer's own team - the latter might be called something like a 'supplier development group', to use the terminology of automotive industry manufacturer Nissan.

'What we are seeing is the growth of relationships where we have multiple linkages, team up against team. Companies are linking their information systems and their logistics systems together, meaning that if I am on the outside, I have got a real problem trying to break into that sort of relationship,' added Prof Christopher.

Summing up, he said he believed the new focal point for marketing would be on 'relationship management'. Those relationships would cover logistics, particularly, together with information systems and product development, plus how those elements were brought into the frame and how they were managed against the customer's requirements.

'That, to me, is what partnershipping is all about. And I think it has got great opportunities, it is not just flavour of the month. In five years' time, we will take partnerships for granted. I do believe, though, that it is a fundamental change in the way we do things.'

Supplier Tiers: the purchasing challenge

The impact on suppliers of 'tiering' as practised particularly in the automotive industry

The expression 'supplier tiers' is now commonplace in the automotive industry, but as with so much modern commercial jargon, the meaning of the phrase is less well understood that its widespread use would suggest.

The Japanese concept of 'supplier tiers'[1] was revealed to the world at large by research undertaken in the 1980s. Around the same time, automotive manufacturers in the US launched their own major cost-reduction programmes in recognition of the competitive threat from Japan within US markets. One aspect of these programmes was a drive towards supplier reduction in order to reduce costs through consolidation of volumes and increased specialisation. This policy has now been adopted by European manufacturers, but is will still be some years before it will be completed. Figure 1 illustrates the extent of some of these programmes and shows the vast difference between traditional Western manufacturers and their Japanese counterparts.

Since the introduction of these policies, automotive subcontractors now commonly refer to themselves as belonging to a particular level or 'tier' of supply. However, implementing a policy of supplier reduction does not automatically create supplier tiers. Figure 2 illustrates a typical Japanese supplier tier structure.

FIGURE 1 The number of first-tier suppliers to European car-makers has fallen significantly in the past decade, but there is further to go to match the Japanese.

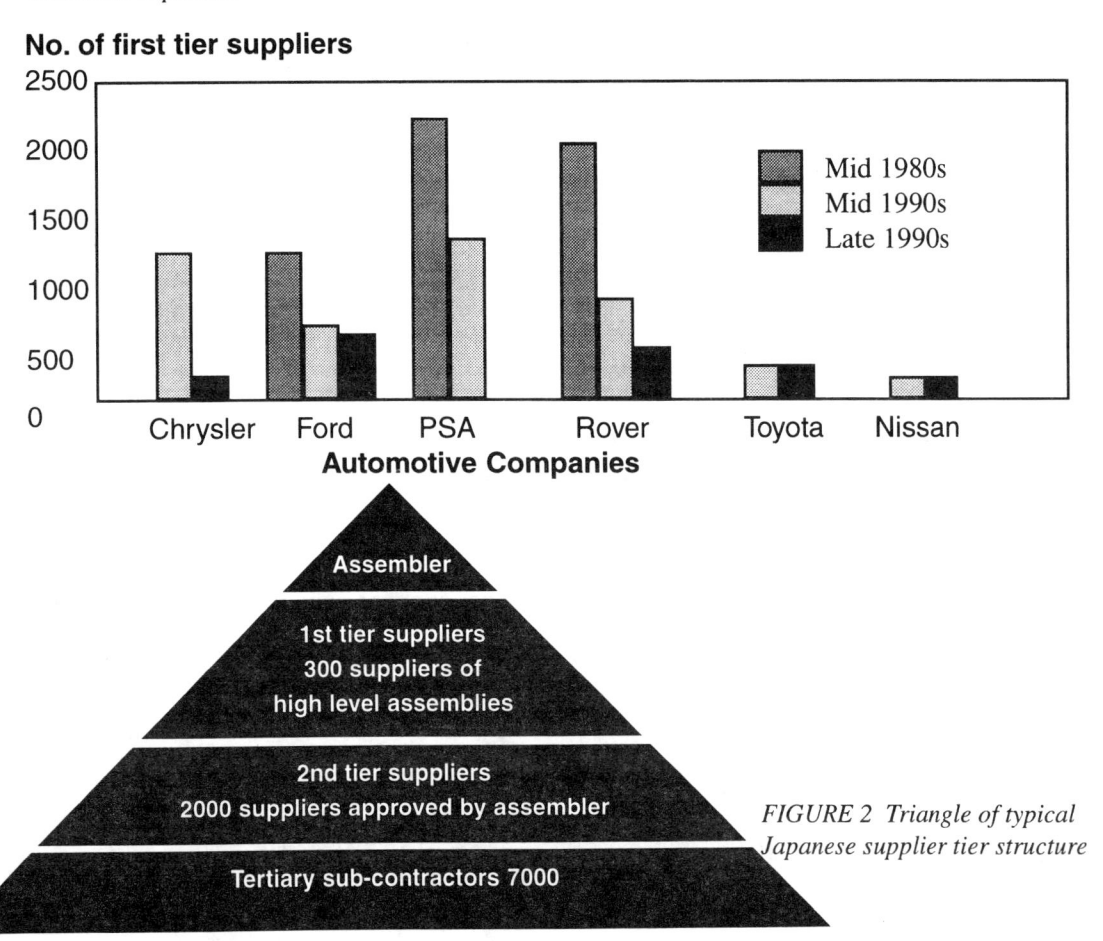

FIGURE 2 Triangle of typical Japanese supplier tier structure

Those companies selected by an automotive manufacturer to deal with it directly are usually referred to as 'first-tier suppliers'. Such suppliers will probably have endured a rigorous selection process and demonstrated their commitment to competitiveness, with an emphasis on continuous cost reduction. They will also have proven track records in quality and delivery, design capability and the ability to implement continuous improvement programmes. This process inevitably leads to many suppliers in the lower tiers losing direct contact with the automotive manufacturer, which in turn means that they have to re-focus their efforts onto new customers - the 'first tier suppliers'.

At the moment, the use of the term 'first tier suppliers' is somewhat tenuous, as full implementation of the tiering process within the European markets still has a long way to go before it can genuinely apply the same nomenclature as is used in the Japanese system. Instead, European operations have tended towards the formation of 'unconnected groups'[2] which view themselves, collectively, as a tier. The vital factor usually missing in Europe is genuine collaboration between several companies, working together towards achieving joint goals such as system design and development or improving supply chains. This is an essential step forward as several automotive manufacturers are steadily moving towards assembly-based operations.

One result of this move is that several major car producers are predicting significant growth in the outsourcing of components while simultaneously reducing the number of direct suppliers. This can be a difficult balancing act, but the two goals are more complementary than might at first appear. A direct consequence of the assembly policy means that first-tier suppliers will need to provide complete systems, requiring no pre-assembly before being fitted to the vehicle on the main production line. This practice will generate further reductions in the inventory through the use of direct lineside deliveries.

The trend towards supplier tiers will also allow manufacturers to reduce the capital investment required in plant and equipment, leading to reductions in factory break-even points which, in turn, allow competitive routes for lower-volume models. It will also release more funds for research and development programmes and reduce management complexity by enabling car makers to focus on their core expertise, and by concentrating their business among fewer suppliers, the automotive manufacturers are facilitating the business confidence needed by direct suppliers to encourage the latter to invest in the technology and equipment needed to meet the greater requirements of their customers.

Another key aspect of the reduction in the number of direct suppliers is the move towards partnership sourcing agreements. Whilst the benefits, or otherwise, of the partnership approach are currently being debated, one aspect that has become clear is that if the process is to succeed, the automotive manufacturers cannot possibly develop successful partnerships with the existing numbers of suppliers (nor would they wish to) and therefore must continue to focus their resources on fewer suppliers. Such strategic, or quasi-strategic, factors are in addition to the basic administrative cost savings which are the normal spin-off from supplier reduction programmes.

Apart from automotive manufacturers, those companies most affected initially by this strategy are those chosen to be first-tier suppliers. Increasingly, these businesses will have to take responsibility for detailed design work and be able to provide complete systems (eg brake or exhaust systems). This will cause few problems for the larger suppliers, who have been doing exactly this - to a greater or lesser extent - for many years; but for others it will be a relatively new experience and will present many challenges, such as increased responsibility for warranty and legal requirements (ie product liability) resulting from the transfer of ownership of design to the supplier.

Within each supplier, one area of business which will be significantly affected is purchasing. Many of the suppliers who previously dealt directly with the manufacturer will now deal with, and be the sole responsibility of, the first-tier supplier, whose purchasing department becomes responsible for managing the cost, quality and delivery performance of companies that the supplier has probably never dealt with before. The new legal and warranty requirements will need to be clearly established and, in many cases, the lower-tier supplier will have been nominated by the manufacturer as the only approved source. Having previously supplied direct to the manufacturer, the lower-tier supplier may now feel aggrieved at a perceived demotion from a first-tier position; and if it was unable to achieve price increases from the manufacturer for a considerable period of time, the lower-tier supplier may well attempt to use the opportunity provided by the new relationship to re-negotaite costs. These are not ideal circumstances under which to start a new supplier/manufacturer relationship and the purchasing manager will have to manage this very carefully.

An obvious knock-on effect of the tiering process will be that many first-tier suppliers will find that they have to increase their own supplier base in order to accommodate the new requirements of systems manufacture and customer-nominated suppliers. This is another substantial challenge for purchasing departments which will no doubt also have embarked upon their own supplier reduction programmes in order to reap the same cost and administrative benefits mentioned earlier. In some cases, major strategic reviews of the supplier base may be required, while new partnerships will need to be developed in order to provide the systems capability demanded by the manufacturers. This process will not happen overnight, but the implications are such that a strategic, long-term view of sourcing policies will be required.

The first-tier suppliers will be under constant pressure to demonstrate cost reduction programmes, and to pass on at least a significant proportion of the savings to the car manufacturers. The first port of call for many executives in first-tier suppliers will be the purchasing department, which typically controls 40-60 per cent of the company's total costs, and the purchasing department will have to change the nature of its relationship with many of the company's own suppliers.

In order to achieve set targets, it will be necessary to introduce many of the techniques and controls adopted by automotive manufacturers. Working together to design to agreed cost targets rather than quoting to a fixed specification, together with collaboration on joint value engineering and analysis programmes with second-tier suppliers will be essential to retain competitiveness. These techniques will seem like a foreign language to many suppliers, and will be met with suspicion and mistrust, but the purchasing department will have to work hard to build confidence by demonstrating the mutual advantages. Figure 3 illustrates the importance of the components sector, the most significant value-adding link in the chain.

FIGURE 3 The components sector is the most significant value-adding link in the chain

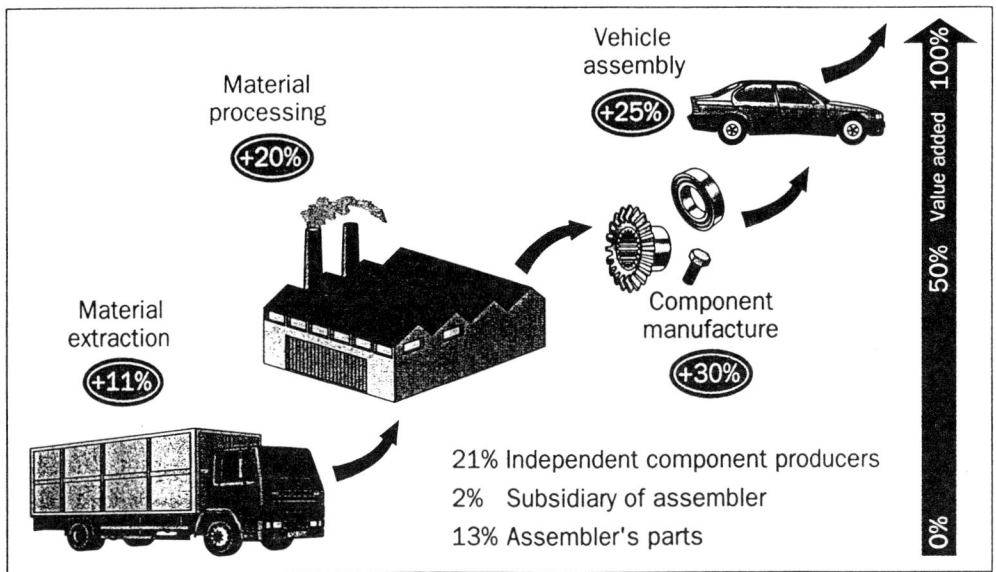

The responsibility for improving quality levels in the lower tiers will also fall on the first-tier suppliers and will need to form a major element of the purchasing policy. Some companies may have lost their status as first-tier suppliers as a direct result of unacceptable quality levels. The chosen first-tier suppliers will be expected to improve the quality levels of the second tier - if they do not, they may find that they soon become uncompetitive as their costs rise due to the level of rejection of items coming in from their own suppliers.

As a consequence, major supplier development programmes never previously envisaged or resourced may become essential to survival. The first-tier suppliers have the advantage of being able to learn the best (and worst) examples of this process from the automotive manufacturers, which should help them in transferring knowledge to the lower tiers. In some cases, a form of collaboration or joint venture with other customers of the same lower-tier supplier would be extremely beneficial, as costs could be shared and the supplier would not receive confusing - or even conflicting - messages. This would be an excellent example of companies operating within a true 'supplier tier' system.

Other developments are also encouraging the evolution of just such a system, for instance the growing success of regional supplier groups, the West Midlands Supplier Network, to name an obvious example, in which knowledge and information are shared to improve the collective and individual competitiveness of the members. The focus group activities initiated by the joint DTI-SMMT industry forum are also playing an important role in this process. Every grouping of this nature provides a forum for a sharing of knowledge, and creates opportunities to develop truly collaborative partnerships that focus on the common goal of satisfying customer requirements. Purchasing managers in each tier must ensure that they play an active role in these emerging associations, as such groups will be essential to achieving competitiveness as well as being a key influence on sourcing decisions.

The key role of the purchasing function has long been recognised among the automotive manufacturers and the largest first-tier suppliers, but the overall effect of tiering is to increase the demands on purchasing in each of the tiers in the pyramid. An increased focus on total costing, supplier development, value engineering and analysis and continuous improvement is essential for the purchasing professional in the automotive components industry, as the success, or failure, of purchasing policies could determine the winners and losers in this process.

References
1 *The machine that changed the world*, Womack & Jones et al
2 *A review of the relationship between vehicle manufacturers and suppliers*, Lamming
3 *Car manufacturers of the world: a MIRA review*, MIRA, 1995
4 *Europe, the battlefield of the nineties*, KPMG

Adding value - the purchasing mission

Stephen Cannon summarises recent thinking

At a time when organisations find themselves under increasing pressure to perform, it is obvious that they must get more for less from every pound they spend. In these circumstances, the purchasing and contracts function should contribute even more markedly to organisational objectives than it has done in the past. It must use its skills and expertise to deliver value to the organisation of which it is a part.

A key feature which underlies the delivery of value is the relationship with the function's internal customers within the organisation. In many cases, purchasing and contracts work is a team activity involving both internal customers who have the requirement (to be satisfied from outside the organisation) and the purchasing and contracts practitioner who has the skills and expertise to ensure the contractual satisfaction of that requirement.

Previous articles have discussed the steps which might require attention in order to maximise the function's role as a contributor of value.
These include:
- defining the value which the function can contribute, improving its own attitudes to change and flexibility, making its mission the servicing of the internal customer
- facilitating and guiding the purchasing and contracts activity, concentrating on those aspects where it can add value
- defining its goals and milestones in quantifiable terms
- measuring and auditing its performance
- enhancing the importance of communication and training, bearing down on its own costs.

Defining the value which the function can contribute

The purchasing and contracts function offers internal customers three qualities: *added value, service* and *expertise*. Expertise is used by the function to help it deliver added value and service (Figure 1).

FIGURE 1 Offering the internal customer three qualities

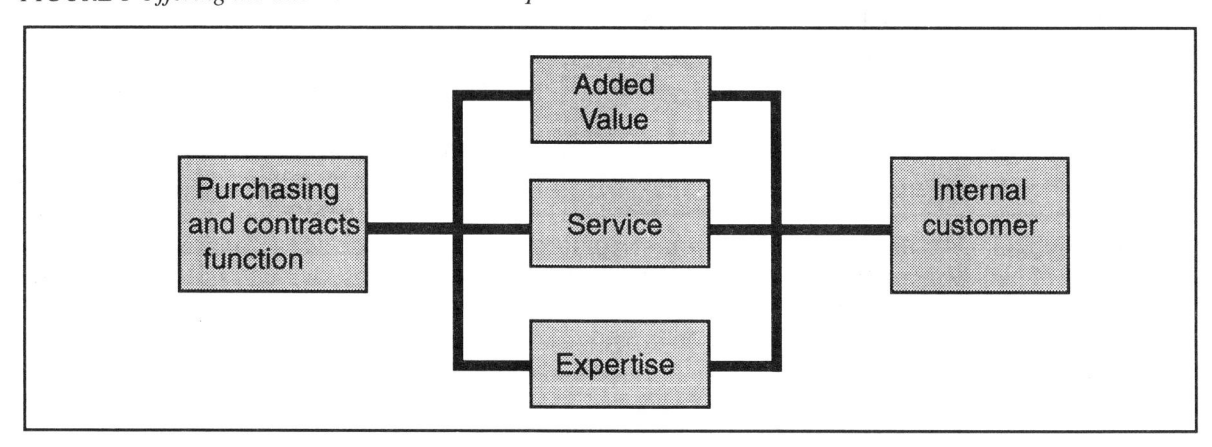

Savings generated by the function are added value. There are many sources of savings and there are many different tools and techniques which can be used to generate them. They can be generated by the practitioners in the function working alone or by practitioners and the internal customers working together or by a collaboration of practitioners, internal customers and vendors.

The added value should be targeted. This means that a value which is required should be determined for a period, most likely the organisation's financial year. This Targeted Added Value should be a combination of a saving required by the internal customers and the cost of the function itself. Achieving targeted added value is thus a means for the function to deliver reduced cost to the organisation and also for it to recover its own costs so that it is essentially a cost-free service to the organisation in which it operates.

The services which the function offers its internal customers need to be broken down into different types and an appropriate level assigned to each type. The important feature about the service types and levels is that they should be money-based. The benefit to be derived by the internal customer receiving the service should be quantified in money terms and so should the cost of delivering it. It is only if there is a net benefit that the service is worth delivering.

It should be noted that the process of deciding money based service levels is collaborative. It involves the internal customer in the decision-making. Money based service levels could be benchmarked against other organisations as a further check of the function's effectiveness.

Targeted added value and money based service levels are the two key sources of value which the function can define both at the generic and at the quantifiable, actual level. These two factors affect the vision, goals and milestones of the function, how it is organised, its relationships with internal customers, vendors and the top management of the organisation, its training and communications role, the size of the function, the remuneration of its staff and yardsticks for self-audit.

Attitude to change and flexibility

An essential first step to implementing any major change is attitudinal change within the function. This really means accepting that there can be no sacred cows and that all previous attitudes, practices and techniques must be open to question, analysis and modification.

The management and practitioners have to be prepared to change the structure of their function and to change their ways of working. Changing the structure could mean the elimination of centralised departments, reduction in staff numbers and the deliberate abandonment of some traditional activities and responsibilities where the value added is small or non-existent. Changing ways of working might involve significant changes in working practices. The manager's role is likely to become more like that of a negotiator, facilitator and guide rather than that of a departmental master. The management style would be supportive rather than controlling.

At the practitioner level, the role changes so that it is more that of a team player rather than functional operative. To find the enhanced value that the organisation will require, the practitioner needs to work with and increasingly rely upon the internal customer whose needs he/she tries to meet.

It should not be taken for granted that the management of the function will internalise the need to change even if it has knowledge of the threats and opportunities facing the organisation/ Individuals at any level in an organisation see change in different ways. Change which is handed down is often seen as enforced.

The degree of internalisation of any change depends often on the degree of involvement of the individuals in making the change. A key to developing commitment to the change process is the early involvement of the practitioners. Much of the responsibility for managing the change needs to be assigned to the practitioners.

In many cases, change will not be possible without altering the attitudes of the internal customers. If the internal customers do not co-operate in the change-making, then the function on its own will have difficulties realising the full potential. Close, collaborative working with internal customers is the essential supply partnership if there is to be a continuous upgrading of the value delivered by the supply chain. Much modern supply chain thinking assumes this relationship exists but it needs to be built and maintained like any other relationship.

Joint working sessions involving the internal customer and the function's management and its practitioners are recommended for exchanging views and clarifying attitudes. They should preferably be held away from the normal working environment and they should be linked to the development of co-operative contracts with internal customers. These describe and agree the change needed and they state their agreed requirements from the internal customer and the practitioner in order to support it.

Making its mission the servicing of the internal customer

Because of the importance of the collaborative relationship with the internal customer, the mission of the function is to service the internal customer's needs better in the belief that this will improve the function's contribution to the organisation. Really understanding the needs of the internal customer and how they deliver value to the organisation is the key to value generation by functional practitioners.

To find extra value continuously, a collaborative effort will often be required with the internal customer. The building and maintenance of this collaboration needs to be adopted as a key task by the triumvirate of the function's management, practitioners and internal customers. As a result, practitioners become members of procurement teams to which they deliver benefits derived from their expertise.

FIGURE 2 Collaborative relationships the key

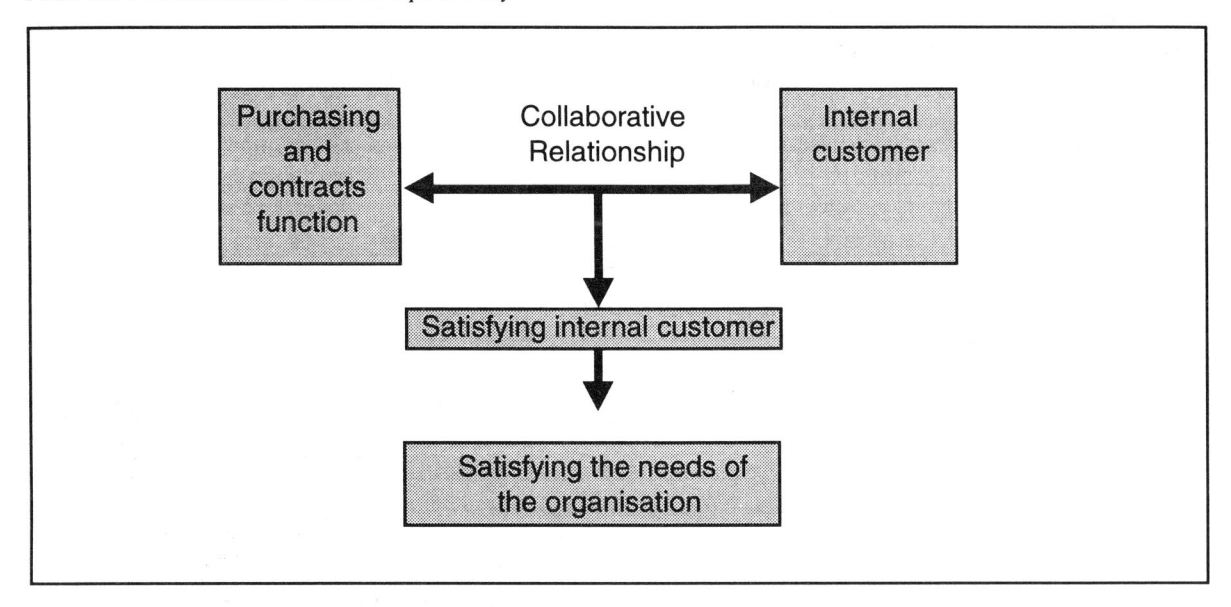

[Figure: Diagram showing "Purchasing and contracts function" and "Internal customer" connected by "Collaborative Relationship", leading down to "Satisfying internal customer", then to "Satisfying the needs of the organisation"]

this changes the roles of the practitioners and the management of the function. It is the job of the function and its management to make sure that these teams work; it is the job of the individual practitioners to make sure that the teams are successful. There are techniques and approaches which help both the function and the practitioners to achieve these objectives.

Highly competitive markets drive the management of organisations to question the contribution of all parts of the value chain. Just to survive organisations need to be bearing down on costs and enhancing the value of their products to customers. To grow, organisations need to be extremely successful both at bearing down on costs and at enhancing value. This state of affairs demands that the purchasing and contracts function manages its activity so as to meet these crucial needs of organisations. Targeted added value and money based service levels are the vehicles for doing this. Possible sources of added value are:
- market imperfections arising from competition
- savings such as value engineering, rationalisation of product range, simplification of specifica tions or terms and conditions etc - usually arising through collaboration with the internal customer.
- savings arising from ad hoc negotiations with vendors
- savings arising from partnership-style arrangements with vendors
- savings arising from discontinuities in the market or technology
- savings arising from new entrants and substitute products.

Facilitating and guiding the activity

The change from practitioners acting as individuals within a function to their being members of a team to which they contribute their expertise can be assisted by dispersing the practitioners among the internal customers whom they serve. In effect, this means eliminating central purchasing departments and situating the practitioners alongside their customers. Such change is difficult and, without the change in attitudes which has been discussed above, it will probably be impossible.

The change of attitude, the co-operative contract and this dispersal are the three main planks to the transformation of the function into one which seeks to facilitate and to guide the purchasing and contracts activity. They establish a basis for practitioners to use their skills in conjunction with those of internal customers and sometimes with vendors to find new sources of value. The practitioners should be supported by an active purchasing and contracts research department which ensures that they remain at the forefront of new developments.

Concentrating on adding value

For the function to concentrate on where it can add value, the procurement needs of the organisation must be reviewed by means of the segmentation technique (Figure 3). This enables these needs to be split into those which can be purchased by:
1 the internal customer with minimal active purchasing involvement from the practitioners in the function

2 which can be undertaken by the practitioners with minimal involvement of the internal customer
3 which should be undertaken as a joint exercise.

In category 1 of the above list, the function limits its role to facilitating purchase by the internal customer. This facilitation might take the form of the provision of such things as a credit card purchasing facility, an IT purchasing system, standard terms and conditions etc. Money based service levels can be used to measure the efficacy of this help.

FIGURE 3 Review by segmentation

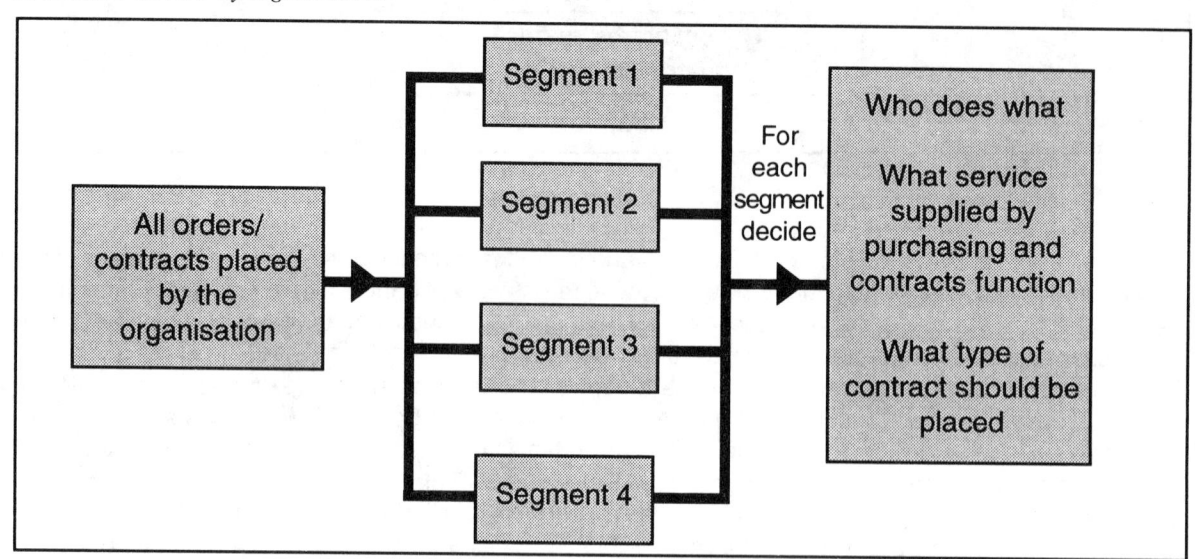

In category 2, the function seeks to find and meet targeted added value requirements as well as provide a service which might again be subject to the discipline of money based service levels. While the involvement of the internal customer should not be great, it is not non-existent. The search for targeted added value will often involve the internal customer, for example in such things as agreeing to rationalisation of requirements, simplifying specifications, use of new materials etc.

Category 3 requires complete collaboration with the internal customer. Again, both targeted added value and money based service levels can be applied. It is quite likely here that partnership arrangements with vendors could be most fruitful.

Defining goals and milestones

In many organisations, the principal management control of the function has been the departmental budget. This is, of course, an important device for controlling manpower and costs associated with the work to be done. It does not target or measure achievement. To do this, it is necessary to define goals and milestones in quantifiable terms.

Goals are derived from mission statements. They are quantifiable targets for the function as a whole. They are derived in collaboration with the internal customer. For the purchasing and contracts function, the goals should include money based service levels and targeted added value (Figure 4).

In the case of targeted added value, the individual goals are determined by the management of the function with the internal customer and then they are apportioned among the practitioners in the function by a process of negotiation akin to that used to agree a departmental budget.

Money based service levels are determined by the Practitioners with the internal customers. Safeguards are required to ensure compatibility across the function.

FIGURE 4 Missions and goals

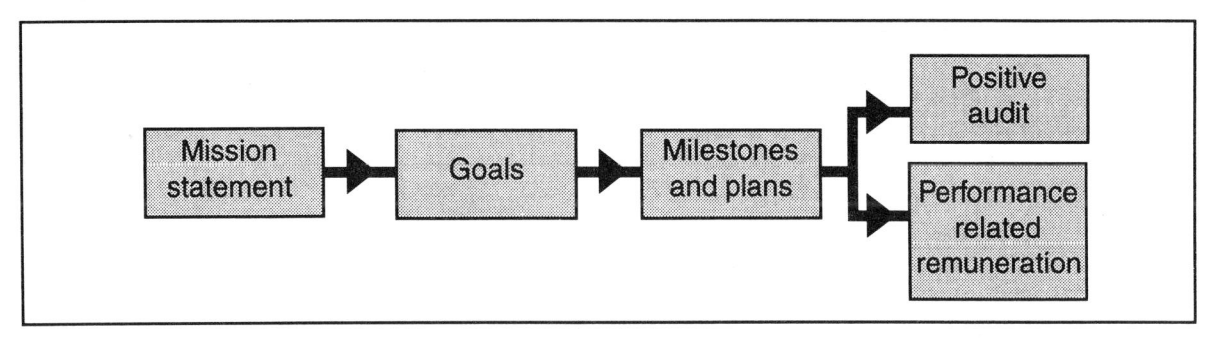

```
Mission statement → Goals → Milestones and plans → Positive audit
                                                  → Performance related remuneration
```

Measuring and auditing

The goals assigned to individual practitioners should be further broken down into milestones which can be used to measure performance. These provider a means for practitioners to measure and to control their own performance which an be monitored by the internal customers and by the management of the function.

Practitioners should be empowered to perform but this does not mean that there should be a total absence of any reporting structure. Both the function's management and the internal customer will want to know what progress is being made in meeting milestones. It does mean leaving the onus for success or failure with the practitioner. Intervention by the management should always be a last resort.

Quantifiable milestones provider a way of auditing the performance of the practitioners and thus of the function. The objectives of the audit are help and improvement. They are not error or fault detection.

The audit team reviews internal customer satisfaction. They monitor cross-functional compatibility and benchmark against external organisations. The audit takes into account the markets and environment in which the organisation operates.

Communication and training

The perceptions of the various levels of management within an organisation to both the purchasing and contracts function and its work are important. The function should ascertain them and also seek the reasons for them. A four-box matrix of the perception of the importance of the activity of the purchasing and contracts function against the perception of the function itself can shed some useful insights which can be used as a basis for the formulation of a communications strategy.

The purchasing and contracts function is in competition with other functions for the ear of top management. To neglect communication is to risk losing or never gaining the support of the top management of an organisation. Training should also be an important part of the function's activities, in fact it should be a core activity as it provides a means both of improving skill levels and of communication. Part of the activity of the function should be to conduct training so that all those involved in the purchasing and contracts activity understand all the fundamentals of what they are doing. This is particularly important for internal customers conducting their own purchasing. The purchasing and contracts practitioner should provide training to support the internal customer.

However, the internal customer is only one of the five client groups which require training.

It is important that the top management are aware of the supply constraints which can affect the high level strategy of the organisation. it is also in the function's self interest to ensure that top management understands the need for a skilfully undertaken purchasing and contracts activity. Training and communication to this level of management are cardinal tasks for the management of the function requiring both imagination and prudent use of opportunism.

The practitioners also need development as the purchasing and contracts field is continuously improving. Much of the training will be the theories and practices of the activity together with the background to them. Some training should be devoted to supporting the practitioner in his/her important role as ambassador of the function.

The two other important client groups for training (and for communication), whose needs are often neglected, are the external suppliers to the organisation and the internal suppliers to the function. it is often assumed that these two groups will pick up what is required of them as they deal with the function. This is no substitute for dedicated training and, in both cases, the training provides a basis for partnership relationships.

Bearing down on the function's own costs

The costs of a purchasing and contracts function are usually people and people-related. It has already been mentioned that the function should provide cost free its services to the organisation as part of targeted added value. This stimulates the need to keep the manning levels low.

Segmentation should mean that fewer clerical staff are needed as much of the purchasing work often undertaken by this grade of staff should be left to the internal customer. This avoids the need for pointless paper processing. Dispersal of staff and their empowerment should eliminate hierarchical structures which could reduce the need for supervisory staff. Money based service levels provide a brake on the costs associated with providing a service/service level because there should always be a net benefit. If there is none, there is no justification for the service/service level. Staff should only be retained provided they contribute to the net benefit.

A further way of controlling staff costs is to people the function so as to be able to achieve a certain defined level of added value. If additional value is identifiable, it should be sought using temporary contract staff and the possibility of peaking work load to make full use of this sort of staff arrangement is worth considering.

Partnerships - what's going on in UK SMEs?

A look at the attitudes of smaller companies in the South-East Midlands

Who should be interested in the state of small and medium-sized enterprise (SME) partnerships? The straightforward answer is: other SMEs. Knowing the standard of one's competitors' practices is the first step to firm survival and prosperity. However, most SMEs are closely linked to larger firms as suppliers and as buyers. Their management practices will have significant know-on effects for larger firms. Thus the answer to the above question is of some interest to all of us.

Unfortunately, most research in the area of purchasing partnerships deals exclusively with larger corporations. For instance, in a recent article Norman Hosford (1) asked 'Partnerships - what is really going on?' and looked at implementation approaches used in medium-to-large manufacturing and service sector companies. Other articles have looked at firms like Xerox (2), Procter and Gamble (3), Rover (4), ICI, and Laing Homes (5), which overhauled their supplier systems in the 1980s. The question of how far such management practices have percolated down to SMEs is unclear. In a recent review of the literature on buyer-supplier relations, Imrie and Morris (6) conclude that SMEs have not moved far towards co-operative relationships.

In this article we report on the state of partnerships in small and medium-sized manufacturers in the South-East Midlands. We seek to assess quantitatively the status of buyer-supplier relations of UK SMEs *in their role as buyers*. We study the prevalence of a number of characteristics that indicate moves towards partnership relations and we utilise these indicators to assess the extent to which SMEs have adopted partnering practices.

We set out to identify whether there has been a significant change in the total number of suppliers and the number of key suppliers used by the sampled companies. Research suggests that a reduction in the number of suppliers and an increase in the number of key suppliers plays a leading role in the movement towards partnerships.

Next we analyse whether there has been a change in other cornerstones of purchasing partnerships (2-7-10), such as long-term contracts (LTC), joint product design (JPD), Just-in-Time delivery (JIT), electronic data interchange (EDI) and supplier site visits (SSV). Their prevalence should give a sign whether any progress towards partnerships has been made.

Lastly, we look at the activities that firms report they are implementing to improve their supplier relationships. These actions should give us another powerful indication about the attitudes of SMEs regarding purchasing partnerships.

In order to elicit the required information we developed a semi-structured questionnaire. Central to the structured part of it was a matrix detailing the formal arrangements with suppliers described above. The term 'buyer-supplier partnerships' was not mentioned in the questionnaire. This was to avoid over-optimistic responses from firms keen on associating themselves with 'modern' management practices.

We got addresses from local business directories. 82 per cent of the companies contacted had fewer than 100 employees. Most firms were in the area of engineering, but sub-contractors and precision engineers were also included. In many, but not in all cases, the name of the managing director or proprietor of the business was available.

The questionnaires were sent out in two waves during the period August/October 1994 to differentiate between the companies where the managing director or proprietor was known in advance and companies where no such information existed.

Targeted areas were Milton Keynes, Northampton, Aylesbury and Luton in the South-East Midlands area of England. 621 questionnaires were posted and the overall response rate was 25.1 per cent, which may be considered high for this type of survey, although some responses were unusable for various reasons.

FIGURE 1 - Number of suppliers (total and key) today and four years ago

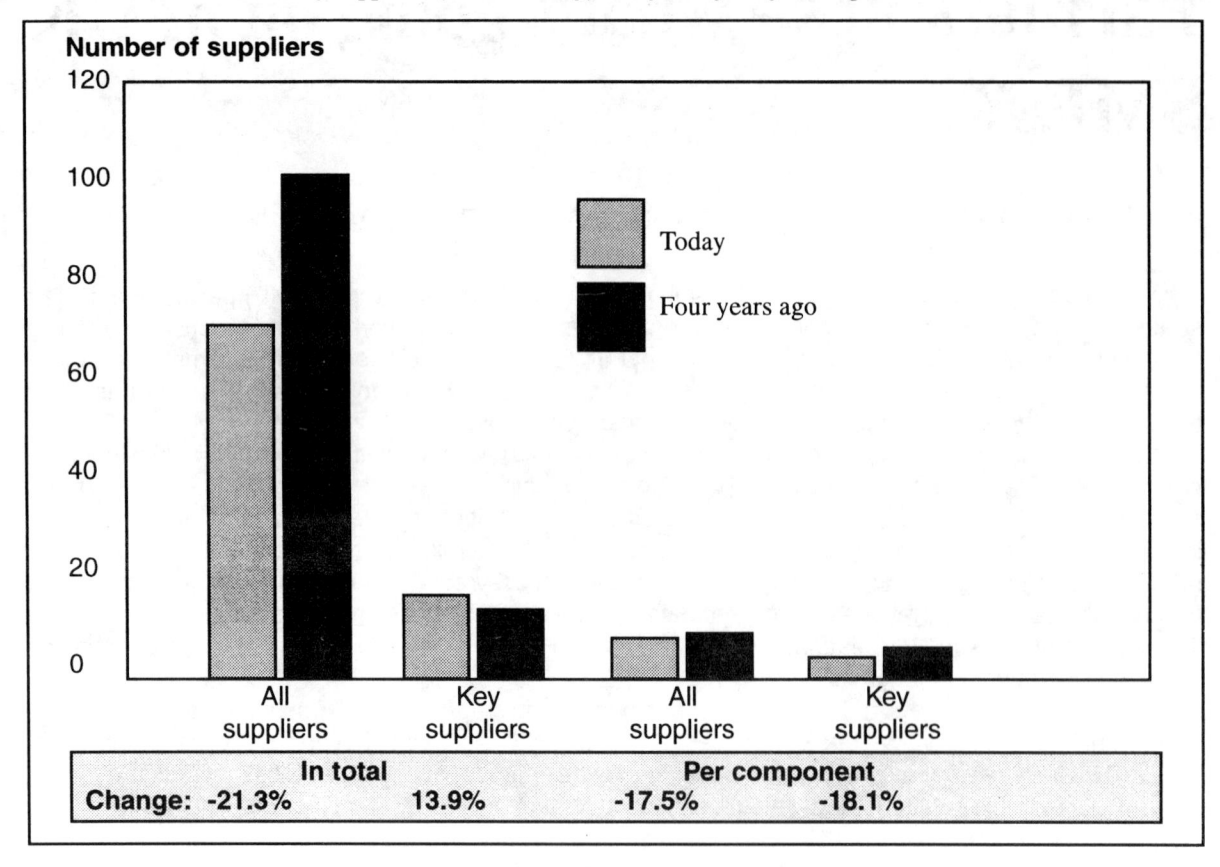

	In total		Per component	
	All suppliers	Key suppliers	All suppliers	Key suppliers
Change:	-21.3%	13.9%	-17.5%	-18.1%

FIGURE 2 - Percentage of suppliers covered by partnering arrangements

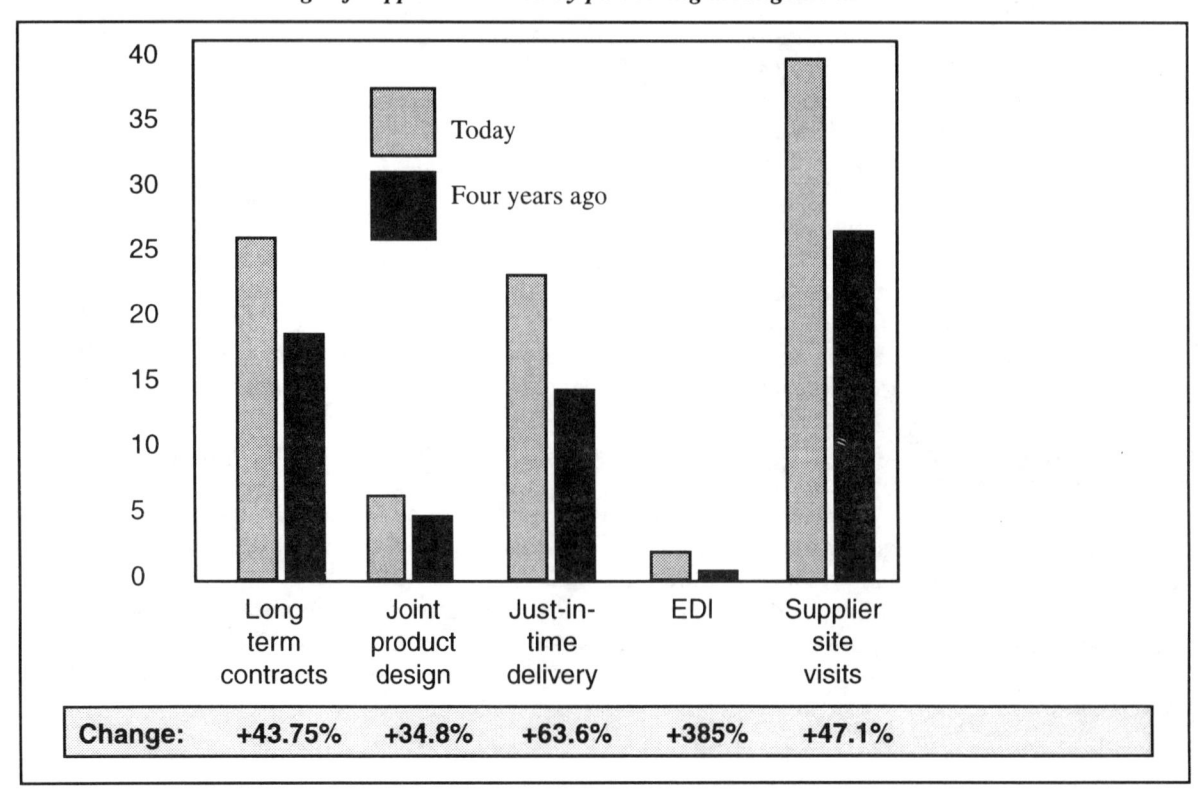

Change:	Long term contracts	Joint product design	Just-in-time delivery	EDI	Supplier site visits
	+43.75%	+34.8%	+63.6%	+385%	+47.1%

Partnership sourcing ideas in SMEs

We find that the total number of suppliers used by SMEs has decreased and the number of key suppliers has increased over the last four years (see Figure 1). The total number of suppliers per component has declined as well. This indicates that the widely reported supplier reduction that has been occurring in large firms over the last decade has a parallel in SMEs.

To examine the development of partnerships in SMEs in more detail, we analyse the use of partnership indictors. Supplier site visits, long-term contracts and JIT deliveries are popular with SMEs whereas EDI is virtually absent. All indicators have increased over the last four years (see Figure 2). The steepest increase is visible in JIT deliveries. Supplier site visits have the highest overall utilisation.

These findings suggest that the building blocks of successful partnerships are appearing in SMEs. While the prevalence of what we would consider 'advanced' indicators like JPD and EDI is still at a lower level, the movement is in the direction of closer supplier relations.

Companies are currently implementing a wide range of activities to improve purchasing performance (see Table). Most of them can be seen as being conducive to the partnership idea. In unstructured comments virtually all respondents indicated that they were implementing such measures. For instance, nearly 12 per cent of respondents said that they were engaged in cost reduction projects of various kinds with their suppliers.

Conclusions

So what *is* going on in SME supplier partnerships? Our results are at once reassuring and sobering. The awareness of the need for better supplier relationships is widespread. So is knowledge of the basic foundations of partnerships, albeit sometimes in a fairly rudimentary form. And the changes all point towards more effective supplier links. However, we cannot disagree with the conclusions of Imrie and Morris (6). The existing level of partnership development is quite low. SMEs have a long way to go, but the good news is that they are moving in the right direction.

Acknowledgements

We acknowledge a research grant from the University of Buckingham and project support from the Milton Keynes Borough Council and the Chartered Institute of Purchasing and Supply (CIPS). The views expressed here are not necessarily attributable to any of these institutions.

Reported improvement actions	% of total
Prompter payment/monthly	13.4
Regular (mutual) visits	13.4
Cost reduction projects (continuous, Kaizen, VANE)	11.9
Improved scheduling/delivery standards	11.9
Direct communication between (technical) staff	10.4
Improved forecasting of future demand	10.4
Develop long term/strategic supplier partnering	9.0
Encourage adoption of ISO 9000/BS 5750	9.0
JIT planning/line supply/review stocks	7.5
Joint design/product development	7.5
Long term contracts/agreements	7.5
Closer working relationship/development policy	6.0
Open negotiations on costs, profit margins, delivery, price	6.0
Reduce supplier base	6.0
Regular progress meetings/reviews	6.0
EDI links	4.5
Installation advice/changed manufacturing techniques	4.5
Iinvited to presentation/supplier days	4.5
Quality surveys/requirements	4.5

Others:
Stop ordering from suppliers that upset us; joint purchasing; customer concern action reports;mention possible competition; target setting; more professional purchasing function; joint marketing.

References

(1) Hosford, N Partnerships - What is really going on? *Purchasing and Supply Management*, July 1994, pp38-40

(2) Sheridan, JH, Suppliers, Partners in Prosperity, *Industry Week*, March 1990 pp 12-1990

(3) Bergman, S, Reverse Marketing in 1991, *NAPM Insights* July 1991, PP 26-27

(4) Turnbull, PN, Oliver, and B Wilkinson, Buyer Supplier Relations in the UK Automotive Industry: Strategic implications of the Japanese Manufacturing Model, *Strategic Management Journal,* 1992, pp 159-168

(5) Partnership Sourcing Limited, *Partnership Sourcing,* 1993, DTI/CBI

(6) Imrie, R and J Morris A Review of Recent Changes in Buyer-Supplier Relations, *Omega*, 1992 Vol 20 No 5/6 pp 641-652

(7) Cousins PD, Choosing the right partner, *Purchasing & Supply Management*, March 1992 pp 21-23

(8) Cousins PD, A Framework for Selection, Implementation, Measurement and Management of Partnership Sourcing Strategies: A Multiple Criteria Objective Modelling Approach, 1992 *University of Bath Working Paper*

(9) Ellram, LM, The Supplier Selection Decision in Strategic Partnerships, *Journal of Purchasing and Materials Management,* 1990 Vol 26 No.4 pp8-14

(10) Harris, D, Own Business, *The Times* 17 September 1993 London

The Japanese system of subcontracting

A look at an essential factor in Japanese v Western performance comparisons

Over the past two decades, the business world has witnessed the dominance of the Japanese in the global market. According to Massayoshi Ikeda (1992), there are four reasons why a large gap exists between the performance of Japanese and Western companies:
- the superiority of equipment and facilities
- the sharing of information between final assembler and supplier
- job rotation in Japanese companies an the consequent multi-functionality
- the active use of sub-contractors

While the Western world considers that the widespread use of sub-contractors in Japan holds a key to its efficiency, it is well to remember that sub-contracting is not merely an integral part of the strategy which could be termed 'Japanese-style Management' but operates as a stand-alone factor (Sato, 1984).

The Japanese context

Before discussing sub-contracting, it is important to have an understanding of the organisational structures and inter-organisational relations that exist within the Japanese business environment. Intrinsic to the Japanese culture has been the establishment of hierarchy and this characteristic is evident with the development of a hierarchical company structure where companies are arranged in groups or *'Keirestsu'*.

Keiretsu (group of companies)
Dai Kigyo (large companies)
Chu-sho Kigyo (small to medium companies).

Interestingly, when the West thinks of Japanese companies, it is very often of the 1000 listed on the Tokyo stock exchange, yet 99 per cent of Japanese industry is made up of *Chu-sho kigyo* and one 1 per cent corporations with factories spanning the nation, rather than the *Dai Kigyo* who are the co-ordinators, assemblers and marketers and not the manufacturers. It is the contractual relationships with the lower level companies which provides the research and development and the production output.

The most common form of contractual relationship between large and smaller firms is the sub-contracting or *shitauke* system.
FIGURE 1 (upper) shows the pyramidal nature of Japanese subcontracting; the table below illustrates the scale of such arrangements.

Subcontracting

The historic need for co-operation between companies can be traced to the 1939-45 was effort when supplies of raw materials were controlled and issued to finished product manufacturers and subsequently to their sub-contractors. The first *kyoriku kai* (supplier associations) resulted from early government intervention to try to take assemblers organise their sub-contractors and increase their supply chain efficiency.

Over the years this contractual relationship evolved in a different way from the typical Western arrangement, where contractors are 'free agents' and able to work for whom they want and when they want. The Japanese arrangement is a long-term commitment. From the day the contractor accepts the contract it is bound to work for that organisation under its terms and conditions.

Shitauke, then, becomes more than the supply of goods and services, it incorporates a partnership where there are inputs from both sides, in terms of information, resources, knowledge and investment (a good example is research and development). Strong ties of loyalty and mutual dependency develop to bind the operation of the two firms (ie 'benevolence for loyalty trade' note 2) which can ultimately benefit both parties.

It is important to note that the Japanese subcontracting relationship is not the same as, nor is it interchange with the traditional view of the 'customer-supplier' relationship; rather 'what distinguishes a subcontractor from a supplier is that the sub-contractor is not responsible for procuring part or all of the material they require for production activities' (note 3).

The sub-contractual arrangements fit with the traditional Japanese company hierarchy where fewer larger companies sub-contract work to many smaller companies. Figure 1 represents the 'layered' approach or pyramid model which exists within the Japanese subcontracting system.

Figure 2 indicates the scale and potential for such contractual arrangements. Note that 65.1 per cent of firms employ only 1-9 people, indicating the extent of small scale operations. To put this into perspective, it is not unknown for there to be 15-30,000 sub-contractual relationships within a *Keiretsu*, with 99 per cent of small and medium businesses (who employ 80 per cent of the workforce) involved in sub-contracting work. Within this union, the power remains with the patent organisation (note 7) allowing it to dictate the final unit costs, production methods and the exclusivity of the smaller firm.

In Figure 1 the hierarchy between the three tiers of sub-contractors is not straightforward, but involves unequal relationships and levels of control. For example, in companies such as Toyota, the first tier could incorporate 200 sub-contractors, but there may only be 12 who are full blown partners. Examples of criteria for partnership include levels of technological development and the global influence of the smaller firm.

So varied are the relationships between firms that descriptive categories have been created according to the stake the parent company has in the smaller company:
Kankeigaisha: Parent company has 51 per cent plus shareholding
Kanrengaisha: Parent company has 20-50 per cent shareholding
Toshigaisha: Parent company has less than 20 per cent shareholding.

It is important to remember that during the Korean war of 1950, sub-contractors were used as a means of increasing capacity without committing to taking on extra labour and facilities an they became increasingly valuable as a source of cheap labour against an environment of continued growth. The sub-contractor system continues to provide advantages to the customer companies in the protection and maintenance of their employment principles.

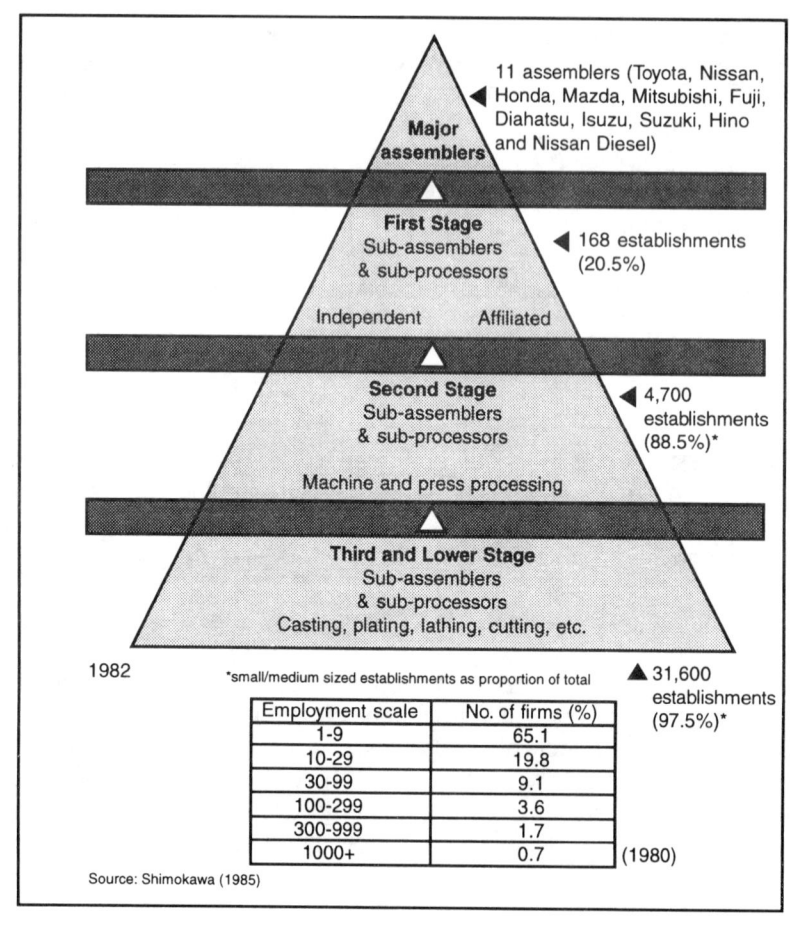

Figure 1 (upper) shows the pyramidal nature of Japanese subcontracting, and the table illustrates the scale of such arrangements

- Major assemblers: 11 assemblers (Toyota, Nissan, Honda, Mazda, Mitsubishi, Fuji, Diahatsu, Isuzu, Suzuki, Hino and Nissan Diesel)
- First Stage Sub-assemblers & sub-processors: 168 establishments (20.5%) — Independent / Affiliated
- Second Stage Sub-assemblers & sub-processors — Machine and press processing: 4,700 establishments (88.5%)*
- Third and Lower Stage Sub-assemblers & sub-processors — Casting, plating, lathing, cutting, etc.: 31,600 establishments (97.5%)*

1982
*small/medium sized establishments as proportion of total

Employment scale	No. of firms (%)
1-9	65.1
10-29	19.8
30-99	9.1
100-299	3.6
300-999	1.7
1000+	0.7

(1980)

Source: Shimokawa (1985)

Advantages to customer companies

In the Japanese style of sub-contracting, companies may sub-contract up to 80 per cent of a product's value added work. Three areas of business can be identified where advantages could be considered; management, technology and finance (note 4).

Managerial advantages

Generally the trend for a Japanese *assembler* is to deal only with first tier suppliers on a long-term basis. This serves to reduce the 'supplier' base and consequently the management effort required.

A resulting increase in mutual dependency is seen to lower the risk of losing supply sources creating greater stability. In Sako's survey (note 5) 88 per cent of large companies cited supply stability as the reason for long-term sub-contractor relationships. Additionally less time has to be spent on finding and assessing sub-contractors and gathering competitive bids. In the MITI White Paper of 1986, 47 per cent of companies sub-contracted on the basis of having had previous reliable dealings with the company.

Because of the closeness of the relationship and the existence of mutual trust, joint planning and information sharing is possible. The joint benefits come from eliminating second guessing and reducing the effect of amplifying order sizes through the supply chain.

'Preferred customer' loyalty generally leads to greater focus on customer needs such as:
- reliability in both lead-times and in meeting deadlines
- priority in times of shortage
- increased attention to solving supply problems.

Often in the Japanese system sub-contractors will supply few customers and will concentrate effort on the most appropriate work. This, MITI found, is seen as an advantage by 48 per cent of Japanese companies who sub-contract. The resulting co-operation and focus by sub-contractors can result in their being much more aware and supportive of their customers' strategies.

Japanese customers gain flexibility from sub-contracting. MITI research identifies that 37 per cent say they have gained flexibility in the size of order they are able to place. By using smaller companies they can reduce the batch sizes and achieve greater efficiencies (31 per cent) and can achieve lower personnel costs and therefore unit costs (37 per cent). this fact is reinforced by Sako research (Survey 1992) where 50 per cent of customers consider that long term sub-contracting relationships produce competitive prices.

The ability to favour sub-contractors close to the client and who tend to group in particular areas provides the customer-client with advantages in both transportation and the ease and frequency of communications.

Sub-contracting continues to have labour implications in its provision of a 'protective belt around its permanent employees' (note 6). Japan is characterised by employment principles such as lifetime employment, seniority pay and the encouragement of the multi-task employee or the 'generalist', all of which carry implications for employers. Using sub-contractors which operate as 'flexible specialists' at the boundary of the business, the company can continue to develop generalists as well as having an acceptable target for cost cutting when necessary, without affecting the secure position of their permanent employees.

Technological advantages

There are striking differences between the Western and Japanese approaches in the sharing of technological effort. In Europe, an average of 54 per cent of the 6800 (approximately) engineering hours needed to produce a new model are contributed by sub-contractors. In the US it is only about 14 per cent of the 4200 engineering hours required. In Japan, the hours required are lower at 3900 and about 72 per cent are contributed by the sub-contractor (note 7). The sub-contractors' ability to participate in product design gives their Japanese customer the advantage of sharing the workload and reducing the 'time to market' through simultaneous engineering (note 8).

It is common for the partners in a relationship to be willing to give access to and share technology with customers. Japanese companies state as the main reason for subcontracting that they gain technical knowledge not available in their own companies.

An advantage of involving sub-contractors in product deign is that it often leads to improvements in quality. Sako's research (1992) cites good quality as a reason for maintaining long-term sub-contractor relationships (74 per cent of customers interviewed).

Financial advantages

The long-term relationships associated with sub-contractors often build up sufficient trust to allow business risks to be shared through joint ventures, joint research and development as well as the sharing of financial risk associated with market changes.

Use of sub-contractor labour in the customer company *(haken)* is widespread and for the customer both cost effective and beneficial to the technological interchange.

Sharing market information and sales forecasts may lead to reductions in inventory levels, especially where Just-in-Time delivery or Kanban quantities (note 9) are achieved. This results in cost reductions across both customer and sub-contractor organisations.

Continuing experience of the sub-contractor in producing a component is expected to lead to a decline in cost and prices over the product life cycle.

The customer is also able to 'share' the effects of a downturn in orders. The customer's contribution to the product work content can be as low as 20 per cent. Therefore, when the market falls it is the sub-contractors who have to deal with excess capacity and resources to accommod the movement.

Advantages to the sub-contractor

Many of the advantages discussed above apply equally to both the customer and sub-contractor. Key examples include stability from long-term contracts and the existence of open, trusting relationships with shared access to information.

To understand the advantages of sub-contractors taking sub-contracting work, the figures from the MITI White Paper (1986) have been used as a source for the following (note 10):

It would appear that the benefit Japanese sub-contractors appreciate most is a steady stream of orders from an assembler (59 per cent).

We have seen earlier that about 72 per cent of the engineering hours needed for component development for a new vehicle is done by sub-contractors. However, sub-contractors themselves consider it to be easier to design and develop products with customers (46 per cent). Perhaps this illustrates the proposition that Japanese feel more comfortable in being developers rather than inventors.

Companies prefer to take sub-contracting work because of difficulties in obtaining orders themselves (42 per cent). The advantage here seems to be that by working in this type of relationship the customer incorporates the function of, and bears the overhead for, sales and marketing. The sub-contractor has the freedom and what is perceived by many of them as an advantage in being able to concentrate on production efficiency and flexibility (39 per cent).

The stability in the relationship benefits the sub-contractor by avoiding exposure to bad debts. Because of the long-term nature of the partnership the customer pays consistently and on time. This was an advantage of 39 per cent of sub-contractors in Japan.

Selection as a long-term sub-contractor to an assembler enhances the reputation of the sub-contractor and prestige is an important factor (26 per cent). This may be understandable given the Japanese Confucian ethic of respecting hierarchy and status. In the UK, sub-contractors may consider such an association as 'good PR' which could be used to attract new business from other quality assembler.

A distinct advantage is the fact that raw materials are supplied as free issue an the sub-contractor does not have to find and manage the sources (22 per cent).

The customer gives technical assistance to sub-contractors to develop processes and production capabilities which result in higher quality and quicker product development.

The process described as *shukko* involves a large percentage of Japanese businesses. In 1980 over 95 per cent of companies with over 5000 employees used
shukko (note 11).

Disadvantages

Japanese writers are not inclined to be negative about their system and the Western texts often seem to view the Japanese approach as a panacea to gain competitive advantage.

There are however, some drawbacks to the Japanese style:

● Disadvantages for the customer

The Japanese approach to sub-contracting with its policy of single sourcing could be dangerous because it appears to be over-dependent on a source, creating unreasonable risks, especially with critical products. Generally the Japanese overcome this by planning capacities with sub-contractors and ensuring their financial stability. They also have sub-contractors with identical capablities who are able to start production quickly.

Single sourcing of an individual part is normal but Japanese companies have possibly three suppliers, making a 'family' of parts. This inter-changeability also allows them to generate real competition for the next generation of parts.

It could be considered potentially dangerous if the customer' sub-contractor relationship became too close for comfort. Price competitiveness could be affected, as both would lose market focus. 'Interchangeability' as practised partly counters this danger.

Rover (note 12) consider that mirroring this style of sub-contractual relationship in UK industry would carry a risk whereby 'technology will stagnate and will not keep pace with competitors who are more expose to market forces'.

For the Japanese customer, there is a danger of over-reliance on a sub-contractor, which would influence their ability to maintain continuous improvement in productivity, quality and technology. Detached from contemporary product technology and processes, the customer may lose the essential skills needed to assess 'quality' proposals, driving product/service standards below competitive levels.

Over-dependence on a sub-contractor's deign capability could create an inertia which reduces motivation to change partners and could be further exacerbated by a financial stake in the sub-contractor. Flexibility to re-source is constrained and as time goes on the exercise would involve increasing amounts of time and money.

The customer has to have additional resources available to assist suppliers with processes, information systems and technological developments. They may also be required to commit financial resources to take a stake in the sub-contractor, limiting their capability to invest in their own processes.

● Disadvantages for the sub-contractor

The power of the final assemblers grew in the last years of the war and for fifteeen years afterwards, and we have already noted that customers were able to use sub-contractors as a source of cheap labour. It was the customer who dictated terms and price levels. Partnership approaches reinforced the power relationship where the sub-contractor was slotted into the 'value chain' owned by the assembler (note 13).

Whilst in the Western world the price power swings between suppliers and customers between boom and recession, the Japanese model remains somewhat biased, with pressure on the sub-contractor to find ways of cutting cost year-on-year. The Japanese expect their sub-contractors to benefit from a learning curve in producing the product, thus improving the quality and cost to them throughout the product life-cycle.

Generally sub-contractors in industries such as vehicles and electronics tend to work for a few customers, 32 per cent of sub-contractors have only one customer and the average dependence on one customer is 62.3 per cent (note 14). This makes the sub-contractor potentially vulnerable to the fortunes and benevolence of the customer - yet the acceptance of this role may be found in the Japanese Confucian heritage which applauds loyalty and serving a sole master. Marks & Spencer in this country also maintain an average dependency in suppliers ranging from 30-40 per cent, but it is suggested that motivation on the part of sub-contractors in this case is driven more by profit than by cultural fit.

The negative consequences of this approach for the Japanese sub-contractor could be that he is committed to a great deal of asset specificity. His processes and equipment are dedicated specifically to producing for that customer and should the work be removed, he could be out of business.

In these circumstances the sub-contractor is totally dependent on his customer, or customers, to provide orders. If they fail to reach the target market, or as mentioned, market forces alter and the sub-contractors are unable to switch production easily, they may be forced to carry the burden of excess capacity or stock.

The sub-contractor is often reliant on his customer for his raw materials and could be unable to produce these supplies. Generally these companies are small with less than 20 employees and would not have the expertise to obtain materials themselves, nor can they build any buying power through volume purchases.

The customer could have a financial stake in the sub-contractor which may be sufficient to influence all the businesses' trading and development decisions. The sub-contractor is in effect tied to the customer, and is not really independent.

It would be difficult for a sub-contractor to end such a relationship, given the strength of the technological links and the bonds of the *keiretsu* and *Kyoryuku kai*. Would other *keiretsu* accept a newcomer? The barriers to exit are matched by the potential barriers to new entrants breaking into a particular business and becoming accepted. It is perhaps these 'glass walls' which keep relationships long-term and ensure the responsiveness of a sub-contractor to the needs of his customer.

Conclusion

The Japanese model of sub-contracting reinforces the key principles which are intrinsic to the culture of the country. The development of long-term partnerships are based on the acceptance of the hierarchical nature of Japanese business and its implications for power exchanges between the larger and smaller companies which exist.

Levels of mutual dependence are created and reinforced against the backdrop of the Japanese ethic of 'benevolence through loyalty'. Each partner's position is protected yet the relationship is driven by the colder business decisions which force pricing, technology and quality to optimal levels.

The existence of the sub-contractor as a flexible specialist operating at the boundary of the firm affords the Japanese corporation the ability to maintain the unique employment attitudes which have been associated with its success. Security for its homogenous staff is guaranteed, whilst the sub-contractor an his heterogeneous agents remains vulnerable as the first cost-cutting target in uncertain times.

We have shown that the sub-contracting system can be insular, restricting flexibility in choice for both customer and sub-contractor. The paradox exists that the same sub-contracting 'network' which promises economic stability and strength can be as limiting as it can be protective. The art remains within its management.

References

1) 'The feudal world of Japanese manufacturing', Sakai, *Harvard Business Review* 1990
2) Friedman 1987
3) 'Prices, quality and trust' Sako, 1992
4) National Association of Purchasing Management - Lisa Ellram PhD 1991
5) 61 per cent of the 2241 large companies surveyed said all transactions are long-term and have been continuous for five years (Sako 1991)
6) Friedman 1987
7) Boston Consulting Group 1993
8) Sub-assemblies developed in parallel rather than consecutively
9) Kanban means 'card control' and the quantity is based on, for example, consumption in two hours
10) Quoted in both 'Creating World Class Suppliers' (Hines 1994) and 'Manufacturers and suppliers in Britain and Japan' (Trevor and Christie 1988)
11) Inagami, July 1984
12) Presentation from Rover Group Purchasing 1994
13) 'Beyond partnerships', Lamming 1993
14) Shoko Kumiai-Chuo Bank Survey, 1993

Establishing and managing buyer-supplier relationships

Vas Prabhu and Terry Miskell

Entering into a relationship with customers operating a JIT/TQM environment does impose a major cultural change on the supplier. Organisational changes are often necessary to meet the customer's requirements of defect-free items delivered in small quantities just in time, and on an on-going basis. This article by VA Brabhu and Terry Miskell of Newcastle upon Tyne Polytechnic and Alan Rayson of ARD Components Limited describes the experiences of ARD.

The UK experience of JIT/TQM appears to be concentrated around original equipment manufacturers in the electronics and automobile manufacturing and engineering industries who are all seeking 'World Class Manufacturing' status. Most of these organisations are naturally seeking to influence the companies in their supply chain in order to reap the maximum gains from JIT/TQM philosophies. Often such approaches are alien to the suppliers, who in order to retain their customers, are forced to make major cultural changes in their organisations. Many suppliers are thus finding themselves in a situation where the need to change is being thrust upon them and these changes in business practices are expected from them in very short periods of time. some results from recent studies (7) of JIT supply relationships seem to indicate that they are very much slanted in the customer's favour.

The article presents the experience of one small supplier,. ARD Components, which, having had some previous exposure of servicing a JIT/TQM customer, took the opportunity of supplying components for that customer's products. ARD Components has been highly successful not only in establishing JIT/TQM relationships with both their customer and suppliers but also in managing them over the past two years. They are now in a position to develop them even further in the form of collaborative ventures with their customer.

Some of the key stages and events in the process, some of the problems encountered, the impact that the JIT/TQM environment has had on the company and what the future holds are described below.

Company profile

ARD Components Ltd, a sub-contract precision toolroom facility based in Washington in the north eat of England, was established in May 1983. The toolroom consisting of precision engineering equipment and producing press tools, mould tools, special purpose equipment builds and general engineering component supply, developed a varied customer base in the north east of England for the first three years of operation. By 1986 the company was supplying Nissan Motor Manufacturing with an increasing supply of special purpose machines/jigs and fixtures and providing a general engineering support,.

However, profitability in the sub-contract engineering market place at the time was difficult - meanwhile TI-Nihon Ltd (Tinuk) a joint venture company between TI Exhaust Systems and Nihon Radiators of Japan was set up in July 1986 in a small factory in Washington to supply assembled exhaust systems to Nissan on a JIT basis. They required someone to provide them with welding jigs, fixtures and general engineering support, and since ARD Components had already established a relationship with their main client - Nissan - they were accepted as Tinuk's supplier.

Tinuk's plan was, as the single source supplier of exhaust systems to Nissan, to supply completely assembled on a JIT delivery basis, to be followed by Kanban, and eventually to provide a sequenced delivery several times a day (at maximum car production - every 38 minutes) by mid-1990.

For the first two years of operation Tinuk sourced all press components direct from one of its partners, Nihon Radiators in Japan, but it was always their intention to eventually source these components locally (within the European Community) when a supplier could be found.,

Search for a supplier

In June 1987 ARD Components were asked by Tinuk if they were interested in setting up a press shop facility to produce the press components. Tinuk felt that the relationship which had been established between the two companies could be developed into the supply of direct materials (their press components). The proposal interested ARD Components for two main reasons:

● The press parts all required new tools to be manufactured. This was welcome new profitable business which at that time was difficult to obtain.

● The potential for establishing long term business relationships using new manufacturing techniques which if introduced correctly would allow steady growth to the business.

At the time ARD Components were approached, Tinuk with the TI Exhausts influence, vetted a number of other potential suppliers known to them in the midlands and north wet of England. These suppliers had already an established customer base with the automotive industry and to take on the Tinuk business with all of the new manufacturing philosophies it entailed, would have required a great deal of commitment on the part of the supplier.

Tinuk's pre-requisite was, as part of the localisation programme to supply parts identical to those already being supplier from Japan on a daily JIT basis even though the volumes at that time were small. By working closely with them to establish good patterns on delivery and quality, Tinuk expected that an understanding would be developed in readiness for the much larger projects to be introduced in 1990. The fact that ARD Components was 'on the doorstep' played an important part in the eventual decision to use them as a supplier.

It was essential that the components supplier were identical to those being supplied from Japan. Their process was set up to handle the Japanese parts and any dimensional/material deviation would have meant further expensive retooling to their existing process.
The timing for introduction of the proposed localised parts was another critical factor. It was planned that commencement of localised parts would be April 1988. This meant that all tooling would have to be built and sample parts produced for trials by December 1987. One of the key factors in Tinuk using ARD Components was that all tooling could be produced in-house, which turned out to be the main issue in achieving the start-up date.

In July 1987, ARD Components were requested to take on the press parts localisation programme with a planned start of production date of 1st April 1988.

Planning stage

Tinuk's method of project planning was used to set up and control the implementation of the project. The stages were:

● A project team sheet was drawn up identifying by name the key personnel to be involved in the project, fig 1. Since this project was to be the base for the expansion of the entire operation, all senior management resources were named to handle key areas of the project.

● A master timing plan listing all actions - including finance, equipment, space, human resources, design, tool availability dates, direct material supply - was developed and agreed with Tinuk management. The time intervals for reviewing the programme were also agreed.

● Since the press components were to be manufactured identical to the Japanese components drawing were based on the actual components themselves and not the original drawings. There is always a risk that process related parts will differ slightly from drawing, and this would case problems in the existing Tinuk automated assembly process.
● Project window sheets, fig 2, which identify key availability dates by components such as the four main evaluation and trial dates, critical to achieving the overall project introduction date were agreed.

● The preparation of the following product planning sheets was actioned:

(ii) process control sheets identifying specially how each component was to be produced.
(ii) a quality plan identifying how the process was to be controlled to produce zero defects.
(iii) material specification for all components identifying any deviations from Japanese specifications.
(iv) preparatory analysis sheets which taker a first look at each component and identify possible design/ manufacturing problem areas and solutions.

It was this strict attention and adherence to the planning detail, which we knew would create major problems in personal workload, that was ARD Component's major concern, but which was essential to the success of the project.

FIGURE 1

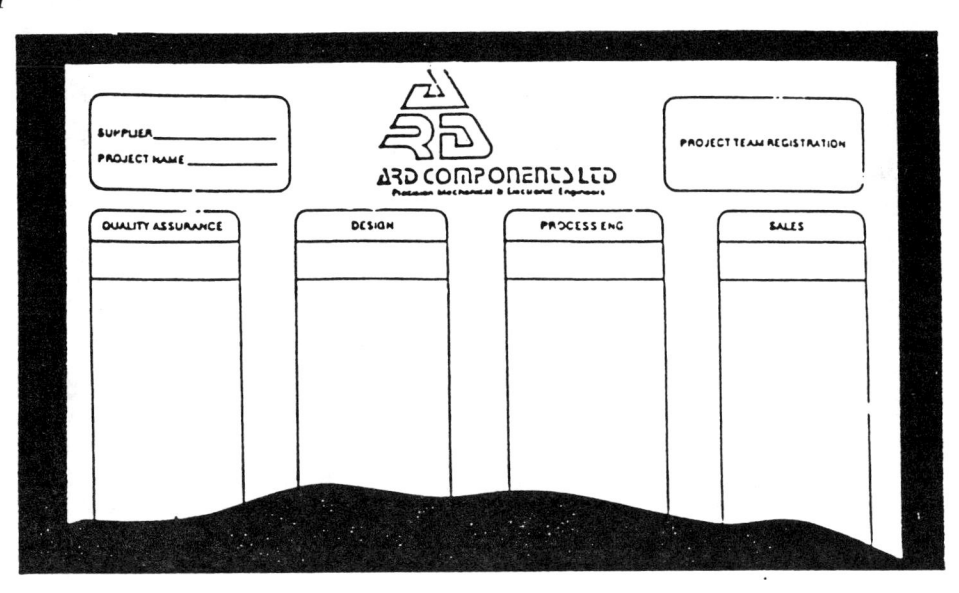

Setting up the press shop

Apart from the problem of tool manufacture timing, the main concern was the financing and availability of capital equipment for the project.

Initial costings had made provision for the purchase of refurbished equipment through an established press supplier who could be relied on to provide a back-up service in the event of equipment breakdown. It was important that the principle of single sourcing and of developing an on-going relationship was adopted with the equipment supplier, as it had been with the direct material supplier.

Refurbished presses were eventually received as one package in November 1987 from a supplier who gave good guarantees and back-up service. Unfortunately, because of financial restraints all capital equipment required to provide full flexibility could not be obtained.

Finance was provided through hire purchase agreements. Additional funding was obtained through regional development grants, selective financial assistance grants - both through the Department of Trade & Industry - besides negotiating additional working capital from increased overdraft facilities.

Space was the next hurdle, and again because of time restraints it was necessary to use a small nursery factory adjacent to the existing premises to handle the immediate needs, with the objective of moving to larger premises when they were available six months into the programme. The space forecast only made provision for the localisation programme at that time.

The supply of direct materials was the next priority, while tools were being manufactured. A relationship needed to be established with a supplier who could supply not only the materials at the right price, quality and delivery schedules, but who was also prepared to accept the total quality policies required in order that prices to Tinuk could be maintained. This policy required the supplier to supply RD Components with defect-free material to a JIT system, and to conform with all other supplier obligations regarding pre-planning information and activities.

FIGURE 2

Figure 2

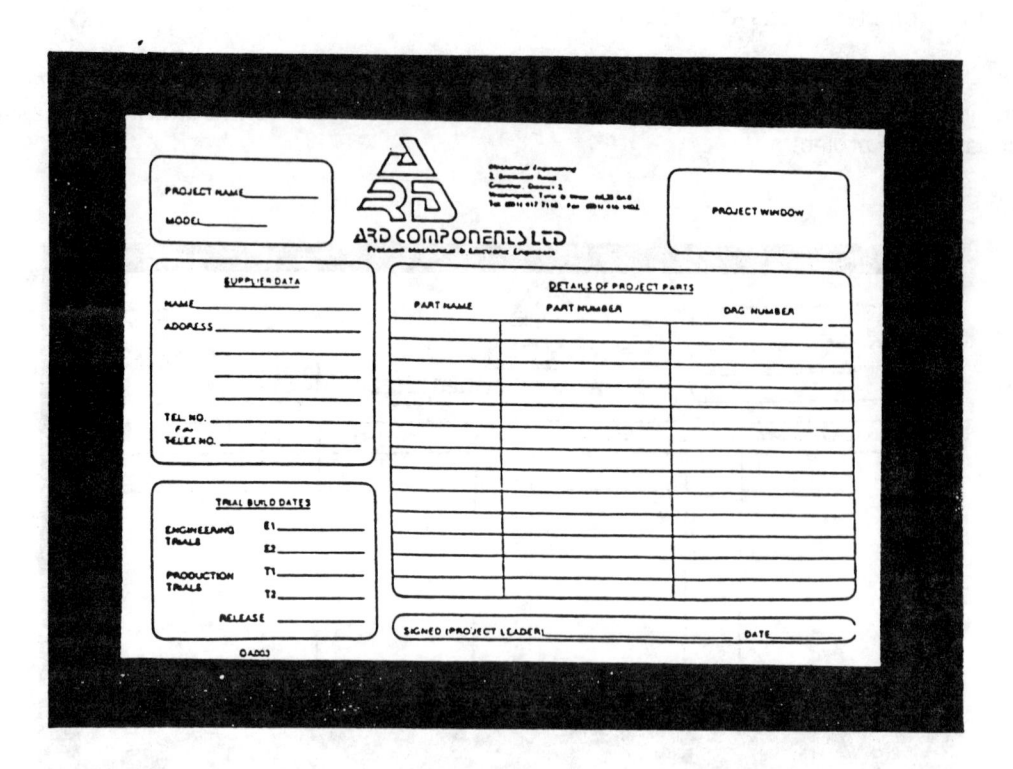

For a small company new into the press parts manufacturing business and with no proven track record, this setting up of suppliers proved to be one of the biggest problems that had to be overcome. Eventually the only solution was to settle for batch deliveries resulting in high inventory levels placing further pressure on our cash-flow. Also one UK stud supplier who failed to achieve the necessary quality standards forced decision to temporarily source from Japan. However, this component has now been sourced from another UK supplier.

By February 1988, the press shop facility was in place. Most of the sample components had been produced, the main material suppliers had been given shipment schedules; the necessary direct and indirect heads had been recruited, and start of production had been scheduled for 1st March 1988 in readiness for first shipments on 1st April 1988.

Start of production

Tinuk required that all deliveries from day one were to be implemented using a tote bin system with standard numbers of parts (SNP) in each bin - determined by ease of handling - and that all such deliveries were made once a day at a specific time.

While Tinuk still continued to receive their supplies from Japan, these would be reduced as confidence was increased in deliveries from ARD Components. By May 1988, ARD were supplying the full complement of parts to ?Tinuk and the Japanese source was cut. Surplus stock from Japan were phased into production over the next six month period.

Introduction of Kanban system

By the lst quarter of 1988 the production was allowing internal stock levels to be reduced and it was at this time that Tinuk requested that the 'Kanban' system of deliveries be introduced by March 1989.

The control of internal inventory levels remained one of the priorities throughout the start-up phase, but because of the production process it had to be accepted that higher levels of work in process (WIP) would have to be accepted through the life of these first phase components.

The introduction of the Kanban delivery system gave Tinuk real benefits, but had little effect on ARD Components other than to tie up the delivering driver for more time than previously, and make him more aware of Tinuk's requirements.

The implementation of the Kanban system has nevertheless made ARD more aware of its benefits and it is planned that with the introduction of new parts in 1990, the system will be implemented internally to control the inventory levels of finished parts stock.

New vehicle, new problems

In February 1989 ARD Components were requested to look at a completely new range of parts for introduction in May 1990.

This programme required that the number of components being supplied be increased from 11 to 32. Costings were supplied to Tinuk using the same manufacturing processes as the existing components, and while the prices were acceptable, the indication were that a request to take a look at cost reduction with some urgency would be forthcoming. Indeed, by November 1989 Nissan requested all supplier to improve their prices by the start of production in May 1990.

The financial resources had already been stretched during the setting-up period and to now invest in automation equipment to bring the unit cost down meant that some support would be required.

A package was prepared to introduce the 'cell lines' approach into the operation. This involved the use of existing equipment where possible, and the addition of some automatic transfer equipment, thereby speeding up cycle times, reducing inventory levels, reducing labour costs and improving product quality consistency.

The financial implications meant that investment was not possible without the support of Tinuk, or the bank, or both, if the automation programme was to be implemented. Both parties were approached and the eventual outcome was that funding was provided by the bank with Tinuk underpinning the borrowing with their guarantees. The automation package is now being implemented and the current range of components will reflect cost reduction by 1st January 1991.

Working together

The relationship between ARD Components and Calsonic Exhaust System (Nihon Radiators changed its name to Calsonic and bought out the complete TI Exhaust interest in Tinuk) has developed to the extent that plans are now being made to move from the existing premises of 10,000 sq ft into a 30,000 sq ft facility adjacent to the Calsonic facility. Turnover has increased from £0.3 million to £1.0 million per annum during the start-up period and it is planned to increase if further to £3.3 million by 1992. Plant capacity will increase three times by automation and reinvestment in further equipment over the next three years to enable the company to be one of the major press components suppliers win the north east of England.

This has been achieved as a result of trust and commitment to one of the top Japanese corporations.

Current developments

With the renewed confidence throughout the organisation, the company now feels that the time is right to progress towards BS5750 quality approval. The help of the Department of Trade & Industry's Enterprise Scheme was sought.

A 'quality' consultant was appointed in January 1990.

Implementation of his proposals is now under way, internal audits have commenced and it is planned that application for assessment will be made within the next two months.

Training at all levels of the company has become another priority. It is recognised that if continued growth is to be maintained, then a good understanding of the company's systems and its culture by all employees, together with good communication must be maintained.

A three year training plan is being drawn up from information supplied by all levels of the company's organisation and from its experiences during the first three years in production. In conjunction with one of the local training agencies, together with help from the Department of Trade & Industry's Business Growth Training Scheme, training will commence during 1991.

Main problems encountered

Prior to its involvement with Calsonic Exhaust Systems, ARD Components had experienced major pressure on its cashflow. Throughout the expansion programme finance played a major part in the company's ability to implement processes and systems, which would allow it to keep pace with Calsonic's growth.

When the first car was being phased out at the beginning of 1990, ARD's sales fell naturally. However, it was only with the help of Calsonic through this unbudgeted period, when they assisted financially with an increase in the piece part prices, that ARD's workforce was kept intact. Training on the production of the new components and the new vehicle start-up was smoothly introduced.

The considerable amount of time and effort spent on 'planning' at the beginning of the programme had imposed a major strain on our personnel resources. But, this investment has proven to be an essential ingredient to the eventual smooth introduction of the project.

Another hurdle to overcome, especially for a small company such as ARD, was to motivate, convince and educate its major material suppliers to adhere to the new systems of inspection-free and JIT deliveries and to maintain strict conformance to product specifications. All direct material supplies are now on a consignment stock basis, resulting in material being delivered against a schedule over and above the month's requirements, but not being invoiced until it has been used.

this arrangement has improved cash-flow and strengthened the relationship between ARD Components and its suppliers.

The impact of JIT/TQM

Changes to organisation - As the company has grown, partial re-organisation has been necessary. The organisation of the direct workforce has remained intact, with the team leaders spearheading the various group. However, with the on-going need to reduce unit costs of components, a greater emphasis on engineering and internal cost control is now being put in place, and changes have already been made to the company's financial management team.

Methods of communication - Regular team briefings form the backbone of all communications. They have worked successfully so far, and will be strongly supported and encouraged in the future.

Change is the only constant - The last three years have been a period of tremendous change for every9one in the company, and it is likely that this will continue as the company grows. The handling of this change has meant everyone making a clear commitment to it, even if in some cases it did hurt.

For better or for worse - The decision in June 1987 to commit the company wholly to Calsonic Exhaust Systems has enable ARD Components to research all the benefits and drawbacks of implementing, from day one, the JIT and TQM philosophy and to set out its stall for the future. Hopefully, it will reap the benefits of continued growth and profit.

Teamwork is an important element in the company's philosophy; every employee in the business knows precisely what is required of him or her. To achieve this, regular team discussions are the norm; they will undoubtedly improve the transfer of vital information in both directions and lead to continuous improvement.

Shortage of skills - As the programme of growth continues, a concern for the shortage of toolmaker skills in the immediate area still has to be overcome. The lack of trained young people with such skills is generally recognised as a problem within the industry, and it has been necessary for the company to include in its training programme plans to address this problem.

Journey to excellence

Trying to carry out business successfully with a customer who demands defect-free components on a just-in-time basis can often be a tall order, especially when there is no previous experience of working in this kind of environment.

It could be argued that ARD's circumstances were unique when it embarked on its application of JIT/TQM principles. They were a very small company at that time and were not saddled with a previous long history of traditional work practices. Therefore, it would have been relatively easy for the company to adopt these new approaches.

However, like most small firms, all its workforce including management had considerable prior experience of working within a typical British industrial relations climate. The problems of change at ARD were therefore not dissimilar to any other small, local (British) manufacturer. Two factors in particular have contributed to their present level of success. These are:

● a total commitment to this approach from the directors and senior management of the company who were enlightened enough to realise the benefits that they would gain from it. Exposure to this philosophy at an early stage in the life of the company had been particularly significant. This determination has enabled them to convince not only Calsonic Exhaust Systems, but the financial organisations including their bank and Department of Trade & Industry that working in harmony with their Japanese customer in the long term was the best solution for ARD Components' future.

● the time and effort spent (by the directors) in convincing the workforce on the most important areas of Japanese philosophy such as:

a) process control and the effect it has on their ability to deliver defect free products
b) teamsmanship and the importance that every individual should understand their role in the organisation
c) the attention to detail, the high level of cleanliness and timeliness, which ensured the quality of their products and customer service.

Looking back over that period it would be fair to say that ARD Components have benefited and grown considerably as a result of building up close relationships with Calsonic and have every intention of continuing to do so. There is still a long way to go down this 'journey of excellence', but the results achieved so far indicate clearly that it is the best way forward for ARD.

Note: *This article is based on the authors' presentation at the BPICS Conference, Customer Focus, December 1990.*

References:

1. Schonberger, RJ. *World Class Manufacturing: The Lessons of Simplicity Applied;* Free Press, New York, 1986.
2. Hutchins, D. *Just-in-Time;* Gower Technical Press, Aldershot, England 1988.,
3. O'Grady PJ, *Putting the Just in Time Philosophy into Practice;* Kogan Page, London 1988.
4. Proceedings of the lst, 2nd, 3rd and 4th International Conference on Just In Time Manufacturing, 1986-1989, IFS Publications, Bedford, England.
5. Voss CAs, *Just-In-Time Manufacture,* IFS (Publications) Ltd; Bedford, England, 1986
6. Case Histories of Britain's Best Factories in the September 1988 and November 1989 issue of Management Today.
7. Baxter, LF, *et al, 'Management Control in Supply Chain JIT' i*n Proc. 4th Int Conf. Just in Time Manufacturing, 145-153, IFS Pub, October 1989.

Buyer Responsibility & Supplier Development

Max Munday reports on a survey which revealed differing national attitudes

Competitive original equipment manufacturers are increasingly forming closer relationships with their main components suppliers. Movements towards 'comakership' or 'partnership' with suppliers is recognised as a departure from more 'traditional' relationships based solely on price criteria and very often mutual distrust. Inevitably for the supplier an orientation towards partnership relations with key customers involves additional obligations as well as rewards. Essentially partnership is built around quality and trust. The supplier will be responsible for delivering quality components in correct quantities at correct times. The supplier may also be involved in technical collaboration with the buying firm, especially in the broad area of component design.

Importantly, partnership relationships are founded on free communication and information sharing between both buyer and supplier. This does not just mean sharing of test and technical data, but also sharing of cost and accounting information underlying component prices. Buyers wishing to consolidate co-operative relationships with key suppliers may thus require information that was previously undisclosed. This article briefly summarises the results of an exploratory survey that sought to examine the extent to which buyers require information on costs underlying quoted and contract prices of components.

Cost information underlying component prices has a number of uses. Data on costs of separate parts of the component production process, together with information on overhead allocation and raw materials costs, can be used within the confines of the buyer-supplier partnership for value analysis and value engineering. Within value engineering the costs of each individual part of the production process are broken down and analysed to identify areas where savings can be made. Ideally both buyer and supplier will work together on value engineering with the end result that long run component costs are reduced. Shared financial data is a valuable addition to this process. Unfortunately cost data shared by the supplying firm may also be used in an unwise manner to simply squeeze profit margin. Trust is thus essential where such data is shared, and it may be contingent on the buyer in particular to ensure that cost information is used in a wise manner.

The exploratory survey completed during the summer of 1991 sought to examine the extent of cost data sharing among a sample of similar suppliers. As a second objective the survey also attempted to analyse supplier perceptions as to the nature of feedback from buyers resulting from the sharing of financial information. The sample of suppliers selected comprised trade plastic injection moulders, mainly to the electronics and automotive sectors, although many of these moulders were involved in other market sectors. This is a sector where there are a large number of clients within not just UK firms but foreign subsidiaries operating in the UK. It is also a sector where closer relationships with buyers have been seen as an important way ahead for the British supply industry *(NEDC, Plastics in IT, 1990)*. 82 questionnaires were sent out, and 33 responses were received, of which 27 were valid for analysis.

Initially, responding suppliers were asked to comment upon the cost information that buyers required from them when quoting for new business or in fulfilling orders. The suppliers were asked to differentiate if possible the information requirements of their UK, US and Japanese clients, if they indeed had business with foreign subsidiaries operating in the UK The responses are shown in Table 1.

A high proportion of UK buyers required information on raw materials grades. In several cases buyers may actually specify grades of plastic granules to be purchased, and will themselves negotiate a price with the upstream chemicals producer. Approximately half of the surveyed moulders reported that UK buyers required details of costs of individual processes in the component manufacture ie the injection moulding of the component, painting, foiling, finishing and various sub-assembly operations. Fewer UK buyers seemed to require further financial data on overhead allocation. Details of scrap and wastage, packaging and transportation costs, with only five firms stating that data on profit element was a requirement.

TABLE 1 Buyer cost information requirements

TABLE 1 Buyer cost information requirements	Total Response	Yes	Details Required No	Unsure/No Resp
UK Customers				
Press Machine Details	27	12	14	1
Raw Material Grade	27	23	3	1
Cost of Indiv. Processes	27	13	13	1
Details of Overhead Allocated to Product	27	6	18	3
Details of Scrap and Wastage Costs	27	8	17	2
Packaging Costs	27	8	16	2
Transportation Costs	27	8	17	2
Profit Element	27	5	20	2

	Total Response	Yes	Details Required No	Unsure/No Resp
US Customers				
Press Machine Details	15	8	2	5
Raw Material Grade	15	11	1	3
Cost of Indiv. Processes	15	7	5	3
Details of Overhead Allocated to Product	15	7	5	3
Details of Scrap and Wastage Costs	15	5	5	5
Packaging Costs	15	6	5	4
Transportation Costs	15	6	5	4
Profit Element	15	3	8	4

	Total Response	Yes	Details Required No	Unsure/No Resp
Japanese Customers				
Press Machine Details	19	13	3	3
Raw Material Grade	19	15	1	3
Cost of Indiv. Processes	19	14	2	3
Details of Overhead Allocated to Product	19	11	5	3
Details of Scrap and Wastage Costs	19	11	5	3
Packaging Costs	19	12	4	3
Transportation Costs	19	11	5	3
Profit Element	19	11	5	3

Those plastic moulders who differentiated the data requirements of their US clients noted a similar pattern. However, a slightly higher proportion of the moulders noted that US subsidiary buyers required more information beyond raw materials grades alone.

Far more significant, however, were the requirements of buyers within Japanese subsidiaries. A high proportion of the responding plastic moulders noted that buyers within Japanese subsidiaries required not only details of costs of constituent parts of the process but also details of overhead allocation, scrap costs, wastage, transportation, packaging and, importantly, the profit element. This would perhaps suggest that buyers within Japanese firms are more exacting in the financial information that they require. However, it may also reflect the fact that Japanese companies have moved furthest in developing the kind of supplier partnership which makes true communication of such information a reality. Statistical tests were carried out on the data and these confirmed that the requirements of Japanese subsidiary buyers were significantly different from the requirements of buyers within UK firms and US subsidiaries.

Where sampled suppliers had shared financial information with their customers they were asked to comment on their perceptions of feedback from buyers and further to comment upon their reactions to this feedback. Table 2 shows perceptions of feedback received from the 25 firms who responded.

TABLE 2 Suppliers' perceptions of feedback following provision of cost information

TABLE 2 Suppliers' perceptions of feedback following provison of cost information	Yes	Total Response
1. Suggestions for the reduction of constituent costs	14	25
2. Pressure to reduce prices	21	25
3. Suggestions for reductions in wastage and scrap	9	25
4. Suggestions for the usage of new types of plastic materials	14	25
5. Suggestions for the improvement of manufacturing operations	6	25
6. Other (packaging improvements	1	25

In a high proportion of cases financial information provision had led to pressure to reduce prices, but, in the majority of cases this pressure was linked to other suggestions from the buying company such as ideas for the reduction of wastage and improvements in operational efficiency. The survey information showed a very definite pattern whereby if feedback was limited to pressure to reduce prices alone, then reactions in the supplier firm were limited to just reducing prices. More detailed feedback with price pressure being linked to suggestions whereby this might be achieved led to a wider spread of healthy reactions by the supplier.

In conclusion, it is noted that buyers are requiring more information on costs underlying component prices, not least buyers within foreign subsidiaries operating in the UK. These exploratory survey findings would tend to indicate that there is a great responsibility for buyers who wish to move to co-operative linkages with their main suppliers. It is the buyer who will be the channel for much of this shared financial information, and it is thus contingent on buyers to ensure that information is used wisely and not solely as a means of battering down prices and squeezing the profit elements that such information discloses. It is also contingent for buyers to provide valuable feedback beyond solely negative signals for price co-operation which in turn is the basis for greater operational efficiency within the component maker. Such an outcome is in the interests of both parties.

Co-makership - a Worthwhile Word

Kenneth Deans and Shan Rajagopal examine the single source purchasing role

A manufacturing operation cannot exist without the support of its suppliers. It is futile for big businesses to reform their production operations without the strong backing of suppliers. In the present fragmented markets, greater emphasis is placed on flexible manufacturing. This in turn requires suppliers who can deliver under pressure, quickly change to new production programs or master new technologies to aid product design. Indeed corporate product design teams, whose lead times are shrinking fast, need all the help they can get, especially the subtle product improvements that only the subassembly and components manufacturers can provide. Hence, strategic manufacturing combined with strategic purchasing requires a special partnership between corporations and usually it is the single source suppliers who are able to meet these demands (1).

This article attempts to highlight the importance of comakership as a strategic tool for purchasing. More often than not, it is neglected by organisations (2). The authors will explore the concept of comakership and assist in the formualtion of a series of steps to achieve a single source strategy. Much has been written about single sourcing benefits that accrue to the buying organisation (3), but the development of a single source strategy has not been explored in the same depth. This article seeks to fill that gap.

Single source management

Current market conditions necessitate a longer planning time horizon than was traditionally employed in the field of procurement. Improved quality, delivery, cost, flexibility, positions in learning curve, computerisations and communications systems all require strategic purchasing to achieve results, and this in turn requires time.

Leenders and Blenkhorn (4) highlighted that companies like Signetics took a minimum of two years to achieve acceptable quality standards from their suppliers. Thus, to discuss any contracts for six months or one year is meaningless. The development costs incurred by purchasing must be recovered and this can only be achieved over longer periods of time. Thus a good supplier and a good buyer will form a long-term comakership agreement, where both parties derive mutual benefits.

The concept of single sourcing is the foundation for a 'win-win' situation where business is conducted in a co-operative manner (5). Single sourcing, as a purchasing policy, has important implications for quality, cost, dependability and flexibility (6). In today's context, single sourcing implies a longer-term relationship and an emphasis on mutual cost effectiveness including quality considerations. The increasing use of the Just-in-Time (JIT) approach to production management has resulted in additional demands being placed on vendors and consequently has added support to the single sourcing argument.

The JIT concept is based on the philosophy of waste elimination, where waste is defined as anything other than the minimum resources required to add value to a product (7)., Typically it focuses on the reduction of inventory levels. This translates into a requirement for frequent, on-time deliveries of materials that are 100 per cent fit for use. Therefore, unless there is a capacity problem, using multiple sources violates the JIT principle of absolute minimum resources. Findings by Andari and Modarras (8) indicate that the most significant problem that arises in the implementation of JIT purchasing is lack of co-operation from suppliers.

They recommend two strategies to help minimise these problems. They suggest the education and training of suppliers and the development of long-term relationships with these suppliers.

According to Butt (1)) there is 'anachronistic thinking' by purchasing managers who advocate the award of two or more contracts for the supply of critical material, usually in the belief that competition drives prices down and helps secure delivery.

A point to note here is that the cheapest component procured from driving hard bargains with multiple sources if not necessarily the least expensive in the long run. Once the cost of poor quality is factored in - downtime on the line, rework, scrap, warranty work, legal fees, etc - the cheapest may well be the most costly.

Benefits of single sourcing

The major benefits of single sourcing (11) can be summarised as follows:

● Product cost reduction through improved communication resulting from (a) close buyer-seller relationship where mutual understanding establishes a basis for co-operative constructive problem solving, and (b) no adjustments to parts/components needed when changing from a part supplied by one vendor to the 'same' part supplied by another vendor.

● Lower prices through (a) reduction in vendor's order processing, sales, transportation, and material handling costs, and (b) fewer reworks and returns.

●1Stbility of supply through (a) long-term agreements, and (b) shipments able to be undertaken with the frequency and timeliness required by JIT.

Some common arguments against single sourcing are:

● Strike or production disruptions can cause major difficulties. However, this can be refuted as an argument because the situation is similar to existing buyer's own production operation. A contingency plan is required in both instances.

● Problems similar to captive (in-house) production where risks are normally greater, due to one production location, whereas with external single sourcing more often than not vendors have different sites capable of producing that part.

● Absence of bargaining power and suppliers developing an unfavourable advantage. This is not really so. The new-style supplier partnerships intensify the dependence of suppliers on major manufacturing corporations and the latter would be well advised not to press this advantage too hard. Companies that become single source suppliers must lock into product programs over which they have no control, with no guarantee that consumers will accept the product enthusiastically enough, or long enough, for suppliers to recoup considerable investment in R&D and setup.

Moreover, suppliers compete intensely at the design stage. They can tie up their design engineers and CAD/CAM facilities for weeks with no assurance of future contracts or of making any revenue. The growing intimacy between manufacturers and suppliers really means that manufacturers are given access to inspect the suppliers' operations in detail. It is not the other way round.

The comakership strategy

The process of formulating comakership is a simple but effective one for an organisation to adopt. it is designed as a two-step approach:

● Classification of purchased material and components in terms of profit impact and supply market.

● Adoption of the comakership matrix.

Classification

The profit impact of a given supply item can be defined in terms of the volume purchased, percentage of total purchase cost, or impact on product quality or business growth. Supply risk is assessed in terms of availability, number of suppliers, competitive demand, make-or-buy opportunities, storage risks and substitution possibilities (12). Within these criteria, the company can sort out all its purchased items into the categories shown in Figure 1: strategic, tactical and operational.

FIGURE 1 Classification for purchased material and components

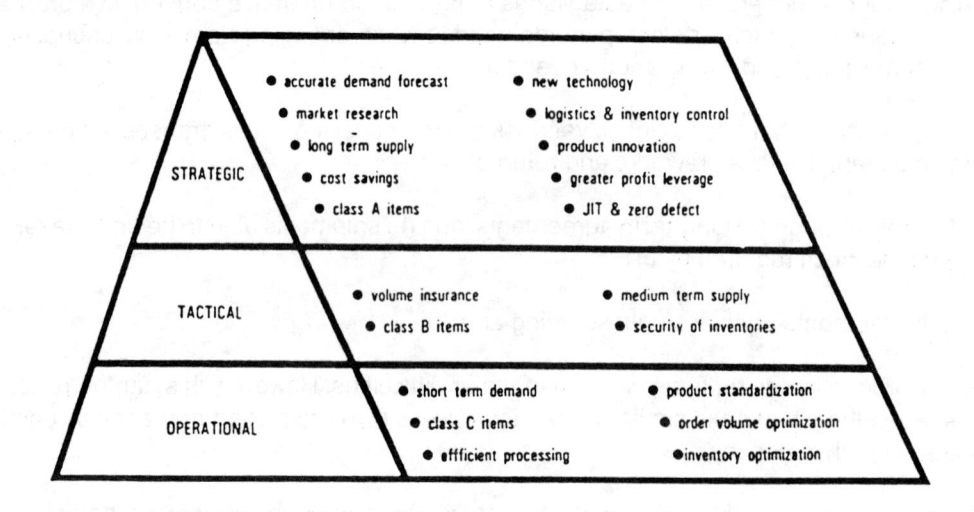

```
                    ╱╲
                   ╱  ╲
                  ╱ STRATEGIC ╲
                 ╱  • accurate demand forecast   • new technology
                ╱   • market research            • logistics & inventory control
               ╱    • long term supply           • product innovation
              ╱     • cost savings               • greater profit leverage
             ╱      • class A items              • JIT & zero defect
            ╱──────────────────────────────────────────────╲
           ╱  TACTICAL    • volume insurance     • medium term supply
          ╱               • class B items         • security of inventories
         ╱────────────────────────────────────────────────────╲
        ╱  OPERATIONAL   • short term demand     • product standardization
       ╱                 • class C items         • order volume optimization
      ╱                  • efficient processing  • inventory optimization
     ╱──────────────────────────────────────────────────────────╲
```

For strategic parts/components, top management decision making (eg Vice President, Director of Purchasing) is required. It involves accurate demand forecast, supply market research and consideration of a long term supply. It also involves greater profit leverage and cost savings through implementation of JIT, zero defect (quality programme) and inventory control.

Tactical classification involves higher level decision makers (eg Department Head, Chief Buyer). It includes volume assurance, medium term supply, control, monitoring and evaluation of vendors and security of inventories.

The operational parts/components are basically non-critical items. Here procurement of standardised parts, monitoring and optimising of order volume all ensure efficient processing of items and inventory optimisation. Shifts in supply or demand patterns can alter a material's strategic category.

The figure 1 structure can be correlated with Leenders and Blenkhorn's (13) supplier pyramid shown in Figure 2.

In this Japanese mode, the first-tier suppliers have close and long term relationships with the manufacturers. They correspond to the supply of parts/components which have a strategic impact on the organisation.

FIGURE 2 The Japanese supplier pyramid

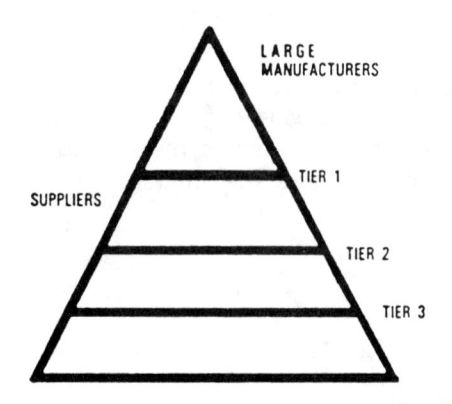

```
                    ╱╲
                   ╱  ╲   LARGE
                  ╱    ╲  MANUFACTURERS
                 ╱──────╲
                ╱        ╲  TIER 1
       SUPPLIERS ────────╲
              ╱            ╲  TIER 2
             ╱──────────────╲
            ╱                ╲  TIER 3
           ╱──────────────────╲
```

84

Approach for comakership

Upon classifying the strategic materials, the organisation must then shift its focus to achieving comakership. This is done through the comakership matrix depicted in Figure 3.

FIGURE 3 The comakership matrix

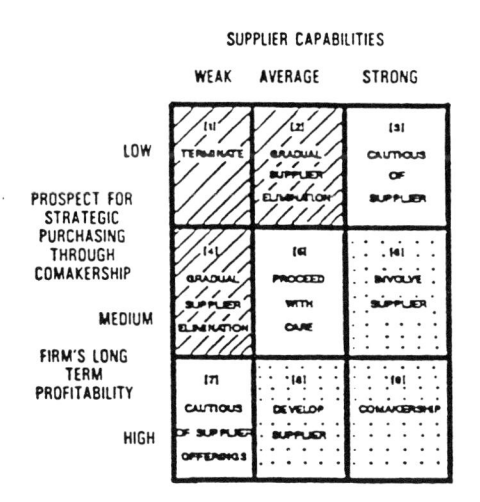

The supplier capabilities can be assessed by their technological facilities (R&D work), management commitments, organisational structure, financial resources, production capabilities and quality management. Though simplified, the capabilities of the supplier can be categorised into weak, average and strong suppliers. Based on these criteria, one can also review the suppliers in terms of small, medium and large vendors.

Quadrant I (Terminate)

As the supplier capabilities are weak and prospect for strategic purchasing low, the purchaser should terminate. There is an immediate need to change supplier. The purchasing organisation needs to start sourcing for new suppliers and its vendor selection needs to be a team effort.

Quadrant 2 (Gradual Elimination)

Here, the process to phase out the supplier gradually needs to be considered. With the supplier capability as average and prospect for strategic purchasing low, periodic evaluation of vendor's production capability and management commitments need to be carried out

Quadrant 4 (Gradual Supplier Elimination)

When the supplier capabilities are weak and the prospect for strategic purchasing is medium, a careful review of other potential vendors is called for. Here, an analysis of supplier's general growth plans, future deign capabilities and strategic planning needs to be evaluated by the purchasing organisation. In the selection process, new geographical sources should be considered.

Quadrant 3 (Cautious of supplier)

As the supplier capabilities are strong, one of the most important elements to be reviewed by the purchasing organisation is supplier management attitudes. For example, if there is any display of 'monopolistic attitude' by the vendor in its bargaining, the buying firm must monitor the supplier's performance closely and begin alternative source searching.

Quadrant 5 (Proceed with Care)

In this sector where both supplier capabilities and purchaser's prospects are average, the purchasing organisation needs to evaluate the supplier's performance continuously. With this position the buying organisation is in a state of 'inertia decision'. It has to decide whether to develop and involve the supplier or gradually phase it out. The supplier's performance and capabilities need to be reviewed on a continuous basis.

Quadrant 7 (Cautious of Supplier Offerings)

With the supplier capabilities weak, and the prospect for strategic purchasing high, the vendors may offer low prices or other incentives to capture a large share of the buyer's business. Caution is needed by the purchasers because the offering by the vendor may 'disguise' a real problem at the supplier's site. Evaluation of supplier capabilities needs to be done with 'team' effort.

Quadrant 6 (Involve Supplier)

In this quadrant, the supplier needs to be involved effectively and early. Invite supplier's engineers to the engineering department and plant. Hold discussions and involve the vendor in value analysis and value engineering.

Quadrant 8 (Develop Supplier)

Supplier development is essential in this sector. The purchase organisation should provide training, management know-how, and general assistance in product design and quality programmes for the vendors. No matter which form this assistance takes, it is important to recognise four facts (14_):

- the assistance may be critical in assuring development success
- there is an actual cost to the purchaser to provide this assistance
- if the supplier had to purchase this assistance in the open market it would probably be expensive in terms of both time and money
- the purchaser's actual cost of providing the assistance may be substantially lower than the vendor's perceived cost for acquiring the same in the open market.

Quadrant 9 (Comakership)

The final quadrant leads to the achievement of a single source strategy. With the establishment of comakership with the supplier, there is vendor involvement at an early stage of product development and other activities of the buyer's organisation. The purchaser's organisation can expect the supplier's to develop quality plans, sometimes to the extent of component design. There may be collaboration with suppliers in the development of initial quality tests, and a progressive striving towards achieving zero defect. In the process of achieving zero defect, purchasing firms can monitor production and quality systems of suppliers by visiting their site periodically and not be inspecting their incoming goods.

A continuous exchange programmes between purchasers and suppliers can be achieved by involvement in both quality and deliveries. The supplier performance is monitored objectively and meetings are arranged with suppliers to discuss their overall performance.

In summary, the assistance provided by the purchasing organisation in developing the vendor to achieve a comakership agreement should be considered, taking account of the following two points:

- the amount and form of assistance needs to be structured as part of the whole deal
- the aid should be dispensed as part of a sound business deal; in return the purchaser should get back the equivalent value. This may be in the form of lower prices, fast delivery, willingness to respond instantly to emergencies, willingness to accept additional orders without quoting ridiculous lead times or prices, or unusually stringent quality standards, or anything that will be of high value to the purchaser.

Progress to achieve comakership can be on an incremental and long term basis. The organisation will have to evaluate, select and develop vendors carefully and learn to overcome any obstacles while striving to attain single source strategy. In the final analysis the rewards are well worth the effort.

References:

I. Burt DN, *Managing Supplier up to Speed,* Harvard Review, July-August 1989 pp 127- 135

2 Rajagopal S and Deans KR, *Strategic Purchasing: a renewed focus for success*, Proceedings of 5th International Marketing and Purchasing (IMP) Conference, 1989 by Wilson DT, Hans SL and Holler GW, pp553-564

3 Juran JM and Gryna FM Jr, *Quality Planning and Analysis*, 1980, McGraw Hill, New York

Sheridan JH, *Strategic Manufacturing: Betting on a Single Source,* Industry Week, Vol v236 No.3, Feb 1, 1988, pp31-36

Hahn CK, Pinto PA and Bragg DJ, *Just-in-Time Production and Purchasing,* Journal of Purchasing and Materials Management, Vol 19 No3, Fall, 1983, pp.2-10

Trevelen M, *Single Sourcing: A Management Tool for the Quality Supplier*, Journal of Purchasing and Materials Management, Spring, 1987, pp 19-24

Farmer DH and MacMillan K, *Voluntary Collaboration vs Disloyalty to Suppliers* Journal of Purchasing and Materials Management, Winter 1976,pp 3-8

4 Leenders MR and Blenkhorn DL, *Reverse Marketing: the new Buyer-Supplier Relationship*, 2988, The Free Press.

5 Newman RG, *Single Sourcing: Short-Term Savings versus Long-Term Problems*, Journal of Purchasing and Materials Management, Summer 1989, pp20-25

6 Trevelen M, *Single Sourcing: A Management Tool for the Quality Supplier*, Journal of Purchasing and Materials Management, Spring 1987, pp19-24

7 Edward JH, *Will the Real Just-in-Time Purchasing Please Stand Up?*, 1984, Readings in Zero Inventory Control Society, Falls Church, Virginia, pp 90-92

8 Ansari A and Modarress B, *Just-in-Time Purchasing: Problems and Solutions*, Journal of Purchasing and Materials Management, Summer 1986 pp 11-15

9 Deming WE Quality, *Productivity and Competitive Position*, 1982, Massachusetts Institute of Technology's Centre for Advanced Engineering Study, Cambridge, Massechusetts, pp 29-30

10 Burt, DN, op cit

11 Trevelen M, op cit

12 Kraljic P, *Purchasing Must Become Supply Management*, Harvard Business Review, Sept-Oct 1983 pp 109-117

13 Leenders MR and Blenkhorn DL, op cit

14 Leenders MR and Blenkhorn DL, op cit

Chapter 3: Environment & ethics

Green paths through the packaging maze

David Henderson looks at the choices facing packaging buyers whose companies want to be green

All the talk about jumping on the green bandwagon has died down. Being green is no longer fashionable or glamorous; it is a fact of life. Now considered by everyone to have a direct impact on profitability, it has been absorbed into business practice. This is backed by a recent survey by the Institute of Directors indicating that 56 per cent of respondents think that the environment will have an increasing impact on business performance over the next five years.

Standing up to scrutiny

Having left the glamour an the excitement of the first phase of the greening of the corporate conscience, we are now in stage two - the detail of implementation. Buyers can't ignore the difference that absorbing green policies has made to them. The need to demonstrate value for money has been joined by the need to demonstrate the green credentials of their suppliers. Business credibility and success can depend on pursuing green purchasing policies that stand up to public scrutiny.

In the context of global warming and the depletion of the ozone layer, packaging may not seem to deserve its high profile. So why its extraordinary ability to grab headlines? Nobody can argue that packaging fulfils its prime function brilliantly - protection, storage and marketing of the product. A look at the reasons why packaging is so high a profile will reveal why the choice of packaging is so critical.

In the early seventies Friends of The Earth dumped a load of one-trip bottles outside the offices of Schweppes. The media loved it, and similar stunts followed to fire the public's indication. The visibility of packaging and the fact that consumer packaging has consistently been used by environmentalists as a metaphor for the 'throw-away society' make it a soft target. Fierce lobbying of the media has made packaging a hot political issue.

The upshot of this is the EU Packaging Waste Directive now passing through the European Parliament to the accompaniment of fierce dissent.

These are the ambitious targets set by the waste directive:
- 90 per cent recovery of packaging waste (including recycling and incineration with energy recovery)
- 60 per cent recycling of each packaging waste material
- only the residues of the collection and sorting processes to go to landfill, and these to be no more than 10 per cent of total packaging waste.

All this to be achieved within 10 years of the Directive coming into force.

You could be forgiven for thinking that there is a political drive across Europe to recycle everything as a matter of principle, unsupported by rational economic and environmental thinking.

Nevertheless, to protect their businesses, companies have had to react to the twin forces of public perception and impending legislation. Throughout the packaging chain manufacturers, fillers, wholesalers and retailers are reviewing and changing packaging buying guidelines before being required to do so by legislation.

Chanting the mantra

The mantra of reduce, recycle and re-use that was first chanted by the environmentalists has been taken up by industry. Most of the high street retailers now have dedicated teams promoting recycling, the use of recycled packaging, the recovery of packaging waste and the elimination of unnecessary packaging.

An increasing number of companies have published corporate environmental statements to explain how they reduce, recycle and re-use, and the subject of packaging is invariably singled out.

It is not surprising then that buyers are turning to their suppliers for help and advice when justifying the choice of particular materials.

In our experience, these are by far the most common questions asked:
a) Can the packaging be shown to cause minimum impact on the environment? (This also includes the transit packaging in which the products are supplied.)
b) Can the company be shown to be creating markets for recycled packaging where possible?
c) Can the used packaging be disposed of effectively?

In each case the buyer needs to know how the answers to each of these questions relate to the general imperative to reduce, re-use and recycle.

As a packaging company involved in plastics - two potentially suspect areas for environmentalists - Plysu has had to establish a watertight case.

Ways to use less
There are three chief ways of reducing packaging:

Removing unnecessary packaging For example, studies have shown that it is possible to pack frozen burgers directly into cartons, dispensing with the polythene flow wrap previously used.

Reduced packaging also includes outer and transit packaging and again, many companies are already working on programmes to dispense with unnecessary packaging and re-use transit packaging.

Lightweighting This is where the amount of material used in the pack is reduced to a minimum without compromising pack performance. This has economic as well as environmental benefits - in that the pack works out cheaper. The best example of lightweighting is probably the ultra-lightweight plastic milk bottles which can be seen on the shelves of supermarkets.

Concentrate packs A look along the household goods shelf in the supermarket will show the extent to which the household chemicals market has gone into small concentrate packs.

So who's recycling?

Only so much can be done to reduce the amount of packaging used. The rest has to be recycled or re-used, but what evidence is there that this is taking place?

Recycling is a sunrise industry and the economics are still being worked out. All packaging can be recycled but the first viable schemes are only now being set up. The recycling logo shown on a product is only meaningful where schemes exist - as consumer pressure groups are quick to point out.

Every bit as important as the existence of a recycling scheme is the creation of a market for that recycled product. The Germany DSD recycling system was a victim of its own success. So many responded to the call to recycle that Germany ended up with mountains of waste for which it had no outlet.

Refusing to incinerate it, the only alternative was to ship it abroad. In doing this they created uproar as the delicate domestic markets destabilised. Vivid lessons came out of the German experience: you have to have a market for everything you collect and you need to create domestic markets, not look to export.

The super model

In the UK there is one brilliant example of a recycling scheme based on proper economics - the scheme run by Milton Keynes Borough Council and centred around a #6M high-tech recycling factory the size of four football pitches.

The factory's capacity is deigned to accommodate waste from Councils throughout the UK and from industry as well as the waste generated by householders in Milton Keynes.

Birds Eye Wall's and other members of industry who are sending their packaging waste to the factory know that everything accepted will be sold on to those for whom the materials have a real value as a raw material for their manufacturing process.

Plysu has a heavy involvement in the scheme. It has sponsored the #500,000 washing and granulating plant for plastics containers. It will also be buying every shred of the plastic which the washer/granulator processes, and this recycled material will be used to make more plastic containers.

The benefits are commercial and environmental. Plysu will have access to a high quality local source of recycled material at a good price. It will also be able to prove beyond doubt to its customers that it is involved in a recycling loop that works.

The availability of recycled containers from a proven closed loop scheme is crucial if Plysu's customers such as Reckitt & Colman, Procter & Gamble and Unipart are to meet the objectives of their own corporate environmental policies. The major high street retailers too are saying that the target for use of recycled packaging on own-label brands is 15 per cent by the year 2000.,

The good news for buyers is that as the packaging manufacturers perfect techniques for producing recycled packs, prices have come down. It is no longer necessary to pay a premium for environmentally friendly packs. Across many packaging suppliers the message if 'green for free'.

Under these emerging conditions there should be no problem in developing markets for recycled materials - provided that companies specify recycled packaging at the time of a product being launched or re-launched.

Re-use and refillables

Refillable systems are also on the agenda. In the UK the only successful example of a refill system is the milk bottle, and even here sales are being undermined, not by any inefficiency in the system but by changing social habits.

In the late eighties much was talked about Life Cycle Analysis (LCA) and cradle-to-grave assessments in an attempt to make a case for refill and return systems.

None of the studies comparing milk bottles, milk cartons and plastics milk bottles has provided conclusive evidence. All have served to throw up more questions than they answer. Where, for example, do you begin and end the analysis?

Abroad, the Dutch government is warning that suppliers must be prepared to supply bulk containers to supermarkets for the consumer wanting to use refill facilities. In the UK the only major chain using refill is The Body Shop. This can hardly be interpreted as a trend, since the Body Shop has carved a particular niche for itself through being seen as very green.

In another sector - this time liquid pesticides - Plysu is working with Ciba in the development of a refill-re-use system. Here both the product and the large, heavy-duty container are expensive to produce an the distribution system clearly defined, so the economy of using the packaging again and again is obvious.

Burning questions

In the case of containers which cannot be used or recycled because of the hazardous materials they have contained, incineration with energy recovery is an attractive option. If the UK follows the rest of Europe, the number of incineration plants in the UK used to power schools, hospitals and housing estates will grow. For example Switzerland recovers energy from 72 per cent of its municipal solid waste, the UK, at the moment, only 5 per cent.

Justifying choices
Ironically, it is the pressure to justify packaging choices that has brought us closer to our customers. To use the term in vogue, there is more of a partnership.

We are regularly invited by buyers to give presentations about the role we play in the supply chain. WE are also working on research projects to reduce, recycle and re-use packaging.

Packaging is set to remain a high profile and complex issue, and companies welcome help as they seek to implement environmental policies.

David Henderson is sales and marketing manager of Milton Keynes-based Plysu Containers.

Waste - a supply chain issue

Harry Whyte looks at the link between purchasing and supply management and waste management

The link between purchasing and supply chain management and waste management is perhaps not one easily made within the structures of the majority of companies. Awareness of the potential implications, both positive and negative, of making such a link should give sufficient proof that it cannot be ignored.

There are several pressures on those involved in waste management within a company, which could be alleviated or removed by consideration during the purchasing and supply chain process.

Legal requirements

The introduction of the Environment Protection Act has major implications on liabilities associated with the management of waste, in particular from the point of production. The Duty of Care Regulations 1992 require all producers, keepers, carriers and disposers of waste to take sufficient steps to ensure the proper control and disposal of waste. Such care includes proper containment, labelling and description of wastes and detailed documentation and transfer to appropriately qualified companies. Hazardous and special wastes, ie those requiring specialist handling and disposal as a result of their toxicity, flammability, physical nature etc are specifically controlled by regulations and through licensing conditions at waste treatment and disposal facilities. Similarly, the storage of special wastes on producers' premises is in some cases subject to specific licensing to ensure environmental protection. These regulations are additional to the duty of care regarding all wastes.

There has for some time been a number of drafts for adoption and proposed EC directives, which will have implications on the longer-term costs of disposal, as a result of reclassification and tighter controls on disposal of wastes and related liabilities in the event of an incident leading to environmental damage. Briefly, the key points for consideration are:

(i) Green Paper proposing civil liability for damage caused to the environment

This has superseded a proposed Directive on Civil Liability for Damage Caused by Waste, to include the wider context of environmental damage, no matter how caused. The document proposes strict liability combined with a 'decentralised Fund' contributed to by each economic sector to cover costs where responsibility cannot be attributed. This would include damage caused by both legally and illegally disposed waste, and would be in addition to any criminal law statutes.

ii) Directive on the landfill of waste

This has been revised several times in response to waste industry lobbying, but was adopted by the Commission this year. No date has been set for implmentation. The directive aims to introduce a system of strict liability for landfill operators and a landfill after-care fund. The directive also initially sought to ban the co-disposal of hazardous wastes to landfill; however, the revised version exempted for five years countries (ie the UK) where co-disposal is practised, after which it will be subject to review.

(iii) Hazardous Waste Directive and European Waste Catalogue (EWC)

The Hazardous Waste Directive was to be implemented in December 1993 and is supported by the EWC. The directive aims to define and classify both hazardous and non-hazardous waste throughout the EC and is likely to restrict disposal routes and hence increase costs for disposal of these wastes.

Individual production/commercial sites may decide upon specific waste reduction policies as a response to regional initiatives or specific waste outlet problems. For example, the scarcity of hazardous waste disposal sites in Scotland is forcing companies in the region to consider waste minimisation as an essential part of cost considerations.

Industry schemes such as BS 5720 and BS7750 are also highlighting the need for an improved approach to waste management subsequent to, in particular, environmental reviews for BS 7750, environmental effects register, with the aim of developing internally set targets for improvement. The achievement of these targets through awareness and commitment from all personnel is the key to company environmental management programmes. It is hoped that, at this stage, the life-cycle analysis approach to the purchase of goods and services can be considered integral to waste disposal practices.

Life Cycle Analysis

Life Cycle Analysis involves assessing the environmental impact of a product throughout its lifetime, from the extraction of the raw materials through to ultimate disposal, sometimes referred to as 'cradle to grave'. This covers the sourcing of the raw materials, manufacturing processes, packaging, distribution and use, re-use, recyclability and ultimate disposal.

Taking stock/your waste on your site

Stock-taking is integral to purchasing and supply chain management, but may currently not extend to stocks of waste. An objective and throrough audit of on-site waste management is vitally imporant as it will provide a basis upon which to build sound waste reduction, reuse and recycling policies and will identify the priority areas for investment-on-site, ie storage facilities, training requirements etc. The following are the suggested steps required:

(i) Identify and quantify all wastes

Once identified, wastes can be put into a number of different cateogies and compared with the original 'mass balance' figure. More obvious classification into solids, liquids or sludges for example can be enhanced by a consideration of handling problems and health and safety issues associated with components. The classification of components will be needed when considering alternative purchasing regimes and/or waste management policies. Almost invariably, wastes are easier to manage when they are segregated at source and the classification of components is a way of focusing on areas where segregation could be improved.

(ii) Disposal contracts should be made to best advantage

Selection of a waste disposal/recycling contractor very often involves little more than looking through Yellow Pages and finding the cheapest quote. However, the actions of a contractor can have major liability implications for an organisation.

Waste or recylcing contractors must be able to fufil certain criteria, as outlined below:
- Registered carrier
- Reliable - on-time, quick call-out if urgent
- Consistent - same driver, same disposal point, same container
- Professional - advice, documentation freely given, disposal site visits.

(iii) Potential for cost reduction

Green purchasing strategies are not in themselves a certain way of reducing financial costs, at least in the shorter term. Similarly, modification of purchasing and supply chain management to achieve waste reduction may not yield immediate cost benefits. However, it is a fact that waste disposal costs have, over the last few years, risen far faster than inflation, as increasingly stringent regulations require waste contractors to invest in their disposal locations with cost increases to their customers. This is a trend that is set to continue.

Re-use of materials currently designated as waste may be advantageous in cost and liability management terms. Purchasing and supply chain managers need to be aware of the consequences of their purchasing decisions in this respect. The selection of office machinery, for example, can have significant implications in waste/re-use of consumables and lifespan of machinery involved. Cost saving associated with such items may have to be viewed in the longer term.

Recycling of materials previously considered as waste can again lead to advantages in cost and liability management. As with re-use, the key is for supply chain managers to find buyers/suppliers who can handle materials in a reliable and safe fashion. In liability terms, it must be remembered that waste destined for disposal will not normally come into direct contract with individuals once it has been placed in a container. In the case of materials destined for re-use or recylcing, it is highly likely that the re-use or recycling will involve a physical contact with the waste. It is therefore vital that segregation of hazardous materials from those destined for re-use or recycling is maintained.

Minimising pressures through purchasing and supply chain considerations

Having described the advantages of considering waste within your purchasing policy, the following are suggested as the key areas for action:

Reduce quantties of hazardous and other wastes:

(i) Purchase materials which will not constitute a Special Waste when disposal is required. For example, buy solvent-free materials: solvents may accumulate as wastes, to become a health and fire risk in addition to having significant costs of disposal.

(ii) Adopt alternative systems to those producing hazardous waste. This relates mainly to production sites and would be identified by the audit as previously described. Many companies have identified significant potential for hazardous waste reduction through no-cost changes in practices.

(iii) Reduce the purchase of unnecessary consumables, for example, use rags for cleaning which can be laundered; reduce packaging requirements to the minimum.

(iv) Consider the recycling of all purchased materials which become wastes including paper, all containers, chemicals, oils etc. This can include waste exchange schemes and novel uses which are good for PR as well as waste reduction.

Consider contractors on-site

(i) Develop contractual obligations regarding waste legislation and ensure they are met by all contractors. As with other purchasing arrangements, be specific concerning exactly what you require. If a particular contractor cannot meet or exceed your requirements, look elsewhere. There are many reputable companies to choose from.

(ii) In order to minimise indirect waste production as a result of your operations, specify materials to be used by contractors on-site, for example during maintenance/redecoration work.

Consider contractors off-site

Prior to any purchase/contracting of waste disposal services, the key issue to be understood is the options available for disposal/recycling of your waste. These options may be different techniques and/or different companies. Criteria will be required for selection of options and companies over and above price, to take account of minimising environmental impact an potential liabilities.

The supply chain manager has therefore an increasingly important role, not only in the purchasing but also in the final waste disposal of goods and materials for his company. By forward thinking and careful purchasing he can improve the long-term contribution to the company not only in financial but also in environmental terms. By careful assessment of waste contractors he can possibly avoid the embarrassment, publicity and costs of legal action should his company be caught out by a contractor taking short custs. It amounts to partnership agreements at both the start and finish of the supply chain process.

This article is based on a paper presented in 1993 by **Clive Rockingham and Nicola Eury**, environmental consultants with Environmental Assessment Group Ltd.

How green are my suppliers? - buying environmental risk

Michael Lloyd believes that real added value can be obtained through proper management of environmental risk

The old adage 'you are what you eat' is applicable also to the procurement of supplies and services for your business. Attention to environmental matters is essential for all companies which have a substantial bought-in component in their business - most manufacturing companies and a high proportion of service companies - if control over environmental risks is to be achieved. However, it is not simply a question of avoiding environmental risk. It is crucial to recognise that in handling environmental issues or in responding to environmental pressures, an organisation has the opportunity to add value to its operation. This contrasts with the narrow views of compliance with environmental legislation, leading to increased costs.

Research in the US, with a longer history of environmental legislation and other environmental pressures on companies, suggests that some 45 per cent of companies are motivated to introduce environmental management systems by the desire to achieve compliance; some 40 per cent by the desire to achieve cost savings; and the remaining 15 per cent by the desire to improve bottom line performance by process or product innovation. It is interesting that, in a country well known for instant recourse to litigation, more than half of the US companies appear to take a strategic view of environmental pressure in the sense of directly and positively attempting to adjust to those pressures by adding value an profit to companies' operations.

None of the above should detract form the obvious importance of compliance with environmental legislation nor of the associated bottom-line benefits of compliance, eg lower insurance premium and protection against legal liability, fines and damages. However, as a Rover company spokesman has said recently, 'The environment is no longer simply a compliance issue for Rover; it is now one of the drivers of the company.'

From a purchasing viewpoint, the strategic approach to environmental management has a number of implications. I want in this article to deal with one area in particular, namely the environmental rating of suppliers. However, before moving on to this issue, it may be useful to deal with more general environmental management aspects as they relate to the purchasing function.

Advice, management strategies and implementation

It is imperative in any organisation to devise a set of management strategies for dealing with environmental issues. One immediate problem is to define, in any given organisation, what are 'environmental' issues. Indeed, there is a case for saying that use of the term 'environmental' to describe a particular sub-set of impacts on the organisation is merely a convenient, or perhaps inconvenient, taxonomy, covering a variety of business areas including waste management, energy, utilisation, quality management, health and safety, insurance, legislative compliance, etc.

However, gathering a number of apparently disparate issues under a single heading does have a significant advantage. It focuses management's attention on the substantial impact that these various areas have on the revenue and cost flows of the organisation. This then should lead to a proper appreciation of the importance of handling the various issues in a strategic manner.

Devising the strategy may be done solely via internal management mechanisms or with advice from external consultants. There are large number of environmental consultants around the UK. Many cover specific areas, eg toxicity of substances, health and safety etc. Some do provide strategic management advice. Few, however, combine advice with implementation in an integrated system. Yet successful implementation is essential to achieving bottom-line performance. In this respect the use and application of information technology to environmental management systems is seen to be an increasingly cost-effective means of achieving not only compliance via auditing and reporting tasks but also procedural benefit via the use of workflow software to define and adapt to changing business process in relation to implementation.

Integration and Information Technology

This is perhraps the key to future success in handling environmental issues, namely to devise the management strategies and procedures required, with or without external advice, and then to use appropriate modern software systems to achieve the essential implementation of the strategies and procedures, including monitoring and compliance procedures.

Now let me turn specifically to consider supplier assessment and improvement over the range of environmental impacts on the supply chain.

Supply chain assessment

First, a caveat: it is not going to be possible to assess exhaustively all your suppliers. However, nor is it essential to do so, at least in the initial phases of establishing a system for managing the environmental impacts of your suppliers on your business. Not only is a stage-by-stage approach the only practicable route, but it is also the most desirable one.

For example, whole life-cycle assessment is a good idea, and ultimately will be essential to achieve full environmental assessment coverage, for the time being a single accepted methodology does not exist. Indeed, currently there are some 10 different ones which are recognised!

Moreover, what welfare economists call 'second-best' solutions frequently, in practice, indicate the right paths to follow. What methods should then be used for evaluating suppliers' environmental performance?

Alternative approaches

Essentially there are two broad approaches. First, an external certification of suppliers via BS7750 or EMAR. Second, there is the approach via questionnaire and audit.

The revised BS7750 standard was published earlier this year. EMAR will not become extant until April 1995. The principal difference between the two lies in the reporting module included in the EMA Regulation.

In deciding which is the more appropriate route to follow, there are a number of pros and cons attached to the two broad approaches.

The EMAR and BS7750 routes tend to involve heavy bureaucracy and documentation for the suppliers, and as far as product quality is concerned, these standards cannot guarantee the meeting of customer requirements.

However, by shifting part of the cost burden of checking internal supplier procedures from the purchaser to the supplier, like BS5750 the external certification approach has much to commend it to the buying organisation.

there is, however, another aspect to bear in mind when considering BS7750 or EMAR.

These standards are intended to act as national/European standards. They are, hence, general and enabling rather than industry or company-specific. However, the tendering to specific industry or company situations is left to the consultants used by the company. As with BS5750 this is not a copper-bottomed guarantee of relevance. Indeed it has led to the development of sub-species of BS5750/ISO 9000, such as the TICKIT standard for the software industry. Other pressures have led even BSI to develop a separate Total Quality Standard.

In relation to BS7750 and EMAR it could be argued that there is even more need to be industry and even company-specific in approach. These comments should not apply, however, to the reporting module of EMAR which clearly should be based on wide national or European standards.

However, if there are limitations and disadvantages to the external certification route which may lead companies to be less than enthusiastic about following it, what is the alternative?

Clearly, a company-specific questionnaire followed in key product areas by a site audit at the suppliers' premises can produce information tailored to the needs of buying organisations. However, there are costs involved. a high proportion of these costs will, necessarily, be borne by the buying organisation. The cost burden is likely to tempt buying organisations to follow with the external certification route in the environmental area.

However, there is one significant difference. The penalties attaching to the buying organisation resulting from inadequate BS5750 certification are not likely to be serious in terms of legal liability or immediate cost penalties or loss of revenue. Failure to ensure that suppliers are environmentally compliant represents a major area of risk. For this reason alone it is likely that more companies will rely on the questionnaire/site audit approach than in the case of quality verffication.

Environmental evaluation criteria

If this is so, then what are the likely criteria to be applied in assessing a supplier's environmental performance? It is not possible to be too specific, but there are some general headings, to be analysed and supplemented, which can be given.

There are likely to be four main headings which provide a high level taxonomy in relation to environmental issues. These are:

- Regulatory compliance
- Environmental effects and performance measures
- Existing environmental management proedures
- Commitment to management and process improvement

The first heating will encompass the various legislative an regulatory issues, some of which, eg specific EPA authorisations, will be mandatory conditions for supplier approval. Other criteria under this head, though not mandatory, may nonetheless have a high weighting, both within this high-level category and for the overall evaluation. For mandatory criteria, it is likely that buying organisations would withold approval/negotiation until such time as the supplier did fulfil the mandatory conditions.

The second category heading covers the various effects and performance measures, such as ecotoxiological information, volatile organic compounds records etc.

The third category heading covers the existing management procedures relating to the existing set of products and processes. This will involve environmental effects register maintenance, energy conservation policy etc.

All the above headings will relate to specific products or sets of products and bought-in materials and components relating to the transformation processes involved in the business covered.

The final category covers the commitment to continuous improvement in both management and transformation processes. These will apply to the supplying company irrespective of the various products and materials which are supplied. The category will include the level of board/senior management practices in the company, as well as issues such as the level of line manager/supervisor knowledge, practice and training.

Some key issues

These issues present themselves as requiring discussion an agreement. First, what level of suppliers/services classification is required for environmental assessment? A minimum of two levels would seem essential, ie a product level and a material or component level. However, it could be argued that three levels may be required, say the product, pipe; the coating metal/polymer; and the substance, aluminium/polyurethane.

Second, should quantitative or qualitative rating be used? Here the answer seems obvious. Whatever value may or may not be ascribed to the final score for a product/supplier, it will not be possible to compare performance in one area with another without a rating system which designates minimal values. Moreover, it will be impossible to produce a sufficiently credible ranking of suppliers without quantitative rating, even though the final ranking itself may be regarded as an ordinal (1st, 2nd, 3rd ranking).

Third, the issue of which criteria will be mandatory must be resolved. Mandate should be restricted to situations where some legal or specifically identifiable financial penalty may be invoked against the buying organisations.

Conclusions

One thing is certain. In the future, environmental pressures will increase. Social, economic, business, financial and legal measures are going to force companies to set up environmental management systems. These will have to include as a key sub-system the appraisal and monitoring of suppliers. CIPS has recently participated in a major exercise with Business in the Environment to provide guidelines for integrating the environment with purchasing and supply. The joint publication *Buying into the Environ-*

ment should be mandatory reading for all involved in purchasing and supply, and perhaps particularly those at board level. This article has attempted to put some flesh on the bones on the issues set out in 'Buying into the Environment'. However, the discussion is now for CIPS members to enter and for practical work on environmental supply chain monitoring and appraisal to commence in their various organisations.

Michael Lloyd is Managing Director of Ceres, a leading UK consultancy in environmental procurement terms and procedures, which has developed the EROS (Environmental Rating of Suppliers) database application. EROS is being officially launched at the ITEMS conference. Details of the system are available from Ceres on 0191-236 7166.

Getting shot of it

Disposal of surplus stock or equipment is an increasingly complex task, writes Martin Beauchamp

One of the more famous disposals of history concerned Alexander the Great in 332 BC. In invading the Middle East as part of his lifelong world tour, Alexander demanded that the cities of Phoenicia (including Tyre) should do him proper obeisance. The other cities had smart businessmen. They opened their gates and welcomed him. Tyre however felt his was an offer they could refuse.

In earlier years the Tyrians had decided their coastal city was too exposed and had moved to a nearby island where their capital was re-erected. With famed Greek pragmatism (though purists might rightly say that Alexander was Macedonian) he tore down the old mainland city and re-using the stones, masonry and debris, built a causeway to the island. Having thwarted various attempts to repel his boarders, Alexander ensured final naval supremacy by drumming up ships from Macedonia and six friendly allied states.

In further idsposing of and re-utilising the debris of the old city, Alexander built floating siege platforms whose battering rams settled the siege outcome. The cost of the disposal to the Tyrians was quite high with 10,000 killed and 30,000 sold off into slavery. The moral is to know when to settle.

Throughout the centuries there have naturally been manyinstances of disposals skills being needed - some more anecdotal than others. More recently however, the sheer breadth of modern technology has created a much more challenging problem.

Waste and environmental strategy

A while ago there was a brave attempt to log and publish information on the literally hundreds (actually more than 1500) of British sites on which dangerous metals and chemical pollutants had built up. This included sites such as former gas holder sites on which allegedly there were heavy metals and other pollutants. The resultant, rather depressing, map looked like a patchwork quilt design spread right across the country. The then government, ever optimistic, failed to understand the pressures that would ensue as thousands of businesses and even more home owners suddenly realised that, with further publicity, their plots might now become unsaleable. Expediency won the day and the scheme to focus environmental awareness on this issue was rapidly faded into the background.

Similarly, I read with some concern but nevertheless amusement that, as Anthony Barry reported in *Procurement Weekly*, the Government's consultative exercise on a wsste strategy for England & Wales has, to mix the metaphors, met with a deafening silence. Key points from the document were the following:

- Waste in landfill to be cut by 10 per cent within 10 years
- 25 per cent of household waste to be re-cycled within 5 years
- Use of recycled waste to rise nearly 90 per cent within 10 years
- 75 per cent of companies with more than 200 staff to publish clear waste policies
- 50 per cent to have introduced waste management systems within 5 years

The obvious difficulty is that companies and domestic consumers will be loath to enact any arrangements that in practice are more expensive than at present, and with the great human capacity for self delusion we all hope the problem will go away. This is naturally flawed logic and it will be necessary for legislation to be introduced forcibly to improve the situation although undoubrtedly it might initially be a vote loser. But pressure groups understandably concerned about the environment will continue through advertising, high profile PR stunts and the electoral system to shape public opinion on the attitudes to and the use and disposal of a wide variety of everyday resources.

We must not, however, expect buyers to be technical experts on all the interactions, uses, properties and risks associated with chemicals, metals, fibres and other base materials, substances and products natural and artifical. Buyers must therefore rely on informed comment from Government, Health &

Safety Organisations, CIPS, the Engineering Institutes and other relevant concerned professional bodies who will publcise findings that may subsequently affect a buyer's positioning on the acquisition and later disposal of various kinds of equipments and products.

Key considerations in disposals

All equipment procured will utlimately fulfill its purpose in the procuring organisation and a decision will finally be reached to effect its removal. The basis of the decision will vary from organisation to organisation, but some of the following may or will be involved:

1   Obsolescence technically
2) Planned use has ended
3) Financially, equipment has depreciated to zero
4) Internal stragegy changes force disposal
5) Stored items are introducing capital holding charges
6) PR value can be leveraged from charitable disposal
7) Market conditions favour rapid disposal
8) Equipment may now be perceived as hazardous
9) Budget considerations may force early replacement purchases
10) Environmental considerations may now exist for safe disposal

Technical obsolescence may be a prime factor in forcing disposals, particularly when there has to be product integration (such as in the Information Technology niverse). Frequently with Informtion Technology related acquisitions, the entire marketplace is leveraged by the large manufacturing principals such that continual product upgrade improvements are constantly appearing and these are co-ordinated in such a way that new hardware will force the acquisition in short order of new operating system and applications software required to run the hardware. Now whether, technically speaking, the dog is wagging the tail or the tail is wagging the dog is irrelevant, it is still a most convenient and desirable arrangement for all parties *except the buyer* who must decide whether he will participate in the race to keep up with the technology or not.

Budget and financially based product renewals are operated in many companies so that when the equipment has been depreciated to zero, there is no further enthusiasm to use it and it is thus removed. This will generally mean a 3 to 5 year owned life cycle for the equipment concerned.

Main Board strategy changes or other policy changes imposed by senior management may mean the replacement at short notice of a whole line of equipment which previously had been serving a specific function within the company. If communications and proper business plans are a weakness in your company, you may be under immense pressure to both procure new equipment at short notice and dispose of the originals with equal despatch. Regretfully this is not a good backdrop for optimising benefits to the organisation.

Charitable disposal may look good from a PR point of view, collecting considerable brownie points in the local press and with local organisations such as the chamber of commerce etc. However in Britain, unlike in America, duties of care exist which mean that under certain sale mechanisms other than Auction (where one can legally disclaim various responsibilities) there are requirements which mean that equipment must be in reasonable working order when disposed of - even if that disposal is charitable and at no charge! Thus if some poor old lady in a hospice were electrocuted by your charitably donated electric toaster, then despite any waivers and disclaimers accompanying the originally donated equipment, you would still be legally liable. This principle at law means effectively that all equip;ment being directly put onto the market should have been verified as to its safety first. This in turn implies checking and safety validation costs that may make donation very unattractive unless there are overwhelming 'political' reasons for so doing.

You might normally have a phased and tightly planned disposal arrangement with the situation where new equipments will be purchased within the current financial year. If however it become apparent that market conditions have created a shortage then it might well be appropriate to accelerate the acquisition of alternative new equipment whilst disposing of the original equipment at a satisfactory premium.

Equipment may be perceived as hazardous. For example, there was recent EEC legislation relating to the new and lower acceptable energy emissions from video (computer) monitors. If staff insist on new safety emission equipment or you realise tht your equipment is not compliant with the new legislation, then rapid disposal (or scrapping) would be a much sounder option than risking prosecution.

Crazy though it may seem in 1995, **corporate budget considerations** still force may unnaturally early and unplanned acequsitions (and thus the correlating dispoasls). It seems extraordinary to think that in a good number of organisations, otherwise very sound commercially oriented managers will be racing round in late March each year desperately spending money because their budgerts have unanticipated sums still remaining in them. As the money can invariably never be accrued, the managers must spent it or lose it and risk budget cuts the following year. Unofficaly, buyers and commercial staffs should prepare annually for such scenarios so that pressured timescales do not force ill-udged acquisitions or poorly handled disposals.

Environmental considerations may shade disposals not just in terms of whether or not there is now appropriate European legislation which is forciung the position, but also in terms of public opinion and perception of your business. Being caught dumping noxious or dangerous chemicals in landfill sittes or down mineshafts is a certain way not just to be prosecuted but to ensure tht your company takes an instant nosedive in public popularity. Ignorance, or at the very least thoughtlessness, is not the perquisite solely of the unenlightened. Many years ago, one famous London College where I once worked seemed blissfully unaware of the dangers of tipping highly toxic chemicals down the drains. They wised up only when two inspection staff were later discovered snoring heavily in a tunnel reeking of potent chemicals. Happily the men were rapidly retrieved and ultimately seemed none the worse for the incident. It was undoubtedly an oversight , but highlighted the need for an enforced written policy accompanied by constant vigilance, consistency and thoughtfulness in the matter of disposals. Buyers must likewise be seen to be covering their organisations back in the area of environmentally friendly disposals.

Methods of disposal

The methods used to dispose of your unwanted stocks or equipment will naturally vary according to the equipment on offer. Very different procedures will affect the disposal of chemicals to those employed for unwanted office equipment, and different again will be the disposal techniques used for high technology engineering or electronics equipment. Some of the principal options are shown in Figure 1
　　In many cases, organisations no longer wish to have staff permanently assigned to the labour intensive activities associated with disposals. If there is a substantial case and the officer concerned id expert on a wide range of differing types of disposals, the arrangements may be different, but increasingly disposal as a skilll is outsourced.
　　If you are outsourcing, it only remains therefore to see whether acution or agency is to be used. Both have advantages and disadvantages. Perhaps two key factors should be that your corporate representative
1) should be legally empowered to take decisions on your behalf
2) possesses the broad bandwidth of skills across differing types of disposals to make a success of each assignment. Both factors can only be effectively utilised if you have given your acutioneer or agent a firm written brief as regards your expectations, and his basis on proceeding and negotiating (or withdrawing).
　　The other types of disposals such as direct bids/sales/trade/counter trade agreements, etc all contain the need for centrally owned control. Some, such as countertrade agreements may be relatively rare and unusual unless foreign governments or companies are keen to obtain second user equipment against a national background where technology is not so advanced.

Contractual considerations

What are some key elements to include in a disposals arrangement? This question will especially come to the fore if you are having a third party do the disposals for you, and you wish to construct a suitble framework agreement - perhaps lasting for a year or more, against which a variety of assignments can be undertaken

FIGURE 1 - Some options for disposal

Disposal Method	Advantages
Direct sale via bids/tenders	Direct control of all assets Single point accountability No 3rd parties to manage
Trade ins	May be excellent if upgrading existing equipment with same company Final disposal by 3rd party
Auction	Hands over responsibilities on a pre-arranged basis Simple to operate
Agency	Agent more flexible than an auctioneer Terms for disposal can be easily varied Selling time can be adjusted to optimise revenue stream
Sales or gifts to staff	Easy disposal managerially Simple direct arrangements May favour staff via undercharging
Charitable donations	Appears socially friendly Gives company good local image Is free publicity
Counter trade arrangements	May get you Eastern European or 3rd world products on preferential terms Is technically a flexible barter arrangement Avoids currency exchange limitations
Fixed price sales	Very simple, can be agency controlled Buyers will probably pay carriage Easy if valuations originally correct

Here are some general principles:

1 Construct a Framework Agreement after consultation with users about their needs
2 Give clear admin procedures on how the scheme will work
3 Reference the points of contact at both ends
4 Consider prior evaluation and assessment of the equipment for disposal
5 Tie up carriage arrangements tightly
6 Build in a competitive basis of fee charging by the agent
7 Arrange for any repairs or refurbishment of eqipment by agent.
8 Decide on a scrap v sale policy for marginal items
9 If scrap - at what level? Down to precious metal extraction?
10 Build in a basis for checking that repair/refurb arrangements are densible
11 Devise strategy on how long stocks are held by the Agent
12 Arrangements where necessary for return (or scrap) if sales not forthcoming
13 Tie up insurance and indemnification arrangements for your assets
14 Arrange for when title and property in the assets will be vested
15 Build in regular reviews, meetings, asset printouts etc
16 Get reimbursement arrangements watertight including actions needed
17 Allow for periodic review and adjustment of the arrangements
18 Ensure terms and conditions are referenced for all transactions
19 Make certain that contractual 'consideration' always exists
20 Wrap up environmental disposal issues as appropriate
21 Monitor the scheme for regular compliance with the agreement

Taking some comments on these headings:

1 A Framework agreement is sensible as it gives an excat view of the forward positioning of procurement on disposals. A small company will naturally have less formal arrangements. it serves in line with 2 above to collate all key details for instant reference and access. As 3 suggests, buyers and sellers' contact details, phone and fax numbers and commercial details should be immediatly to hand

4 Sending equipment to an agency only to find it is unsaleable or worthless is poor policy. Charges will already have been incurred in single or dual carriage costs, plus insurance on the goods in transit. This is unacceptable If it is not economic on a disposal for the agent to send his representative to value the goods *in situ,* then at least a good description of the goods and their condition must be phoned to the agent so tht he can make an enlightened guess as to ther relative worth, pending final examination. The asset owner can then decide *before a courier is sought* whether the tentative valuation on the goods is worth proceeding with and whether further costs should be incurred in their disposal.

6) If running a period-based agreement - the original agreement should have been on the basis of a good competitive market analysis. Verify periodically that this basis still relates to the realities of the market.

7) Repairs or refurbishments to potential sale equipment naturally lower its value but may be crucial. Press for sufficient details to be fully initially satisfied and obtain documentation of auditing work undertaken.

8) Internal clients tend often to over-value favoured equipment. If scrapping is suggested, get a fully documented rationale open to a second opinion (as required) and simply agree the specifics of the mechanism and the resulting value. Encourage internal customers to be realistic and not incur unnecessary further agency admin charges.

11) Market conditions may normally favour disposal but there may be a short term glut of similar or identical equipment. Have a flexible stocking policy so that an agent can sell at the optimum time. If time (or space) is ofthe essence you will probably have used another mechanism such as auction to dispose of the goods. This will constrain return cash values to the value 'on the day.'

13 Assets must be insured the instant they ar off your property until sale has been accomplished Obtain annual rolling indemnification and insurance from your vendor to cover the risks. Be certain it covers the contingency of unsold goods being returned to you.

14) Title and property will likely be retained in equipment until the moment of sale, at which point you will vest it to the agent for obvious reasons of transfer. If the sale fails or payment is not forthcoming within the contrat terms, title and property should re-vest to you forthwith.

17Periodic review and adjustment allows for finessing and changing of long-term agreements (ie agreements more than 6 months) to reflect changing market realities and any new wishes of each of the parties. It can also cover any changes in technology or adjustments necessitated by new environmental legislation or other considerations.

What a disposal vendor offers

Naturally there are many areas for disposal and many vendors operating within each. To pick an example, in information technology, here are some typical services offered by a well-known professional company in this area: Dataserv Ltd:

- Data eradication on personal computers for disposal
- Check on transfer of proprietary (licensed) software
- Asset analysis
- Co-ordination and packaging
- Disposal v scrapping

- Second-level disposal (environmentally driven)
- Wide ranging IT disposals due to strong financial base
- Administration and management
- Dedicated unique solutions for you
- Modifications and upgrades to leverage re-sale value
- Bar-coded stock identification and tracking
- Serial number level audit trail reporting
- Market intelligence
- Tailored regular reporting programme.

Many of these are clearly added value services of the kind that might not be available from a smaller company in the arena. Such added value services can usually be customised and tailored according to your requirements. Within the disposals arena, whether we are talking office equipment, major constructions disposals or whatever else, the principles are the same - todispose safely, environmentally acceptably, economically and where possible with a positive cash inflow towards your further procurement expenditure.

Understanding difficult technologies

Sometimes buyers get ousted from areas of proper corporate concern (such as acquisition and disposal of IT assets) because it is claimed that technical experts are more qualified to make judgements than the buyers are.

I believe this to be false reasoning. It is easier in my view to give intelligent buyer several years of suitable background in IT and engineering issues and the assoiated equipment and then to apply their skills in this area than it is to train engineers to become really commmercial and to participate in highly creative procurement positioning - including control and shaping of the market.

However, buyers should be aware that where they have deficiencies they should look to improve their technical and product knowledge by reading up and by attendance at seminars and exhibitions of the relevant product groups. They should also not be afraid to ask seemingly simple technical questions of 'experts' within their organisations in order to increase their comprehension and grasp in the vital product and technology areas concerned.

this will then have the effect that in due course the buyers will be able to take an increasingly authoritative role in the acquisitions of new technology so that well procured results are obtainable and disposals can also be meaningfully and professionally handled.

Increasing the Efficiency, Lessening the Impact

by George Hazle

Environmental responsibility is a process of ongoing education. Awareness of the effect of distribution activities on the environment has steadily grown over the past five years - particularly regarding any potentially negative impact. Government regulatory bodies, pressure groups, and operators themselves have all taken steps to lessen that impact, and further steps are set to take place. What are the environmental pressures facing the logistics practitioner? What are their implications? How can companies prepare for the changing face of distribution which is set to result?

When the Royal Commission's report on transport and the environment was published in Autumn 1994, it recommended sweeping moves to drive traffic off the roads and lessen the impact of distribution on the environment.

Calls for an increased shift of freight from road to rail, a radical increase in the price of fuel, a reduction in the Government's road building programme, and for large vehicles and distribution centres to operate well away from local communities. These were some of the recommendations made which, in the view of some people, may lack in commercial awareness. But they have, unquestionably, focused public awareness on the environmental impact of distribution activities on the environment.

Perhaps less well known is a report by SACTRA, the Standing Committee on Trunk Road Assessment - published in late 1994. The report states that, in certain circumstances, the extra building of roads can generate induced traffic resulting in extra vehicles on the road network and adding further to congestion.

While the British Roads Federation took the opposed view, the Government has subsequently announced cutbacks in its road building programme which may, in part, be due to SACTRA's report.

Declining Investment

So, while the amount of freight on the roads increases to ever higher levels, and business continues to demand smaller, more frequent, precisely timed drops, investment in the infrastructure is set to decrease. And all this as technology is being perfected to charge for the use of the road network.

The need for utmost efficiency in our use of that network and the vehicles we run on it has never been higher. Strategic placement and utilisation of the distribution centre - the hub of any company's operation - is vital, as is the careful specification of cleaner, greener vehicles which can be effectively routed and scheduled for optimum efficiency.

And, with work already taking place to constantly maximise the use of resources, such importance is set to increase as further restrictions come into place.

Consider local authorities who, exercising their right to protect their residents, are putting more restrictions on commercial vehicle movements. Surrey County Council has proposed that certain roads south of the M25 are restricted to HGVs either at specific times or days of the week such as weekends. Ministers are considering giving local authorities powers to lower speed limits and ban cars without catalytic converters from cities during long periods of air pollution.

An even more controversial proposal is the blocking of motorways running through high density urban areas - such as the M5 and M6 through Birmingham - on days when air quality is poor.

The likelihood of such restrictions is likely to grow if levels of air quality in Britain continue to deteriorate. When, for instance, vehicles in the 40-44 tonne range are allowed greater freedom on Britain's roads, as aniticipated at the beginning of 1999, this could potentially bring further restrictions.

Future patterns

Frank Worsford, from the University of Westminster's Transport Studies Group, has worked with Exel Logistics on research into distribution activities and environmental impact. He predicts that the permitted use of 40-44 tonne vehicles will be restricted to the primary road network - trunk roads and motorways - where they will load or unload at road freight interchange points. Onward urban deliveries or collections, he believes, will only be allowed in smaller vehicles, probably below 16 tonne maximum permitted weight, which will be forced to operate on low emission fuel or clean alternatives such as compressed natural gas or even electricity.

While the view may be futuristic, the implications of its implementation for any company with operations in urban areas is considerable.

Consider the future visualised by Frank Worsford, and then include the increased planning restrictions imposed by the Department of Environment's PPG13 - large warehouse developments attracting large fleets of vehicles must be located well away from residential locations, or include provisions to radically lessen their environmental impact - and the full picture begins to emerge.

It is clear that, in line with all this, the distribution centre must be strategically placed and operated to be as environmentally friendly as possible. The most efficient use must be made of a road network which is facing increasing restrictions and potential congestion must be minimised. The fleet which serves the centre must be as clean and green as possible, fully utilised to minimise journey numbers and therefore lessen environmental impact and cope with increasing restrictions.

Clean operations, in terms of low emission fuels and environment-friendly alternatives, are a must. Information technology packages, which optimise vehicle utilisation and thereby minimise the number of vehicles on the road, will come into their own.

Into action

But how can logistics decision makers be sure that the distribution operation they plan today meets tomorrow's increasing restrictions? How can they be sure that they are constantly up-to-date?

The first step is education - making themselves aware of the pressures likely to have an impact, and the steps which can be taken now to ensure environmental acceptability tomorrow.

For managers seeking such education, the transport and logistics trade press is a valuable source of ongoing information and topical debate.

Looking more specifically, a new guide published last year: Best Environmental Practice: A Manager's Guide for Transport Distribution Centres, by Frank Worsford, is useful reading.

The guide is jointly funded by the Department of Transport and the Engineering and Physical Sciences Research Council and is issued by the Department of Transport with all operating licences.

It provides managers wishing to lessen the impact of existing sites, or planning to develop new sites, with techniques to enable them to carry out best environmental practice and prevent adverse local impact. It lists current environmental legislative controls and the administrative bodies which can impose conditions on site activities.

It also outlines measures which eliminate, minimise, reduce or avoid environmental impact in terms of noise, smell and visual impact on the local community.

A second publication: Best Environmental Practice at Distribution Centres, also by Frank Worsford, is available from Croner's Road Transport Operation. This looks at the role of trucks, distribution centres and best environmental practice in more detail.

Need to consider

Location is clearly important, as both publications make clear, but other aspects should be considered too. Decision-makers should take a close review of their fleet. They should begin making themselves acquainted with new environmentally friendly technology to maximise the utilisation of that fleet.

At Exel Logistics, we have recently developed a new in-cab computing sytem. Called 'Mercator', the system employs technology to fully optimise the utilistion of vehicles, fuels and human resources through constant monitoring and reporting on operational information and vehicle/driver performance.

The quantifiable, commercial benefits the system will bring in terms of lower fuel and maintenance cost, improved fleet security, flexible vehicle scheduling, increased sales opportunitis and better customer sevice, are all balanced by sound environmental benefits.

The proven 5-10% reduction in fuel consumption which the sytem can achieve clearly has positive environmental implications along with lower, better quality emissions and, most importantly, minimising the fleet sizes required.

Logistics managers should make themselves fully aware of the availabilities and the environmental benefits of such systems. They should also start to look at the new greener fuels available and their alternatives - low sulphur diesel, compressed natural gas, and electricity.

Pressure to use such fuels is likely to increase, and logistics managers need to be aware of the options available. There is increasing documentation available on the market which offers guidance and help, and which is well worth reading.

Exel Logistics, in conjunction with Boots the Chemists, has recently completed research into the effectiveness of low-sulphur city diesel. The report on the results makes useful reading for managers in the retail industry considering alternative environment-friendly fuels. Managers should take advantage of such reports, capitalising on the experience of others to benefit their own operations and to bring wider benefits to the environment.

They should talk with third-party logistics providers and benefit from the experience available. Responsible operators will be happy to demonstrate their track record and their own environmental policy, and to put companies in contact with academic experts to offer further advice as necessary. This will help provide a wider view of the total supply chain and the areas where environmental improvements can be made - minimising packaging waste, for instance, and developing relationships with suppliers which encourage environmental co-operation.

The future

One of the few certainties in today's dynamic arena is that environmental pressure is going to increase and that the consumer will demand ever-increasing levels of environmental responsibility. Distribution patterns are set to change fundamentally in line with this, and the core of our business - the logistics function - will be subject to increasing regulation.

The very best that logistics managers can do in such an arena is arm themselves with the knowledge they need and talk to the people who can support them, and who can utlimately help them implement the best environmental distribution operation for their requirements.

For further information on the reports discussed in this article contact: Alison Hibbard, Exel Logistics, Tel 01234 273727.

About the author: **George Hazle** is Executive Director, Exel Logistics. He has more than 30 years' experience in the transport and distribution industy. He was instrumental in developing Exel Logistics' own environmental policy which was launched six years ago. He now heads the company's environmental policy team.

Green supply: getting a grip on whole-life costs

Steve New, Ken Green and Barbara Morton discuss how the first step towards green supply is whole-life costing. The authors all work at the Manchester School of Management, UMIST, where they are engaged in a wide range of research on supply chain and environmental management.

Purchasing managers are becoming increasingly aware of the importance of environmental issues, but there are few tools for turning concern into action. This article discusses one of the most powerful approaches to tackling the green agenda: whole-life costing. These words, however, can be used in many different ways, and the first stage is to understand what interpretation is relevant to a particular situation.

The recent debacle for Shell UK in regard to the Brent Spar platform is a powerful reminder of the influence of environmental groups on business behaviour. Such pressures are likely to grow over the foreseeable future, and also be accompanied by legislative and regulatory controls. As these forces become institutionalised, environmental awareness becomes less of an optional marketing ploy, more a necessary pre-requisite for business. Furthermore, the costs of not being 'green' will make environmental approaches simply good financial sense.

The Buying into the Environment initiative has provided purchasing managers with a useful toolkit for getting started in this field. One danger, however, is that managers may be unable to sustain a case for green purchasing initiatives without translating the argument into tangible bottom-line benefits. This is why taking a holistic approach to costing is so important. In one way, the green approach to whole-life costing is merely an extension of an established idea; in another sense it require managers to take a radical view of their operations.

Something old

The old idea is that purchase decision-making should be based on more than the headline price. Successive attempts at making purchasing a 'strategic' function have drawn more issues into the orbit of the analysis. Table 1 illustrates this as a progression from 'traditional' to 'strategic advantage' thinking, with each stage bringing more information to bear on the buying decision. In the caricatured 'traditional'

TABLE 1 A framework for the perspective of costs

Perspective	What costs	Who pays?
ONE	The Total Costs generated in the supply chain up to and including the organisation	The organisation
TWO	The Total Costs generated by the organisation, its suppliers and its downstream customers	The final consumer
THREE	The Total Costs to the organisation to all its downstream customers and to the Earth	The whole earth

approach, the key information is simply the price paid to the supplier. This has the important advantage of simplicity and immediate economy. However, this does not match the ideas of the 'quality revolution'; organisations which buy on price alone are encouraging expensive quality problems. Following Dr Deming, firms need to base purchasing decisions on the price, the cost of quality - which includes all the costs of, for example, inspection, scrap and rejects. One difficulty is that these costs are generally difficult to measure accurately.

The commonsense approach to quality also applies to other types of costs associated with a purchase, and so can be extended to a general 'systems thinking' which considers the 'total cost of ownership' or the 'total cost of acquisition'. For example, a firm may purchase a low price tool for a machining centre, but then need to run the machine at a slower rate: it may be cheaper overall to buy a more expensive item in the first place.

This is, of course, an obvious principle but one which is often very difficult to apply. It normally requires data about the use of a product or service which may not be readily available to the purchasing department. Furthermore, high technology products or systems are often difficult to assess because future use or developments may simply be unknown.

The final approach extends this even further, and considers intangible 'costs' which may be even more difficult to quantify. These include the opportunity costs associated with an option, for example in lost sales. Component A may be cheaper or even better than component B, but the final consumer may believe - perhaps irrationally - that products which include B are preferable.

These last two approaches in this framework are immediately relevant for understanding environmentally-aware purchasing. For many buyers, the total cost of ownership may include the cost of compliance to environmental legislation and of disposal. Furthermore, the adoption of 'green' sources of supply may be an important factor in an organisation's marketing activity and competitive positioning.

Something new

Expanding the scope of costing is a well-established idea, but environmental issues also bring the need to consider *perspective*: costing cannot be considered separately from the question of 'who pays?'. Table 2 presents three options for answering this issue.

TABLE 2 A framework for the scope of costing

Approach	Key criteria for purchasing decisions: the "Total Cost"	Comment
"Tradition"	Price	Simple and relatively cheap
"The Quality Revolution"	Price + cost of quality	Deming's Point Four: but difficult to calculate
"Systems thinking"	Price + total cost of ownership (inc. quality costs)	Holistic approach
"Strategic Advantage"	Price + total costs of ownership (inc. quality costs) + opportunity costs (e.g. cost of lost sales)	Holistic approach accounting for intangibles

The table illustrates that the 'life-cycle' costs associated with a purchasing decision can be seen in different ways. Firstly, the costs can be considered as all the costs associated with a product from an individual firm's perspective. For example, Kirschner (1994) describes how Dow Chemicals try to charge cost of waste treatment back to particular production lines. Keene (1994) describes the use of life-cycle costing in regard to the maintenance of vehicles. This total reflects the activities of the organisation concerned, and (in the prices paid) all the preceding suppliers. At each stage in the supply chain, the costs accumulated are passed on (with a premium for profit) to the next link.

Perspective Two expands this by adding in all the costs incurred by the downstream customers. Recent examples from this perspective include the use of life-cycle costing to evaluate building materials (Mahmoud et al 1994; anon 1994).

Perspective Three takes this further by recognising that the costs actually charged and paid at each stage may not reflect the true environmental costs. For example, in some cases the price of hardwoods may not reflect the true environmental cost to the planet; the cost of fast food may not fully reflect the cost of clearing up litter generated afterwards. The trouble is that many of these costs are not picked up by the relevant stage in the supply chain, but absorbed by society in general, and generations to come.

This third perspective is the focus of the technique called Life-Cycle Analysis (Franklin and Hoffsommer 1994). there is as yet no robust or universal way of applying this - Gray and others (1993) cite the example of comparing the 'true' environmental costs of disposable versus traditional nappies. The major difficulty is deciding at what point in the analysis to stop, and where to draw the boundaries around the system.

Traditionally, purchasing has focused on Perspective One. In what situations is it appropriate for an organisation to adopt Perspective Two and Three?

Two scenarios suggest themselves:
- where customers' total cost of use is likely to increase due to environmental pressures from regulators and consumers
- when taxation, insurance premiums and other fiscal devices are used to apportion the full environmental costs to the relevant stages of the supply chain.

In these situations, organisations may need to adopt a more far-sighted and proactive approach to Life-Cycle Costing which will need to draw from detailed Life-Cycle analyses and overall impact assessments.

It should be stressed that this does not rely on corporate altruism or ethics, but concerns hard commercial decisions made to maximise profits. Adam Smith is alive an well, but is adjusting to a trading game in which the rules are continually changing.

References:

Anon (1994) Roofing costs by life cycle ENR 232:25 Jun 20 p65

Keene, D (2994) 'A leader in service' *Fleet Equipment* 20:11, p24-27

Kirschner, E (1994) Full-cost accounting for the environment *Chemical Week* 154:9 p25-26

Franklin, W E, Hoffsommer, KK (1994) Using life cycle analysis as a decision making tool *Environment Today* 5:4 p38-39

Gray, RHI, Bebbington, J and Walters D (1993) *Accounting for the environment* Paul Chapman Publishing Ltd, London

Mahmoud, MA A-R Al-Hammad, A, Assaf, S, Aref, M (1994) An evaluation and selection model for floor finishing materials' *Cost Engineering* 36:9, p21-24

Code or Codswallop - the relevance of Ethical Codes

Business ethics is a boom subject. Stark (1) reports that in 1993 over 500 business ethics courses were being taught in USA campuses; fully 90 per cent of the nation's business schools provided some kind of training in the area and at least 16 business ethics research centres were in operation. In the UK the Institute of Business Ethics established in 1986 aims to 'clarify ethical issues in business; to propose positive solutions to problems and to establish common ground with people of all faiths' (2). A Chair of Business Ethics has been instituted at the London Business School and the holder, Professor Jack Mahoney advocates that ethics should be compulsory rather than an elective element of the School's MBA. The Cadbury Report of 1992 (3) recommends that every major company should adopt an ethical code. A survey conducted by Edinburgh University in 1988 of 200 of the largest UK companies reported that of 74 respondents the numbers with and without codes were 31 (42 per cent) and 43 (58 per cent) respectively (4).

A later report (5) estimates that over half of all organisations with over 500 employees have codes of ethics, rising to 80 per cent of those with over 50,000 employees. This does not mean that those without such codes are not ethical. A 1992 Loughborough University made a survey for the *Economist* of eleven British companies most admired for community and environmental responsibility. Six of the companies had, and five did not have, codes. The five without codes were Marks & Spencer, Anglian Water, RTZ, Glaxo and Pilkington (6).

From the days of Hippocrates (c460-375 BC) doctors have had an ethical code, the possession of which is listed by Millerson (7) as indispensable to professional recognition. Today occupations from accountants to travel agents have such codes which indicate an agreed pattern of behaviour for the roles undertaken and the responsibilities involved. Such codes provide simple moral direction. They provide guidance regarding what the accumulated wisdom of a given profession has found to be good and appropriate. They can also be a means of some form of disciplinary action from the profession's controlling body.

Purchasing is, of course, no exception to this trend. Many national professional purchasing institutions have prepared such codes. These include those of the National Association of Purchasing Managers of America (NAPM), the UK Chartered Institute of Purchasing and Supply (CIPS) and the International Federation of Purchasing and Materials Management (IFPMM). But what is the practical value of education in business ethics in general and of codes of purchasing ethics in particular? Stark (8) for example, observes that while managers welcome help in identifying ethical courses of action in difficult grey area situations and in navigating situations where the right course is not clear, the insights of business ethics are more of academic interest than practical use. Previous articles by Ramsay (9) and Arkinstall (10) suggest that purchasing ethics is regarded as little more than an examination subject and that, in practice, the CIPS code of ethics is ignored. This article aims to examine some of the advantages that ethical codes can provide to employees including to those engaged in purchasing. It also seeks to look at some of the criticisms directed at ethical codes. A later article will make suggestions as to how ethical codes can be made more relevant and of greater practical use.

The advantages of codes

Manley (11) following a two-year interaction with the top executives of 145 British and multinational companies, identified no less than eighteen major benefits that a code of conduct provides to a business firm. Most of these 18 points are directly or indirectly relevant to purchasing including:
- Providing guidance to and inculcating the company's values, cultural substance and style in managers and employees.
- Signalling expectations of proper conduct to suppliers and customers.
- Pre-empting legal proceedings
- Nurturing a business environment of open communication.

It would, however, be tedious and, to some extent, meaningless to quote all Manley's 18 advantages without his supporting comment. A more succinct statement by Karp and Abramms (12) applicable to

both organisational and professional codes is that there are advantages in:
- *Providing a basis for working together.* Most codes require that people treat each other with respect. Thus, the NAPM Code specifies that subscribers shall 'accord a prompt and courteous reception, so far as conditions will permit, to all who call on a legitimate business mission'.
- *Setting boundaries as to what constitutes ethical behaviour as determined by organisational and professional values.* The guidance provided by the CIPS Code relating to declarations of interest, confidentiality of information, competition, business gifts and hospitality are examples of such boundaries.
- *Providing a safe environment for all subscribers.* Codes remove uncertainty about what the organisation or profession regards as ethical behaviour. With the guidance provided by a code employees are always subject and accountable to the value system of anyone in a higher position.
- *Providing a commonly held set of guidelines* that enable what is right and wrong in a given situation to be judged on a consistent, value-driven basis. Codes also provide a reference point to suppliers and others which they can quote if the company or individual is in breach of ethical conduct. Manley (13) reports a high correlation between undertakings with an ethical business culture and their long-term financial success. Such undertakings also appear to be more successful in recruiting and retaining high calibre staff.

Criticisms of codes

If ethical codes are so advantageous why, in practice, are they so frequently regarded as theoretical or worse still, mere window dressing? In the writer's experience, criticisms of codes can be categorised under two headings: *content* and *context*.

Content: From an organisational standpoint purchasing or 'relationships with suppliers' is usually a sub-section of a more comprehensive document. Atherton (14) makes an important distinction between the moral dimensions of the organisation and moral behaviour in the organisation. Statements of the moral dimension of the organisation usually relate to what are frequently termed the 'social responsibilities of management' and are aimed at a wide range of constituencies. Clutterbuck Dearlove and Snow (15) for example, identify eight social responsibilities: (1) customers, (2) employees, (3) suppliers, (4) investors, (5) the political arena, (6) the broader community, (7) sponsorship and (8) the environment. Suppliers and the environment are of particular interest to procurement. Under suppliers the writers specify:
- practical help and advice to smaller suppliers;
- purchasing policies that ensure that small and local companies have a fair share of the business.
- monitoring suppliers social responsibility performance
- payment policies that help small businesses;
- closer arrangements with suppliers through partnership agreements. Responsibilities to the environment include:
- demanding that suppliers do not use environmentally harmful products;
- energy efficiency;
- encouragement of environmental initiatives.

An excellent discussion of the ways in which purchasing can contribute to environmental issues has been published by the Department of Trade and Industry (16).

The above are wider, macro ethical issues as distinct from moral behaviour *in* the organisation which relates to individual rather than corporate vehaviour but there are three reasons why such professional codes must take cognisance of wider organisational issues. Social responsibilities are utlimately individual responsibilities. Social responsibilities change. The concept of supplies work has, for example, considerably broadened from when the CIPS code was formulated about 1971. Procurement is now a strategic issue and ethical considerations are important when formulating strategies. New issues such as international partnership, single sourcing, post-gender negotiation and counter-trade require greater in-depth consideration of ethical issues that the cosy trotting out of accumulated wisdom found in most purchasing texts. Above all, codes, whether organisation or professional, must take cognisance of contextual factors.

Context
Probably, most purchasing people think of ethical codes as remote from the real world. This may be because work often leaves little time for reflection. The requirement to maintain an unimpeachable standard of integrity in all business relationships is fine until one questions the meaning of integrity and to whom

the duty of integrity is due. What if there is a clash of loyalties between personal and organisational integrity? Farmer (17) quotes Baumhart (18) who concluded that *It is easier to be ethical in jobs involving fiduciary relationships such as the accountants' or engineers' than in those jobs involving competitive relationships, such as the salesman's or the purchasing agent's.*

It is also a fact that codes of ethics are associated with larger undertakings. Brigley (19) in a survey of ethics in management considers that codes are easier to introduce and implement in larger organisations than in small undertakings where there is generally a preference for informal approaches to ethical issues. Brigley also reports that within organisations, senior management's attitudes and tactics and conflicts of values with senior management are most prominently cited obstacles in managing ethical matters. When there is a conflict between their own or their profession's ethical code and the ethics of their organisation or their immediate superior, employees may have to choose between remaining silent or speaking out and faicng the consequences of being seen as disloyal or even the termination of employment which under conditions of redundancy and restructuring is not be lightly contemplated. Some comments of Bigley's respondents include:
- High unemployment affects your ethics - cynical but true
- What people say and what people do are very different
- People suppress their own ethical values to be generally accepted and to get on in business.
- The more senior you are, the easier it is to maintain an ethical stance. The NAPM Code, for example, lays down that subscribers must denounce all firms of manifestations of commercial bribery. But, what do you do, knowing full well what happens to 'whistle blowers', if you discover that your boss or a colleague is receiving bribes? In summary, it seems that to be effective, both organisational and professional codes need to be made more relevant to those to whom they apply and supported by administrative procedures designed to assist in creating an ethical culture. This in turn means that purchasing ethics to be effective requires appropriate training and education.

References

(1) Stark A What's the Matter with Business Ethics. *Harvard Business Review*, May-June 1993, pp 38-44, 46, 48

(2) *Institute of Business Ethics*, Mission Statement

(3) Report of the Committee on the Financial Aspects of Corporate Governance, *HMSO,* 1992

(4) Quoted in Ryan LV, Ethics Codes in British Companies, *Journal of Business Ethics*, Vol 3, No 1, 1994, pp54-64

(5) Brigley S, Walking the tightrope, *A survey of ethics in management.* Institute of Management/University of Bath, 1994, p 39

(6) Ryan LV, Ethics Codes in British Companies, *Journal of Business Ethics*, Vol 3, No 2, 1994, pp 54-64

(7) Millerson G, *The Qualifying Associations*, Routledge and Keegan Paul, 1964, p4

(8) Stark A, What's the Matter with Business Ethics, *Harvard Business Review*, May-June 1993, pp38-44, 46, 48

(9) Ramsey, J, No Bribes Please, We're Professionals. *Purchasing and Supply Management,* October 1994 pp12-13

(10) Arkinstall D, Ethics in Practice, *Purchasing and Supply Management,* October 1994, pp 12-13

(11) Manley WW, *The Handbook of Good Business Practice - Corporate Codes of Conduct,* Routledge, 1991, Cap 1

(12) Karp HB and Abramms, B, *Doing the Right Thing, Training and Development* (USA) Aug1992 p37-41

(13) Manley WW, *The Handbook of Good Business Practice - Corporate Codes of Conduct,* Routledge, 1992, Chap 9.

(14) Atherton J, The Individual and the Organisation, *Expository Times*, Vol 105, Sept 1994, pp 356-362

(15) Clutterbuck D, Dearlove D and Snow D, *Actions Speak Louder - A Management Guide to Corporate Social Responsibility,* Kogan Page 1992, Chapters 4 and 9

(16) Department of the Environment, *Environmental Action Guide to Building and Purchasing Managers,* HMSO, 1991

(17) Farmer D, Ethical Issues in Purchasing in Farmer (Ed) *Purchasing Management Handbook*, Chap 22, p 433, Gower Publishing 1985

(18) Brigley S Walking the Tightrope, *A survey of Ethics in Management,* Institute of Management/University of Bath, 1994, p36

(19) Baumhart R, *Ethics in Business,* Holt Reinhard and Winston, 1968.

Chapter 4: Non-traditional acquisition

Contract hire - bed of roses or bed of nails?

Simon Marks looks at the snares and pitfalls in this popular approach to company car finance

Contract hire is the most popular acquisition route for company cars after outright purchase. In most cases, the package includes full fleet management, with the cars provided at the start of the hire period and all risks carried by the lessor until the lease ends when the car is collected, all this being provided for a fixed monthly rental payment.

As a product, contract hire is sold hard because, like third party maintenance for computers, Mercury telephone lines and stationery sold off the page, the marginal cost of managing your contract is fairly small by comparison with the venue it generates. The sales person will make the benefits sound almost too good to be true, but few will warn you of the downside; and the magazine articles you read are normally written by people selling the benefits of contract hire. I will try to redress the balance by sharing my experience of some of the pitfalls of *running* a medium size mixed fleet of outright purchased and contract hire cars supplied by a number of contract hire companies.

Firstly, the question 'Why contract hire?' The two main replies are financial and operational, or a combination of both. I will not be addressing the financial aspects except in passing, but they cannot be ignored completely, so the next paragraph provides a very brief overview.

Contract hire is an operating lease and gets your cars off the balance sheet. It reduces gearing/improves cashflow, depending on your viewpoint. Beware of purchase and leaseback deals, the contract hire company will ensure that it covers all its risks involved in buying 'second hand cars'. The only other way of running cars off the balance sheet is contract purchase (see P&SM, April 1991), which is an accountant's device that operates in the same way as contract hire but with different tax treatment. If your business is a charity, does not pay VAT and/or corporation tax, other factors apply, but I do not intend to address them; see your accountant.

'Fixed cost motoring' allied to vastly reduced administration is the way the operational benefits are most frequently sold, and the packages look very attractive, but have you ever heard a salesman tell you the problems upfront? He wants his bonus or commission and the company want to make a profit, which it does in a number of areas.

Whether set up as cost or profit centres, the contract hire business has a number of discreet major profit opportunities in a normal 'with maintenance' contract. These include:
- New car supply - the margin between the actual price paid and the price written in the contract
- Funding - providing money upfront recovered from monthly rentals
- Maintenance - keeping actual costs below budget by controlling the servicing garages and maximising warranty claims
- Disposal - obtaining a better price at disposal than the contract residual value
- Management fee - it's in there somewhere to pay for the administration required.

They will also try to hand on other 'services' including relief vehicles, breakdown cover, accident management, fuel cards etc, in addition to the basic contract. The points above exclude the costly hidden extras which we will deal with later.

Let us assume that for 'financial reasons' you are required to move to contract hire as quickly as possible. Every contract hire company will produce a proposal in a different format, using different cars, over different time/mileage combinations, with different terms and conditions. Trying to produce a valid (price) comparison, based on supplier presentations is like trying to untangle spaghetti, but producing a workable tender document is nearly as difficult unless you have done it before.

The key to producing a meaningful tender document is knowing the problems that will be encountered running a contract hire fleet and ensuring you know how your potential suppliers will respond before placing your business. Each supplier will quote a monthly rental figure, your 'fixed cost of motor-

ing', the Holy Grail that you didn't know you were chasing. This monthly sum will incorporate all the cost elements previously mentioned, but how is it established and what else do you need to know?
The monthly charge depends on the factors below:

The specific car and its specification

Every car will attract a different monthly charge. The charge for a Cavalier 1800 GL 5 door will be different from that for a Rover 216 SLi. A Rover 216 SLi will be different from a Rover 220 SLi, and a 5 door Rover 220SLi will be different from a 4 door Rover 420 SLi. The difference will result from the different purchase price, maintenance costs and residual value, and each company will view each element differently depending on the special deals they have with the manufacturers and their own historical data. Contract hire suppliers will always quote for cars where they feel they have an advantage to show themselves in the most competitive light. The pricing policy operated by each company will be determined by their ownership. They may be part of a financial institution, owned by a manufacturer or an arm of a multi franchise dealer group, and therefore have different objectives.

To ensure that quotations are comparable, you must ensure that you state the specification of the cars which will constitute the bulk of your fleet and that such a quote includes the list price on which the quote is based to avoid 'mistakes and misunderstandings'.

The contract term

The contract term is fixed at the outset and the car is yours for that period. The cost of the car to the contract hire company will be calculated at the outset, and the appropriate monthly charge established to cover the costs. Once the car is purchased for your use, they will ensure they recover their budgeted profit.

If the car is stolen, written off or no longer required, you either pay the monthly rental to the end of the term or agree an early termination. Be assured it is extremely painful having to pay in the region of 75 per cent of the outstanding rental value to hand back the car because you no longer need it. You should understand the basis for early termination before signing any contract.

If the car is stolen, written off or no longer required, you either pay the monthly rental to the end of the term or agree an early termination. Be assured it is extremely painful having to pay in the region of 75 per cent of the outstanding rental value to hand back the car because you no longer need it. You should understand the basis for early termination before signing any contract.

The contract number of miles

The contracted mileage is also fixed at the outset as this will affect the maintenance cost and residual value of the car at termination. While depreciation is under-recovered during the early part of the contract, service costs which are mileage related are over-recovered. The mileage will be stated either as a total contract mileage or an annual mileage, and there will be a mileage adjustment formula which may or may not be stated upfront. This is likely to be based on pence per mile in excess of contract mileage but can be manipulated in the contract hire company's favour in a number of ways. The least likely is by reference to annual mileage with a charge made for each year's excess mileage, which is definitely to be avoided. More likely the rebate for under-mileage may be credited at a lower value, a fixed level of under-mileage disallowed against credit, an additional loading on cars substantially over-mileage, or a combination of these and other mechanisms.

If the contract is written for too few miles you will overpay for the additional miles covered; if you over-estimate the mileage, you pay an excessive monthly charge. The only solution is to estimate correctly the mileage of each car on contract hire, or manage the fleet to achieve the objective.

Some companies 'pool' mileages for cars terminated close together and these arrangements should be explored in advance.

Payment terms

Payment terms normally quoted are three months' deposit then 33 monthly payments (for a 3-year contract) with the final two months free, /To ensure quotes are comparable the terms must be the same, but it does not end there. If you finish the rental before the 1,095th day, does the rental for the unused period get rebated? You may be sure that if you keep the car after the rental period, you will receive a supplementary invoice. If, for operational reasons you choose to exchange a batch of cars at the same time rather than on the third anniversary, do not assume the 'swings and roundabouts' principle will prevail because they have already got your money for the early terminations.

Other factors

Other factors cover the way contract hire companies make their profits that are not covered by the monthly charge. This can be by avoiding costs and/or making extra charges. Some contracts are written making the user responsible for costs incurred other than by way of wear and tear. If you get through more than one set of tyres or clutch or have headlamps or windscreen damage, you may be liable. There may be a service charge levied for passing unpaid fixed penalty tickets through to your fleet administration, and detailed management reports may be chargeable.

On termination, contract hire companies may (legitimately) charge for rectification work to put right abuse the car has suffered at the hands of the user, which may be difficult to dispute. Costs may be avoided, for example, by 'encouraging' you to use a nominated garage for servicing and restricting the drivers' choice for replacement tyres, and then only when at the legal limit.

Outsourced everything else? Why not purchasing?

Martin Beauchamp thinks the unthinkable - could the purchasing function itself be suitable for outsourcing?

The amusing story of the inexperienced but exuberant apprentice in Dukas' famous overture 'The Sorcerer's Apprentice' underlines the chaos that can result from an imperfect grasp of key management essentials. In due course, the hapless apprentice realised that he had much to learn about management skills.

In a sense our whole modern business age parallels Dukas' story. The days of certainty and security and relatively stable business patterns are over, and we are being constantly cautioned to accept change and, indeed, to thrive on it. Thus if we are not able to approach and handle these changes from a basis of true business comprehension with management certainty, we may suffer the same fate as the sorcerer's apprentice.

With regard to purchasing and the skills related to the acquisition of goods and services, how should be strategically position ourselves nowadays and how should outsourcing be viewed? Even more provocatively, we might ask: 'Is there a place for outsourcing or facilities managing purchasing and procurement itself?

I think that this question looks like commercial heresy to many n purchasing and procurement, leaving them feeling that same kind of anxiety that the Eastern Europeans felt when the Mongol hordes appeared over the horizon.

TABLE 1 What the market is driving to

The Market is Driving to:			
Downsizing	Reducing staff where possible so to implement	Least Cost	Greatest efficiency solutions
Devolution	Decentralisation of staff and tasks unless provably better otherwise	Outsourcing	For temporary or regular section needs
Analysis of	Cost Centre vs Service Centre vs Profit Centre approaches	FM	Externally for large requirements or to devolve entire departmental responsibilities
Logistically	Balanced Operations	Comparisons	Of internally re-charged operations with best value external competitive tenders
Continuity	Seamlessness of Purchasing Production, Distribution if manufacturing based	Justification	For jobs & clearly delineated rationale for future staff needs

However, there are strong reasons why the purchasing fraternity must take on board and develop their positioning on outsourcing, as its use is rapidly becoming a key consideration in modern business management.

Why consider outsourcing?

● Market conditions are dynamically changing very quickly nowadays. Whilst monopolies still exist and may introduce some apparent stability and a measure of job security, there is nevertheless in modern business a considerable perceived overcapacity and overmanning in many market sectors. Where circumstances thus allow, market conditions will push towards corporate downsizing.

- Desire to impress shareholders will cause some companies to perform commercial sleights of hand which, while legal, are nevertheless subtly contrived so as to make results look optimal in terms of turnover and profitability and the strength and depth of corporate assets. Put simply, a policy of reducing staff whilst retaining and improving profitability and turnover will obviously vastly improve perceived shareholder perceptions of corporate standing, leading to a strengthening of the business through increased investment.

Allied to certainties of the points above is the issue of concentrating on core business. If you are a company selling consultancy services why do you need in-house departments covering accounts management, health and safety, procurement, legal services, public relations and the like? Or if you are a local government department, why have in-house expertise on engineering and building services, administrative services, travel services, office services, purchasing, facilities services and the like? It is a question of identifying needs and services that are core to the true nature of the business. Beyond these, other requirements can be outsourced.

- There are genuine possibilities of added value through concentrating resources. Obviously if procurement staff are needed in a business and are freed from routine purchasing, they can work on higher added value activities, thus creating maximum impact from their roles.
- Outsourcing and facilities management are related. Whilst some facilities management (FM) can effectively be run internally in a company by using external resource, the other option is to segregate the desired department or discipline and make it entirely external to the company. The finesse between outsourcing and FM is difficult to define exactly, but in general terms, whereas outsourcing may imply anything from a day or two's external help in assisting with defined tasks up to a much fuller and broader remit, FM implies a substantial and probably total handing over of services, requirements, and needs to an external organisation, perhaps even to the extent of entire departments being managed externally.

Organisations which specialise in FM solutions are generally highly skilled (outsourcing may require less skills but this is not necessarily so) and these FM providers can work on or off your premises in providing the cover required. The key perception gained by your directors and shareholders is that the FM or outsourcing service providers are not adding to your headcount and thus absorbing potential profits.

- Outsourcing in very general terms (and FM is included for the sake of the argument here) works best in purchasing rather than in procurement. I will amplify this later.
- Outsourcing can be infinitely adjustable. Once permanent staff are working in your organisation in purchasing or procurement remit, there is naturally a learning curve effect if they are continually moved around to differing product and service areas. This can be offset and mitigated by outsourcing.
- Outsourcing is likely to be the future wave. Like the concept or not, it is here to stay. Thus it is wise to examine it carefully and see how its benefits can be harnessed where appropriate.

As business decisions have to be taken in the logarithmically accelerating dynamics of the modern marketplace, they must be handled swiftly, surely and often intuitively in order to control the commercial out-turn. This background favours product and skill specialisation, which in turn favours considered and well-judged outsourcing.

What can be outsourced?

As I have stated elsewhere, purchasing, although possibly of very high value, calibre and intrinsic importance to an organisation, is basically less complex and diverse a remit to oversee than is procurement.

It is the capacity though to define more easily the requirement underlying the purchase and the higher possibility of the repeat nature of the business which makes purchasing as a skill stand out. Whilst purchasing is employed in the service sector it is also intimately associated with manufacturing and production, so whatever flavour of materials processing you use - JIT, Kanban, MRPII, Theory of Constraints (OPT) or whatever else - the throughput and effectiveness of purchasing, stocking (or not), production and materials management will be according to time-tried management principles, however subtly these are shaded.

But procurement is about defining, sourcing, contracting for, project managing and obtaining complex systems, with all the difficulties of relevant high level internal sponsorship, project board establishment, business need analysis, pilot studies, specification analysis and writing, production, testing, acceptance and system integration routines and the attendant difficulties. This kind of acquisition is unique for each need and has to be customised at all levels and processes on each occasion. Thus outsourcing in areas of highly complex and unique need with leading edge technology can be extremely difficult to achieve.

To outsource against requirements of high technological speciality with contract terms and conditions having to be uniquely written (or at least uniquely customised) will require a very high level not only of contracting skills but also of all the requisite specialist knowledge associated with the product groups required.

FIGURE 2 - Rationally effecting job protection

RATIONALLY EFFECTING JOB PROTECTION

01 Examine personal current skills	08 If shortfalls are sectional or departmental (rather than personal) have you the clout to approach directors 1:1
02 Be ruthlessly honest as to your indespensibility or otherwise	09 If NO to 8 above, consider moving before senior management sweeps you away with the ineffective department
03 Examine skills in your Section & make the personal comparisons	10 Be careful of innocent looking schemes dressed up as company re-organisation or performance appraisal which actually are designed to log all aspects of your work
04 Examine Departmental skills & make the comparisons	11 Consequences of 10 adove could be Outsourcing or FM of your section or department including you!
05 Examine how all skill sets aline with stated corporate policy	12 Gain all possible relevant experience so that if FM or outsourcing comes you have diverse options to consider
06 If shortfalls are personal ask: Can I obtain relevant training? How do I best read up on crucial areas? Can I be positioned temporarily alongside an expert willing to divest knowledge?	13 If your section/department is to be FM'd consider joining the FM company if your skills are good and all your rights (salary, leave entitlements, pension etc etc) are protected
07 If the immediately above are impossible, consider transferring to another company who are more interested in your training	14 If skilled, alternatively consider joining or establishing an agency to market your talents and abilities

Additionally and equally vital, is a full comprehension of how the feasibility, deigning and specifying, risk analysis, prototyping, piloting and acquisition of a key technology system will contribute to filling the requisite business need and influence the shape of corporate strategy. Far too many project sponsors have been caught up with almost apocalyptic visions of marvellous technological innovations whose implementation will revolutionise the way their company operates, only to have the project crash around their ears as an expensive disaster with no key objectives realised.

As high technology strategic procurement is an extremely skilled remit involving highest level liaison with and specialist advice to senior managers and directors, one also requires an understanding of the complex technology and engineering decisions under consideration. It is unlikely that general outsourcing agencies will have the levels of expertise to cover the breadth, depth and diversity of such complex procurement requirements against the variety of technological bases and market sectors needing assistance.

After all, if you have the capacity to earn, say > #30,000 pa because of having very high procurement and business skills, it will be unlikely that you will place yourself in the hands of an agency which, having recognised your skills, will fully utilise you but subsequently take circa 20 per cent off the top as the price for administering your working fortunes. The possession of highest level skills will enable you to write your own ticket!

What agencies may offer

Agencies and consultancies may offer some or all of the following:
- feasibility and research studies
- analysis/positioning/rebuilding of your purchasing and/or procurement function
- specialists who can join your organisation for specified periods
- courses both internal and external
- procurement skills
- purchasing skills
- stock analysis and profiling
- quality and standardisation analyses
- product of purchasing procedural and policy manuals
- development of sources
- international buying
- negotiation expertise
- organisational purchasing/procurement positioning studies

Top flight management consultancies such as Andersens, Peat Marwick, Coopers & Lybrand, price Waterhouse and the like (to name but a handful) will give you high level advice but in general, although they will take on many differing kinds of remit, it is best to remember that their role is perceived as mainly offering strategic, policy and operating consultancy and advice at senior manager and director level. Their interest is thus more in the creation, alignment and forward strategy of purchasing and procurement in your organisation than for example in providing practitioners to effect current outsourcing needs. That is not to say that they cannot or will not do so, only that their key role is more tightly focused. If you wanted, for example, a feasibility study into the pros and cons of centralisation versus devolution (for a multi site company), then such consultancies would be in their element in creating the ambience and climate for a fruitful and considered investigation at all corporate levels with appropriate research and analysis leading to specific tailored recommendations.

Outsourcing agencies and their staff

Agencies which are not into management consultancy but which are concerned more with the provision of contract staff or in covering outsourcing requirements will be more usefully placed to remove temporarily or permanently the commercial and purchasing load from their pressured clients.

Agencies will wish to keep permanently on their books skilled practitioners whose abilities are beyond dispute and whose presence on key tasks will enhance the standing of the agency with the employing organisation, thus leading the client to appoint the agency as a preferred supplier in due course. Many companies, including large blue-chip organisations, may well want preferred suppliers. Equally, government departments, utilities or para-government quangos may wish the same, but if their subject specific purchasing turnover puts them under the new European law (relating to the acquisition of business services), they may well shrink from the prospect of an 'open call for competition' in the *Official Journal* producing hundreds of enthusiastic agencies which will hammer at their door creating an impossible business analysis situation on each occasion.

Outsourcing agencies may therefore competitively bid to be amongst those who are effectively 'pre-qualified' under the European legislation (thus obviating the above noted nightmare) and if successful in this regard with the client organisations, may be selected from occasion to occasion by those under the European directives who have need of their services.

Purchasing requirements and outsourcing

As noted, true outsourcing favours more the high-workload, lower-skill combinations of corporate purchasing requirements. The following uses for outsourcing could therefore be fruitfully considered:
- purchase orders, one-off and repeat needs
- locally and nationally procured needs (international sourcing and procurement may be rather specialised for outsourcing)
- low-value or low-valu/high volume acquisitions

- high-value but easily specified acquisitions
- brand-name requirements
- call-offs against internally approved agreements
- set-up of commodity or service based purchase contracts
- obtaining goods for batch or volume manufacturing
- stocking and profiling for private/public sector needs
- finessing computerised purchasing or software based manufacturing procurement
- all administration and paperwork associated with purchasing needs
- supply of stores staff at varying levels of skill
- multi-disciplinary and multi-departmental outsourcing

There are obviously other areas that could be considered. All the areas above should be concerned with operations which, although skilled, are not of such complexity and demand such a learning curve that it will be virtually impossible for an external organisation to run an outsourcing brief.

to illustrate effectiveness here, consider corporate contracts. Using these, allied perhaps to call-off arrangements, it may well be that the level of personal contacts generated by the external company together with its historic ability to handle high value purchasing requirements will have led to your obtaining terms and discounts more favourable than your company would normally warrant in view of its regular turnover. Such would therefore be an effective use of outsourcing.

Effective outsourcing

There will be no point to outsourcing unless you can obtain a better result than could have been obtained internally. As you will to a greater or lesser extent be handing over responsibilities, it is essential that this is on terms no less favourable than would normally be obtained contractually by your company. A checklist of key matters to consider about outsourcing should include the following:

1 Professionally agreed results spelled out in the contract
2 Liquidated damages for failure, lateness (or against other unmet targets - provided these are not penalties).
3 A written warranty under contract from the supplier as to its ability and confidence in performing the specified services
4 Suitable indemnification and insurance against business risks, loss, damage, injury, death etc.
5 How you will determine, quantify, specify and describe the service
6 What key performance areas and critical success factors can be isolated to enable performance measurement
7 Suitable performance bond and/or parent company guarantee
8 Prior intensive financial and trading analysis
9 Access to agency's customer base (so that appropriate succinct questioning may take place and referees questioned)
10 Full analysis of agency's working documents, procedures, modus operandi, O& M etc
11 Ownership and rights to intellectual property (where applicable)
12 Removal and replacement of staff
13 Statutory regulations and compliance therewith
14 Full definitions and description of the agency's legal and contractual obligations as your agent
15 Confidentiality and issues of public domain
16 Assignments of rights or vesting
17 Constitution of *force majeure* situations
18 Relationship of outsourcing agency to your departing staff

Will I be outsourced?

In conclusion, this is the question that must occupy the minds of many who are now in purchasing and procurement positions in the private and public sectors.

There is obviously no immediate simple and all-embracing answer. I think that, eventually, only very high profile skills will keep procurement experts in their original companies instead of being put out to the market.

Obviously, no company will fire its own procurement staff if it is clear that it will take many, many months or even a year or two to update alternative agency staff as to their real use, role, responsibilities, capacity and interactions within the relevant organisation. All retraining and repositioning lowers your immediate business efficiencies and can be most deleterious to an organisation's forward commercial movement.

Thus the acid test has to be the question: How many weeks or months would it take for my company to create a full replacement for me in my current purchasing or procurement role? It is best to be realistic here. We all like to feel we are indispensable, but in reality with the current recession still ongoing and thousands of qualified purchasing people across the country, we must be realistic and not overstate our importance. Ask yourself what your manager' or director's response was last time you were sick for a week or two or last time that you had a vacation lasting several weeks, or the last time that you were on secondment for a period to another part of the business. Were they devastated? Really delighted to see you back? Did they comment that your absence had left the whole department in a mess?

If you genuinely have had these kinds of plaudits, you have nothing to worry about. But many buyers and even managers (who in today's world are very exposed) will not se that kind of response and have that comfort factor. An additional risk is ignorance on the part of senior management as to your true worth to the company. If your manager is not an excellent communicator, you could be doing a wonderful job, but this could all be totally invisible to your directors who might simply be looking to reduce the corporate headcount. Thus, balanced self-publicity both individually and departmentally is absolutely vital. if procurement does not advertise itself effectively, you can be certain that production or finance will not jump up to correct the anomaly.

What then is the solution? Well, very simply, provided you have the requisite skills for survival, you need have no further anxieties. Whether purchasing is outsourced or not (I do not consider procurement will be, for the reasons mentioned earlier), you will survive and come up smelling of roses.

If you detect, as I suspect is true of many organisations which should know better, that your training and experience are inadequate and particularly if you simultaneously perceive evidence of managerial inadequancies, you must start making the case for filling your particular needs now before your directors begin to question the entire internal worth of your purchasing department. To fail to do so would be to lead an illusory existence before your senior managers wield the axe and put you onto the market, where you might then find that the interview and job offer process painfully establishes your true level of competence and real worth.

The rigours of such a potential humiliation can be avoided by ascertaining what the market demands in terms of real skills at your salary level, and then ensuring that by obtaining further training and experience, you fully and satisfactorily meet the requisite profile.

Letter from Paul Chadwick, Hampton on the Hill, to Purchasing & Supply Management, September 1994:

Outsourcing the purchasing function

The excellent article on outsourcing purchasing by Martin Beauchamp (July/August 1994 *Purchasing & Supply Management*) has rightly brought out into the open a subject that is raised in boardrooms more frequently than most CIPS members would realise.

As a senior manager with one of the 'top flight management consultancies' mentioned in the article, I am aware that directors of well-known companies are constantly challenging their business strategies, processes and functions. Purchasing is not immune from the make-or-buy decision itself and sometimes only survives the axe through the business need to retain a close link with technological innovation which it may find in the supply base, and thus may lose if the purchasing department (the 'eyes and ears' of some businesses) were to be outsourced.

It is a gross overstatement, but if your industry does not require technological innovation or is not subject to time-to-market pressures, your purchasing department is at risk! In several (non-purchasing) outsourcing deals concluded, often the change becomes one of employees changing employer but retaining virtually identical terms of employment and performing almost the same job (at least until the re-engineering gets underway). Clearly others are not so fortunate.

What should concern all procurement professionals is not the outsourcing issue itself, but the continuing low regard in which their efforts and skills are held by the key business decision-makers. As Mr Beauchamp rightly states, the need to communicate upwards the successes you have achieved is vital to raising the function's and individual's profile. Sadly there are far too many UK buyers who are not performing and are taking the ostrich's way out, assuming that they are invisible. Well to those it may concern, you may not be physically visible, but you do appear on headcount charts and key decision-makers are asking questions such as: 'What do all these people do all day?' and 'Can't we automate it or get someone else to do it for us?' Make no mistake, the directors of your business have been, or will be, discussing your future.

All is not lost. By delivering the business objectives (and making sure people know about it), there is more opportunity for you to demonstrate added value and thereby be in a strong position to influence your future. Who knows, you may even be chosen as the preferred leader of an outsourced unit with a guaranteed level of work with significant scope for expansion by providing the service to other companies.

Investing in capital assets

Like puppies capital investments aren't just for Christmas, they're for life. Surinder Mehta looks at the total cost

Machinery and plant are important assets of an industrial enterprise. Procurement of these expensive assets, which form the backbone of manufacturing operations, has escaped the attention that it deserves. Avoidable expenditure in purchase of these assets does not appear prominently in the balance sheet of an industrial enterprise and thus escapes the critical scrutiny of the shareholders. The strategic role of materials management/purchase management is now being appreciated by enlightened and well-managed companies. Therefore, the purchasing department must be allowed to play its legitimate professional role in procurement of such vital and costly assets, instead of being assigned the role of a mere contracting agency for purchase.

Procurement of machinery and plant is not a route activity similar to that of purchase of raw materials, components, consumables, spares etc required to sustain the manufacturing operations. Its impact on the profitability of the enterprise can be profound. Instances are not rare where excess capacities or extra-high speeds have been produced and paid for without being needed. A critical appraisal of the various factors which influence purchase of machinery and plant and the considerations underlying these is necessary. A fresh approach to the entire issue is called for, to ensure that scarce financial resources of the enterprise are invested optimally and produce the desired return on investment. Over-capitalisation in the form of excess capacity in machinery and plant or fancy features in the garb of 'state of the art technology' have ruined many an industrial enterprise.

In many industrial undertakings, the task of identification of machinery and plant, determination of its vital parameters such as manufacturing capacity, speed of operation etc is assigned to either the manufacturing department or the engineering department. These departments, though fully competent to identify their needs, may not be adequately trained and equipped to fix all the parameters, particularly those which are techno-commercial in nature, and have a direct bearing on the total cost of the equipment. Since these departments do not have expertise in the design of machinery and plant they may not be aware of the impact of various design features on its overall cost. They are thus, consciously or otherwise, influenced by the smooth talk of the salesman who is out to see his equipment

A multi-disciplinary approach is, therefore, desirable. It will be in the overall interest of the enterprise to nominate a multi-disciplinary committee to appraise and size the equipment to be procured. A senior materials/purchase manager, preferably with a technical background, be nominated as a member of this committee. It goes without saying that the purchase/materials manager must be well conversant with machines and their operations, and aware of the various techniques adopted by sellers of such equipment in padding up the total cost by offering various additional features, accessories, spares etc which may not be required.

The foremost task of the committee will be to 'size' the equipment or determine its manufacturing capacity which should be adequate to meet the current demand for the product to be manufactured plus a margin of 10-15 per cent. With the rapid changes in technology and the consumer-driven market of today, it is not advisable to purchase extra capacity to meet the likely demand for the product two or three years later. Such extra capacity, which represents unproductive locked-up capital, may not be physically available, even if required, after two or three years due to wear and tear of the equipment and other factors. Redundant equipment capacity must, therefore, be avoided as it represents avoidable expenditure. The actual physical output will in reality become the manufacturing capacity of the equipment. Additional future demand for the product, up to a certain extent, can be met by operating the equipment extra time. If the demand at a later date really outstrips the capability of the equipment it will be worthwhile to buy additional equipment to meet the additional demand.

The next important decision of the committee will be regarding the operating speed and other parameters of the equipment. Instances are many where machines with excessive speeds and feeds have been purchased though such super features were not required to produce the desired output within the available time. A trade off between such superlative features and their high cost and less sophisticated features and their lower cost may turn out to be cost effective. The committee will have to address itself to such options.

The committee must also appreciate the pricing strategies adopted by the machinery manufacturer(s), and their likely impact on the proposed purchase. It has been observed that manufacturers of machinery and plant, as a business strategy, differentiate their product from that of their rivals by providing super features which are not of much practical utility other than as a mechanism through which the salesman can impress the production or manufacturing manager, influencing him to identify his requirements with the particular features of the machine in question. A committee is thus extremely useful in arriving t a proper conclusion. It will be appropriate for the committee to scrutinise carefully the parameters of similar equipment being marketed and if necessary consult existing users before deciding on the parameters of the equipment proposed to be purchased. The committee must differentiate between 'desires' and 'needs'. Any special features or accessories required to enhance the capacity or capability/versatility of the equipment must be properly evaluated and identified. The committee can then proceed to lay down various features and parameters of the proposed machinery and plant and also its performance specifications.

The next step is invitation of bids, either through open competitive bidding or through restricted competitive bidding from short-listed vendors considered capable of fulfilling the requirement. Though invitations to bids will legitimately be handled by the purchasing department, their evaluation by the multi-disciplinary committee is highly desirable. The equipment identified for purchase must have 'lowest total cost' and be suitable for manufacturing operations. While analysing and comparing the bids the following important techno-commercial considerations, which have a bearing on total cost, must be kept in view by the committee and must form part of the evaluation criteria.

1 The cost of equipment should include not only the cost of the basic machine/plant but also the cost of essential accessories required to achieve the desired operating capacity/capability; charges for transport, installation/commissioning; charges for initial fill of oils, lubricants, hydraulic fluid etc; charges for supply of operating/maintenance/spares manuals. To identify the equipment with lowest total cost it is essential to know the operating cost of the equipment.

An equipment, though apparently cheaper in initial cost, may be expensive in operating costs, being less efficient in use of energy and raw material.

It would, therefore, be necessary to ascertain the consumption and costs of power, compressed air, steam, water etc; oils, lubricants, hydraulic fluids and the frequency of their replenishment/replacement; any other consumables required and their cost.

2 Frequently the vendors quote separately for essential maintenance spares to be supplied with the equipment. The real need such spares and their cost must be closely scrutinised. To remain competitive some sellers of equipment try to recover part of the total cost through cost of spares. 'Essential' spares requirements will merit even more critical scrutiny when the equipment is to be imported from another country, as logistical delays will be crucial in the event of a sudden breakdown of the equipment. The vendors must also provide details of spares not manufactured in-house by them, and their sources, so that they may be obtained direct when required or where commercially advantageous.

3 Performance of the same or similar equipment supplied by the vendors to other customers must be taken into account to assess the reliability and provenness of the equipment. Besides obtaining performance reports from other users a visit to their plant and interaction with operating/maintenance personnel will bring out facts which may not figures in the performance report.

4 The willingness of the vendors to demonstrate and prove the performance of the equipment and guarantee the same over a specified time frame should form a part of the evaluation. The vendors must also assure continuous availability of spares, manufactured either by them or their sub-suppliers so that the equipment always remains operational.

5 Eco-friendliness of the equipment must also receive proper consideration. The equipment should employ environmentally sound technology and must not produce effluents which are either hazardous or polluting in nature. It must not emit excessive smoke, dust, fumes, noise or infringe any anti-pollution laws. The extra cost of effluent disposal, if any, must form part of total cost.

6 The safety of operators and others coming in contact with the equipment as well as long and short-term effects on their health must also be properly evaluated and costs, if any, associated with them assessed and used for comparison.

7 As far as possible the equipment should be capable of normal operation in a factory environment. The cost of supplying and maintaining such special facilities as pressurised air chambers, air conditioning etc must form a part of the total cost.

8 The expenses for travel and stay of the personnel of the vendors during the period of installation and commissioning/proving-out trials of the equipment as well as during the warranty obligations need to properly identified. These, at times, can be substantial and become a matter for dispute. If they are payable by the purchaser they need to form part of the comparative evaluation.

9 The cost of training of operating/maintenance personnel, if any, must be worked out. If such personnel have to be trained by or at the vendor, such costs may be substantial.

10 Any other services which the purchaser may be required to provide during installation/commissioning of the equipment must be identified.

11 After-sales service, including response time during warranty and subsequently, must also be taken into consideration while evaluating the offers. The willingness of the vendor to take up repairs and maintenance of the equipment, if requested to do so, and to share all vital information about design and process improvements effected by the vendor in machines made subsequently also merits consideration by the committee. No less important will be the efficiency in supply of spares.

12 The frequency and complexity of maintenance schedules and time intervals during which the equipment will remain out of operation also need careful evaluation.

Global purchasing and the rise and rise of countertrade

Barter is as old as trade, but John Stevens argues that its sophisticated modern derivatives are an essential of global purchasing.

In my article in the January 1995 issue of *Purchasing and Supply Management* entitled 'Global Purchasing in the Supply Chain', a distinction was made between global purchasing and a mere 'buy foreign' policy. The former was seen as a planned strategy, and a number of companies in various stages of developing an organisational structure successfully to meet such a strategy were given as examples. This current article warns of some of the wider influences that will affect global purchasing decision-making.

Purchasers are 'Traders' and so too are our marketing brethren. 'UK Ltd' is also a 'Trader', and so are all of our international competitors. Some of our customers have no money to spend, or wish to supply us goods to get into our markets as suppliers - hence the increase in trading deals which may not be within the control of individual purchasers or marketers, or indeed individual companies. The rise of countertrade will impinge upon us all.

What is countertrade?

There is no generally accepted definition of countertrade - terms vary from country to country, and by author to author - even within the same country. However, countertrade may broadly be defined as: 'A commercial transaction in which provisions are made, in one or a series of related contracts, for payment by deliveries of goods and/or services, in addition to, or in place of financial settlement.' A counter trade arrangement, therefore, goes beyond a straightforward commercial transaction by virtue of the fact that buyers and sellers accept reciprocal deliveries in part or full settlement of the value of their deliveries.

Before the various forms of countertrade are considered, a look at its growth would be appropriate, in order to underline its importance as a trading method. In 1972 there were just 15 of them engaged in counter-trade. These were Albania, Australia, Bulgaria, CSSR, Cuba, China, East Germany, Hungary, India, New Zealand, Poland, Romania, USA, USSR and Yugoslavia. By 1979 the list had increased to 27 countries, by May 1984 88, and by 1989, 94 countries from Algeria to Zimbabwe, and including as partners all the more developed nations as well. It is estimated that now over 140 countries are involved in countertrade, and the newly independent states in what was the USSR have generated a new impetus as regards countertrade opportunities.

From its early days, when it was restricted mostly to Eastern European states, countertrade has enveloped the world, spreading over all five continents. In 1989 Okorafo said that countertrade was between 20 per cent and 25 per cent of the value of total world trade, so the above facts suggest that it will be more than likely that a business will be involved in countertrade.

What sort of transactions are included? Like the definition of countertrade itself there are differences as to the meaning of the rest of the terminology, the descriptions that follow probably have the widest acceptance, and some have been used by the United Nations.

Barter trade

A barter trade transaction is the direct exchange of goods having offsetting values, without any flow of money taking place. A barter trade transaction can be categorised by the following:
- it is a one-time transaction rather than an ongoing dynamic relationship
- only two parties are involved in the transaction
- only one contract is drafted covering the offsetting deliveries of goods between the two parties
- the good to be exchanged are specified at the time the export contract is signed; only good are involved
- it takes place over a relatively short time, hence there is little time-lag between offsetting deliveries of goods

- it is limited in commercial applications because of the difficulty of finding matched 'needs' and 'wants'
  These transactions are shown diagrammatically in Figure 1

FIGURE 1 A barter transaction

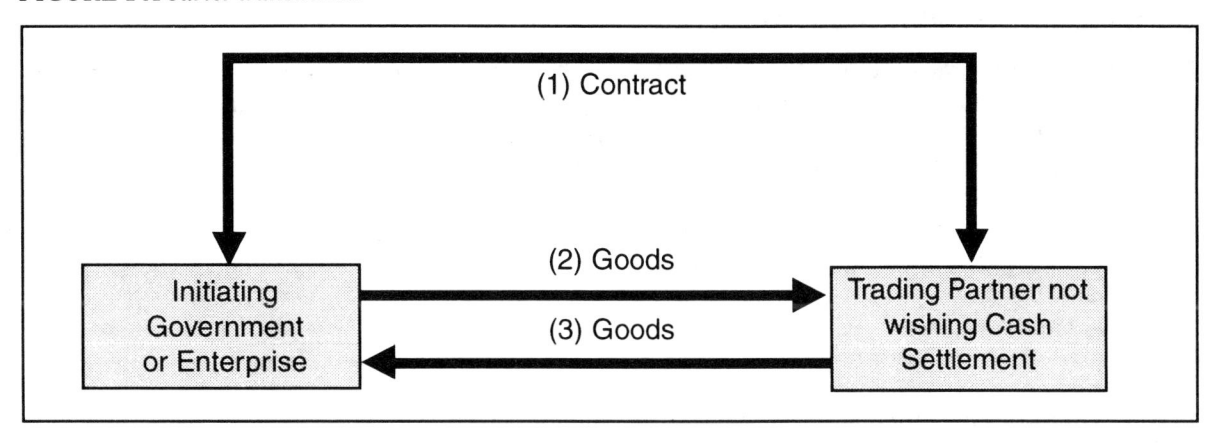

```
                        (1) Contract
        ┌──────────────────────────────────────┐
        ▼                                      ▼
  ┌─────────────┐      (2) Goods      ┌─────────────────┐
  │ Initiating  │────────────────────▶│ Trading Partner │
  │ Government  │                     │  not wishing    │
  │ or Enterprise│◀───────────────────│ Cash Settlement │
  └─────────────┘      (3) Goods      └─────────────────┘
```

Commercial example:

Volkswagen (West Germany prior to unification) exchanged automobiles with East Germany for canned ham. Iranian oil was exchanged for New Zealand lamb.

Compensation agreements

As with barter, the obligations of the two trading parties are set out in a single commercial contract and the original seller may agree to accept full settlement in the form of goods for what is intended to be sold (this being known as total compensation). In contrast with barter, the supplier, under a compensation deal, may negotiate a settlement on the basis that part will be in currency and part will be in the form of goods (this being known as part compensation).

(i) Full compensation

When considering a description of full compensation, in the first instance it may be concluded that it is identical to barter. However, full compensation differs in a number of respects from barter. Two key differences are that:
(a) with compensation, the goods being exchanged are valued in terms of currency; and,
(b) there is a remittance of currency between the two parties.

(ii) Part compensation

With part compensation, the original seller negotiates on the basis that the company wishes settlement to take place partly in a convertible currency and partly in goods. The initiating business will receive the currency in accordance with the agreement with the counterparty (ie to time and amount of delivery of currency). The amount so received will be split. The proportion which is to be used as the part cash settlement can be credited to the seller's bank account and this can be drawn on that amount as soon as it has been cleared. The balance will be held in a special bank account. Thereafter, when goods are shipped by the counterpart, their value can be claimed from the amount which is held in the special bank account.

There is usually a limit imposed on the counterpart as to how much time there is to ship the goods and there may be terms in the contract which state that the goods provided by the counterpart must come from a specified industry or economic sector.

Commercial examples:-

Full Compensation

A UK frozen food company made an arrangement to supply frozen spinach to an Eastern European country in return for non-frozen preserved fruit over a period of years.

Part Compensation

General Motors sold $12M of engines to Eastern Europe and in exchange took $4M of tools, but with the remainder in cash.

(iii) Compensation Agreement with a 'Buy Back' or 'Take Back' deal

This form of counter trade involves the purchase of resultant products, often ass the outcome of the sale and delivery of complete plants, equipment and production lines on the one hand, and the subsequent purchase of product manufactured or raw materials extracted by means of that equipment, on the other.

Such a compensation agreement may be explained step-by-step as follows:

l Initiator contracts to sell plant and equipment to 'Non-Cash' partner.
2 Initiator simultaneously contracts to purchase some of that plan's output, ie (resultant product), once production has begun
3 'Non-Cash' partner negotiates with bank, probably in initiator's country for credits with which to purchase plant and equipment.
4 Bank in initiator's country extends purchase credits to 'Non-Cash' partner.
5 Initiator despatches equipment to 'Non-Cash' partner.
6 Bank in initiator's country pays initiator for deliveries.
7 When production has begun, 'Non-Cash' partner delivers part of the output to the initiator.
8 Initiator pays 'Non-Cash' partner for deliveries of product
9 'Non-Cash' partner repays the bank credit in initiator's country.
This transaction is shown diagrammatically in Figure 2.

FIGURE 2 A compensation (with buy-back) agreement

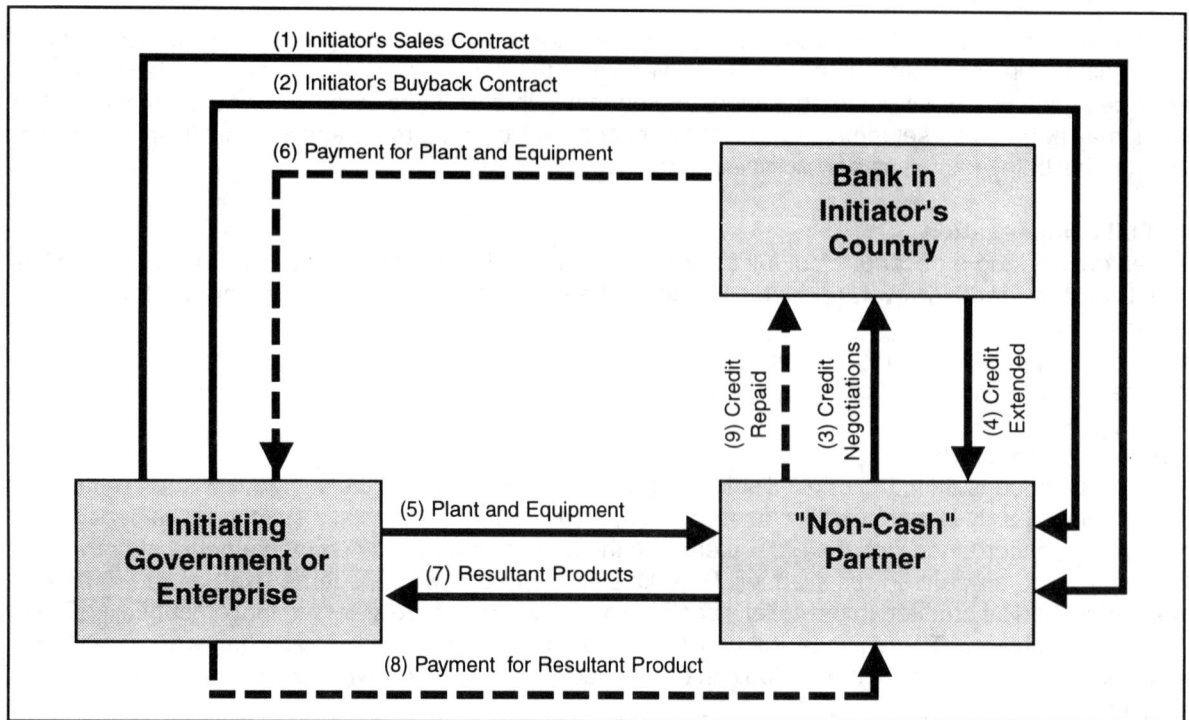

Commercial example:

Wilkinson Sword built a razor blade plant in Russia, as payment Wilkinson Sword agreed to accept back some of the blades produced in that plant.

Variants to this buy-back form of countertrade might be when instead of a factory or hardware being supplied, the offer is know-how. this could be technical or commercial, ie marketing know-how, and in return goods might be supplied specifically from that business. Fiat took cars built in Russia, and Levi allowed products from a Hungarian plant access to Western markets.

Compensation agreement with a switch deal

These originate from bilateral agreements that were made between two sovereign states. Payments for the goods which are imported and exported between the two countries are made in non-convertible 'clearing units', these are just entries or units of account.

Frequently the bilateral trade accounts become out of balance as often in the case of Eastern European or developing countries they are unable to deliver the goods required by the trade partner, or are unable to find the foreign currency to make settlement.

The 'switch trader' can then make arrangements to use these imbalances to obtain commodities from developing countries or Eastern Europe states so that their debts are paid in hard currencies.

The increase in companies willing to investigate all of the forms of countertrade is partly due to the growing number of barter-brokers. These middlemen find a match for clients by using computerised databases, from which they can locate potential exchange partners quickly and cheaply. As a result of this the risks associated with countertrade are reduced. Apart from this, these databases provide an opportunity of finding out which materials are coming into the UK, probably at competitive prices.

Counterpurchase or parallel trade agreements

Counterpurchase can be defined as 'commercial transactions concluded through several related contracts whereby the seller agrees as part of the contractual obligations to purchase goods and services from the buyer to an agreed percentage of those to be delivered'.

The most frequent type of counterpurchase occurs when the supplier (or party designated by the supplier), commits to buy goods from the importing organisation for amounts of equal or partial value to those being sold. Goods accepted in fulfilment of counterpurchase obligations may be related or unrelated to the normal line of business of the exporter. When unrelated goods are accepted, complicated commercial arrangements have to be worked out to dispose of the goods on the market and that is why third parties - usually specialised trading houses - have to be brought into the transaction.

This has become a popular form of countertrade technique. Unlike compensation agreements there are two separate commercial contracts entered into, (although each contract will refer to the other). Such transaction might involve the following steps:

l) Initiator contracts for the sale of, say, plant and equipment to a 'Non-Cash' partner.
2) 'Non-Cash partner negotiates with a bank, probably in the Initiator's country, for credits with which to purchase Initiator's plant and equipment.
3) Bank in Initiator's country extends credits to 'Non-Cash' partner.
4) Initiator arranges delivery of equipment to 'Non-Cash' partner.
5) Bank in Initiator's country makes payment (either full or partial, depending upon the type of counterpurchase arrangement involved) to Initiator for deliveries.
6) Initiator contracts with 'Non-Cash' partner for the purchase of materials to be supplied.
7) Initiator pays 'Non-Cash' partner for materials.
8) 'Non-Cash' partner repays Initiator's credits
9) If the Initiator cannot use or sell the 'Non-Cash' partner's materials it may negotiate directly with another company, or with a home trading house which will handle the sale of the 'Non-Cash' partner's products. The 'Non-Cash' partner delivers materials to either:
10) a) The Initiator partner, or
    b) Another designated party that the Initiator stipulates.
11) The Initiator receives payment either directly from other parties the Initiator has stipulated, or from 'home' trading houses.

The transaction is shown diagrammatically in Figure

Counterpurchase/offset agreements

Governments purchasing high value military equipment or turnkey projects often insist that suppliers purchase equipment or components locally or assist exporters of local goods. These 'offset' policies are to increase or protect local equipment or develop export industries rather than to reduce foreign exchange costs. **Commercial example:** *Boeing sold AWACS to the UK Ministry of Defence and agreed to buy 130 per cent of the value of the transaction in British goods. Such trading agreements benefit therefore both individual firms and nations.*

FIGURE 3   *A counterpurchase transaction*

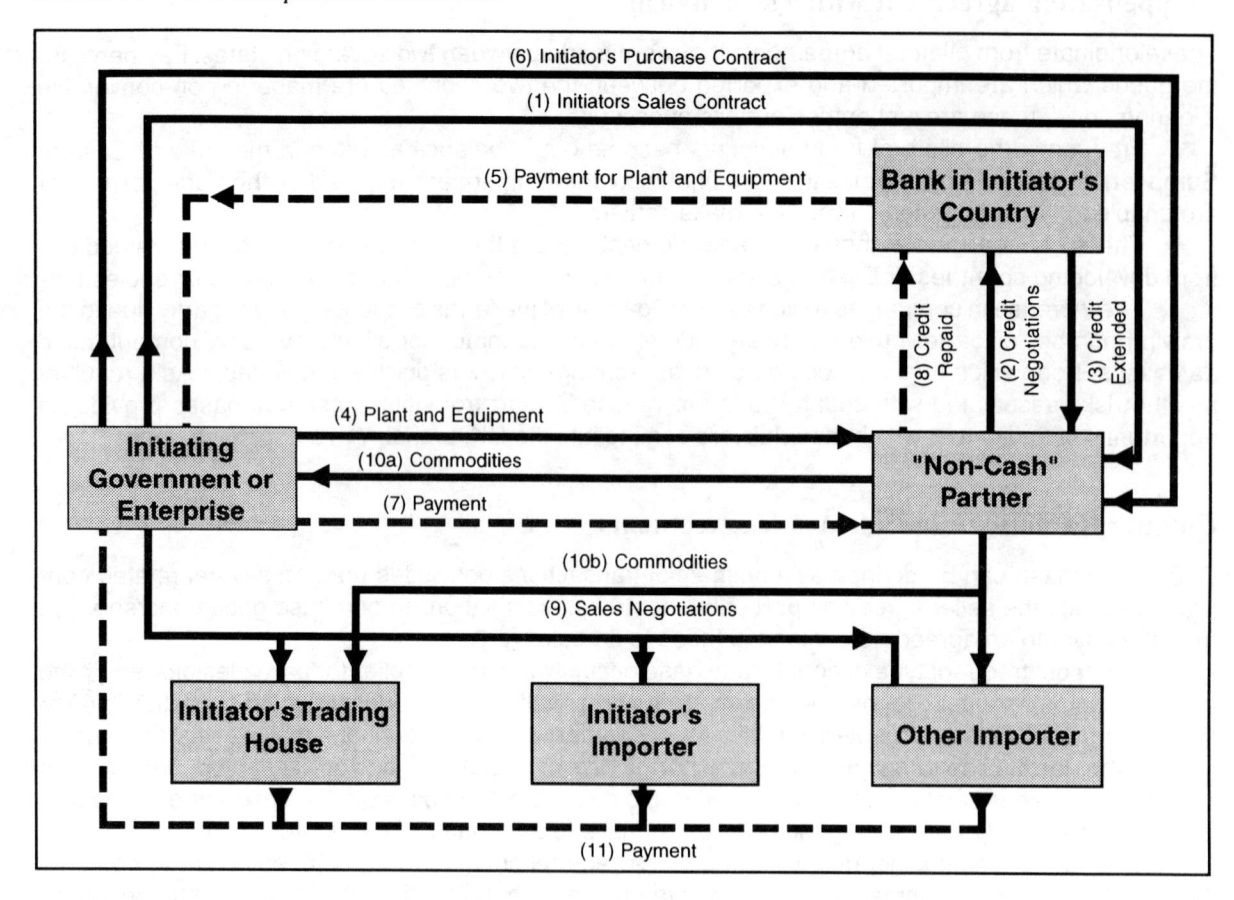

```
(6) Initiator's Purchase Contract
(1) Initiators Sales Contract
(5) Payment for Plant and Equipment → Bank in Initiator's Country
(8) Credit Repaid / (2) Credit Negotiations / (3) Credit Extended
Initiating Government or Enterprise
(4) Plant and Equipment → "Non-Cash" Partner
(10a) Commodities
(7) Payment
(10b) Commodities
(9) Sales Negotiations
Initiator's Trading House | Initiator's Importer | Other Importer
(11) Payment
```

FIGURE 4 *Main categories of transaction covered by the countertrade concept*

TYPE OF COUNTERTRADE TRANSACTION	NATURE OF COUNTERTRADE DELIVERY FROM A CUSTOMER WHO IS NOW A SUPPLIER
1. Direct exchange of products	Delivery of Products in total settlement of the transaction. Delivery of Products in partial settlement of the transaction.
2. Purchase of products by the seller (or a person so designated) from the buyer (or accepted 3rd party) up to a given % of the initial transaction.	Purchase prior to the sale of products. Purchase concomitant with sale of products or within a specified time period.
3. Purchase of products manufactured on the basis of technology and/or by means of equipment or installations supplied to	Purchase exclusively of resultant products. Purchase of resultant and non-resultant products
4. Reciprocal deliveries as part of industrial co-operation (subcontracting, co-production and specialisation	Deliveries of manufactured products on the basis of instructions provided by the seller. Deliveries of products in the framework of jointly agreed or jointly co-ordinated manufacturing programme.
5. Co-operating in marketing	Sales of products on the partner's markets up to a given percentage of the initial transaction. Sales of products on third markets up to a given percentage of the initial transaction.

The future and some advice

We have seen how countertrade has become a growing feature of international business. Maier 1988, predicts that countertrade will account for about 50 per cent of world trade by the 21st century. Now, 'domestic' reciprocity, (ie within one state) had long been initiated by the marketing function. Dean Ammer as long ago as 1962 argued that purchasing should have an input into this issue to arrive at an objective and optimum decision. The same applies to countertrade, which has been driven by marketers needing to sell in export markets. Here are some guidelines for purchasers who wish to argue that their function should have a legitimate role in any countertrade proposal.

1) The buyers are best equipped to choose products to counterpurchase and to price them for the home market. They will know if a product can be used in-house or if it must be disposed of to a third party, and if so, whether modification costs will be involved, and what the logistics costs might be.
2) By sourcing information from barter brokers and having access to their databases buyers will know if other companies are interested in these counter-purchases, and the countertrade market in general.
3) They will help in eliminating bad deals because the total costs of counter-purchases will be evaluated professionally.
4) They will have an ongoing opportunity of assessing any additions to suppliers
5) Often 'Non-Cash' Partner quality standards are lower than UK standards. The purchaser can monitor quality levels, deliveries and after-sales service. They will best know what steps must be taken to rectify problems, and supplier development exercises can be put in place.
6) Buyers may have the responsibility for the disposal of products to third parties. Establishing what products are offered by 'Non-Cash' partners and new potential customers for those products will make such jobs truly entrepreneurial.
7) A survey conducted by the Centre for Advanced Purchasing Studies USA found that purchasers who were experienced in countertrade had a more positive outlook as regards its potential. The lesson for purchasers: involvement is a necessity.
8) Marketers may find that they might fail to get business if they refuse to countertrade. They may find they can get higher prices if they are prepared to counterpurchase. The acid test, however, is that any company must be able to show a net gain for entering such as agreement. This may be a fiscal profit; the bait to secure long-term markets or a flow of spares orders; use spare capacity in the company; to achieve economies of scale; to spread R & D costs; to extend the product life-cycle of a mature product, etc. All of these may be generated from successfully marketing to the customer market.

Purchasers must be involved too - to make assessments of any downside from a supply market that happens to be the customer market as well! Figure 4 shows what has to be assessed.

Chapter 5: Logistics

3C - A method to reach total customer service

By Miguel Fernandez-Ranada, F Javier Gurrola-Gal & Enrique Lopez-Tello. This article introduces an entirely new Materials Management (MM) theory called 3C. This is the result of more than three years of scientific research applied to the MM systems. The authors used hypothetical and actual data from complex manufacturing operations.

Our conclusions are also supported by the experience of a real-life implementation that has been running for more than two years under the 3C principles. Our studies clearly indicate that 3C can produce significant improvements in customer service and inventory turns for businesses that service highly unpredictable and therefore difficult to forecast customer demand.

3C operates with a whole new set of rules, very different from the ones used in industry today. The 3C theory is simply based on the maximum selling *capacity* of the business, a complete exploitation of the *commonality* content present among finished goods sold by the business and, lastly, the concept of consumption, which requires a radical change in the planning/purchasing functions of the business. this change consists of literally replacing what we do today with a safer method that simply replenishes the actual material *consumption*. The combined usage of these 3Cs produces the elimination of the main root-causes of material shortages and has a direct, positive impact on the company's bottom line.

The purpose of this article is to deliver a high-level but clear understanding of how 3C uses *Capacity, Commonality* and *Consumption*, and to expose the strategic business advantages that it can generate. The benefits of 3C are measured in terms of Turn Over Ratio (TOR) and customer service and are presented as a benchmarking exercise that compares the performance of 3C against one of the most popular methods currently used, MRP.

Why an alternative?

Achievement of 'Total Customer Service' is a key competitive advantage seriously pursued by many businesses today.

'Material Shortages' are often addressed as the main cause of customer service failures. Countless expensive approaches have been tried to solve the problem. Some of these attempts have only produced marginal improvements, the majority have not succeeded at all; still there was no solution in sight. An honest look at many of today's modern factories provides living proof of this judgement.

The MM methods and systems now in use, as well as the philosophy on which they are based, just do not seem to be suitable to appropriately support the markets of today. Today's approaches to manufacturing systems are largely based on 20 year old MRPII concepts that, when integrated with present-day real-time competitive demands, have created unnecessarily complex systems. Maybe it is time to question some of the foundations upon which MRPII systems were developed and to examine new approaches/systems which will survive in the 1990s.' (Lee Kneppelt, APICS - *The Performance Advantage*, October 1991)

Before changing - why are current strategies failing?

There are at least three main causes that negatively affect the MM systems in use today:
- complexity,
- uncertainty,
- and a new more demand concept of customer service that has emerged through an ever-increasing, more aggressive and strong *competition*.

Complexity

Any materials management system needs to have an efficient and reliable execution. The purpose of any

MM system is highlighted as follows: Guarantee an efficient supply of materials, work in progress and finished goods by being able to answer the basic replenishment and manufacturing questions: What, when and how many materials to buy, and what when and how many end-products to make. this purpose must be accomplished with the maximum simplicity and minimum effort and cost, and with such service quality, that the business has a competitive advantage.

Unfortunately, the complexity of many modern MRP systems results in poor execution of the basic function for which they were created. Too often they take too long to answer the basic questions or, even worse, some endemically provide the wrong answers, creating significant economic disadvantages.

Right now the answers these systems provide have been made to depend on just 'too many things,' which are characterised by high degrees of uncertainty. The question then is: Why get so precise and specific when the base is so shaky?

Uncertainty

It is impossible to predict the future. Time-phased sales forecasts at the end-product level of detail rarely become a reality when compared to what the customers truly need and want, when the appropriate time comes.

High-level sales forecasts are needed for many reasons, such as strategic planning, resource and capacity planning and budgeting, to name but a few. Using them as the basis to purchase materials, however, can be too costly and highly inappropriate for certain types of businesses in the market conditions of today. 'The downfall of MRPII, of course, is in the inevitable inaccuracies in the sales forecast data which, together with the 'firm orders', determine the units needed- -by date in the system's build plan.' (Bob Wilhite, APICS - *The Performance Advantage*, September 1991)

It is not uncommon to find businesses where the MPS quantities compared to the actual customer demand vary in ranges from minus 100% to plus 300% - even over planning horizons as short as the immediate month.

General managers pound on MM managers: 'How come you have so many million dollars in inventories? We have customer orders and manufacturing capacity, yet we are hardly shipping anything!'

Result: Everyone blames the marketeers and the sales force for their inability to predict what the customers want. After this, new money and resources become engaged in projects 'to improve' forecast accuracy. this has been our endless loop, without results, for too many years now.

Competition

MRP systems are based on 'planning cycles' (competitive disadvantage) as opposed to the desirable 'continuous planning' mode (competitive advantage).

TABLE 1 Main differences between MRP and 3C

Main Differences between MRP and 3C	
Current Characteristics under MRP	**Current Results**
1 Sales forecast needed for material management 2 Planning based on end-product with no usage of 'Commonality' 3 Planning cycles 4 Allocations of materials 5 High level of bureaucracy 6 Many, multiple and complex BOM levels 7 High overhead expenses 8 Treat all PIs equally	**Continuous and costly Material Shortages and Poor Customer Service performance**
New Characteristics under 3C	**New Results**
1 Planning approach based on 'Capacity' 2 Complete exploitation of 'Commonality' of materials 3 Continuous material replenishment based on 'Consumption' 4 Materials are never allocated, just used when needed 5 Bureaucracy removed and replaced with simplicity 6 Just one, easy-to-understand level in the BOM 7 Overhead expenses are lower than those of other methods 8 Treat PIs differently, based on a fast and slow classification	**Main root causes of Material Shortages eliminated** **Improved Customer service and Bottom-Line performance**

Some businesses have 'eliminated' the problem of 'material shortages' at the expense of either increasing inventories in finished goods or sacrificing customer service. WE are talking about factories that 'freeze' the MPS during a time period often referred to as 'time-fence'. These factories report a 100% fulfilment of their production plans. They, of course, always have the 'exact and right materials' to make what was planned and they go ahead and work hard, and are even rewarded to make that plan a reality, no matter whether the reality is different from the plan.

This approach certainly eliminates the problem of 'material shortages', but it can also produce extremely damaging results for the business, such as the creation of unnecessary inventories of finished goods that the company has to carry until they are sold. In some cases these goods are either scrapped for obsolescence or sold at a lower price. Furthermore, customers are told that they cannot change their mind. What was ordered will be manufactured Just-in-Time, and delivered Just-in-Time as the *promised* due date (sometimes called committed due date). Someone in your company should be able to measure and show you where your business really stands with respect to customer service. You might find out that only between 40 per cent to 50 per cent of customer orders are actually delivered JIT at the 'Customer Requested Date'. Although is is rapidly changing, many copies are still referring to the 'Customer Promised Date' when they talk about their JIT delivery performances. Businesses can only get away with this in a monopoly or while high demand/low supply conditions exist.

The concept of Frozen MPS has created millions of pounds' worth of unnecessary stocks of materials and finished goods for many businesses. This is not a good alternative in today's highly competitive environment. Lastly, this approach to eliminate material shortages makes the sales function more difficult and ultimately results in loss of revenues and market opportunities.

We have devoted a big proportion of this article to discussing what we have grown to believe are common and real-life problems of all real factories. We used the space to disuss them, because 3C has a tremendous impact on all of them, and actually eliminates many of them.

The so-called 3C alternative

The 3C alternative provides businesses with flexibility levels that represent a competitive advantage, while delivering global economic improvements.

How is 3C different from what we are doing todayl? Table 1 gives a high level view of the main differences between MRP and 3C, and the consequences.

All eight items shown in Table 1 can be quantified and benchmarked. This article, however, only covers the first three points.

3C - capacity, commonality and consumption

Detailed and more formal documentation on 3C will become available with time. For this introductory article we have chosen to use a simple example as an attempt to explain the basic concepts.

Imagine a very simple business that sells only two 'different' end-products. The end-products of the example are puzzles that assemble into a 'Giraffe' (referred to as G from now on) and an 'Elephant' (E, for short).

Each one of the end-products G and E requires certain amounts of three different kinds of raw materials, each called a Purchasing Item (PI. Table 2 contains drawings of the end-products G and E, the unit cost of materials and the corresponding Bill of Materials (BOM).

The First C: Capacity

3C supports the manufacturing system with one stable and relatively constant parameter for each end-product. This parameter is called TOP (Table of Pulls). The TOP is the maximum volume of sales of an end-product that the business decides to support. The TOP values are assigned, based on various reasons. For example, the maximum quantity that a resource can produce in a mono-product mode and at full capacity or the maximum estimated market size of the product. For non-strategic products, an arbitrary number can be assigned to their TOP. TOPs are expressed in units/day.

The example used assumes that 'Total Customer Service' is pursued very seriously. It also assumes we have the selling capability of five puzzles/day (maximum market size) and a manufacturing facility with an average capacity also equal to five puzzles/day. The problem is that we have no idea which puzzle and what quantities the actual customer will demand.

Instead of spending time, money and permanent overheads producing sales forecasts and guessing the expected product mix each month, we use 3C and avoid the risk of missing the market because of inaccuracies. In addition, we save the overheads needed to handle the numerous problems created with the other approach. So, we define the TOPs of our example as follows:

TOP for end-product G = 5 units/day
TOP for end-product E - 5 units/day

TABLE 2 Bill of Material (BOM)

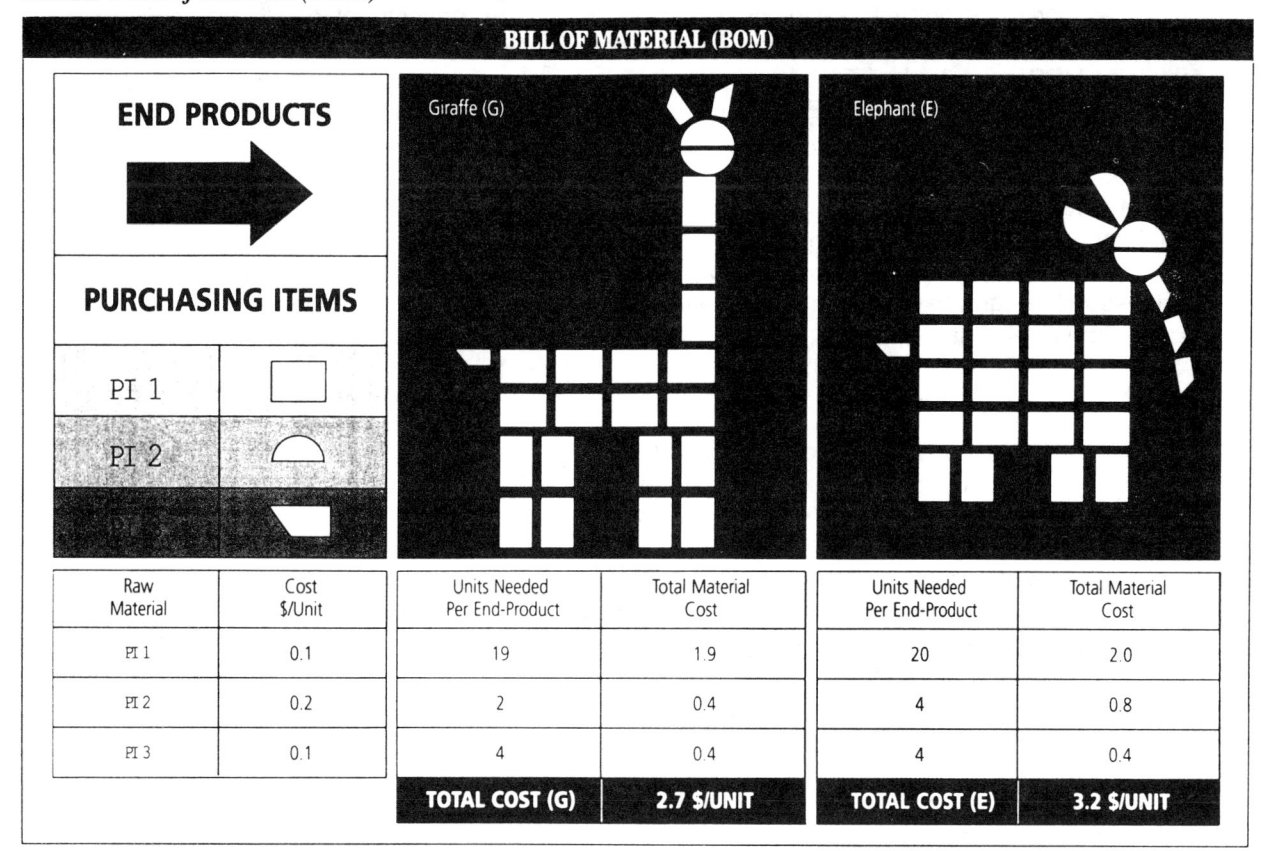

Raw Material	Cost $/Unit	Units Needed Per End-Product (Giraffe G)	Total Material Cost	Units Needed Per End-Product (Elephant E)	Total Material Cost
PI 1	0.1	19	1.9	20	2.0
PI 2	0.2	2	0.4	4	0.8
PI 3	0.1	4	0.4	4	0.4
		TOTAL COST (G)	**2.7 $/UNIT**	**TOTAL COST (E)**	**3.2 $/UNIT**

The second C - Commonality

3C takes full advantage of any presence of 'Commonality' in the end-products through the calculation of a set of values (one of each type of PI) that we call the 'Rate Bill (RBILL). RBILL is the peak consumption of material 'M' that might be expected per day. The actual calculation of the RBILL for real and complex systems requires several and more complex mathematical considerations. Just to convey the point, however, and thanks to the simplicity of the example, the RBILL is determined by performing the following two steps for each PI.

1) The number of units of each purchasing item contained in each end-product is multiplied by the TOP of the end-product. This calculation is done for all end-products.
2) The RBILL for the PI is then set to be equal to the largest value found in the calculations at Step 1.

TABLE 3 The impact of commonality

THE IMPACT OF COMMONALITY
Units of Material Needed to Provide 100% Product-Mix Flexibility and therefore 100% Customer Service Level in our Example

Purch Item (PI)	MRP No Use of Commonality units/day	$/day	3C Full Use of Commonality units/day	$/day
1	39 x 5 = 195	19.5	20 x 5 = 100	10.0
2	6 x 5 = 30	6.0	4 x 5 = 20	4.0
3	8 x 5 = 40	4.0	4 x 5 = 20	2.0
Total	265 units/day	29.5 $/day	140 units/day	16.0 $/day

Table 3 shows the impact of 'Commonality' in the example by comparing the estimate of the usage rate of a typical MRP system and 3C when both systems prepare materials for full flexible coverage of any possible end-product mix.

The numbers in Table 3 were arrived at as follows:

MRP: Because of the premature allocation of materials and the commitment to at least satisfy the MPS, the only way to cover the TOP of the end-products of the business at a 'high customer service' level is to make the MPS equal to the TOP, completely ignoring the commonality that is there. We then do the 'explosion of materials' using the BOM of each end-product, arriving at the values given in Table 3.

3C: 3C recognises that the final products G and E have materials in common and fully exploits it. 3C prepares the system for the 'most demanding pull' (or usage). The 'most demanding pull' that P1 1, for example, can ever experience is 100 units/day (now constrained by manufacturing capacity). So the RBILL for material 1 is set to exactly that 'most demanding pull'.

For the example used, at full product-mix flexibility and total customer service, 3C supports the business with roughly half the inventory investments of the same business supported by MRP. Therefore, at the same level of sales, the 3C usage of 'Commonality' will double the TOR of our business example.

The Third C: Consumption

Tables 4 and 5 summarise the set of practical rules that 3C uses to respond to the three basic questions of manufacturing and replenishment functions that any MM system should support. (Notations: BTOB means 'Build To Order Business', BTSB means 'Build To Stock Business', MOQ means 'Minimum Order Quantity').

As claimed in Table 1, the concept of making consumption drive the purchasing actions has a great impact on the elimination of the main root-causes of material shortages. Based on the descriptions provided for each one of the 3Cs and the list of main root-causes of shortages, it should be easy to understand. Main root-causes:

1 Inaccuracy in sales forecast
2 Differences between the MPS product and volume mix, and actual product and volume mix really needed
3 High complexity and bureaucracy in the order realisation process
4 Working with planning cycles
5 Inaccuracies in the data bases of the information systems
6 Poor delivery performance of suppliers of purchasing items
7 Poor and unpredictable quality of purchasing items

3C contains internal mechanisms that cost-effectively protect the business against 'material shortages' triggered by the first four root-causes listed.

TABLE 4 - Practical rules - manufacturing

Practical Rules - Manufacturing		
Question	MRP	3C
What to make	The MPS if materials arrived as planned	Next customer in a BTOB or what was sold in a BTSB
When to make	By the due-date posted in the shop order	Immediately
How many to make	As indicated in the shop order	The amount requested by the customer order in a BTOB or the amount consumed in a BTSB

TABLE 5 - *Practical rules - purchasing*

| Practical Rules - Purchasing |||
Question	Current MM Systems	3C
What to buy	Answer depends on the BOMs, dependent and independent demand, OH inventories sales forecast, rough cut, (assumed constant and uniform) capacity	The PIs for which there was consumption
When to buy	According to an MPS and depending on the PI's 'Lead Time' (LT) from the supplier, etc. Every time the MRP system is run	When the consumption of PI is equal to the PI-MOQ of the supplier or weekly
How many to buy	Answer depends on the BOMs, dependent and independent demand, OH inventories, sales forecast, Lts of PIs, rough-cut capacity, open purchase order etc.	The PI-MOQ or actual PI consumption during the week

In conclusion

3C has the potential to generate improvements, when it is applied to businesses dealing with unreliable forecasts. Studies indicate that 3C can improve the Turn-Over Ratio by up to one order of magnitude when there are high levels of 'Commonality' and the business is executing an MRP-based system with *monthly* planning cycles. 3C can produce the transformation of a highly complex and poorly performing environment into a highly simplified and better performing operation.

We do not claim that 3C applies absolutely everywhere all the time. In this article, we have only shown a simple case for which 3C outperforms the MRP method. Individual characteristics, such as the system utilisation, product mix of sales and the presence of material 'Commonality' among the end-products of your business are determining factors as to how good 3C can really be for your operation.

The MRP practices have been so deeply embedded in the manufacturing culture for so long, that we now face the difficult challenge of finding the way of changing that mind-set without causing intermediate chaos.

Miguel Fernandez-Ranada is the Manager of Logistics at AT&T-NS-ES in Spain with responsibilities for all industrial operations, including production planning, manufacturing, purchasing and all inventory investments.
F Javier Gurrola-Gal is currently managing part of a manufacturing excellence project at one of the largest AT&T manufacturing locations.
Enrique Lopez-Tello is the Factory Planning Manager at AT&T-NS-ES. His responsibilities include the complete production and inventory management functions. He is the author of a successful already-operational software implementation of 3C called HERMES.

Development of Pan-European distribution strategy

by Kirsten Tisdale

Locating your warehouse in the optimum position can lead to huge cost savings. Sophisticated models can be built, using extremely detailed data, that will allow any number of complex scenarios to be explored. But what can you do if your company is considering its very first acquisition in Europe, and the data required is just not available? How can you tell if it will fit into a longer-term strategy?

At this early stage, your commercial colleagues may only be able to give you a fairly broad brush picture of future markets. But, before you can consider distribution infrastructure, you need to have a more detailed idea of where your customers are likely to be, and in what concentration.

A Pan-European demand model can be produced without access to sophisticated modelling techniques, and with access to relatively little data, using this stage-by-stage procedure. The model can then be used to explore location and service strategies, and can be refined as more accurate data becomes available.

Start at home

Before attempting a pan-European model you need to be able to build a demand model for your existing marketplace, which for the purposes of this exercise, I'm going to assume is the UK

Step 1: You need to understand your customer base - who buys whatever it is that you make or sell.

Most companies' marketing departments analyse their sales, using either census-type classifications if they sell to individuals (eg ABC1 etc), or Standard Industrial Classification (SIC) codes, or similar, if they sell to other companies.

Step 2: You now need to source some measure of the geographical concentration of different types of customer - not for your company, but generally. It needs to be a measure which is publicly available and which will not just be available for the UK, but for any country in which you are likely to be interested.

Assuming that we are looking at a manufacturing company with industrial customers, a suitable and readily available measure might be 'number of wage and salary earners' by region (see Figure 1). Obviously this produces distortions in favour of labour intensive and bureaucratic industries, but it is a measure for which information is widely available, at the very least for all EU countries.

Step 3: The final stage is to combine your own company's sales analysis, from Step 1, with this general geographical concentration, from Step 2, into a spreadsheet format (see Figure 2).

The calculations within the boldly outlined area are a direct function of your sales volume to customers that are in, say, the building trade, and the proportion of building workers that are generally found in the various regions of the country.

Validation

The figures that result from your spreadsheet give a theoretical view of where your company's geographical strengths and weaknesses are likely to lie. How do they compare with the actual volumes that your company delivers into these regions?

You will I want to examine various measures in Step 2 and choose the one (or combination) which give the best correlation with your actual geographical spread.

FIGURES 1 & 2 - Building the model

BUILDING THE MODEL

No. of Wage & Salary Earners £000s	United Kingdom			
	South West	South East	East Anglia	Etc.
Agri, Forest, Fish	44	69	34	-
Fuel & Power	24	104	8	-
Industrial	363	1405	187	-
Building	70	310	38	-
Etc.	-	-	-	-
	-	-	-	-
	-	-	-	-

Extract: Eurostat Statistical Year Book

	% of Sales	UNITED KINGDOM			
		South West	South East	East Anglia	Etc.
Agri, Forest, Fish	5	0.7	1.0	0.5	-
Fuel & Power	10	0.4	1.9	0.1	-
Industrial	35	2.4	9.4	1.4	-
Building	50	3.5	14.7	2.0	-
Total	100	7.0	27.0	4.0	-

These figures will not be an exact match. The important aspect of the comparison is to identify both the differences, and the reasons for them - be prepared to list both subjective and objective reasons. Do you service Scotland through a distributor based in Carlisle? Is East Anglia looked after by your best salesman?

There will be some differences where no reason can be suggested. Equally, some differences will be caused by your method of 'spreading' (steps 2 and 3 above) - head offices in London are unlikely to take large deliveries of, say, animal feed, but may be classified as part of the 'agriculture' industry.

FIGURE 3   Window for DC location

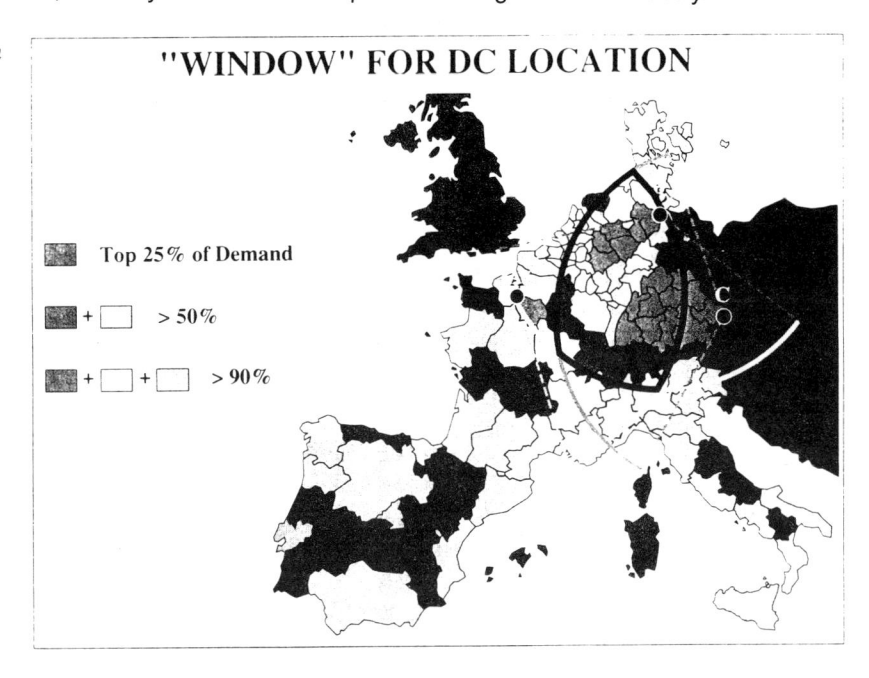

"WINDOW" FOR DC LOCATION

Top 25% of Demand

■ + □ > 50%

■ + □ + □ > 90%

European model

You now need to source the single most difficult piece of information in this exercise - likely market penetration on a country-by-country basis that you believe will have been achieved in, say, five or 10 years' time.

You may be able to source industry specific information - for example, the Germans eat twice as much canned food as we do in the UK.

You can also get country-by-country trends in consumer spending, and forecasts for broad consumption areas eg food/drink/tobacco.

You need to bear in mind different weather conditions and the changing age profiles of the various nationalities.

When you have made all your assumptions on market penetratation, you can then generate a model for Europe in the same manner as the UK.

At this point, mount your figures on a map using colour coding to denote concentration of likely demand.

Already, just from visual impact, you will be able to start forming a view as to the areas of strategic importance.

Servicing demand

There are three areas that need to be considered prior to using the model:
- traffic type
- peripheral regions
- order to delivery cycle

Traffic type: What kind of freight are you likely to generate out of whatever locations you have - full loads? part loads? parcels?

Are your volumes likely to warrant outbases, to which you can trunk overnight? Will you want to tap into an existing parcels network?

Peripheral regions: What is your attitude to the peripheral regions in the UK - do you offer customers in the Scottish Highlands and Islands the same service as those in Central London?

Be careful here - remember that in the UK we do not have any particularly large cornubations on our islands. Palma de Gran Canaria and Palma de Mallorca are both among Spain's top ten cities - neglecting them would be like neglecting Bristol or Coventry respectively.

Order to delivery cycle: What order to delivery timespan do you intend to offer to customers? How much of that timespan is taken up by administration, picking and load consolidation? How much will be left for the distribution and delivery element?

The answer to these questions will determine the 'radius' that each Distribution Centre is able to service.

Using the model

A couple of comments with respect to Figure 3:
1 I have made the assumption that all areas of peak demand (shown in blue) are to be a maximum of 12 hours from the DC. Those 12 hours represent overnight trunking to an outbase, and then onward delivery as part of a multi-customer trip the following day.
2 I have assumed that we can adequately model the area that can be serviced by using average day and night running speeds, and using 'crow-fly distance plus waggle factor' - I've been relatively conservative with the road speeds in this example.
3 Rather than starting from a 'sensible' DC location and working outwards with a circle to see what area can be covered from each prospective DC location, I have started from the edge of each area of peak demand (points A, B, and C in the diagram) and have worked inwards. This allows me to see the swndow of opportunity for the DC - the boldly outlined area.

The same exercise can also be carried out for the remainder of customers to be serviced, probably representing a reduced level of service and certainly narrowing the window further.

All the stages in the modelling so far have concerned demand and customer service. You also need to overlay the same results from examining the sourcing side of the equation.

Assessing the results

Assuming for now that you have a single theoretical window of opportunity, look at it from a practical point of view - how suitable does the area indicated look:
- Is the road network good?
- Or is the area mountainous or uninhabited?
- Where are your competitors based?

You will want to consider other factors influencing warehouse location:
- workforce availability and skills

- labour and property costs, including grant availability
- local transport links, including access to public transport
- sophistication of local telecommunications
- crime levels

Whatever the result, you need to do some sensitivity analysis on the assumptions you have made:
- market penetration
- road speeds
- service levels to peak and peripheral regions

Use the various causes that contributed to differences in your earlier UK validation exercise to explore the type of impact those same factors might present in Europe. You can also explore the impact of the opening-up of Eastern Europe.

I have been referring so far to the easiest scenario - ie, when the results of your modelling indicate an appropriate area for one DC. Of course, if you are considering the whole of Europe you may well end up with the model indicating that more that one DC is required - are you happy with that?

Remember that the results are merely a function of the information and assumptions from which you have built the model - by changing your service level criteria slightly, for instance, that single DC might be an achievable goal.

Moving away from the model, you will want to cost-out a number of scenarios, albeit that it may have to be at a fairly high level.

Refining the model

You are likely to want to refine the model at some stage.

Perhaps the validation was not sufficiently close to actual for the UK and you wish to refine the method of generating concentration of industrial activity across the regions.

Information which is both extremely detailed, and as up-to-date as you could wish, can be sourced on individual industries. The Department of Trade and Industry's Export Market Information Centre in Victoria is an excellent source of data (not just for Europe), particularly if you speak several languages - the more detailed the data for each country, the less likely that it is published in English.

You may also wish to refine your use of the model, by using a simple road network based package to produce isochrones to replace the circles used earlier. Isochrones are 'contours' of equal travel time from a particular point.

So, you have some idea of where you might want to be in five or ten years' time. What about that first acquisition that you're considering today?

What the model allows you to do is to explore whether the locations and properties that go with today's acquisition are likely to fit into a longer-term strategic plan. Are the locations likely to feature in five or ten years' time? Are the facilities themselves going to be able to accommodate the throughput - use the model to calculate the likely demand to be serviced by a particular location.

And, finally, remember that ultimately the most important factor is that the acquisition is the right decision today.

About the author:

KirstenTisdale is a member of Marks & Spencer's Physical Distribution Group. Since joining the ompany in 1989, she has concentrated on the international side of the business.

This article is based on consultancy work carried out when Kirsten worked for P-E International.

Working as one

Recently, directors of 19 UK companies met with a team of five from Manugistics. Chaired by David Harland, Gillette, and supported by Alan Braithwaite, Logistics Consulting Partners, the charter of this 'Executive Council' was to form a 'think tank' to facilitate debate on current and future topics and issues related to the management of the total supply chain.

These companies represented a number of diverse industries, including food, drink, 'white goods', automotive spare parts and 'HiTech'. Although there were many inherent differences in external business pressures and corresponding supply chain metrics across these sectors, it was quickly evident that all concerned saw an increasing convergence towards a similar, consumer or customer-driven supply-chain strategy. For example, over the past few years many 'HitTech' sectors - such as manufacurers of PC, terminal and server equipment or components - have been evolving their business model and corresponding supply chain business practices and processes to align themselves more with the consumer manufacturers than with their specialist technology origins.

A common ingredient to all present at the 'think tank' was the recognition of and dependence on the effective management of the supply chain as one of the core business processes to enable growth and to effectively manage both customer service and market share. As was witnessed by the seniority of the attendees, there was also consensus on the elevation of these issues to the boardrooms of major corporations.

Interestingly, one other common factor was the focus on the integration of the operational planning processes along the entire supply chain. This was recognised as being in stark contrast to the almost exclusive focus until a few years ago on the transactional or execution aspects of the supply chain as the foundation for integrated supply chain management.

Trends

Many of the trends emerging in the marketplace, some of which originate from, or bear similarities to, primary customer/supplier initiatives in progress in North America - such as QR (Quick Response), ECR (Efficient Consumer Response), VMI (Vendor Managed Inventory) and CRP (Continuous Replenishment Planning) - were identified as being fundamentally facilitated by tight integration of the operational planning of the supply-chain, rather than driven or supported by the underlying transaction or execution layer, see Figure 1.

FIGURE 1 Process integration vs systems integration

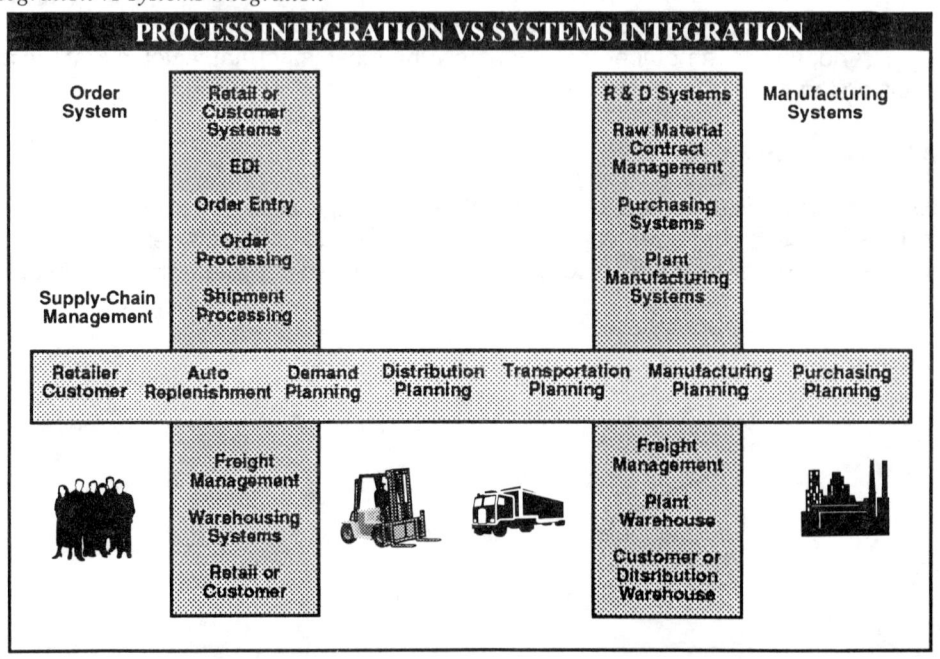

It was recognised that most large companies, operating in similar markets and sectors to those present, were now working on a 'two-layer' style supply chain model with a formal recognition of the two fundamental supply chain processes: planning and execution, with the planning layer increasingly being recognised as the facilitator of supply chain integration.

When Manugistics first started working with leading-edge corporations addressing the integration of the supply chain, companies were either focused on the forecast as the only driving mechanism for the supply chain - and specifically to determine manufacturing plans and schedules - or, on the 'Master Schedule' as the control of the feasibility as well as the efficiency of manufacturing facilities which would, in turn, determine what would be supplied to the distribution network. Corporations have evolved to an understanding of the benefit of a balanced demand and supply plan - neither exclusively driven by the manufacturing plan nor the demand forecast and/or stock cover plan, but rather as a balance of supply and demand across and throughout the whole supply chain based on 'one number'.

the enterprise today increasingly extends beyond the manufacturer or distributor to the integration of some level of market or customer data, see Figure 2. In this situation, the forecast needs to become more sophisticated, particularly in evaluation of detailed short-term trends as well as the 'automatic' evaluation of causal factors in the determination of the short and medium term forecast. It also needs to integrate even more closely with the distribution, manufacturing and transportation plans and schedules as well as with firm and tentative short-term actual demand.

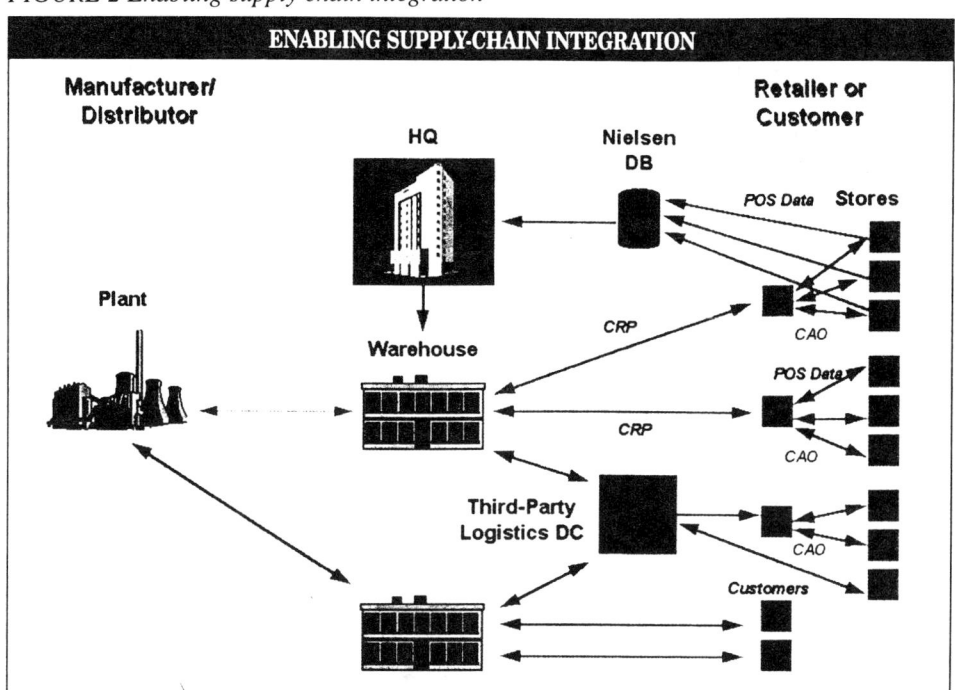

FIGURE 2 Enabling supply chain integration

In addition, as the cycle times reduce and the demands from the customer increase, there is increasing pressure to incorporate detailed external market trend and promotions data into the demand driven plan. Finally, all of this demand driven planning needs to be at an increasingly more detailed level; both in terms of demand forecasted items, customer/channel and distribution point focus as well as increasingly shorter time intervals.

This has dictated a far more sophisticated planning process which can only be facilitated by more sophisticated planning tools and technology. This is primarily focused on the fast-increasing complexity at the front - demand - end of the supply chain. However, the long term goal is clear, companies are increasingly looking for ways to remove functional barriers along the supply chain and allow their organisation to 'work as one'.

Author **Arthur Vonchek** is Director of Northern European Operations, Manugistics. He chairs Manugistics' European Management Committee. He has experience in developing long-term integrated logistics strategies for multinationals throughout Europe.

Benchmarking warehouse operations

By Christine Rowat. The plethora of conference papers and journal articles on benchmarking have tended to concentrate on its use in assessing logistics and supply chain performance. A conference organised by the National Materials Handling Centre narrowed the focus to benchmarking warehouse performance and identifying reliable performance measures.

There was a general agreement by all speakers that before embarking on a benchmarking exercise managers should be committed to continuous improvement. To quote Professor Martin Christopher, one of this country's leading exponents of benchmarking logistics operations and the opening speaker: 'By undertaking a benchmarking exercise the company is embarking on a journey that will fundamentally change the way it sees itself. Such companies can never stand still. For them the phrase 'continuous improvement' is not just a cliche, but a way of life ... Benchmarking can lead to the elimination of a practice or the redesign of the supply chain ...'

Interestingly, when asked by show of hands, only one-fifth of delegates could confirm their company's involvement in, or intention of, benchmarking their logistics process, including warehousing. In Professor Christopher's view, a disappointingly low percentage - showed a true reflection of industry's concern. Similarly, when Bill Brockbank, Leading Consultant, Logistics Consulting Partners, advocated stock accuracy as an important measure, very few delegates could confirm that their company had a stock accuracy standard.

Starting point

The first two speakers, Professor Christopher and Alan Braithwaite, Managing Partner of Logistics Consulting Partners, urged delegates to understand that before starting a benchmarking exercise it is essential to:

o Be well organised - prepare thoroughly. Understand the aims and objectives of the exercise; select the appropriate measures; identify the resources and processes which impact on the desired outcome. Customer service is one of the outcomes of benchmarking logistics. See Figure 1

FIGURE 1 What to benchmark?

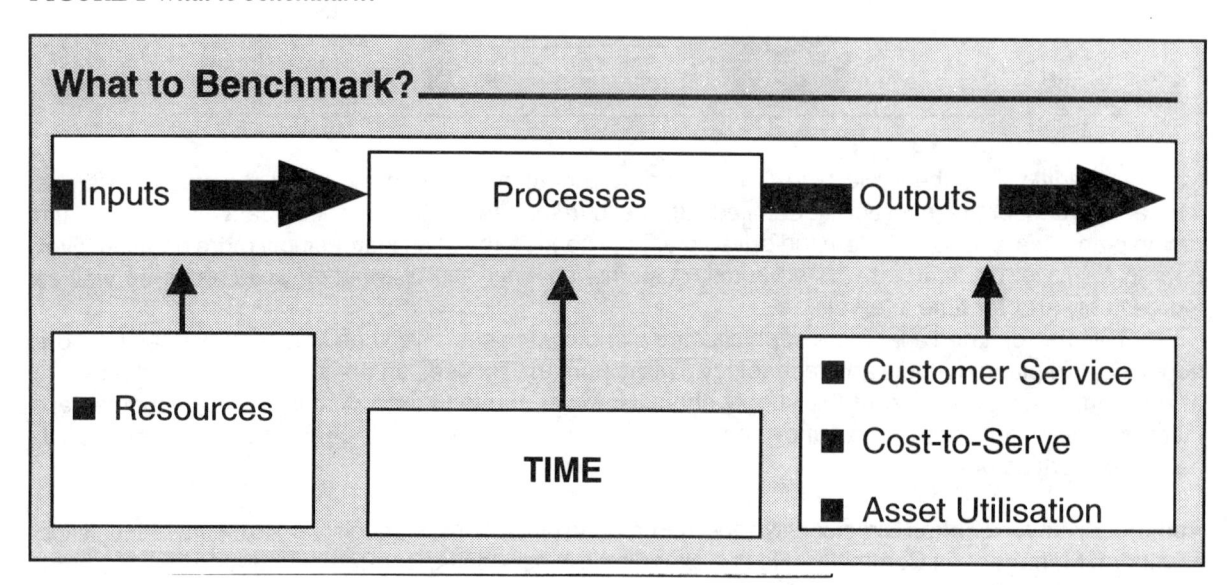

- Priorities - it is impossible to measure every dimension of an organisation or operation.
- Identify companies for comparison. These should be 'best in class' not just immediate competitors; for example, when Xerox Corporation wanted to improve order processing, they benchmarked against a mail order company.
- Understand that measurement for its own sake is a pointless exercise. The outcome should be continuous improvement.

Professor Christopher proposed that companies start by asking themselves three basic questions:
1 How relevant are out standards?
2 How do we justify the way we do things?
3 How competitive are we?

All three questions had to be answered by Texas Instruments in the USA after they failed to win a federal contract because their warehousing costs were too high. A benchmarking study to identify 'best practice' has resulted in process and productivity changes raising performance by 40%.

Key parameters

The three key parameters of logistics performance, identified by Professor Christopher and developed by the other speakers, are:
- Customer Service
- Cost-to-Serve
- Asset Investment Utilisation

According to Alan Braithwaite, the warehouse is a functional component of the 'Cost-to-Serve'. In Figure 2, he details the factors which drive warehouse costs. The 'Cost-to-Serve' components in the centre column were described by him as 'constraints which can be managed but probably not significantly changed by the warehouse management.' It is the management determinants - the design, customer commitment, orders and inventory and efficiency and effectiveness - which impact on the 'Cost-to-Serve'. Figure 2 demonstrates that 'the warehouse is a complex environment with many dependencies.' He reminded the delegates that as a result care must be taken to ensure that 'unreal comparisons' are not made.

FIGURE 2 Warehouse Cost-to-Serve

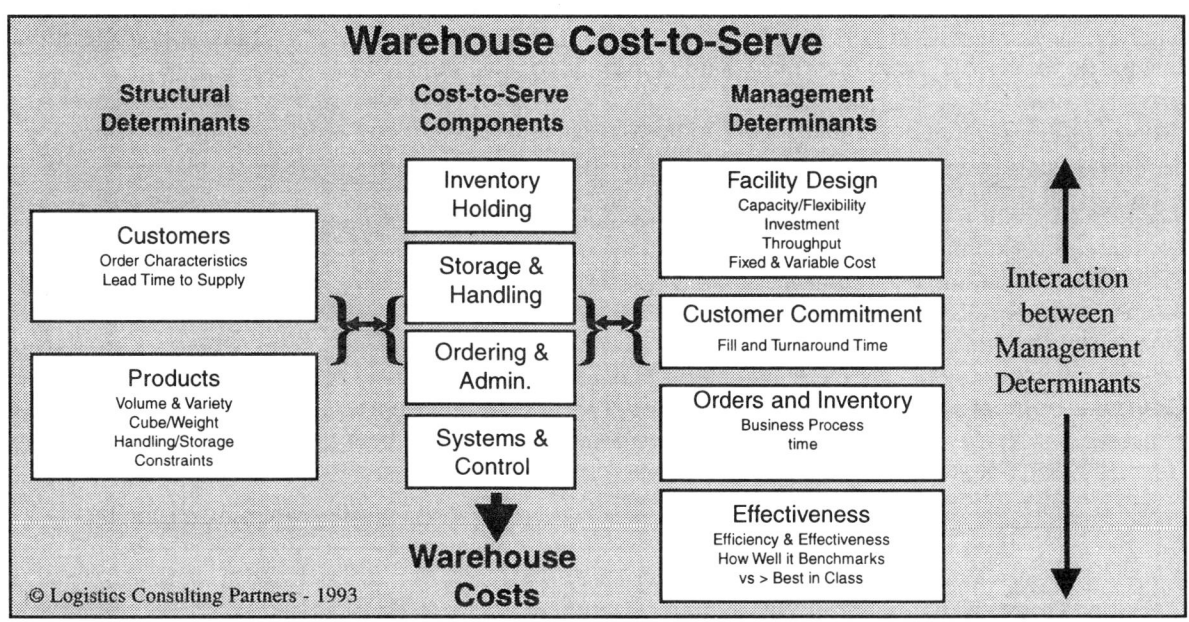

His key measures to evaluate benchmark performance are customer service and productivity, which incorporates Christopher's 'Cost-to-Serve' and 'Asset Investment Utilisation'. He demonstrated how the internal performance of the warehouse can impact on the profitability of the company. For example, the speed and accuracy of order fulfilment can raise customer satisfaction; high stock accuracy leads to improved productivity; lower inventory reduces space costs. Under present accounting rules these benefits are not obvious.

Customer service measures, such as first time order fill rate, order to delivery cycle time and line item availability, to be meaningful, should be measured against customer perception of, for example, the product, the speed of response and quality of documentation. Failures which appear can then be fixed. He quoted a company which appeared to complete orders first time on 98.2% of occasions; on-time performance against commitment was 92.3% - not bad, but performance against what the customer actually asked for was 45.5% - catastrophic!

Advertised as a pragmatic day, the speakers provided a range of performance measures against which to benchmark. Bill Brockbank proposed that a first measure should be stock accuracy as net stock errors are what the customer sees. Stock accuracy has benefits upstream and downstream as the manager of ASDA's Beers, Wines and Spirits store noted when mis-picks were down to 0.0015%

Compatibility of measures

Another recurring theme was the need for care when comparing measurements. Bill Brockbank suggested that they should reflect like-for-like, operations in a manufacturing company warehouse should not be compared with those of an importer. The Dexion benchmarking project has demonstrated that, even when comparing warehouse operations within the same company, measures may not be compatible. Stephen Newlands, the production manager, described how within Dexion it became apparent that there was a need to establish comparable definitions, even to the degree of 'what is a warehouse?' The company's UK warehouse operations are more diverse than in Germany.

Measures also differed between sites in the UK; for example, at Gainsborough, where high value products are handled, compared with Redirack, which handles simpler products manufactured to customers' orders. Gathering the data is only the beginning of the improvement cycle.

An audit of grocery distribution depots undertaken by staff at Cranfield University, and described by the university's Alan Rushton, demonstrated the extent of the data collection and analysis necessary to ensure meaningful results. The results of the study, not surprisingly, identified order picking as the highest operational cost area in all the depots. Picking performances varied from less than 100 cases to more than 320 cases per man hour. To understand the results, the different handling and information systems as well as lines per order and picks per order must be taken into account. A study of this type can be used to highlight major high cost or low performance elements in a single depot. But, as Alan Rushton stressed, care should be taken to ensure that differences can be adequately explained. To do this the benchmarking team must understand the logistics environment in which the warehouse is operating.

In conclusion

Agenda for action - 'Whilst the benchmarking process only reveals the performance gaps, it does present management with a tangible agenda for action'. *Martin Christopher*
From the customers' viewpoint - 'The best performance measures must always start from your customers' viewpoint.' *Bill Brockbank.*
Challenge the measures - 'Complacency must not creep into a benchmarking exercise - challenge every step of the way the measures being used.' *Alan Braithwaite.*
Compare against best in class - 'It is important to understand customer service measures in the context of external standards, a 48-hour delivery from order receipt is not appropriate if the competition is gearing up to next-day delivery.' *Alan Braithwaite*

About the author:

Christine Rowat is the Technical Development Director of the Institute of Logistics.

The roles of stock in logistics, the supply chain

by Anthony H Lines

The desirability of linking together the manufacturing and distribution activities of a business (now termed a 'supply chain') into a single, centrally co-ordinated system has long been recognised. JR Magee (Production Planning and Inventory Control - McGraw Hill 1960) described the design of a stable production and finished goods inventory control system and JW Forrester (Industrial Dynamics - MIT Press 1961) demonstrated the effect different forms of information and decision procedures can have on the inventory levels in a multi-stage distribution system and its associated factory workload. However, in all but the simplest of businesses, the adoption of these teachings has only become practical with the arrival of cheap and reliable computers and efficient means for communicating between them.

In logistics, as in other fields, unaided advances in computer hardware change little. The catalyst compelling industry to take logistics and supply-chain technology seriously - witness the dramatic growth in Institute membership - has been the transformation over the last decade in Western Europe economies from the situation where production facilities are often insufficient to meet customer demand, to today where, in many industries, there is a surplus of capacity. The recent recession has had some role in the reversal of a sellers' to a buyers' market but this has obscured the huge strides in production technology which have made the transformation to a buyers' market a permanent feature of Western economic life.

The industrial customer has become aware of his growing strength *vis-a-vis* his suppliers by the teaching of the concepts of Total Quality Management and Just-in-Time. The relatively high interest rates prevailing in the Western World have emphasised the importance of keeping inventories as low as possible and of making the maximum possible use of manufacturing equipment and other costly assets. The customer has learnt to look to his supplier to meet his requirements at very short notice and, in effect, to do the stock-keeping which, hitherto, he himself undertook.

Today, the manufacturer is thus faced with the following situation:
a) Customers expect to have their needs met at short notice
(b) In almost all cases, there are several alternative suppliers for any product, all of whom can offer similar quality of design and manufacture
c) Consequently, if a particular manufacturer cannot supply at short notice precisely what the customer wants, a satisfactory equivalent is almost always readily available
(d) There is now little product loyalty.

Many in industry now recognise the need to closely reconcile production plans with customer demand. The old production department attitude of 'we make it, you sell it' is giving way to a team approach where market needs and production capabilities are considered together and a balance struck which seeks to maximise overall company performance.

this article aims to examine the tasks of co-ordinating manufacturing and distribution activities so as to serve the end-customer efficiently and reliably at the least possible cost.

Pipeline or Supply-Chain concept

The flow of materials through a manufacturing or trading business from the supplier to the ultimate customer can be likened to that of a liquid through a network of pipes. The task of materials and manufacturing management can be thought of as co-ordinating decisions and actions such that an unimpeded flow through the factory and distribution system is achieved (see Figure 1).

In practice, the nearest this ideal is approached is in the process industries; some chemical transformations do proceed continuously from raw materials to finished products, and in a few instances distribution of the finished product is actually made by pipeline.

the majority of manufacturing and almost all distribution (except utilities) is conducted in batch mode, the consequence of which is to break up the flow into a staccato pattern. The more irregular such patterns, the more difficult it is fully to utilise production and distribution facilities without incurring penalties in terms of delays and inventory. Considerable efforts are currently being made to find ways of 'having one's cake and eating it', ie keeping facilities fully employed, customers well served and inventories low.

FIGURE 1 The pipeline of inventories

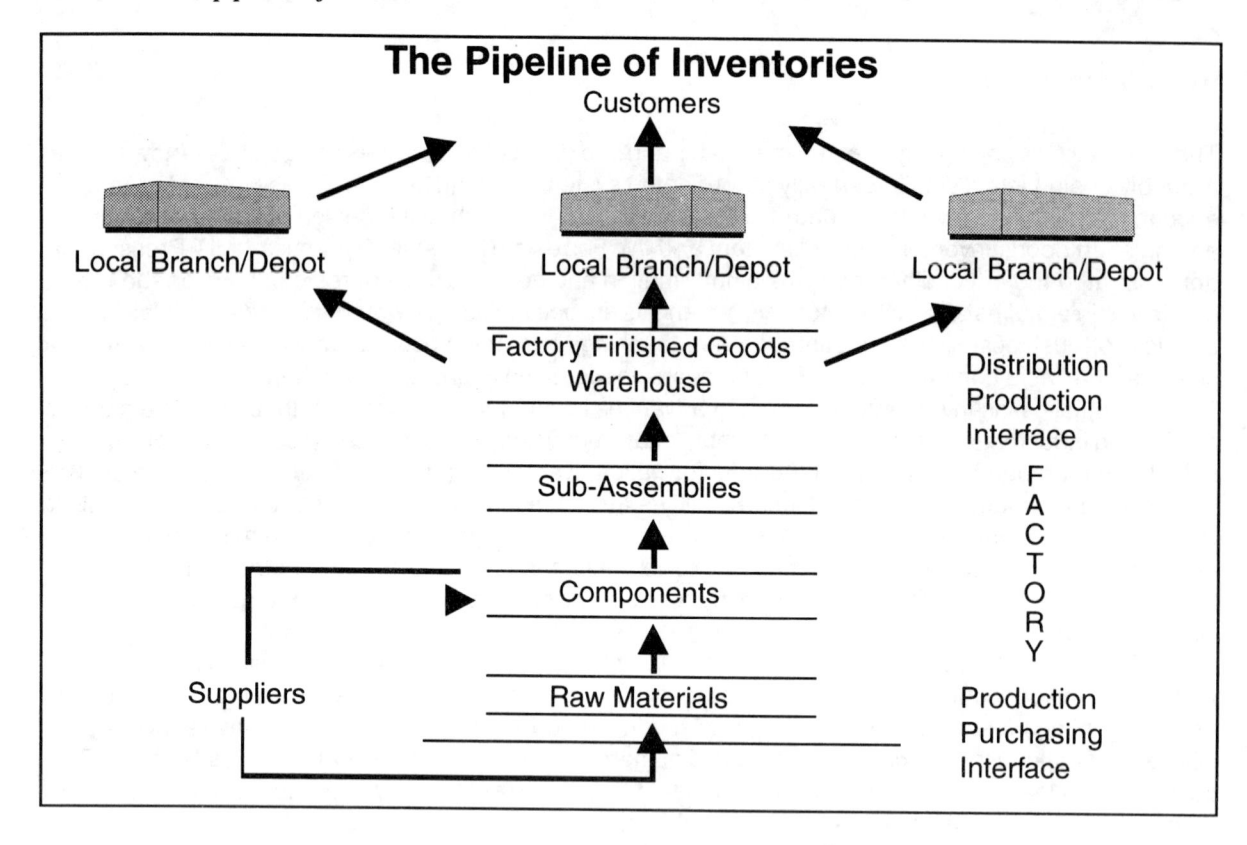

The Pipeline of Inventories

```
                        Customers
                           ↑
  Local Branch/Depot   Local Branch/Depot   Local Branch/Depot
         ↖                   ↑                   ↗
              Factory Finished Goods          Distribution
                    Warehouse                 Production
                        ↑                     Interface
                   Sub-Assemblies              F
                        ↑                      A
                                               C
                    Components                 T
                        ↑                      O
                                               R
                                               Y
  Suppliers         Raw Materials           Production
                                            Purchasing
                                            Interface
```

As customers for the manufactured products have become more conscious of the cost of carrying their own inventories, service has become as important as price in winning business. by 'service' is meant an amalgam of three features concerning the supply of goods.
1 Availability from stock (the percentage of demand met, on average, immediately from stock).
2 Speed and frequency of delivery (on demand, once a week, etc).
3 Reliability of delivery (eg within plus or minus two days).

The emphasis on these three aspects of customer service will vary with different customers and their market environments. to some, reliability of delivery will be more important than speed. This implies delivery from stock, even though delivery frequency may not permit immediate supply. In other situations, a fast, even if incomplete, response may be preferred.

An additional factor is the extent to which goods are made to order or assembled to order instead of being supplied from stock. This lengthens the delivery times; but, where product variety is large, it may be the only economical way for the manufacturer to operate. Thus, a 'trade-off' between product cost and customer service has to be made. If the market demands both low cost and prompt service, then manufacturers may have to specialise and confine their product ranges to what they can afford to make for stock.

Product range, whether made to order or supplied from stock, and the speed and reliability of customer service are three aspects of business strategy which influence the nature and the scope of the supply-chain management task. These factors are inter-related across the operational functions of:
- the distribution of finished goods
- manufacture
- materials and components purchasing

The order of the above list emphasises the 'pull' philosophy of supply-chain management. The customer dictates what is to be made and supplied, and when. Competitive forces have thus compelled many businesses to make the change from 'push' methods of operating.

The shift in objectives of manufacturing companies towards customer service and a 'pull' approach has led, in turn, to the re-appraisal of the suitability of many of the existing methods and techniques employed in the day-to-day planning, execution and control of production. In seeking to achieve a high level of customer service, the effective use and control of inventories is of particular importance.

The 'pull' approach makes necessary a re-appraisal of the role of finished goods stock in manufacturing. Previously, in some businesses at least, the finished goods warehouse was simply a staging post between production and customer. Now it has become the prime instrument in producing a reliable service too the customer. Since customer demand is mostly erratic and unpredictable, unless the finished goods stocks are sufficient to absorb the shocks and uncertainties of such demand, some of this variability will get passed through to the factory. Factories work most efficiently if their workload is kept even. Finished goods stocks, therefore, have the dual role of providing service to customer and ensuring that the factory workload is kept steady.

Service-driven Finished Goods Inventory Management

All companies record levels of stocks. The control of the levels, however, is often left to managers to decide on the basis of their experience and judgement. It is only when the general level of inventories exceeds set financial limits, however, that control is genuinely exercised - usually in the form of a directive to reduce the value of all stocks by some percentage figure. In contrast, an effective, scientifically designed control system aims to make certain that stocks held are at all times logically in line with what is required to meet the stated objectives, usually in terms of stock availability or 'service'.

One factor which makes effective inventory control a difficult task is that the replenishment of finished goods stocks either from a supplier or from one's own factory must be initiated before customer orders are actually to hand. The customer will not wait. Consequently, such demand must be forecast. For inventory control purpose, forecasts are only required for the period covering the time necessary to manufacture or to obtain replenishments, plus the time interval between successive reviews of customer requirements and stock levels.

Manufacturing is, or should be, initiated by the drawing up of a short-term production plan or Master Production Schedule (MPS). this is a statement of what has to be made to replenish stocks of finished products and/or to meet customer orders made to order. Its preparation entails first making a forecast of demand for each individual product.

A comment often made by factory managers is 'If only Marketing Department could forecast sales more accurately all would be well.' There may be little resemblance, in fact, between the forecast and what the factories are eventually asked to produce, frequent changes of schedule and panic action being the usual experiences.

The way such forecasts are prepared is often at the root of the problem. Traditionally, marketing departments have used the 'collective opinion' approach supplemented by discussions with their larger customers. This may suffice to provide 'broad brush' estimates for annual budgeting and sales targeting purposes, but is inadequate for inventory control and MPS. At best, collective opinion forecasts are inadequate for inventory control and MPS. At best, collective opinion forecasts are prepared quarterly and by product group, whereas for stock and production purposes they need to be by individual code number by month (in some cases by week). Lacking better information factories are often compelled to break down the marketing department forecasts themselves into the level of detail they required (how many green ones, and how many blue?) The 'top down' approach is highly unsatisfactory since it can only provide a forecast of the average level of demand, it can give no clue a to the size of error to be expected in the forecast for individual products. At individual product level and over short periods of time, a sales pattern may be very variable. If the sales of individual products are aggregated into a product group, this variability will become less pronounced and by the time the aggregation has reached company level, the sales pattern can look extremely stable. 'Bottom up' aggregation can provide an insight as to the variability to be expected at product group etc level but a 'top down' forecast cannot be used to determine the variability to be expected at individual product code number level.

Experience has shown that the best way of providing such detailed short-term forecasts is by extrapolation from past demand/sales/usage history supplemented by marketing information when unusual events, such as a promotion or price change, are planned. A considerable number of statistical forecasting techniques have been devised ranging in sophistication from simple moving averages to Box-Jenkins. One such method is that of lead squares by which a 'trend' line is fitted to historical data, as Figure 2 shows. A forecast is then produced by extrapolating the line forward over the period of time for which the forecast is required. The point to be considered is just what this forecast actually means. It is seen from Figure 2 that not one of the points on which the line is based actually lies on the line, some are above and some below. Consequently the forecast itself is unlikely to be correct. What one can say, however, is that if an envelope is drawn as shown, then there is a good chance that the forecast will lie between an upper limited 'A' and a lower limit 'B' and the range AB depends on the variability of the sales pattern on which it is based.

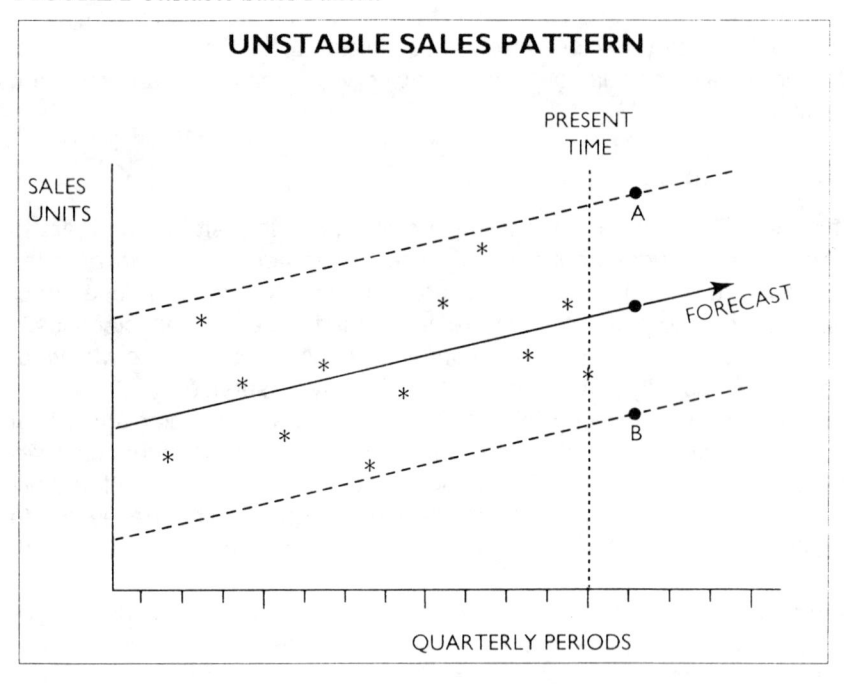

FIGURE 2 Unstable Sales Pattern

If the aim is to meet all, or most, customer demand from stock, then the size of such stocks has to have regard to the maximum likely level of sales not just with the average level. Statistically-based methods of stock control provide the means for determining how much more stock has to be carried (safety stock) than one expects actually to sell. In general, the greater the variability of the sales pattern on which the forecast is based, the greater the forecast error which can be expected and the larger the safety stocks that have to be carried to ensure that any specified level of customer service is actually met. Only by analysis of the actual variability of the individual product (and in the case of multi-warehouse distribution at each individual warehouse) can the size of forecast error and hence safety stock, be determined.

Forecasts by themselves, do not provide the factory with the proper basis on which to prepare a Master Production Schedule. This is because:

1. The factory needs to replenish stocks to the levels which will maintain the desired level of service to customers. This level depends on the forecast of demand, the safety stock, any change in safety stock necessary to maintain service targets, and any change in lead time.
2. Production has to be initiated before the time the stocks are needed to meet the sales forecast after allowing for stocks in the bin, on order or in process of manufacture.
3. If production is in large batches, two or three review cycles may elapse between the manufacture of successive batches.

For these reasons, Master Production Schedules cannot be prepared from forecasts alone but should be derived directly from the output of the inventory control system used to control finished goods stock levels.

Procedures for the calculation of the stock level required are well established. The amount of stock needed depends on the desired service level (see Figure 3), the level and variability of demand, the lead time and its variability, the time between successive reviews of stock and the average size of replenishment order. Figure 4 shows how, for example, lead time affects the size of safety stocks needed to achieve a given level of service.

The ideal system regulates stock control levels automatically, ensuring that customer service targets specified for each product are achieved and maintained, no matter how circumstances change. In fact, systems which incorporate control engineering principles (known as 'Hands-Off' systems) can almost achieve this goal. But, there are three practical factors which mean that automatic re-ordering cannot always work. The first is: The need to over-ride forecasts because of disturbances such as promotions and price changes. The second: Inaccurate computer data. The third: The supply source - especially one's own factory - being unable to deliver what has been ordered and within the expected time. Some of the steps which can be taken to match factory activity to customer demand more closely are discussed below and in the case study which follows.

FIGURE 3 Effect of Service Level on Safety Stocks

FIGURE 4 Effect of Service Level and Lead Time on Safety Stocks

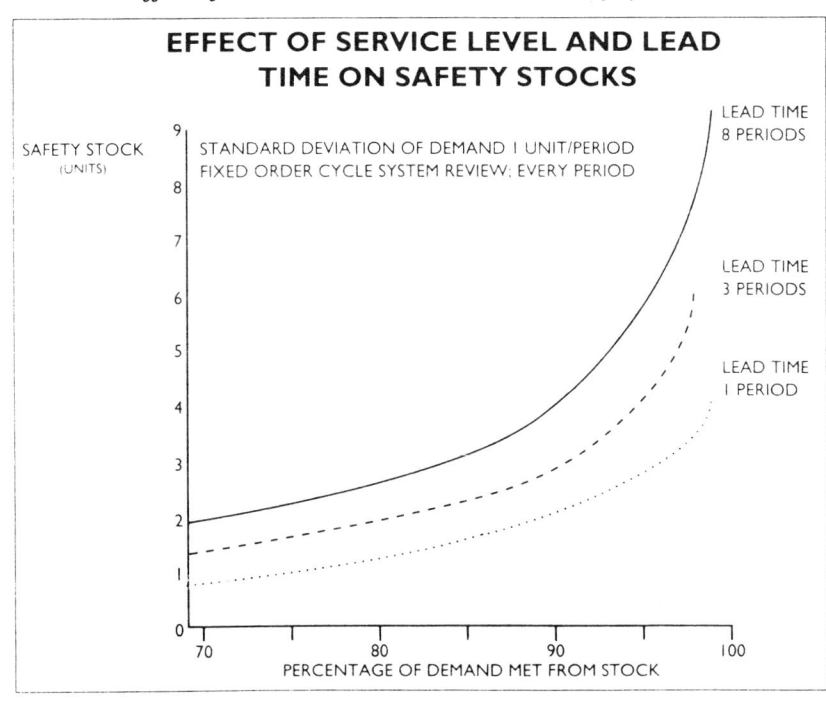

Influence of Production Decisions

Relating decisions concerning what to make, when and in what quantities with customer requirements and marketing objectives, has traditionally been a source of friction between the respective departments. Years of teaching Economic Batch Quantity theory (the Camp Wilson EOQ formula) and cost accountancy methods of analysis (which emphasise the need to get every last ounce of production out of each manufacturing asset) have led to many companies erring on the side of large batches.

ESAB Limited, the British part of the ESAB Group, who manufacture a wide range of welding rods, materials and equipment, have recently completed some studies on the effect of batch size on finished goods stocks, customer service and production performance. At their Waltham Cross plant they manufacture 580 types of manual metal arc electrodes, a large proportion of which are for sale from stock. Their aim is to meet 95% of customer demand for these products from stock, on average, and to this end they have installed a scientifically designed system of (finished goods) stock control. The vast majority of their product range is made to discrete batches as the demand for any one type is insufficient to justify continuous production.

Primarily to limit the load on quality control and the number of set-ups, the company determined that the number of separate production orders they would manufacture - and hence the number of set-ups and quality checks - should not exceed their current average. The question to be considered is: Could inventory levels be reduced, on average, while customer service is maintained? Would it be more economic therefore, to manufacture the fast selling items more frequently and the slow ones less often, in terms of the months of stock (MOS) which resulted?

Table 1 sets out the results of analysing the effect of batch size on stocks for a fast selling product, Product A. /This product averages sales of about 1400 cartons per month, its production is replanned weekly and the lead time from deciding what to manufacture to receiving the stock is 0.6 months.

These figures demonstrate, for the product in question, that the size of the batch has relatively little effect on the resulting level of finished goods stocked (MOS).

Table 2 shows the same calculations for Product B, which is much slower selling and whose sales average 1.6 cartons per month. Currently, this product is also re-planned every week and its lead time is 0.6 months. Table 2 shows that its average stock is very much more sensitive to batch size and the optimum batch size is one carton. The conclusion is that the slower moving items should be manufactured in much smaller sizes of batch more frequently, whereas for the faster selling products the size of finished goods stocks is not nearly so sensitive to batch size, at least within reasonably broad limits, to achieve the same level of service.

TABLE 1 Effect of Batch Size on Average Stocks of Fast-selling Product A

Effect of Batch Size on Average Stocks of Fast-selling Product A					
Batch size (Q) in cartons	1400	1000	718	500	325
Safety stock, for batch size Q	330	424	518	612	707
Average stock (SS + Q/2) cartons	1030	924	877	862	869
Average MOS	0.73	0.65	0.62	0.61	0.62

TABLE 2 Effect of Batch Size on Average Stocks of Slow-selling Product B

Effect of Batch Size on Average Stocks of Slow-selling Product B					
Batch size (Q) in cartons	100	50	25	1	0.37
Safety stock, for batch size Q	0	0	0	3	5
Average stock (SS + Q/2)	50	25	13	4	5
Average MOS	31.25	15.63	7.81	2.41	3.38

In most companies, the ESAB is no exception, average stocks are greatest for the slowest moving items as a comparison of Table 1 and Table 2 shows. This is because manufacturing departments believe it is not cost effective setting-up to manufacture except in a quantity which represents a certain run time on the machines. For ESAB the resulting MOS increases exponentially as the value of the sales by item reduces (see Figure 5 overleaf).

The point has already been made (Figure 3) that the amount of safety stock required varies with the square root of the lead time. ESAB explored the fast moving Product (A) the effect of cover period (lead time + review time) and batch size on the resultant average stocks. Table 3 shows just how important is cover period on the average stocks needed to maintain a 95% service level.

TABLE 3 The Effect of Cover Period on Stock Level (Stock to maintain 95% Service Level

The Effect of Cover Period on Stock Level (Stock to maintain 95% Service Level)						
Cover period	*Batch Size (cartons)*					
		1000	750	500	250	100
0.83	Safety Stock	424	518	612	754	942
	Half Batch Size	500	375	250	125	50
	Average Stock	924	893	862	879	992
	MOS	0.65	0.63	0.61	0.62	0.70
0.65	Safety Stock	375	417	500	625	792
	Half Batch Size	500	375	250	125	50
	Average Stock	875	792	750	750	842
	MOS	0.62	0.56	0.53	0.53	0.60
0.45	Safety Stock	243	312	381	520	624
	Half Batch Size	500	375	250	125	50
	Average Stock	743	687	631	645	674
	MOS	0.53	0.49	0.45	0.46	0.48

A major influence on manufacturing lead times is machine capacity utilisation. As utilisation levels are increased, the length of time each batch waits for its turn on the next machine also increases, as with any queuing situation (for example, traffic lights or supermarket checkouts). Higher utilisation, in general, leads to longer lead times, which, in turn, lead to the need to carry higher stocks. It follows that for some businesses it may be advantageous to invest in additional capacity in order to reduce lead times and so achieve lower levels of finished goods stocks. The value of the stock savings can outweigh the investment needed in additional capacity.

When one analyses the role of the factory in the supply-chain, decisions about capacity and the way it should be utilised in the factory often run counter to accepted practice and to the cost accountant's analysis. Good service to the customer can be provided with low stocks if the factory manufactures in small batches, keeps its lead times short, frequently reviews its production plans and, above all, sets capacity utilisation targets around the 70% - 870% level rather than at 90%-95%.

Continued...

Figure 5 Effect of Sales Volume on MOS

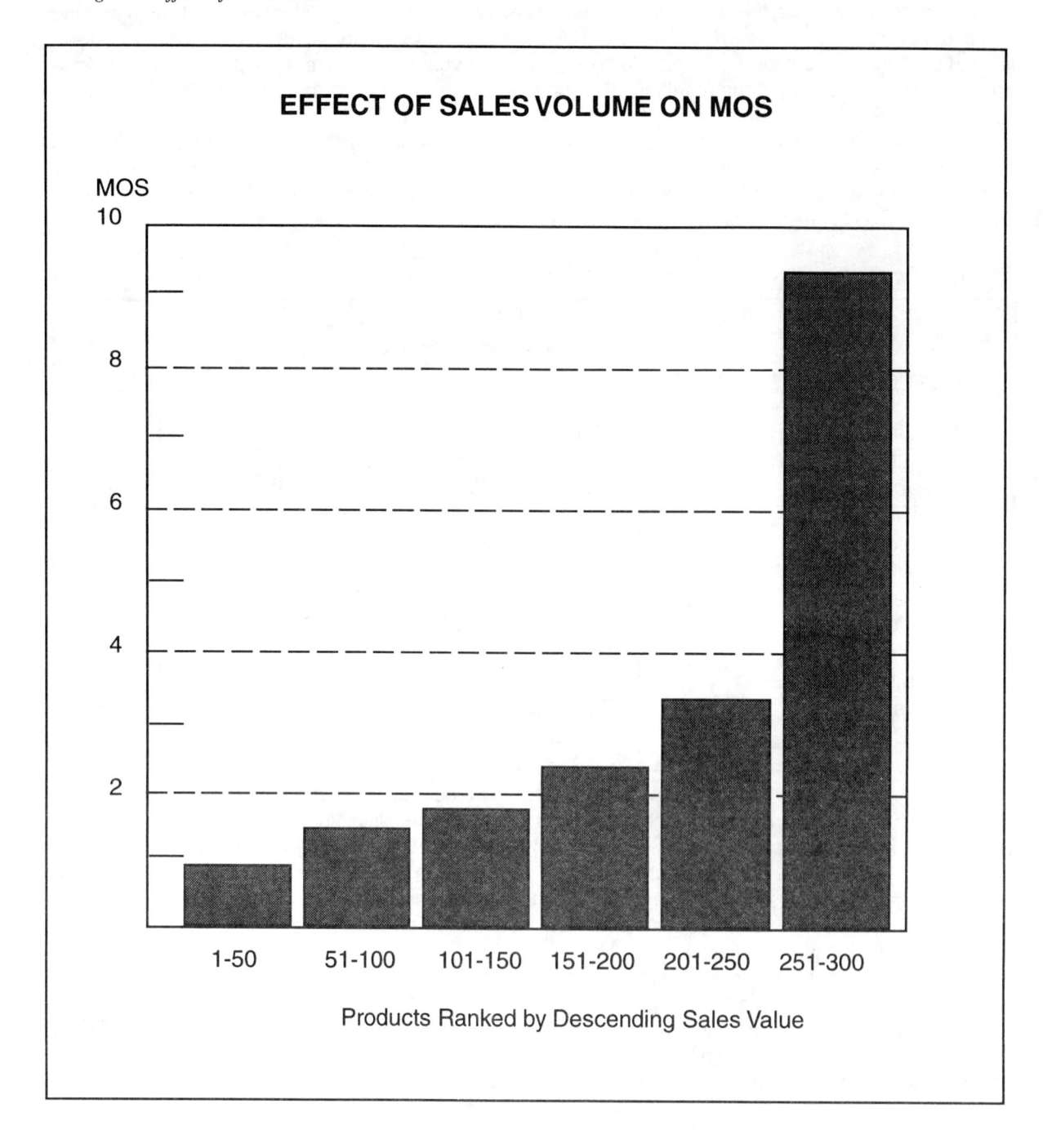

Case Study:
Co-ordinating the Supply-Chain

The study concerns Bonded Fibre Fabrics Ltd, a manufacturer of non-woven fabrics. Various grades of cloth are manufactured from the two main raw materials of rayon and polyester fibre into rolls of base fabrics which are either sold directly to other manufacturers or further processed and converted to consumer products. There are production constraints which dictate the scheduling sequence. There are two types of customer:
1 Industrial, supplied on a make-to-order basis.
2 Consumer product, supplied from stock.

The consumer product market looks for a high and reliable level of service and business is quickly won or lost, depending on the quality of the service provided.

Hitherto, the company initiated its production by preparing a weekly manufacturing plan. The plan was based on confirmed orders in the case of made-to-order fabric and production for stock was determined on a multiple of anticipated weekly retail sales. The sales forecast was simply the collective view of marketing and sales personnel. Mathematical methods of forecasting were not used and the accuracy, or otherwise, of the forecasts was not monitored. In consequence, the factory was often busy producing products for which there was no market whilst stocks of the currently popular items were insufficient to meet demand. For ex-stock items the company was only achieving a 70% level of service whereas customers are looking for 98%. The industrial business was also at risk because firm delivery dates could not be given to customers when an order was placed because the production schedule was only known for the current week; there was no guarantee that the order could be scheduled for the following week.

A statistically-based, service-level driven system of forecasting and inventory control was installed with priority given to the implementation of the high volume retail products sold to the most important customers. Initially, production capacity was dedicated to manufacturing the critical products for stock to the levels recommended by the new system - the strategy being to stabilise the supply to the main customers as quickly as possible and then to concentrate on bringing the remainder of the stocks in-line with current customer demand.

A feature of the new system was the generation of recommended forward stock replenishment quantities over a rolling six month horizon, updated monthly. These forecast replenishments were downloaded into a spreadsheet capacity planning system to calculate the likely production line and conversion machine utilisations. Made-to-order products were also set-up on the system so that forecasts for baseline production could be included in the capacity calculations.

Production could then confidently be moved to a monthly planning cycle for both base fabric and the downstream conversion processes. This gave sales order processing staff the benefit of being able to advise made-to-order customers of expected delivery dates.

At the outset, manufacturing lead times for the purposes of inventory control calculations were set conservatively and the company accepted the corresponding increase in inventory was the price worth paying in order to get customer service under control.

In the first two months of operation, finished goods stock increased overall whilst stocks were adjusted to the correct levels for the fast moving lines. Within nine months, all stocked items had been brought in-line with demand and finished goods inventories had been reduced dramatically by 50%. Service level targets of 98% had been achieve consistently and sales had, in consequence, increased.

Once the system had become stabilised, attention could be focused on fine-tuning and the scope for further improvements explored. For example, after a few months when the planning procedure had reached a steady state, it became evident which products tended to be scheduled for manufacture throughout the month and which tended to be scheduled for specific weeks. Lead times could be reduced from the original conservative values with consequential savings in safety stock. Another benefit of correctly controlling finished goods stocks which became apparent was the scope this gave for smoothing off the production workload. previously, when management spent their time battling to meet an ever-changing order boo, the perception was that there was insufficient production capacity.

Looking back from the perspective of a stable production environment has revealed that there is capacity for more machine set-ups and shorter runs. The company is know considering the possibility of moving back to a weekly production review cycle without the need for further investment in plant.

UK logistics excellence

by Douglas Marr. Throughout the 1980s, the commercial challenge for logistics was the application of a national strategy based upon a reduction in stockholding locations and fast response time affected by night-time trunking and high utilisation of vehicles. These developments were spearheaded by United Kingdom brewers and retailers and facilitated by the large mainframe computer systems that provided and transferred information upon which accurate decision making replace physical effort and inventory.

In achieving such national integration, the UK led Europe, possibly the world, and hence we developed national pride regarding our logistics competence compared to that of other European countries.

In my view, the national pride in our logistics competence that wass justified in the 1980s has developed into unjustified arrogance regarding our European competitors. The widely perceived view in the UK is that European logistics development and intellect lags behind our own.

In retrospect, the only salient feature of the integration of national logistics that can be attributed to the UK only was the emergence of 'cost-plus' logistics contracts. These could allow extravagant solutions to be provided at the expense of a principal locked into a long-term relationship. In mitigation, some of the reason for the establishment of such arrangements stems from a legal system in England which is unique compared to other European countries, in that it allows landlords to lock tenants into long-term leases unrelated to individual business needs or national business cycles.

FIGURE 1
The Euro-Groupage Alliance

The challenge

In 1991, I was appointed by a large German transport company, Thyssen Haniel Logistics GmbH, to establish a Contract Logistics Division in the UK. This was part of a plan to expand impressive national warehousing, transport and contract logistics operations into an integrated pan-European network with similar logistics activities across Europe to complement those in Germany.

My challenge was to attempt to sell the facilities and know-how of a European logistics company to a potential UK customer-base influenced by national prejudices and pre-conceptions.

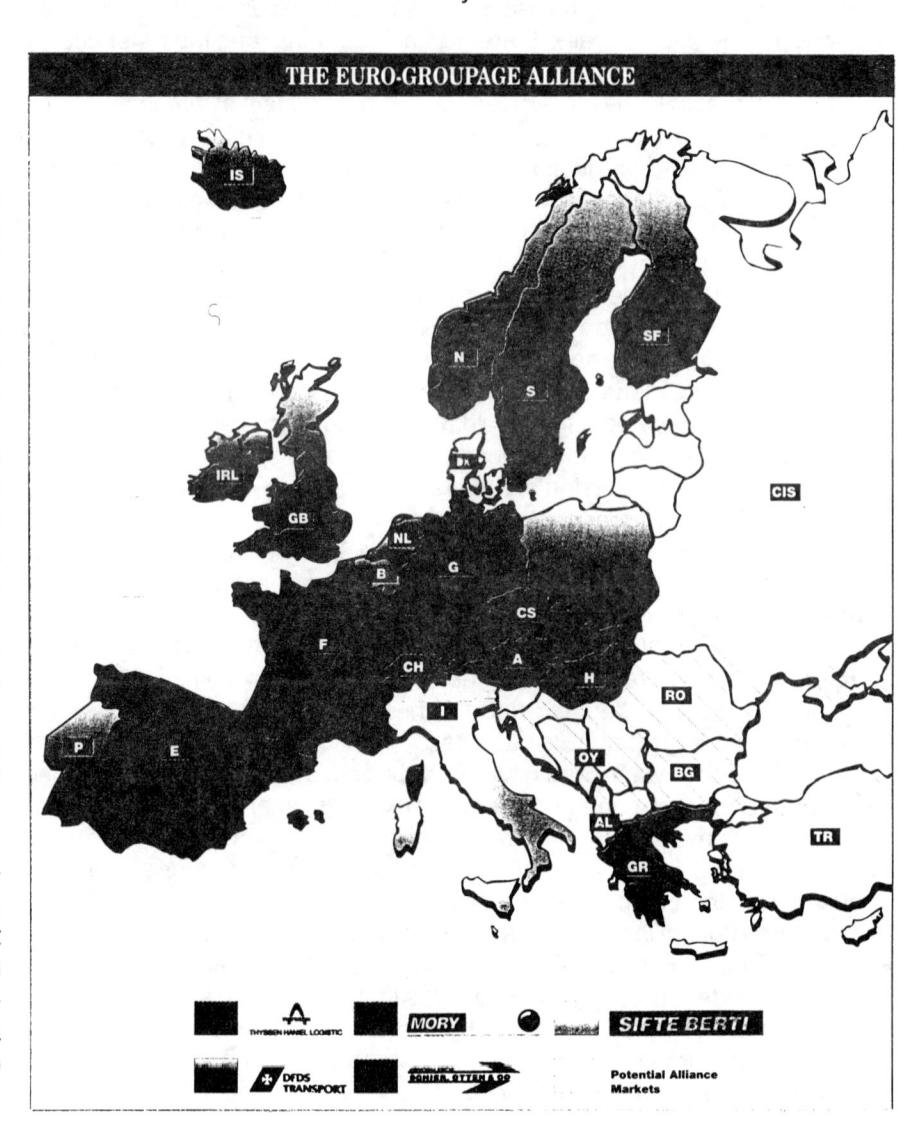

Political and economic change in Germany, linked to an appreciation that the integration of European operations requires a cultural strategy alongside a commercial one, led to the formation of TEAM, see Figure 1, in 1992. This alliance led to the transfer of my division across to the ownership and control of the Danish-owned DFDS Transport, another key member of the companies that make up the pan-European TEAM alliance, see Figure 2.

FIGURE 2 The Euro-groupage alliance

	THYSSEN HAMEL LOGISTIC	DFDS DFDS TRANSPORT	MORY	SCHIER, OTTEN &CO	SIFTE BERTI	TEAM EURO Groupage Alliance
Employees	6.460	6.100	5.868	400	300	18.128
Turnover (in Mio DM)	3.400	1.550	2.700	190	80	7.920
Terminals (in Europe)	65	45	110	8	11	239
Warehouse (in m²)	360	100	350	35	83	928
European Traffic	450	50	100	70	48	718

THE EURO-GROUP ALLIANCE

My brief, however, remained constant: to establish long-term logistics contracts in partnership with major blue-chip manufacturers. Generally, expansion of the division's activities via UK-owned and controlled companies has been difficult as a result of the preconceptions and prejudices to which I have referred.

Manufacturing opportunities

For this reason, I realised early in my new position that UK expansion would best be achieved via contacts established in mainland Europe via my Danish and German headquarters. I therefore sought to establish pan-European logistics projects involving large value-added activities in our UK depots.

Much of the supply chain integration that has been achieved in the UK has been led by retailers involving simple pick, pack and handling operations. My view then, and now, is that the major opportunities in the UK for supply-chain integration are in the manufacturing sector. The application of late configuration to reduce inventory holding and transport costs can now be affected as a result of the IT revolution of the last ten years.

To succeed in gaining third-party contract business for DFDS in the UK, it was essential that I found a niche that was not presently filled by any of our large UK based competitors. They could easily steal my thunder by taking any potential customer to another similar example of the required activity on these shores!

Case Study

There, in Germany in 1992, I initiated discussions with ITT Automotive in Bergneustadt to develop a concept for late configuration and sequenced JIT supply of bumpers on to an assembly tract to be commissioned in Coventry to produce the X300 model for Jaguar Cars. This model was to be the first of a new generation of cars behind the famous name manufactured under the guidance of Ford in the USA.

The project involved achieving quick response to the launch of a car body onto the Jaguar track in Coventry and initiating the sub-assembly of components in DFDS Birmingham depot with the subsequent delivery of this colour co-ordinated bumper set, to permit fitting when the car being assembled arrived at stations 104/105 on the Oracle. The possible different bumper derivatives totalled 136, according to the colour required, construction requirements for the country of use and whether a power-wash fitment was required. Each bumper involved the sub-assembly of up to 27 individual components sourced from factories in Germany, Sweden, Holland and England.

It was of paramount importance to Jaguar Cars that the volume requirement for bumpers be fulfilled to their exacting quality standards, which would achieve 'best practice' for a model range designed to compare favourably with the best from Japan, USA and Europe.

In action

In May 1994, as a result of two years of analysis, discussion and co-operation with ITT Automotive, DFDS Transport established a sub-assembly plant in its Birmingham Depot. This operation carried out the late configuration of components into the X300 finished bumpers for delivery into the Jaguar plant, regularly following receipt via modem of colour and specification details. The key to success was to successfully integrate Logistics operations with those of manufacturing.

To achieve this, DFDS recruited assembly staff made redundant by the company collapse at nearby Leyland DAF. Although the management-led LDV operation had emerged from the ashes of Leyland DAF to re-employ some staff, additional skilled operators were surplus to requirements and were snapped up by DFDS.

The management mix between DFDS and ITT proved the key to a successful operation. After several months of experimentation and division of project responsibilities between different managers from both companies, a sound management structure and division of responsibilities was confirmed. The key principle adopted was that ITT should lead the management and communication with Jaguar, supported in a seamless manner by DFDS. In this way, the correct controls and relationship were maintained between ITT and its 'Principal'. DFDS provided the facilities management, controls and transport co-ordination required to safeguard the interests of ITT Bergneustadt.

Logistics revolution

The key characteristic of the process of bumper supply to Jaguar is the 'pull' methodology compared to the 'push'. Before the logistics revolution, manufacturing companies operated to production plans and procedures which pushed products down the supply-chain, with a certainty based on the maintenance of volumes at optimum plant capacity and justified by sales forecasts over-ridden by operational expediency.

the brewing industry in the 1970s for example, was dominated by the influence of the 'Head Brewers'. The result was slack in the total system and inventory of finished product, which varied in quantity according to the time in the month, or the day of the week. Since then the 'Customer is King' philosophy has been facilitated by the logistics, IT and communication revolutions. Together they have allowed a system to develop where an end-user can now 'pull' products and components through the supply chain, when required, without the inventory inefficiencies previously present.

Our bumper operation, which applies the same methodology for all required components, is but one small part of a similar process carried out by our 'principal', Jaguar Cars, who 'pull' cars through their plant according to demand from their customers.

Space Race

A key personal objective that I identified early in my discussions in Germany was to introduce the efficiency of Japanese transportation expertise into the project. Anyone who has opened a container from Japan loaded with hi-fis or TVs will have observed the very high utilisation of container space that is achieved with fairly few centimetres of space between products and container. Such efficiency in space utilisation arises from its planning at product design stage.

We employed similar methods at the start of our co-operation with ITT. As a result of DFDS' influence from day one, stillage sizes were modified and trailer design changed to maximise cubic space to ensure that for all component transport between Germany and England, vehicles were full in the same manner as that achieved by our Japanese competitors.

In conclusion

I believe that the operation now established in Birmingham is the first example in the UK of an integrated manufacturing and logistics partnership, where the value-added activity of the company fulfilling the contract logistics forms a significant part of the end-product.

A truly integrated manufacturing supply chain process has been created. However, the operation established in Birmingham results from co-operation between a German-base manufacturer, a Danish-owned logistics company supported by companies in Sweden, Holland and Germany responding to the visionary approach to sourcing of an American-owned automotive manufacturer.

Therefore, when attending the Institute's Logistics Conference or even monthly regional meetings, where we reflect on our logistics excellence in the UK, it is important to be cognisant of our partners in Europe and competitors elsewhere in the world.

Douglas Marr is Divisional General Manager - Logistics, for DFDS Transport (UK) Ltd. He has particular involvement and experience in overall business development strategy for companies deriving and implementing pan-European based supply chains.

Chapter 6: Performance

Adding value - the purchasing mission

Stephen Cannon summarises the themes he has explored over the past year

At a time when organisations find themselves under increasing pressure to perform, it is obvious that they must get more for less from every pound which they spend. In these circumstances, the purchasing and contracts function should contribute even more markedly to organisational objectives than it has done in the past. It must use its kills and expertise to deliver value to the organisation of which it is a part.

A key feature which underlies the delivery of value is the relationship with the function's internal customers within the organisation. In many cases, purchasing and contracts work is a team activity involving both internal customers who have the requirement (to be satisfied from outside the organisation) and the purchasing and contracts practitioner who has the skills and expertise to ensure the contractual satisfaction of that requirement.

Previous articles have discussed the steps which might require attention in order to maximise the function's role as a contributor of value. These include:
- defining the value which the function can contribute, improving its own attitudes to change and flexibility, making its mission the servicing of the internal customer
- facilitating and guiding the purchasing and contracts activity, concentrating on those aspects where it can add value
- defining its goals and milestones in quantifiable terms
- measuring and auditing its performance
- enhancing the importance of communication and training, bearing down on its own costs.

Defining the value which the function can contribute

The purchasing and contracts function offers internal customers three qualities: added value, service and expertise. Expertise is used by the function to help it deliver *added value* and *service* (Figure 1).

Savings generated by the function are added value. There are many sources of savings and there are many different tools and techniques which can be use to generate them. They can be generated by the practitioners in the function working alone or by practitioners an the internal customers working together or by a collaboration of practitioners, internal customers and vendors.

The added value should be targeted. This means that a value which is required should be determined for a period, most likely the organisation's financial year. This Targeted Added Values should be a combination of a saving required by the internal customers and the cost of the function itself. Achieving targeted added value is thus a means for the function to deliver reduced cost to the organisation and also to recover its own costs so it is essentially a cost-free service to the organisation in which it operates.

The services which the function offers its internal customers need to be broken down into different types and an appropriate level assigned to each type. The important feature about the service types and levels is that they should be money-based. The benefit to be derived by the internal customer receiving the service should be quantified in money terms and so should the cost of delivering it. It is only if there is a net benefit that the service is worth delivering.

It should be noted that the process of deciding money-based service levels is collaborative. It involves the internal customer in the decision-making. Money-based service levels could be benchmarked against other organisations as a further check of the function's effectiveness.

Targeted added value and money-bases service levels are the two key sources of value which the function can define both at the generic and at the quantifiable, actual level. These two factors affect the vision, goals and milestones of the function, how it is organised, its relationships with internal customers, vendors and the top management of the organisation, its training and communications role, the size of the function, the remuneration of its staff and yardsticks for self-audit.

Attitudes to change and flexibility

An essential first step to implementing any major change is attitudinal change within the function. This really means accepting that there can be no sacred cows and that all previous attitudes, practices and techniques must be open to question, analysis and modification.

FIGURE 1 Offering the internal customer three qualities

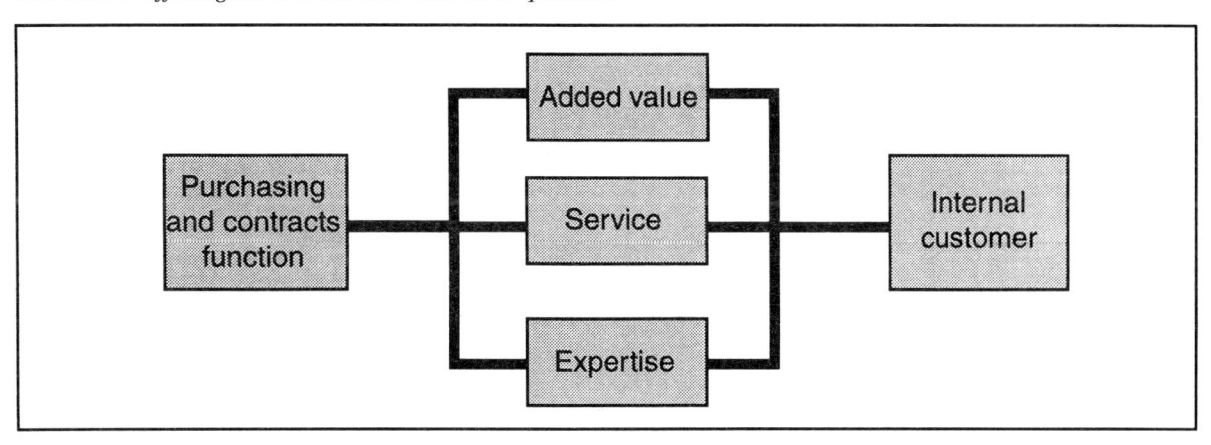

[Diagram: Purchasing and contracts function → Added value / Service / Expertise → Internal customer]

The management and practitioners have to be prepared to change the structure of their function and to change their ways of working. Changing the structure could mean the elimination of centralised departments, reduction in staff number and the deliberate abandonment of some traditional activities and responsibilities where the value added is small or non-existent. Changing ways of working might involve significant changes in working practices. The manager's role is likely to become more like that of a negotiator, facilitator and guide rather than that of a departmental master. The management style would be supportive rather than controlling.

At the practitioner level, the role changes to that it is more that of a team player rather than functional operative. To find the enhanced value that the organisation will require, the practitioner needs to work with and increasingly rely upon the internal customer whose needs he/she tries to meet.

It should not be taken for granted that the management of the function will internalise the need to change even if it knows the threats and opportunities facing the organisation. Individuals at any level in an organisation see change in different ways. Change which is handed down is often seen as enforced.

The degree of internalisation of any change depends often on the degree of involvement of the individuals in making the change. A key to developing commitment to the change process is the early involvement of the practitioners. Much of the responsibility for managing the change needs to be assigned to the practitioners.

In many cases, change will not be possible without altering the attitudes of the internal customers. If the internal customers do not co-operate in the change-making, then the function on its own will have difficulties realising the full potential. Close, collaborative working with internal customers is the essential supply partnership if there is to be a continuous upgrading of the value delivered by the supply chain. Much modern supply chain thinking assumes this relationship exists but it needs to be built and maintained like any other relationship.

Joint working sessions involving the internal customer and the function's management and its practitioners are recommended for exchanging views and clarifying attitudes. They should preferably be held away from the normal working environment and they should be linked to the development of co-operative contracts with internal customers. These describe and agree the change which is needed and they state the agreed requirements from the internal customer and the practitioner in order to support it.

Making its mission the servicing of the internal customer

Because of the importance of the collaborative relationship with the internal customer, the mission of the function is to service the internal customer's needs better, in the belief that this will improve the function's contribution to the organisation. Really understanding the needs of the internal customer and how they deliver value to the organisation is the key to value generation by functional practitioners.

To find extra value continuously, a collaborative effort will often be required with the internal customer. The building and maintenance of this collaboration needs to be adopted as a key task by the triumvirate of the function's management, practitioners and internal customers. As a result, practitioners become members of procurement teams to which they deliver benefits derived from their expertise.

FIGURE 2 - Collaborative relationships: the key

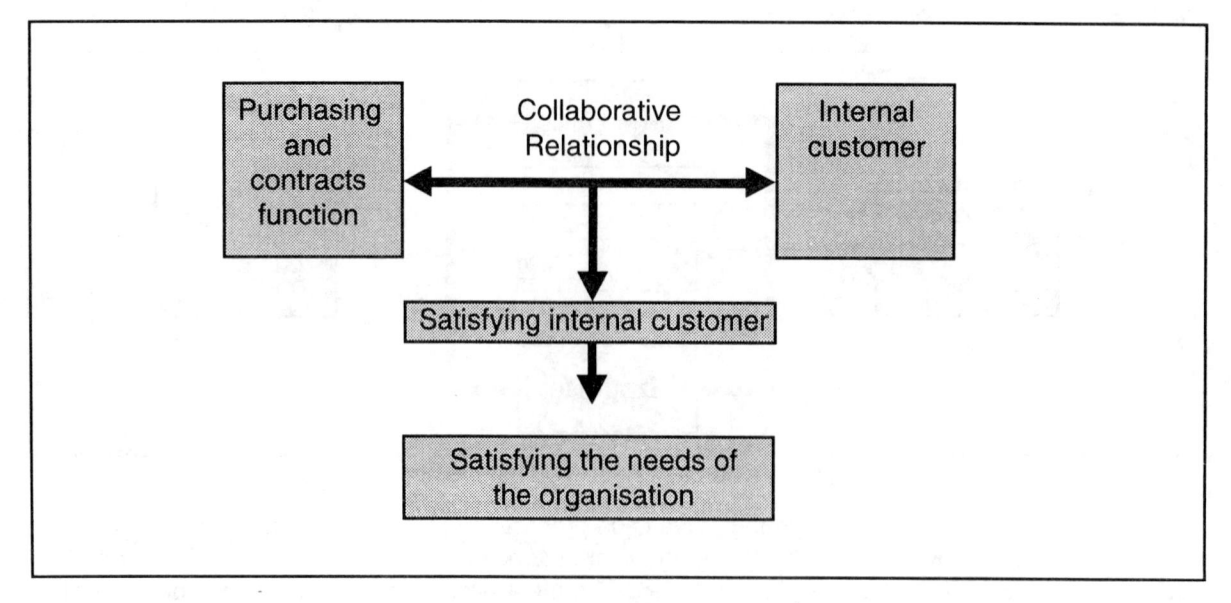

```
            Purchasing      Collaborative      Internal
              and    <——— Relationship ———>   customer
            contracts              |
            function               |
                                   ▼
                       Satisfying internal customer
                                   |
                                   ▼
                         Satisfying the needs of
                             the organisation
```

This changes the roles of the practitioners and the management of the function. It is the job of the function and its management to make sure that these teams work; it is the job of the individual practitioners to make sure that the teams are successful. There are techniques and approaches which help both the function and the practitioners to achieve these objectives.

Highly competitive markets drive the management of organisations to question the contribution of all parts of the value chain. Just to survive, organisations need to be bearing down on costs and enhancing the value of their products to customers. To grow, organisations need to be extremely successful both at bearing down on costs and at enhancing value. This state of affairs demands that the purchasing and contracts function manages it activityto meet these crucial needs of organisations. Targeted added value and money-based service levels are the vehicles for doing this. Possible sources of added value are:
- market imperfections arising from competition
- savings such as value engineering, rationalisation of product range, simplification of specifications or terms and conditions etc - usually arising through collaboration with the internal customer
- savings arising from ad hoc negotiations with vendors
- savings arising from partnership-style arrangements with vendors
- savings arising from discontinuities in the market or technology
- savings arising from new entrants and substitute products.

Facilitating and guiding the activity

The change from practitioners acting as individuals within a function to their being members of a team to which they contribute their expertise can be assisted by dispersing the practitioners among the internal customers whom they service. In effect, this means eliminating central purchasing departments and situating the practitioners alongside their customers. Such change is difficult and, without the change in attitudes which has been discussed above, it will probably be impossible.

the change of attitude, the co-operative contract and this dispersal are the three main planks to the transformation of the function into one which seeks to facilitate and to guide the purchasing and contracts activity. They establish a basis for practitioners to use their skills in conjunction with those of internal customers and sometimes with vendors to find new sources of value. The practitioners should be supported by an active purchasing and contracts research department which ensures that they remain at the forefront of new developments.

Concentrating on adding value

For the function to concentrate on where it can add value, the procurement needs of the organisation must be reviewed by means of the segmentation technique (Figure 3). This enables these needs to be split into those which can be purchased by:
1 The internal customer, with minimal active purchasing involvement from the practitioners in the function
2 which can be undertaken by the practitioners with minimal involvement of the internal customer
3 which should be undertaken as a joint exercise

In category 1 of the above list, the function limits its role to facilitating purchase by the internal customer. This facilitation might take the form of the provision of such things as credit card purchasing facilities, an IT purchasing system, standard terms and conditions etc. Money based service levels can be used to measure the efficacy of this help.

In category 2, the function seeks to find and meet targeted added value requirements as well as provide a service which might again be subject to the discipline of money base service levels. While the involvement of the internal customer should not be great, it is not non-existent. The search for targeted added value will often involve the internal customer, for example in such things as agreeing to rationalisation of requirements, simplifying specifications, use of new materials etc.

Category 3 requires complete collaboration with the internal customer. Again, both targeted added value and money based service levels can be applied. It is quite likely here that partnership arrangements with vendors could be most fruitful.

Defining goals and milestones

In many organisations, the principal management control of the function has been the departmental budget.

FIGURE 3 Review by segmentation

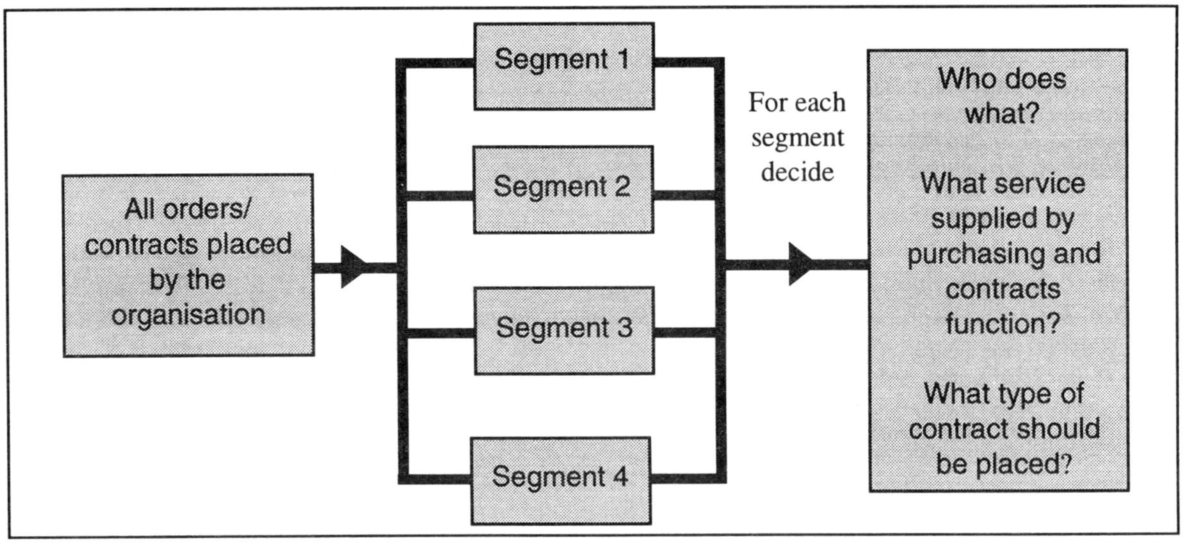

This is, of course, an important device for controlling manpower and costs associated with the work to be done. It does not target or measure achievement. To do this, it is necessary to define goals and milestones in quantifiable terms.

Goals are derived from mission statements. They are quantifiable targets for the function as a whole. They are derived in collaboration with the internal customer. For the purchasing and contracts function, the goals should include money based service levels and targeted added value (Figure 4).

In the case of targeted added value, the individual goals are determined by the management of the function with the internal customer, and then they are apportioned among the practitioners in the function by a process of negotiation akin to that used to agree a departmental budget.

Money based service levels are determined by the Practitioners with the internal customers. Safeguards are required to ensure compatibility across the function.

Measuring and auditing

The goals assigned to individual practitioners should be further broken down into milestones which can be used to measure performance. These provide a means for practitioners to measure and to control their own performance which can be monitored by the internal customers and by the management of the function.

Practitioners should be empowered to perform, but this does not mean that there should be a total absence of any reporting structure. Both the function's management and the internal customer will want to know what progress is being made in meeting milestones. It does mean leaving the onus for success or failure with the practitioner. Intervention by the management should always be a last resort.

Quantifiable milestones provide a way of auditing the performance of the practitioners and thus of the function. The objectives of the audit are help and improvement. They are not error or fault detection.

Quantifiable milestones provide a way of auditing the performance of the practitioners and thus of the function. The objectives of the audit are help and improvement. They are not error or fault detection.

The audit team reviews internal customer satisfaction. They monitor cross-functional compatability and benchmark against external organisations. The audit takes into account the markets and environment in which the organisation operates.

FIGURE 4 Missions and goals

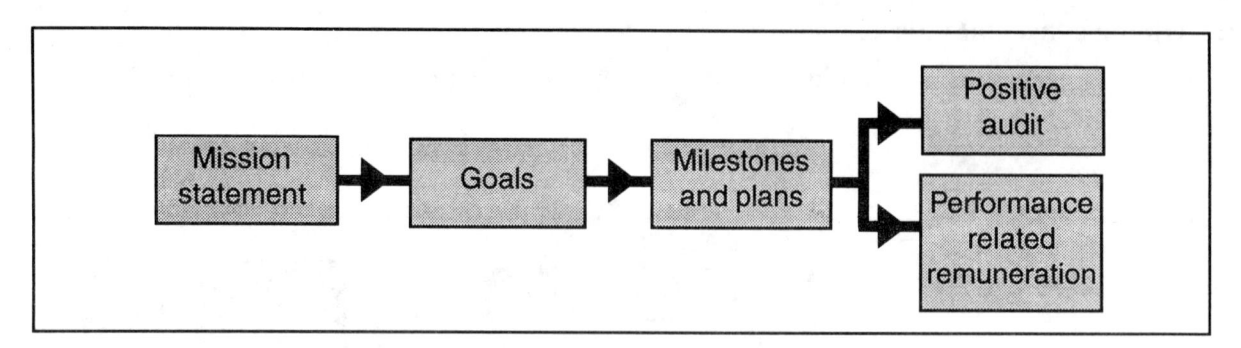

Communication and training

The perceptions of the various levels of management within an organisation to both the purchasing and contracts function and its work are important. The function should ascertain them an also seek the reasons for them. A four-box matrix of the perception of the importance of the activity of the purchasing and contracts function against the perception of the function itself can shed some useful insights which can be used as a basis for the formulation of a communications strategy.

The purchasing and contracts function is in competition with other functions for the ear of top management. To neglect communication is to risk losing or never gaining the support of the top management of an organisation. Training should also be an important part of the function's activities, in fact it should be a core activity, as it provides a means both of improving skill levels and of communication. Part of the activity of the function should be to conduct training so that all those involved in the purchasing and contracts activity understand all the fundamentals of what they are doing. This is particularly important for internal customers conducting their own purchasing. The purchasing and contract practitioner should provide training to support the internal customer.

However, the internal customer is only one of the five client groups which require training.

It is important that the top management are aware of the supply constraints which can affect the high-level strategy of the organisation. It is also in the function's self interest to ensure that top management understands the need for a skilfully undertaken purchasing and contracts activity. Training and communication to this level of management are cardinal tasks for the management of the function requiring both imagination and prudent use of opportunism.

The practitioners also need development, as the purchasing and contracts field is continuously improving. Much of the training will be the theories and practices of the activity together with the background to them. Some training should be devoted to supporting the practitioner in his/her important role as ambassador of the function.

The two other important client groups for training (and for communication), whose needs are often neglected and the external suppliers to the organisation, and the internal suppliers to the function. It is often assumed that these two groups will pick up what is required of them as they deal with the function. This is no substitute for dedicated training and, in both cases, the training provides a basis for partnership relationships.

Bearing down on the function's own costs

The costs of a purchasing and contracts function are usually people and people-related. It has already been mentioned that the function should provide cost free its services to the organisation as part of targeted added value. This stimulates the need to keep the manning levels low.

Segmentation should mean that fewer clerical staff are needed, as much of the purchasing work often undertaken by this grade of staff should be left to the internal customer. This avoids the need for pointless paper processing. Dispersal of staff and their empowerment should eliminate hierarchical structures which could reduce the need for supervisory staff. Money based service levels provide a brake on the costs associated with providing a service/service level because there should always be a net benefit. If there is none, there is no justification for the service/service level. Staff should only be retained provided they contribute to the net benefit.

A further way of controlling staff costs is to people the function so as to be able to achieve a certain defined level of added value. If additional value is identifiable, it should be sought using temporary contract staff and the possibility of peaking workload to make full use of this sort of staff arrangement is worth considering.

Managing quality and change - improving the purchase process

Bob Gilbert discovers that internal customers of a purchasing department do not value its services and his research shows major systems problems and no culture of continuing improvement

Dr Juran believes that it is imperative to develop the habit of making annual improvements in quality and reductions in quality costs. Without these, he suggests, an enterprise's market position can be eroded by competitors which have the habit.

This article looks at a sub-system providing goods and services to a typical service organisation where no such habit has developed. It suggests practical ways to improve the system that will show immediate benefit - without having to deal with the organisational inertia and complexity that can make revolutionary process re-engineering so painful..

Although the survey conducted for this article cannot be said to be academically rigorous, its results do suggest that purchasing has many 'soft' properties in the eyes of its customers. It also highlights the difficulty customers have in identifying quantifiable measures of output with which to measure the effectiveness of the process - or changes to it. Nevertheless, ways are identified by which customer perception of the service offered can be improved. Instances such as the customer interface, bottlenecks constraining the capacity of the system, resource wastage and the correlation between purchasing and the needs of its customers are important subjects to consider in improving performance and image.

The environment

No purchasing system can operate without regard for the internal and external business environments facing its customers. To take one example, if purchasing in BT took no account of recession, regulation and competition on the one hand or growing global communications opportunities on the other, it would not be serving the needs of its customers. But it is also true that a purchasing department divorced from the internal company environment would be equally out of touch.

Keeping in touch can involve considerable change. In BT's case, for instance, purchasing has had to move from a mechanistic to a dynamic process as it seeks to cope with globalisation, increase efficiency, reduce staff numbers and adopt modern staff practices. Alongside such changes a competent purchasing organisation will avoid the danger of over-emphasising internal demands, perhaps politically inspired, at the expense of managerial responsibility for a never-ending kaizen or Deming-like obsession with quality improvement focused on delivering long-term and sustained benefits.

The customer interface

As Bitran and Lojo point out in an article well worth reading, the customer interface is the 'interaction that will shape to a great extent the customer's perception of the service received, and so it can be viewed as the firm's 'moment of truth'[1].

But as Clark points out, the idea that a supplier or service provider serves the market is challenged by the concept of the providers' capabilities driving the market [2]. How often are potential customers driven to expedient solutions by time and resource bottlenecks in the purchasing system? The survey revealed that customer time spent 'queuing' is a pervasive element of the process.

If any customer has to wait, for even a short time, the quality of the service offered is inevitably compromised, at least in the eyes of the customer, through the failure to offer promised services dependably at the required time. According to Bitran and Logo this is a major weakness; they view reliability as probably the single most important dimension of quality. No matter how well the process caters for such elements of the interface as responsiveness, empathy, assurance, courtesy, credibility and security, any failure to deliver service when requested undermines quality offered elsewhere in the system. In today's economic climate, the time of purchasing staff is a scarce resource. Making more of available to customers dramatically improves the perceived quality of the service.

This truism is particularly relevant for purchasing since at the point of service delivery the needs and expectations of a customer are for outputs which can neither be judged for quality before consumption nor stored against future demand. Purchasing's outputs are 'perishable' and 'intangible'. This suggests therefore that a key purchasing output needed by customers is psychological support or reassurance.

This was investigated by asking a random sample of customers a range of questions about their qualitative needs as customers in such areas as:
- their perceptions of what makes a successful purchasing system
- what criteria they use to determine the success and failure of purchasing
- what criteria they use to measure quality in buying
- what criteria they use to measure the performance of purchasing
- what bottlenecks exist in the system today
- what added value purchasing gives
- what current purchasing activities do not add value
- what waste occurs

Output	% mentioning the output
regular feedback	80%
support and advice	70%
management information	55%
specialist knowledge and expertise	50%
contract library	40%
standardisation of contracts	35%

Although the results obtained are not statistically valid, they do indicate, among other things, that 'support and advice' was the second most frequently mentioned output (70 per cent of respondents). This, and the 80 per cent mentioning 'feedback' act as a challenge to traditional ideas of purchasing's role of 'purchasing and supply'.

Customer needs identified in the survey reinforce this challenge. 'Negotiating' for example was mentioned by only 60 per cent of respondents, whilst 'placing contracts' scored lower still. Even 'specialist knowledge' was mentioned by no more than half of respondents.

Need	% mentioning the need
removal of burden	85%
problem solving	75%
meeting agreed timescales	70%
gaining competitive advantage/negotiating	60%
specialist knowledge and expertise	50%
placing contracts	50%
anticipating problems	40%
managing suppliers and relationships	25%

Customers appear to want support, psychological and physical, rather than 'purchasing and supply'. other findings support the argument that purchasing needs to adapt to the needs of its customers if it is to enjoy success and support within customer and parent organisations.
- about one-third of interviewees by-pass the purchasing system from time to time to meet urgent requirements
- about two-thirds of interviewees were confused by the purchasing process and almost half did not understand the financial authorisation process
- most people felt they have no influence over rationing and prioritisation of resources within purchasing
- four-fifths of interviewees felt the process was too slow.

Bitran and Lojo offer six phases in a typical service encounter:
  1 access   4 service delivery
  2 check in   6 check out
  3 diagnosis   7 follow up

They argue that maximising customer satisfaction involves designing quality into the system delivering each phase. How does your organisation deliver them? Most purchasing organisations observed by the author can offer no more than ad hoc reactions.

Hughes suggests organisations are diverse and complex beasts operating in an uncertain and changing environment. He argues they have to meet many competing demands from customers, employees, the state and shareholders. In such circumstances Hughes believes that: 'it is simplistic to think that there can be a single, overriding objective. As a consequence, organisations have to develop a series of objectives to cope with their various responsibilities'(3).

But such a diversity of objectives can lead to purchasing being out of step with its customers. Such disharmony is common; and it leads to a lower perceived quality of service. Goal alignment is an important step in improving the quality of service offered. Without clear and formalised links with customer departments, purchasing's influence on planning and action is at best marginal. Without documented objectives agreed with customers it is unlikely that improvement targets will coincide with customer needs. If purchasing sets objectives for itself without reference to those of the system it serves, it cannot be said to be part of the system.

FIGURE 1 shows the current purchasing process

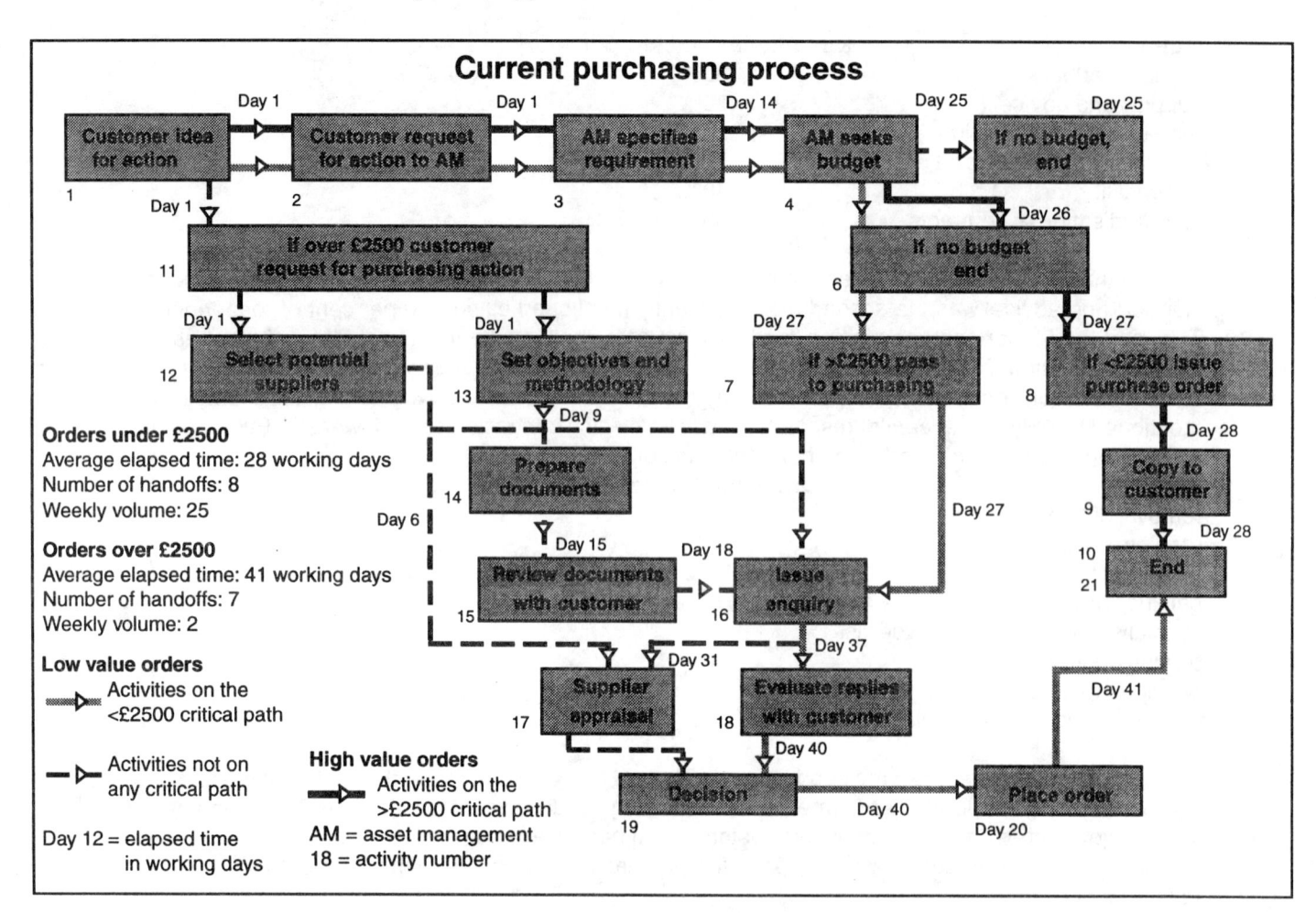

The current system

All purchasing systems are sub-systems of their parent company. As such, its task is to support the company 'primary activities' through its 'sharing activities' and its involvement in 'transferring skills' across the company value chain (4).

Purchasing in a service industry can be categorised as a continuous batch system. A typical system, illustrated at Figure 1, on average consumes over 5 weeks, *not including the time from order to delivery,* in processing a customer order.

Although often a complex task, a flow diagram of the process can identify such horrors as the lack of feedback loops and the baleful influence of sub-systems such as those managing assets, specifications and compatibility and obtaining financial authority.

Operations control defined by Ray Wild as '... concerned with the implementation of a predetermined operations plan or policy and the control of all aspects of operations according to such a plan or policy'(5) is often entirely lacking. Without an aggregate capacity plan and a master operations schedule purchasing will always be a system that is reactive and ill-matched to the demands made upon it.

System capacity

The capacity of a system is ultimately determined by the capacity of the bottlenecks within it. There are bottlenecks visible in Figure 1.

Given customer expectations of the service (see tables above), it is unlikely that they will see much added value in it. It is neither timely nor informative. It could hardly be called supportive, and the atmosphere of delay in the service encounter is not likely to delight the customer. The process wastes huge amounts of time, in queuing, in hand-offs, in specifying requirements and in obtaining authority. It inevitably wastes manpower - either through excess capacity or through reacting to external stimuli caused by insufficient capacity. In either case, it is due to a lack of capacity planning. It is wasteful of methods through its reliance on a sequential process flow from one department to the next when parallel activities could be arranged and it also wastes the time and resources spent on around 10 per cent of customer input which fail to receive financial sanction. The cost of these to the organisation should only be calculated by those with strong nerves!

FIGURE 2 reveals the proposed purchasing 'ideology'

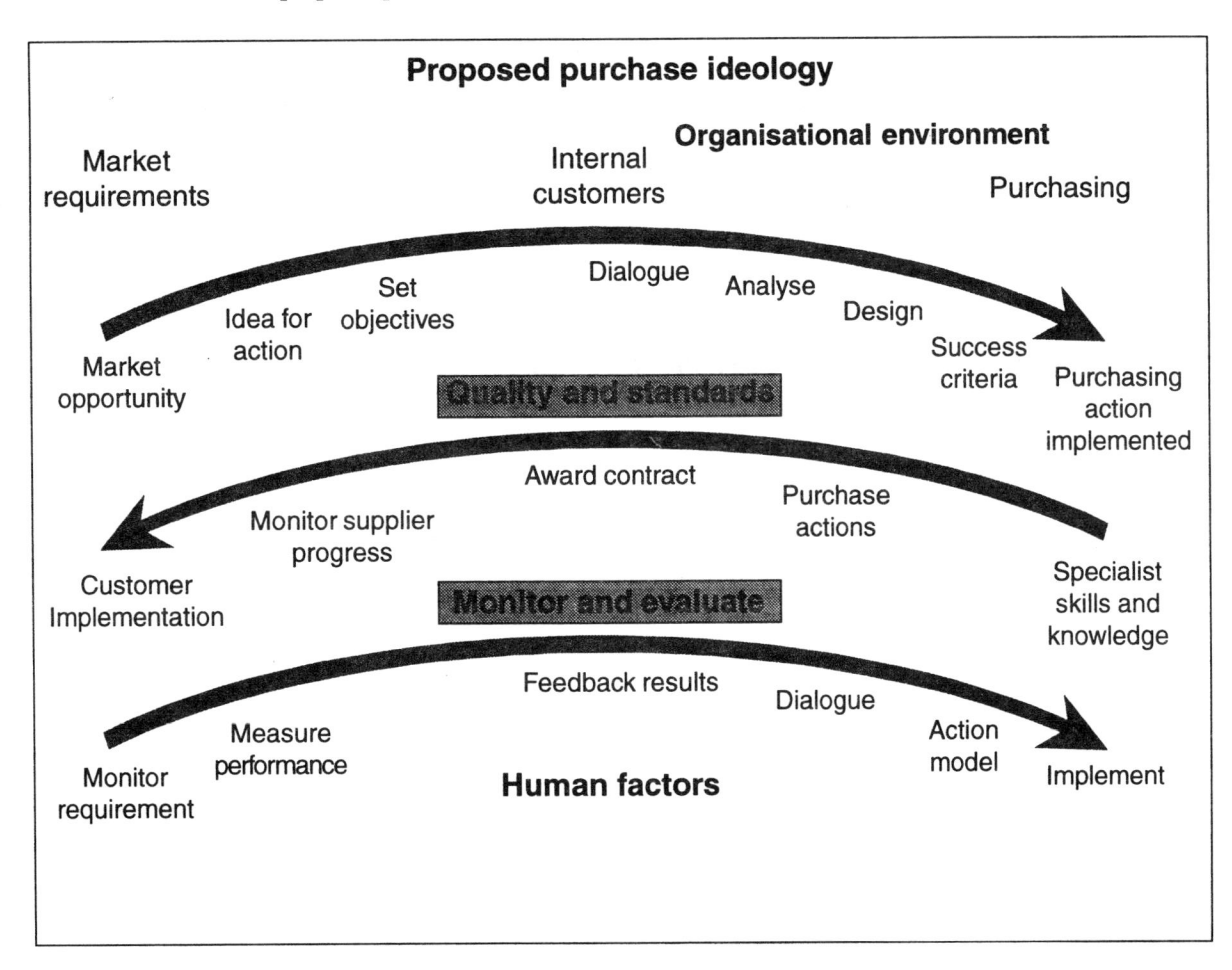

Proposed purchase ideology

Organisational environment

Market requirements — Idea for action — Set objectives — Dialogue — Analyse — Design — Success criteria — Purchasing

Market opportunity → **Quality and standards** → Purchasing action implemented

Customer Implementation ← Monitor supplier progress ← Award contract ← Purchase actions ← Specialist skills and knowledge

Monitor and evaluate

Monitor requirement ← Measure performance ← Feedback results ← Dialogue ← Action model → Implement

Human factors

Waste exists at all levels and each and every cause of it should be targeted for improvement and change. After all, even at the simplest level, as Bitran and Lojo point out 'just improving the customer's waiting experience offers great potential for increasing satisfaction'.

An improved process

Ripley & Ripley suggest that 'all employees must be allowed to share in the responsibility for quality improvement and customer satisfaction'. They continue: 'Competitive strength is now derived from the ability to deliver quality, variety, customisation and convenience in a timely manner'(6). This suggests that the vision of purchasing should bee to deliver its outputs in a way that involves employees in satisfying customers' needs.

Without such a vision, purchasing will not know if its direction is that which customers want. Without it, process improvements will be reactive and late. The development of a vision is crucial to the longer-term success of even the most short-term improvement.

Such a vision is suggested in Figure 2. It proposes a draft ideology for purchasing. It should be viewed as a continuum along which market requirements, internal customers and purchasing travel from identification of a need to its fulfilment. The degree of involvement of each will vary as activity moves along the continuum, but all parties at all times have a stake in and can influence the process. Capacity planning and operations scheduling underpin achievement of the vision.

Developing and achieving such a vision will cost resources, but not providing them will result in change efforts being no more than empty exhortations. This, in Deming's view, is useless, meaningless and no more than an abdication of management responsibility since '....it takes no account of the fact that most of the trouble comes from the system'(7). Most purchasing processes have dissatisfied customer. Despite difficulties, they must change. If purchasing does not change, customers will by-pass them

References

1) 'A framework for analysing the quality of the customer interface', Gabriel Bitran and Maureen Lojo, European Management Journal, Vol 11, No 4, December 1993, p385
2) 'Managing change: back to basics or quantum leaps?' GJ Clark, *Management Services*, September 1993, p12
3) 'Operations management - an introduction', Christopher Hughes, *The Breakthrough Series*, p48
4) 'From competitive advantage to corporate strategy', Michael E Porter, *Harvard Business Review*, May/June 1987
5) 'Production & Operations Management' Ray Wild, 4th Edition, *Cassell Educational*, 1992, p290
6) 'Empowerment: the cornerstone of quality', Robert E Ripley and Marie J Ripley, *Management Decision* 39, p2
7) Quoted in 'Managing for total quality', N Logothetis, *Prentice Hall*, 1992

The road to purchasing excellence

Russell Syson looks at the problems of measuring purchasing performance

It has been said that where you find change, there you should also find measurement. The two go together. There is no aspect of management that has changed more rapidly in recent years than purchasing, and in no field has interest in performance appraisal been stronger. Yet, although largely as a by-product of the introduction of computerised processes, most organisations have at least some kind of measurement system in place, it is generally agreed that there is no single accepted overall framework. There is also a particular difficulty in a number of specific areas. For example, everyone claims that integrating the supply chain brings big benefits, but how do we know? John Crampton, partner at Ernst and Young, claims that manufacturing companies can make savings equivalent to some 30 per cent of total costs. Terrific if you can do it! Even more terrific if you can prove it!

To help bridge the gaps in our understanding, CIPS staged a major conference in London in September 1995. This was designed to examine the kind of performance measures currently used by leading companies and to critically evaluate how well they work. EDI, purchasing performance in high tech companies and the provision of services figure among the many topics came under the spotlight, as will the secrets of setting up and developing meaningful measurement systems. Fourteen professionals shared their experiences, warts and all, in the cause of raising standards in the profession.

Underlying the conference is the realisation that in the modern organisation, purchasing is presented with challenges which are quite different to anything that it has faced in the past. Probably more than any other area, purchasing holds the key to many of the problems posed by fierce global competition and to the ability to sustain or improve profitability. Generating innovative solutions to the problems posed by customers calls for an in-depth understanding of developments in supply markets, for close integration and risk-sharing with suppliers, and for the ability to assess just how well you are doing.

Key issues in purchasing

To play a full part in achieving corporate success, purchasing people need to address a number of key issues. Specifically there is a need to understand just what the core competences of purchasing really are. Are buyers simply negotiators, always on the lookout for a good deal and a saving or is there something more? There is a lot of talk about partnership and supply chains. How well equipped are we to quantify the benefits? And in an age of corporate re-engineering how do we come to terms with new structures which by their very nature can make the synergy and the leverage which we prize so highly more difficult to achieve?

Central to this whole question of the role and future of purchasing is measurement, and here it is possible to argue that in many companies we suffer not from too few measurements but from too many; and those that we have are frequently the wrong sort. Most computer systems, whether designed to provide company-wide management information or as part of MRP approaches, produce basic purchase data. Much of this is used for purposes of comparison against internally determined standards hopefully providing evidence both of transactional efficiency as well as highlighting commercial 'successes'.

As however purchasing becomes more central to the achievement and maintenance of competitive advantage, so it becomes necessary to develop new metrics which are both more relevant and more sophisticated. Qualitative assessments of key areas are needed which compare not just with internal standards but also with best practice in the wider world. Benchmarking becomes an integral part of strategies deigned to gain and maintain competitive edge through mapping the current position against competitors as the prelude to setting realistic 'stretching' targets. It generates a mind frame for continuous improvement by stimulating challenge in an organisation.

Achieving best practice in purchasing

As essential preliminary to any assessment of measurement practices is to identify a coherent framework within which measures may be systematically related to other purposes which they are intended to serve. There is little point in assembling a ragbag of measures related neither to each other nor to business need. Performance measures must meet the requirements of the organisation whether it be in the public or private sectors. Moreover they must also reflect changes in those requirements and be the basis for both development and improvement.

So what determines the kind of buying best suited to any organisation? In essence three main factors may be identified. The most important of these and indeed the main driver of change in purchasing is the degree of competition which is being experienced in the end market. It is no coincidence that the electronics industry is held up so often as a breeding ground for good purchasing practice. The forces of competition force this. Businesses which are competing on the basis of flexible response to customer need and of product innovation, businesses which combine high development costs with ever-shorter product life cycles, need to push their own expertise up the supply chain to chosen suppliers. This process of itself destroys the old notion that, as competition has its own inbuilt performance safeguards, there is no need for other forms of measurement.

The rate of technological change also forces organisations to review the place of purchasing within the organisation

Take aerospace as an example. The place of procurement in Rolls-Royce today bears no comparison with even 10 years ago, and the monitoring of purchase performance there reflects the sophistication of the industry. With some 75 per cent of an aero engine fabricated out-of-house, Rolls-Royce know full well that the performance of its suppliers is crucial if it is to compete with its rivals and that adequate performance measures are central to its success.

Complexity in supply markets also helps to shape the role and place of purchasing. Advanced processes require advanced suppliers. Quality is everyone's byword today, and quality of supplier performance demands quality of buyer performance.

Customer-supplier relationships based upon analysis of the supply base and upon actively practised supplier management call for purchasing professions with a flexible approach founded upon multi-functional and multi-cultural experience. Such people rightly reject the notion that there is but one approach to the supply base. It is as simplistic to imagine that partnership is a universal panacea as it is to think that competition in either its traditional form or in the guise of 'Lopezism' represents the key, But in any event, performance standards must be set and agreed with suppliers and their ability to meet those standards monitored.

A framework for purchasing management

The factors described determine the internal focus of purchasing and are central to an understanding of the process of effective measurement. Internal focus (Figure 1) defines the relationship of purchasing to the needs of the business. From it we can derive both critical success factors and also the changing kinds of supplier relationship. These three factors must be brought into balance with each other.

FIGURE 1 Making the transition (by courtesy of Serevent)

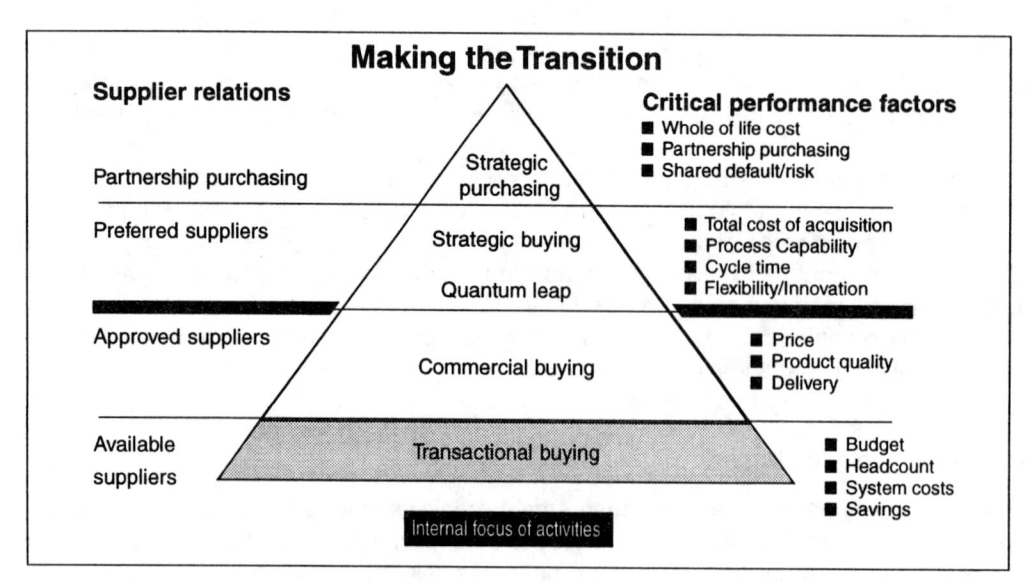

Making the Transition

Supplier relations	Pyramid level	Critical performance factors
Partnership purchasing	Strategic purchasing	■ Whole of life cost ■ Partnership purchasing ■ Shared default/risk
Preferred suppliers	Strategic buying / Quantum leap	■ Total cost of acquisition ■ Process Capability ■ Cycle time ■ Flexibility/Innovation
Approved suppliers	Commercial buying	■ Price ■ Product quality ■ Delivery
Available suppliers	Transactional buying	■ Budget ■ Headcount ■ System costs ■ Savings

Internal focus of activities

Organisations which, through neglect or ignorance, allow them to drift apart face either a loss of competitive edge or a period of trauma as some new broom (probably drafted in from marketing!) attempts to redress the years of neglect. This can also of course be the outcome of business process re-engineering but in either case the underlying requirement is the same. Purchasing must be positioned to reflect the needs of the business, and as those needs change, so purchasing must change with them.

Purchasing focus is in fact not only the key to purchasing appraisal but also to that programme of continuous development which leads to best in class, and ultimately to world class. All organisations should seek the former, but in reality only a few either can or need to aspire to the latter. Those who do should reflect on the words of Senor Lopez. He claims that improvements (in cost) of 5 or 6 per cent per annum are not enough. Change of the order of 30 to 40 per cent is needed. Kaizen, he has said, is out: the quantum leap is in. Of course, Lopez speaks in the context of an industry under threat from the Pacific rim and from the position of being a market-maker but his sentiments contain a message for us all. The quantum leap in the area of purchase is the change from commercial and transactional buying, practised by over three-quarters of organisations, to the strategic buying which tomorrow needs. The quantum leap is not just a question of techniques or skills. It demands a fundamentally different vision of the future and the drive to turn such vision into accomplishment. Measurement provides the yardstick, but it also initially identifies the size of the challenge which purchasing faces.

Making the transition

The different areas of focus and the critical success factors attaching to each provide us with a coherent framework for measurement. Transactional buying still characterises most smaller businesses as well as much of the public sector. With a focus on order placement purchasing is organisationally fragmented, seen as an essentially clerical activity, with little coherent management information. Purchase activity is virtually an overhead with the cost of buying and, in particular, headcount the principal preoccupation. The growth of computerised systems has however led to the replacement of the view that costs should simply be related to the volume of throughput by one which relates departmental cost to savings. Keki Bhote has for example said that in Motorola, a figure of 4 to 1 applies, whilst a savings to purchase cost of 3.7 to 1 was attributed to Mobil Europe in 1993.

Some three-quarters of all purchase organisations have a transactional or commercial focus. All too often measurements in the latter home-in simply on price based savings, not wasting too much time considering whether this is the most appropriate basis. Of course no-one denies the importance of availability but, based on inspected quality and progress-based delivery, its measurement can be rudimentary and often uninformative.

Performance measures of this type are short term and in many cases damage the cause of professional purchasing by pandering to that macho view of supplier relations which still dominates much management thinking. Purchase co-ordination in these cases is largely restricted to major spend items. There is inadequate understanding of the importance of supplier selection, whilst failings are largely obscured by old-style expediting and progressing. Whilst some basic management information is produced, the costs of such non value-adding activities are rarely highlighted or related to the areas which give rise to them.

The change from commercial to strategic buying is both a question of style and substance. There are great differences in the vision, the ambitions and, above all, the calibre of purchase management. This is reflected not just in the greater awareness of underlying issues but also in the much higher profile of the measurement process.

Strategic buying calls for active supplier management, for a change of approach from price to cost-based buying. Total acquisition costs are relevant to all organisations practising strategic buying, whole- life cost to those with project or capital equipment orientation. Cycle time progressively becomes more important than simple supplier lead time, whilst in the domain of quality the emphasis moves from an emphasis on product quality to process capability. It is recognised that the product can be no better than the process, and that the right relationship between the latter and the purchaser's specification is the key to satisfaction. Effective operational and management information systems are in place, augmented as appropriate by reference to outside expertise through the use, for example, of operational audit.

Up to 25 per cent of purchase organisations fall within this category, and it is not too fanciful to suggest that up to another 25 per cent ought to do so. The final 5 per cent which look to world class performance through strategic purchasing are actively engaged not just in developing individual suppliers but in managing whole supply markets. When organisations are working with their suppliers upon jointly capitalised ventures, purchasing must become an integrated activity supporting business strategies and contributing in a very direct way to overall performance. Measuring that contribution is both complex and time-consuming. It involves the assessment of whole of life costs, for the evaluation of approaches to supplier management and to partnership and, increasingly, for qualitative judgements based on comparison with both competitors and best practice. It represents the pinnacle of the measurement process (Figure 2).

FIGURE 2 What must be measured (by courtesy of Serevent)

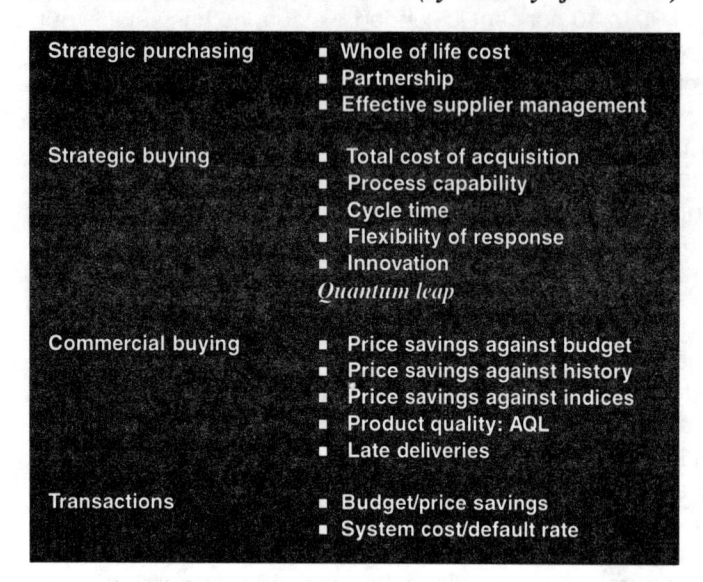

Strategic purchasing	■ Whole of life cost ■ Partnership ■ Effective supplier management
Strategic buying	■ Total cost of acquisition ■ Process capability ■ Cycle time ■ Flexibility of response ■ Innovation *Quantum leap*
Commercial buying	■ Price savings against budget ■ Price savings against history ■ Price savings against indices ■ Product quality: AQL ■ Late deliveries
Transactions	■ Budget/price savings ■ System cost/default rate

Benchmarking strategic purchasing

Benchmarking is in many ways the most effective means of assessing the quality both of strategic buying and of strategic purchasing (Figure 3). When organisations such as IBM declare their conviction that purchasing has become a major competitive weapon, the need to evaluate activities and processes against the performance of other organisations, ideally those achieving international best practice, becomes obvious.

FIGURE 3 The road to world class (by courtesy of Serevent)

THE ROAD TO WORLD CLASS

Strategic purchasing
- Purchasing organisation supports business strategies
- Suppliers partnership
- Purchasing contributes to overall business performance in terms of cost, quality & service
- Benchmarking

Strategic buying
- Supplier management being practised
- Seen to cut total acquisition costs
- Emphasis of cycle time
- Effective operational and management information systems

Commercial buying
- Focused on price reductions/negotiations
- Some co-ordination (major spend items)
- Basic management information
- Availability on demand

Transaction buying
- Focused on order placement (clerical)
- Organisationally fragmented
- No management information
- Purchasing seen as an overhead

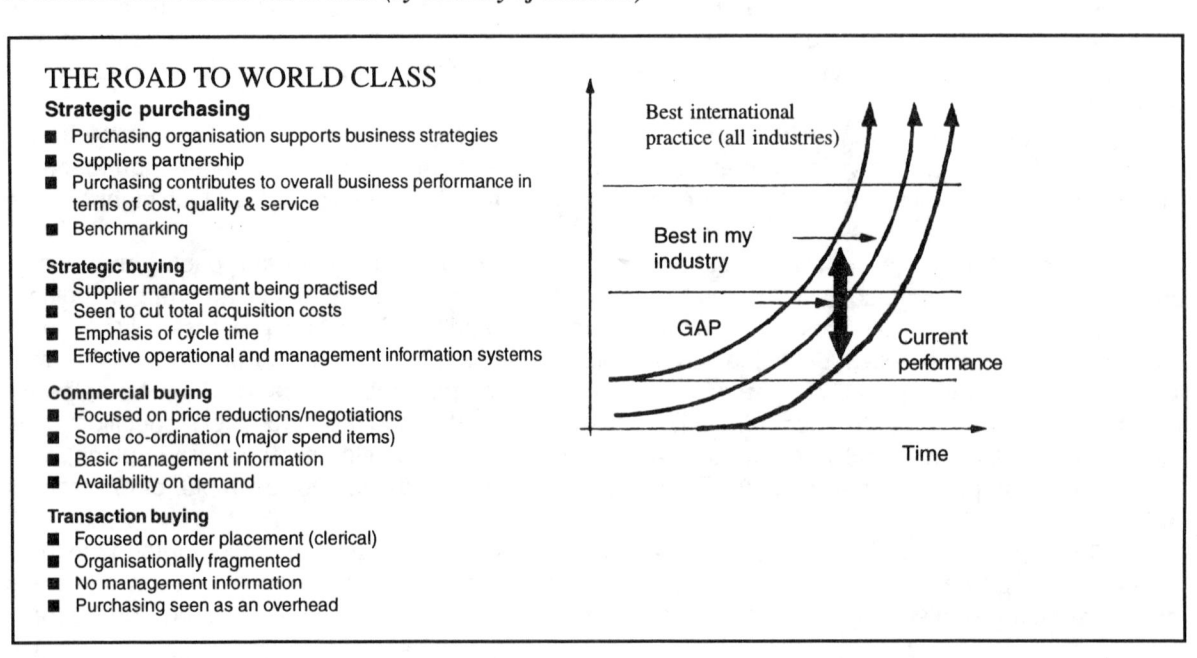

Benchmarking calls for the analysis of processes into activities, which may be compared with best in class. The secret is to focus on carefully selected areas which will produce both those 'quick wins' which will secure senior management commitment and also a steady benefit stream in the medium to long term.

Benchmarking calls for the analysis of processes into activities which may be compared with best in class. The secret is to focus on carefully selected areas which will produce both those 'quick wins' which will secure senior management commitment and also a steady benefit stream in the medium to long term.

Benchmarking is too frequently misunderstood, and it is important that it should be underpinned by an objective audit of purchase functions. This will identify those areas where competitive comparison is most needed. Outside assistance is here usually beneficial as is the search for those against whom comparison will be made. So far as the latter is concerned, firms like Motorola have found that the confidential sharing of experience on a reciprocal basis, even amongst potential rivals is less uncommon than might be supposed. It is this step however that frequently seems to pose most problems to would-be benchmarkers and where consultant assistance can be most valuable.

From comparison emerges the performance gap and with it must come an understanding of the practices which create superior performance. Based on this understanding is the identification and implementation of such remedial measures as may be necessary. This is not a one-off operation and involves the continual monitoring of performance.

Benchmarking for the purchasing process

Open your minds to the possibility that others may have better ways of buying, says Eric Evans

For at least the last 15 years management consultants have been describing purchasing in negative terms. Marketing consultants have said that purchasing decisions are heavily influenced by apathy and inertia, corporate planning gurus have described the function as administrative and even purchasing consultants have labelled purchasing as reactive and unimaginative. But in 1994, purchasing has been dragged, in some instances by the scruff of the neck, to the point where it is truly concerned with managing external manufacturing and service provision. Purchasing is now contributing to organisational wellbeing by improving supplier quality, instituting Just-in-Time delivery, establishing electronic trading and quick-response supply links with suppliers, and of course reducing total cost of bought-in goods, equipment, materials and services.

These improvements have flowed, in part, from greater managerial awareness of topics such as TQM, Supply Chain Management and Just-in-Time. Managers addicted to continual improvement have continued to search for better ways of doing the basic things. These managers are neglecting the conference venues and learned journals in favour of visits to other organisations. Benchmarking has arrived.

How widespread is it?

In 1991 the International Benchmarking Clearing House conducted a survey into the extent of benchmarking in the US. The figures suggest that it is of increasing significance to American industry:
- more than 75 per cent of respondents believed that benchmarking activity had increased within their firm over the past year
- 96 per cent of those respondents expected the level to continue increasing
- almost 80 per cent of respondents believed that firms would have to benchmark to survive
- 95 per cent of respondents believed that most companies do not know how to benchmark.

In the UK a survey by the CBI in 1992 revealed that:
- 66 per cent of survey respondents said they were benchmarking
- 82 per cent of these said that it was successful
- 68 per cent said that they would be doing more benchmarking in the future.

What is benchmarking?

The finding in the American survey that 95 per cent of respondents believe that companies do not know how to benchmark is not surprising. There is much confusion and misunderstanding of benchmarking. It is not industrial tourism, it is not industrial espionage, and it will not provide quick-fix solutions to problems.

It is easier to define what benchmarking is by looking at its history. In the 1950s Japanese industry was still trying to re-establish itself. In the eyes of the Western world, products from the Far East were cheap and unreliable. The Japanese approach to these problems was to visit European and American businesses and learn as much as possible about the business processes used by other organisations. At the time many critics accused the Japanese firms of copying products. While this certainly happened, the biggest benefits which Japanese firms secured was an understanding of how Western businesses differed in their approaches to marketing, manufacturing and distribution. In addition to copying, the Japanese improved the processes they saw. They did not content themselves with observing processes in their own industrial sector, but sought to drag best practice from one industry into another. Thus were the seeds of benchmarking sown.

Rank Xerox in the late 1970s found that its dominant position in the photocopier market had been lost to Japanese firms. Its response was to benchmark its key business processes and to adopt better business processes wherever this would be beneficial to the company. Ford in the late 1970s and early 1980s followed a similar path with its 'After Japan' campaign, which sought to appraise critically its key business processes in comparison with other firms and to absorb and adopt changes which increased its competitiveness.

Benchmarking is an approach to continual improvement. Where it has been most successful, it is a structured, rational process which has senior management support and which involves the establishment of standards and targets. There are examples in purchasing where companies have attempted to benchmark by comparing prices paid for purchases. This can be beneficial, but it is an area fraught with problems. The most powerful form of benchmarking is concerned with comparison of processes, rather than input or output measures. By benchmarking processes a manager will frequently identify a better way of doing a task which will impact upon prices, stockburn or perhaps staffing levels.

So how do you benchmark?

As with most things, a structured and planned approach will yield a higher return than simply setting out to visit other firms. Figure 1 suggests an eight-stage approach which has been proved to work and deliver significant improvement.

A pre-requisite of benchmarking is to secure the commitment of the senior management team within the organisation. Quality gurus will tell you that quality improvement projects are apt to fail without senior management commitment; so it is with benchmarking. The reasons for this will be made clear later.

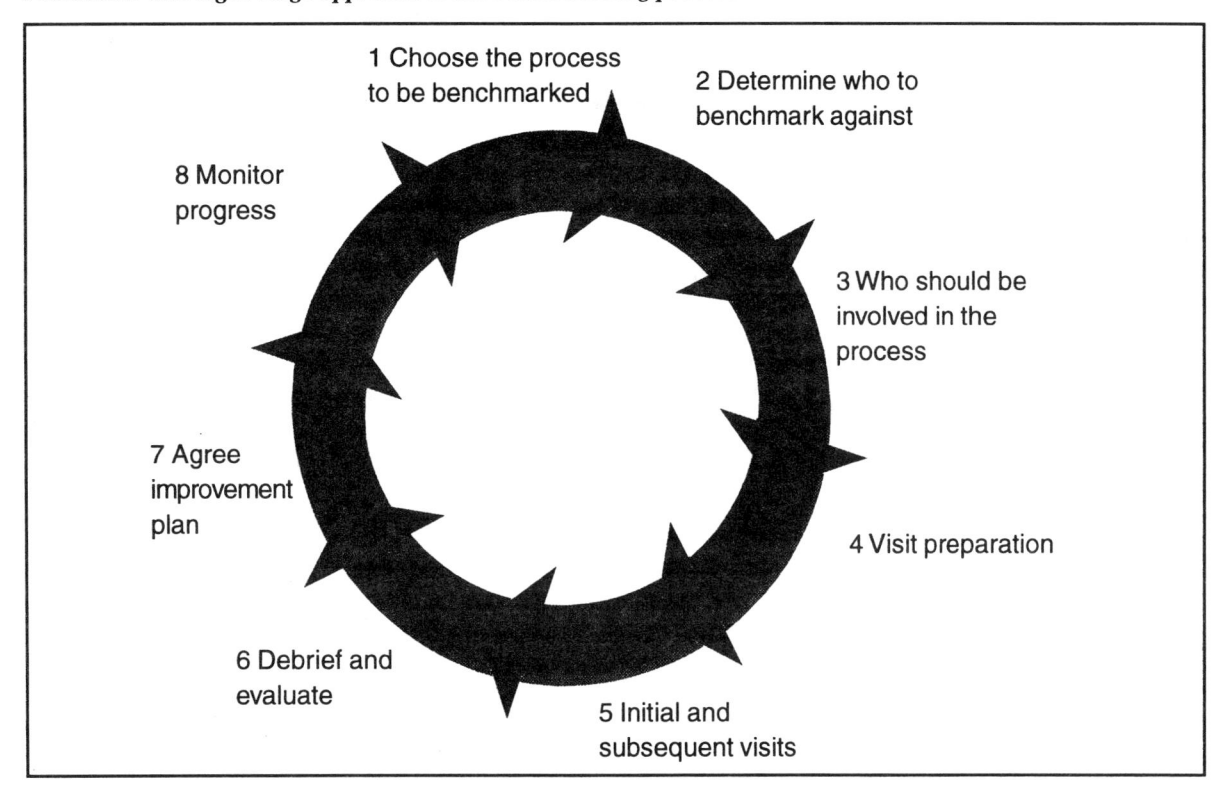

FIGURE 1 The eight-stage approach to the benchmarking process

1. Choose the process to be benchmarked
2. Determine who to benchmark against
3. Who should be involved in the process
4. Visit preparation
5. Initial and subsequent visits
6. Debrief and evaluate
7. Agree improvement plan
8. Monitor progress

1 Choose the process to be benchmarked
If the purchasing function has a carefully thought-through strategy, it will have identified a number of critical success factors which are central to maximising its support of corporate and internal customer requirements. These critical success factors could include:
- improving supplier quality
- reducing stock levels
- shortening time-to- market times for new products
- reducing staffing levels

The critical success factors should lead to easy identification of the processes which will benefit most from benchmarking. It is wasteful and inefficient to benchmark where improvement will not create leverage for the organisation.

Some organisations have benchmarked on a commodity basis. The purchase of IT has been benchmarked with leading IT purchasers from whatever industry. The NHS Supplies Authority, for example, is currently benchmarking on both critical success factor and commodity bases.

2 Determine who to benchmark against

Picking the wrong firm to benchmark against will almost inevitably lead to failure. Four options exist at this stage. These are represented pictorially as Figure 2.

Internal benchmarking may be a possibility if geographically-based divisions or comparable product-based divisions exist. This is often the easiest form of benchmarking to arrange as comparison with other parts of the same organisation should be feasible with no restrictions on availability of information.

Industry benchmarking is often the most difficult form of comparison. Competitors are careful about giving away competitive edge. This can result in industrial benchmarking being limited. Trade associations may, however, be able to provide information on industry-average performance, but this tends to be general rather than purchasing-directed. Desk-based research, using the services of an information scientist, can lead to a fair amount of purchasing information being delivered. Recruiting members of staff from competitors can also lead to a perspective on competitor purchasing.

It is surprising that more use is not made of this approach in non-competing industries such as local and central government and public service industries such as local and central government and public service industries, where profit is not an issue, or where the customer base is geographically-determined and competition is more imagined that real. There are considerable variations in purchasing practice within, for example, the local government sector. Although some limited price comparison services are used by local authorities, more could be done to graft best purchasing practice from one organisation to another.

Over the last six months I have been involved in the development of a number of **Best Practice Clubs** where companies with a common desire to appraise their own buying processes have got together to share information and approaches. Typically, club members are from different industries, and there is no element of competition to cloud the issues under discussion. Normal practice is for six organisations to meet in such a forum and at first they may seem strange bedfellows. One such club includes members from pharmaceuticals, household goods, the retail trade, financial services, the public sector and engineering. It is not uncommon to hear consulting clients say that such comparisons are invalid because such an industry is different and techniques from one trade will not work in another. The Best Practice Clubs show the fallacy of this argument.

Two recent consulting clients were looking to improve their stock control performance. One insisted on benchmarking against industry competitors and convinced himself that his stockturn of eight was capable of being cranked up to ten. This, he felt, would put him in the top quarile of performance in his industry. A competitor benchmarked himself against the grocery trade. Rather than retreat into talk of 'different industries', explored the possibilities of applying retail practices to his own company. The target he is diligently and successfully working towards is a stockturn of 20.

Most talk of benchmarking is related to **World Class Performance**. This involves identifying organisations which excel at one particular aspect of purchasing and comparing their process with yours. Once again, desk research can provide a valuable insight into best practice in a range of buying processes. Distinctions do need to be made, however, between organisations which are truly world class at some aspect of their business, and organisations which trade on the back of an effective public relations function. Particular facets of world class purchasing are often found outside the blue chip sector, where there is genuine belief that trying harder overcomes the lack of a blue chip name.

Whichever approach is adopted, and the ideal might be a combination of all four, it is important that there is a clear link between the critical success factors which are being benchmarked and the organisations which are to provide the benchmarks.

Suppliers should not be neglected. Some purchasing organisations have used close relationships with key suppliers as a means of benchmarking. Partnership relationships are founded on mutual benefit, and either working with one supplier or working with a forum of half a dozen should provide a friendly and supportive environment for benchmarking. Suppliers may also be able to recommend benchmarking partners who excel at particular aspects of purchasing. Their knowledge of the buying processes adopted by their other customers is an invaluable source of benchmarking target companies.

FIGURE 2 Four options

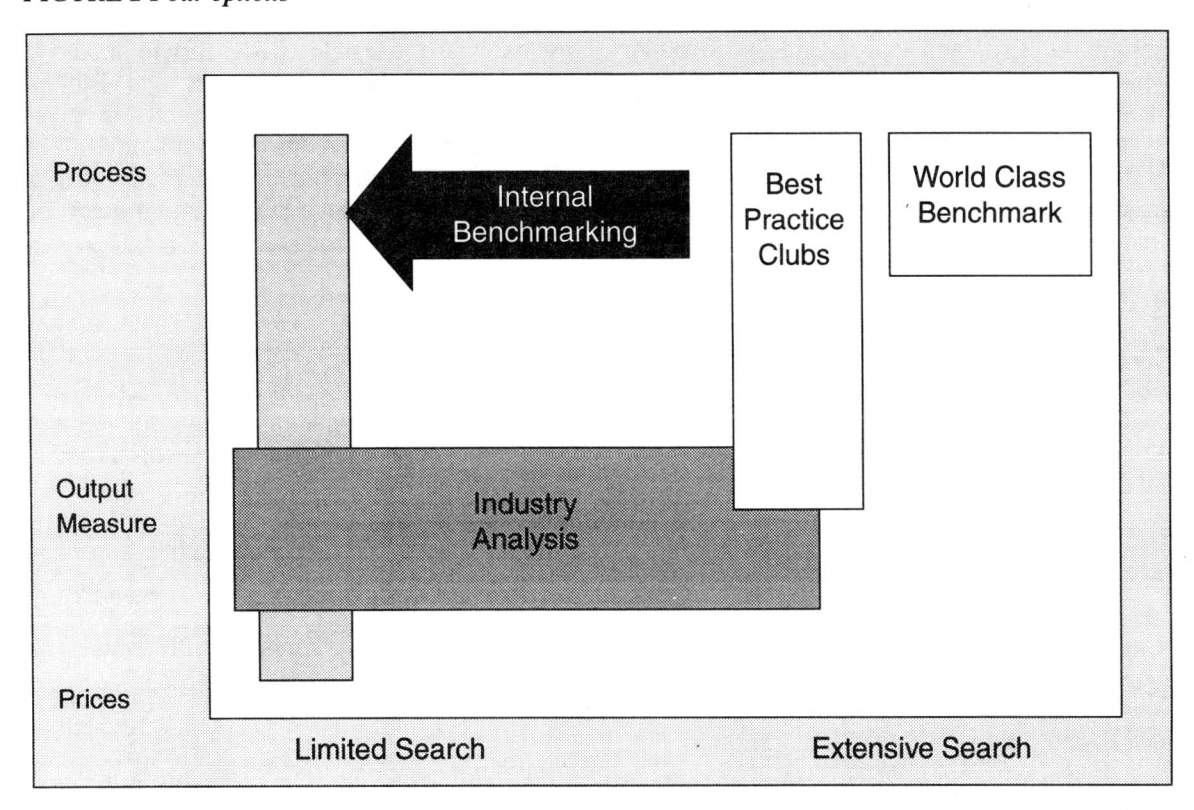

3 Who should be involved in the process?

A small and effective working group will make more progress on benchmarking that an individual acting on his own initiative. There is a need for one person, preferably the purchasing manager, to 'own' the initiative. Support may be needed from colleagues within the company with links to the process being reviewed. Depending upon the process being benchmarked this could be a customer department, design or engineering, or even training. It is always easier to get commitment to change at an early stage by involving those most likely to be affected, and this is the strongest reason for involving others in the process. Buyers wishing to amend the invoice clearance process, for example, would be foolish not to involve finance staff. An external facilitator with experience of benchmarking may help to ease the process through to a successful conclusion.

4 Visit preparation

The effectiveness of the benchmarking visit will inevitably depend upon the extent of the preparation that has been done. Playing it off the cuff is not to be recommended. Typically the company's own purchasing process if 'mapped' using business process re-design tools. Inputs and outputs to the process need to be defined and the metrics associated with the process need to be documented and understood. It is helpful to prepare for a visit by providing the benchmarking 'partner' with this process map before the visit, or alternatively to provide a pre-visit questionnaire which will provide a set of background facts for the visit.

5 The visit

On some benchmarking assignments we have introduced a quality control check after completion of the preparation and before the visit which ensures that the visit takes place only after sufficient preparation has been done.

In practice there are likely to be a series of visits if the benchmarking relationship proves to be of value. The visits will prove to be valuable if the research has been adequate, the pre-meeting planning has been thorough and the meetings are well structured.

6 De-brief and evaluate

Process comparison and widespread dissemination of the results of the visit are necessary to ensure a healthy debate on the process being benchmarked. It is also necessary to satisfy the high level visibility which should accompany the senior management buy-in to the process.

It is at this stage that a degree of positive thinking is necessary if the benefits of benchmarking are to be anything other than marginal. It is all too easy to focus on the reasons why a practice from a different industry will not work, but an approach based upon 'What do we have to do to get the sort of benefits they get?' will be far more productive.

7&8 Agree improvement plan and monitor progress

On benchmarking assignments over the last nine months, 85 per cent of visits have led to some observable opportunity for improvement. Involvement of others within the organisation associated with the process being benchmarked pays dividends at this stage. The benefits of senior management support for the project are also apparent at this stage. Senior management review of the benchmark visit can be useful in ensuring management weight is thrown behind any changes which are felt could be beneficial.

Clearly defined improvement plans need to be drawn up with responsibilities allocated. The improvements will be driven by the establishment of minimum standards and performance improvement targets. Over the last nine months, improvements have been implemented in a range of purchasing processes as a result of benchmarking. These include:
- supplier vetting and monitoring, where a turgid bureaucratic process was replaced with something simple, streamlined and effective
- vendor rating, where a computerised vendor rating system was scrapped in favour of a supplier-administered system
- negotiation, where a pharmaceutical industry client developed a list of 120 concessions which are possible in supplier negotiations, with dramatic effect
- public sector tendering and adjudication, where non-added value activities were reduced to an absolute minimum without transgressing public sector guidelines
- expediting, where a system was introduced where suppliers progress their own orders
- stock control and electronic trading, where orders of improvement which were unimaginable have been produced
- dealing with low-value purchases in such a way that Pareto 'C' class items require the minimum amount of management
- supplier development, where monopoly supply problems have been overcome using supplier engineering techniques.

These improvement projects can take up to nine months before a significant improvement is noticeable. Clearly, improvements can be made more quickly than this, but it would be wrong to raise senior management expectations of 'quick hits'. Having gone through the process once, it is then necessary to recalibrate the benchmark an seek another partner, if appropriate to generate further improvement.

Case studies

There is a growing body of organisations which have successfully implemented benchmarking projects that have led to performance improvement. Rank Xerox has removed a layer of stockholding and streamlined the information flows between the centre and its field operations. The Rover Group has used process benchmarking to improve material utilisation, raw material levels and tool manufacturing lead-times. These and other case studies, including BOC, Hewlett Packard, Abbey National and IBM, are well documented. The following case study is intended to give an example of the way in which benchmarking can be used to improve performance.

A large retail player in clothing and textiles had developed a corporate strategy. A key part of the strategy was an improvement in quality at all levels of the operation. Merchandise was to be taken up-market, store ambience was to be improved and staff were to be trained in customer service. All these things would help to justify higher margins which were considered essential if the firm was to survive in its present form.

The buying function looked closely at merchandise quality and accepted that it was following industry practice. Most quality problems were identified either by staff handling the products or by customers who had purchased the products. The cost of poor quality had not been identified but it was accepted as being very significant.

The buying director decided to adopt process benchmarking as a way of improving performance in this area. She did this initially in Best Practice Club and then by selective benchmarking with leading lights in the automotive and electronics industries. This led to the introduction of statistical process control as a tool for building quality into the product with a reduced number of suppliers.

The supplier selection and quality management processes are markedly different now, and sales staff have recorded a 38% reduction in the amount of merchandise returned by customers. The volume of business with the reduced number of suppliers has led to an average increase of 3% in gross margin without any adjustment in selling price.

Conclusion

There are many who regard benchmarking as a fad, another in a long line of techniques touted by consultants and conference-providers. Results achieved by a growing number of organisations suggest otherwise.

For purchasing managers, process benchmarking provides comparisons which can lead to startling improvements. It helps managers to get a handle on best practice and measure the gap between this and current levels of performance. The most noticeable successes have been found in companies or organisations which have a 'burning platform' - an urgent need to introduce change, either to match the competition or to stave off the effects of the recession. If process benchmarking can work in these circumstances, there is no reason why it cannot work in less demanding environments.

Electronics heading for Sunshine state

Malcolm Wheatley finds that Sun's vendor appraisal system is much appreciated - even by the competition

The value of vendor appraisal remains under-appreciated. Everyone is leaping into business re-engineering - but only purchasing professionals seem to get excited about vendor appraisal. The rare exceptions generally fall into three broad categories: retail chains and automotive and electronics industries.

So true to form, it is a US-based electronics company - computer manufacturer Sun Microsystems - that has been one of the most recently vocal converts to the approach. Sun's experiences with the technique date back three years; enough, say the company for it to be able to bear out the two principal claims made for vendor appraisal. Firstly, it does demonstrably raise suppliers' performance. Secondly, suppliers in turn benefit from, and appreciate receiving, performance tracking.

Although the company is not especially well known, it is big. It doesn't make mainframes or PCs, but a range of minicomputers, file servers and CAD/CAM workstations that site between these two computing extremes, attracting considerably less attention. Sun's machines are based around its high-speed, number-crunching RISC-technology 'SPARC' chips, and are sold to an impressive global customer base. Key facts: Sun is ranked 139th in the Fortune 500, employs nearly 13,000 people worldwide, and had annual sales in 1993 of $4.3bn, 20 per cent of which comes from Japan.

Supplier effectiveness is crucial to the survival of the business, explains Mel Friedman, vice-president of corporate supplier management, for the company has traditionally fought shy of a heavy manufacturing involvement. Consequently, it is unusually dependent upon externally sourced components. '55 per cent of every revenue dollar goes to suppliers,' says Mr Friedman. It is unique amongst the group of companies that it competes with, he points out, for operating without any chip fabrication facilities of its own - remarkable for a business which is essentially leveraged upon the capabilities of those very chips.

Sun's standard 'score card' on suppliers is renewed quarterly

SCORE CARD REVIEW		Q FY Completed: /93
SUMMARY — EUROPEAN RESULTS		Commodity Rated: PCBAs

	Data	Max Pts	Actual Pts	Score
QUALITY PERFORMANCE				
Total Failure Rate (DPM)		25.0		
Failure Analysis		5.0		
Field Issue, Purge, Stop Ship		(15.0)		
Quality Subtotal		30.0		pts
DELIVERY PERFORMANCE				
Leadtime		10.0		
On–Time Delivery		15.0		
Flexibility		5.0		
L/D/F Subtotal		30.0		pts
TECHNOLOGY PERFORMANCE				
Capabilities		6.0		
Corrective Action/Failure Analysis		10.0		
Continuous Improvements		9.0		
Technology Subtotal		25.0		pts
SUPPORT PERFORMANCE				
Purchasing / Materials Support		10.0		
Sustaining Technical Support		5.0		
Support Subtotal		15.0		pts
PERFORMANCE MATRIX TOTAL		100.0		pts
PRICE INDEX		1.0		
SCORE = PERFORMANCE MATRIX x PRICE INDEX		100.0		
TOTAL COST OF SUPPLY = $\left(\frac{100 - SCORE}{100}\right) + 1$		Goal: 1.0		

Prior Performance Matrix Score:
Prior Price Index:
Prior Total Cost of Supply:

In part, the strategy has paid off. Sun's steady revenue growth has outstripped that of its competitors - the more vertically-integrated IBM, DEC and HP - by several orders of magnitude. But earnings per share have been more erratic, and four years ago prompted the company to seek an improved, and more consistent, performance from its suppliers. Given its high level of dependence on suppliers, the company was also determined to monitor their effectiveness over a broader spectrum of parameters than just price, quality and delivery reliability. Given the nature of Sun's business and the mission-critical characteristics of its products, the company took the view that it was the total cost of dealing with a particular supplier, including on-going technological development and backup support that mattered, explained Mr. Friedman.

The performance of what he terms the 'top 40' suppliers is seen as especially critical, although he remains close-lipped about the proportion of annual spend that these 40 make up. For these suppliers, each company's performance against Sun's 'scorecard'(see picture) is reviewed quarterly with the supplier's personnel. Periodically, several such scorecards are combined, and a more strategically-oriented review held with members of suppliers' senior management teams. Loosely speaking, quarterly meetings examine the past, whilst the strategic meetings look at the future - unless, says Friedman, the performance in the recent past merits such senior management attention. Such instances are increasingly infrequent as a supply base consolidation exercise weeds out the under-performers. The long-term objective is to dispense with periodic measurement have the data on-line, Mr Friedman explains, adding that compared with three years ago, 'we are now having discussions about what the data is telling us, rather than about data integrity.'

Several things make the Sun scheme stand out. One is the way that it has been extended beyond the core of suppliers who just produce parts to go inside computers; airlines and car rental companies have been assessed, although the detail on the scorecard differs. As these are not 'top 40' suppliers, these exercises are more infrequent, and in any case have been limited to the 'top 20' non-component suppliers. Nevertheless at the meeting held with United Airlines to review the results, United's representatives included the vice-presidents of worldwide sales and pricing.

Another area in which the Sun scheme stands out is the extent to which the company has gone to avoid making fuzzy measurements, even in areas such as technical capability. Although the company looks at suppliers' investment levels and what Mr Friedman describes as their 'technological road map', precisely formulated expectations underpin that roadmap. With printed Circuit boards, for example, particular levels of expertise - half-micron technology, four-layer capability, 'chip-on-board' and so on - are set as minimum standards.

Also key is the way that the targets are constantly made tougher: three years ago, 'on-time delivery' meant delivery within a time band stretching from three days early to one day late. Now it means two days early and zero days late. Moving the goalposts has disguised progress: although suppliers' scorecard performance has only improved from 1.33 to 1.23 (1 is a 'perfect' score, 2 is complete failure) since the scheme's inception, this is misleading.

On a constant measurement criteria basis, claims Mr Friedman, suppliers' performance has shot from 1.33 to 1.00 - in other words, to a level that Sun regarded as perfection three years ago. That performance *has* worked through to the bottom line: cycle times have shrunk from 274 days to 139; inventory turns more than doubled from 5.5 to 11.6, and $1bn added to the balance sheet in just three years, although the contribution of other ongoing initiatives to these improvements must be acknowledged.

Nor does the company spare itself from the targets that it expects its suppliers to meet. Sun's California base is a key supplier to its overseas subsidiaries' factories, and Mr Friedman insists that these measure the parent as they would any other supplier. 'The internal score card sessions are the toughest,' he says, whilst denying that this is because punches are pulled with external companies. Instead, the aggressive tack taken is meant to balance any suspicion that in-house relationships, as opposed to arm's length ones, are inherently less competitive. In fact, reckons Mr Friedman, 'you demand more from inside the family'.

Interestingly, the scorecard has prevented the company falling prey to what it regards as a delusion common in the industry: that a single supplier can be a global partner. Having the capability to measure in detail suppliers' performance at various Sun site, experience has shown it that the same company's performance can differ widely.

'Even some big household names don't have the global capability we require,' Mr Friedman says. Nevertheless, he is alert to the dangers of a fragmented reliance on what he terms 'geospecific suppliers', so the approach being adopted is to use vendor appraisal to harmonise suppliers' performance across the entire organisation. The fact that many key component technologies are multi-sourced from large corporations helps with this, and comparable manufacturers are shown each others' performance on an anonymous 'best of breed' basis.

Suppliers' attitudes have been very positive, insists Mr Friedman. 'It's a symbiotic relationship,' he argues. 'The attributes we measure help the supplier.' Alastair Kelly, Managing Director of Design to Distribution Ltd, UK computer supplier ICL's newly autonomous subcontract manufacturing operation, agrees. The volume of Sun business that he undertakes has grown tenfold to $34 million since 1990, and he has now imposed the Sun vendor assessment approach on his own suppliers. 'It's the best bit of free benchmarking I get. The minute we stop improving, we start going out of business.' Non-ICL business is scheduled to grow to 50 per cent of the company's operations by 1995, and Sun's endorsement is seen as key to helping the company make headway in the US marketplace.

That endorsement is very public: an annual awards ceremony and full page advertisement in the *Wall Street Journal* trumpet the scheme's star performers. There may be a downside to this. 'Just the other day', muses Mr Friedman, 'I got a letter from a company thanking us for doing all their supplier selection for them.'

Life cycle costing and its benefits

Bob Fox summarises the importance of the LCC approach to the procurement of major capital projects

The total cost of maintenance is essentially built in when a plant is designed and specified. A comprehensive maintenance design brief can optimise cost savings at the initial design phase. In fact, the greatest impact on cost savings occurs during initial design and prior to equipment specification and procurement, which can greatly affect the total life cycle costs in Figure 1.

Selection by design

A maintenance design brief is based on the actual strategy for carrying out the maintenance in the operating plant. For example, a piece of equipment having an absolute criticality rating may need to be 'maintenance free', but will obviously cost more than lesser options. However, when analysing annual maintenance costs against full life cycle costing there may well be factors which economically influence equipment selection.

Added value enhanced profit

From this, the overall value of the assets can be enhanced considerably, with both cost reductions and increased availability contributing added value to enhanced profit margins.

Where a facility is being expanded through the addition of new process units, then consideration needs to be given to the maintenance function on the existing units to maximise integrated maintenance effectiveness.

FIGURE 1 Total life cycle costs

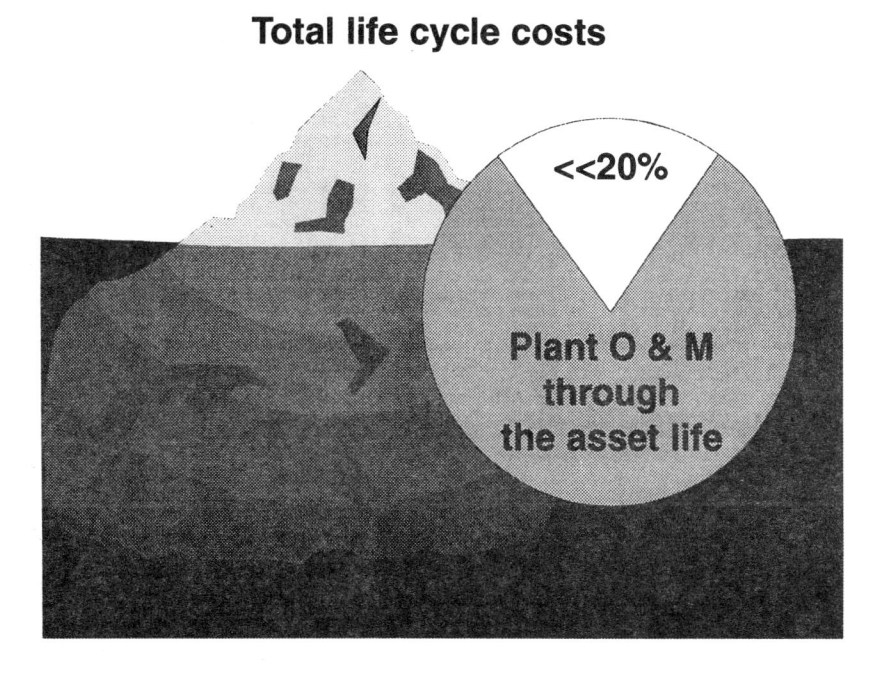

Full life cycle costs

Few users have knowledge and proven expertise in the area of plant engineering which, coupled with skills in other areas, representing a full service capability embracing engineering, procurement, construction, operation and maintenance. The range of services focus on full life-cycle costs of the assets and is a major distinction giving a significant competitive advantage to the owner of the facility.

The summary flow chart in Figure 2 outlines the essential steps of the work process to use in order to capitalise on an integrated maintenance effectiveness programme for major facilities, where new plant is being added to old, and a seamless connection is of paramount importance.

'Design in' new maintenance strategy

This ensures that throughout the deign, specification and construction phases, the total life cycle maintenance cost is optimised and evaluated against a definitive business strategy. It will be based on historical data and up to date technology and will include the following maintenance design brief specification:
Organisation
Maintenance plans and manuals
Planning and scheduling
Materials management
Resource requirements
Training needs
Document system
Maintainability
Operability
Safety management effectiveness
Environmental management effectiveness
CMMS
Diagnostic maintenance

FIGURE 2 Integrated maintenance

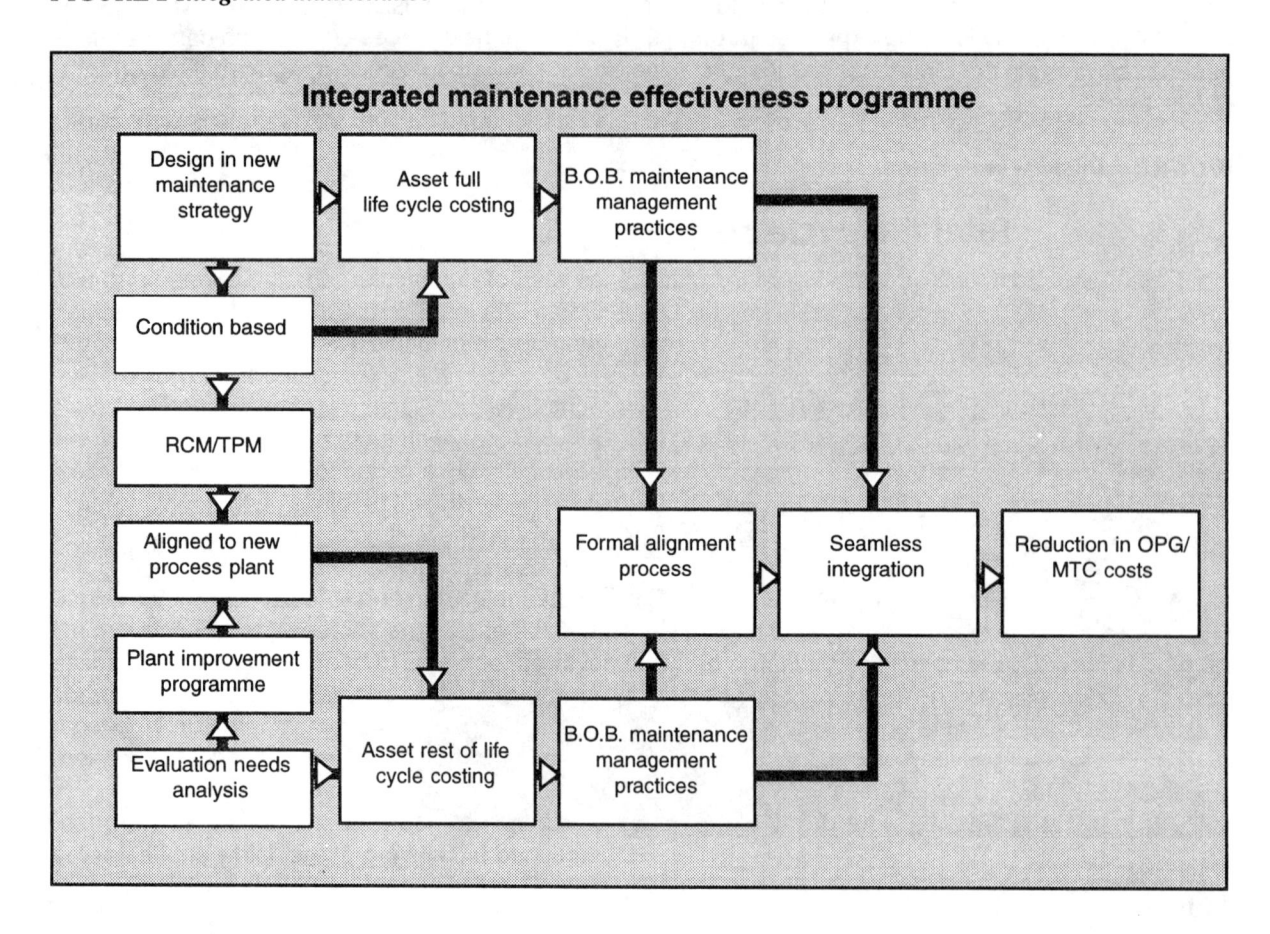

Condition based

From a critical equipment assessment it can be established what benefits can be gained from condition monitoring as shown in Figure 3 and economic justification for the additional rest can be evaluated on a

basis of permanently installed or hand-held applications. It would be normal, as a minimum, to give consideration to the following:
- critical equipment assessment
- vibration monitoring
- thermography
- non-destructive examination/corrosion monitoring
- permanently installed

Maintenance Methodology

It may be appropriate to consider some form of advanced maintenance methodology addressing the following aspects:
- critical equipment assessment
- failure modes/effect
- team concept/multi skilling
- transition process

FIGURE 3 Condition based monitoring

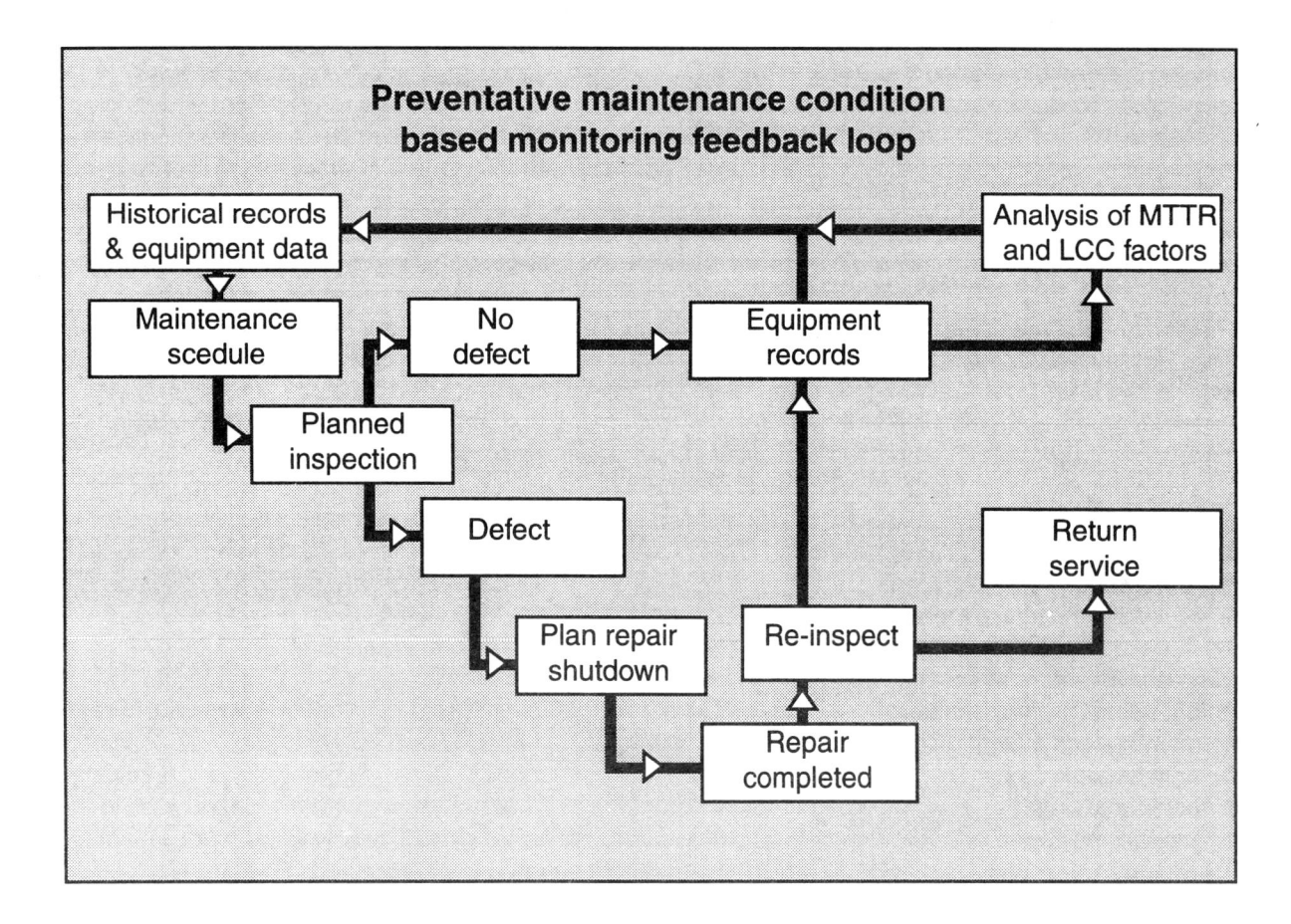

Preventative maintenance condition based monitoring feedback loop

[Flow diagram: Historical records & equipment data → Maintenance scedule → Planned inspection → No defect / Defect; No defect → Equipment records; Defect → Plan repair shutdown → Repair completed → Re-inspect → Equipment records / Return service; Equipment records → Analysis of MTTR and LCC factors → Historical records & equipment data]

Asset full life cycle costing

The fundamental elements of this process will include the following:
- equipment selection
- annual projected maintenance costs
- spares holdings/availability
- depreciation levels
- identification of 'true' maintenance costs.

See figure 4

187

FIGURE 4 *Asset full life cycle costing*

Total life cycle cost

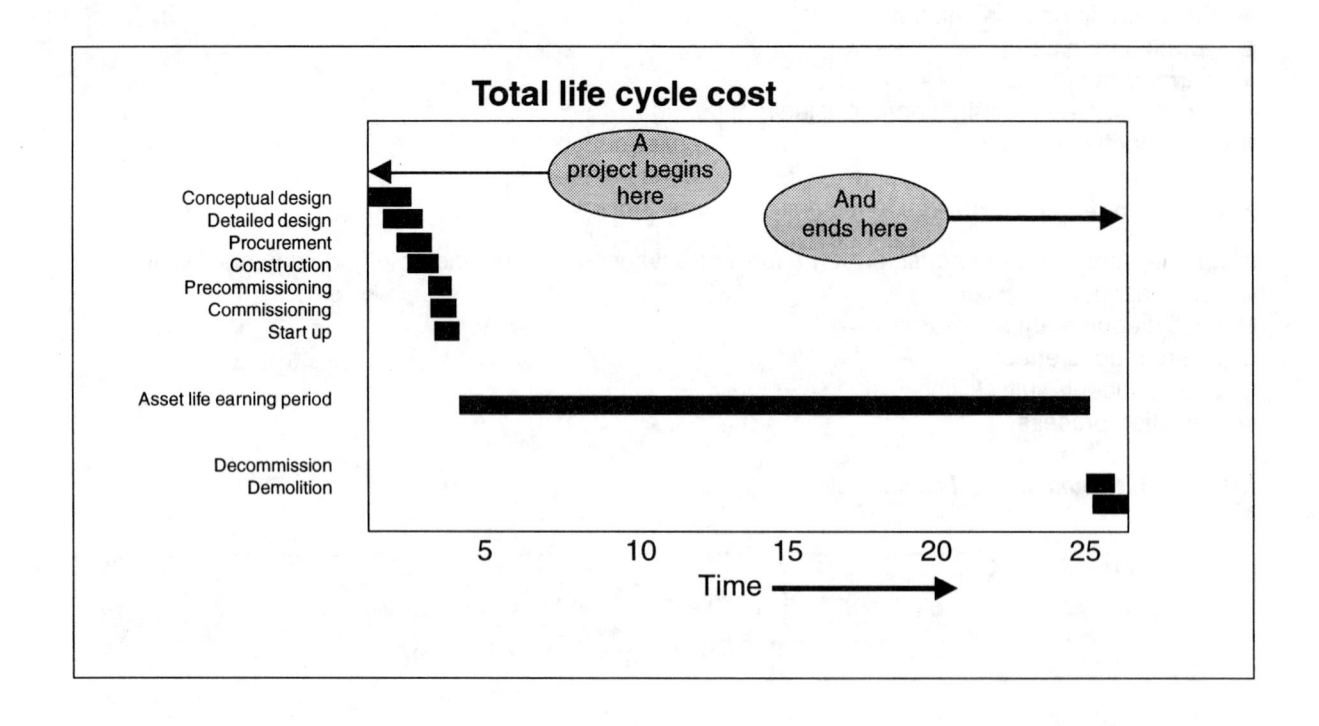

Conceptual design
Detailed design
Procurement
Construction
Precommissioning
Commissioning
Start up

A project begins here

And ends here

Asset life earning period

Decommission
Demolition

5   10   15   20   25
Time →

Evaluation needs analysis (ENA)

The design brief maintenance specification for the new process plant will, to a great extent, benefit from lessons learned and operating experience gained on the existing process plant. The input for that design brief comes from a detailed needs analysis of the existing plant which also provides the basis for a plant improvement programme geared to upgrade the maintenance strategy and ensure it is in line with the application of up-to-date technology as applied to the new process units.

It is important for the evaluation needs analysis to be comprehensive and our experiences have shown the following to be among the most critical of issues:
- current operations and maintenance
- future needs with 'new' plant
- equipment historical records
- breakdown history
- spares inventory/stores holdings
- maintenance effectiveness
- maintenance planning and scheduling
- maintenance costs
- benchmarking

Plant improvement

A plant improvement programme is developed from detailed needs analysis and is customised uniquely to embrace technical, cultural, operational and process related issues as they affect both physical and human resources. The key elements in the detailed scope based on ENA:
- critical path schedule
- fast track execution plan
- milestones
- metrics
- feedback
- continuous improvement

Aligned to new process plant

Whatever up-to-date technology is applied to the new process plant, it may be appropriate to apply similar technology to the existing plant. This is particularly relevant when there are interdependencies between the existing and new plants and where critical items of equipment are found in both areas. The aligning of both strategies an the merging of these into a single strategy can ensure that the application is fine-tuned for maximum maintenance effectiveness. Other areas of alignment could include:
- condition-based maintenance methodology
- team concept/multi-skilling
- transition process

Asset rest of life costing

In order to gain maximum benefit from this part of the process, some research of historical costs is essential, together with the following key elements:
- expenditure to date
- annual projected costs
- updates/modifications
- spares availability/usage/holdingl ongoing depreciation
- identification of true maintenance costs

World class and best of best practices encompass many aspects, some common, but some plant specific, all of which fall into the following categories:
- people organisation
- systems design
- maintenance technology application
- plant engineering management

Best of best maintenance management

Various benchmarking reports exist which provide good performance indicators, however, it is particularly misleading to draw comparisons and force rank stands, when different measurements are being applied. At best, benchmarking provides:
- computerised control
- material costs
- quality management
- constantly 'as-built'
- supervisory/craft ratios
- multi skilling
- technical training
- ongoing alignment of objectives
- effective communications
- team ownership of assets
- planning and scheduling
- pro-active condition base
- dynamic leadership
- high level process awareness

Alignment process/seamless integration
the formal alignment process has a unique application to ensure seamless integration of work processes into both existing and new process units where the ultimate objective is to achieve a smooth start-up to the operations. Part of a simple transition process will address the need for pre-start up maintenance planning and will form part of a detailed schedule where consideration is given to the following:
- clear roles and responsibilities
- clear common objectives
- agreed integration schedule
- realistic milestones

- simple transition process
- continuous improvement
- smooth start of operations

Added value through cost reduction

The diligent approach mentioned in the foregoing text describes a proven process with measurable benefits in the following areas:
- elimination of non-productive practices
- improved utilisation of workforce
- controlled downtime
- increased availability
- enhanced productivity
- greater profitability

Life cycle cost analysis (LCCA)

- projected life expectancy of assets
- initial investment capital cost
- maintenance cost tracking
- economic evaluation of modification/overhaul
- beneficial return on investment (ROI)
- focuses on acquiring, using, maintaining and disposing of the asset
- high cost impact during early detailed design this criteria also applies to existing assets - the rest of LCCA.

LifeCycle Costs (LCC) = cost of operation + cost of ownership as in Figure 5. A powerful tool giving a high control of overall cost.

FIGURE 5 Life cycle cost - the big picture

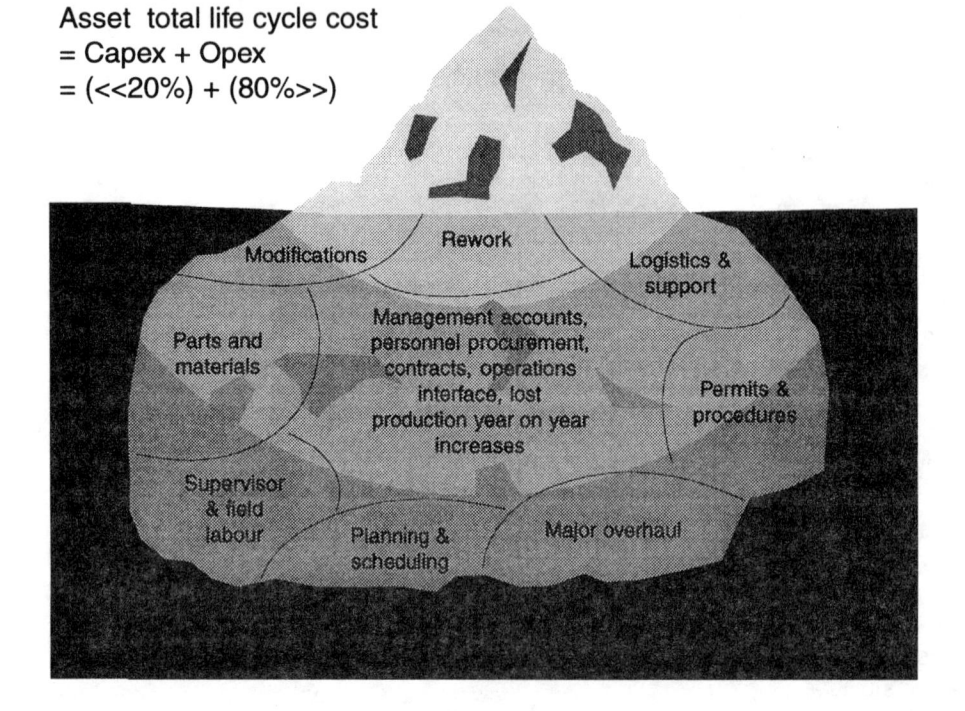

LCC analysis - the big picture

Asset total life cycle cost
= Capex + Opex
= (<<20%) + (80%>>)

- Modifications
- Rework
- Logistics & support
- Parts and materials
- Management accounts, personnel procurement, contracts, operations interface, lost production year on year increases
- Permits & procedures
- Supervisor & field labour
- Planning & scheduling
- Major overhaul

Chapter 7: Specification and Quality

Product change without supply chain tears

Brian Davidson looks at how purchasing can cope with the vagaries of design staff

In a manufacturing setting the product design and introduction have the most important effect on how the supply chain operates. The purpose of this article is to identify supply chain issues which arise from the product change process. After exploring some of the problems, the article concludes by recommending a way to manage product change which gives sufficient integration between the supply chain itself and the technical elements of the product change process.

Product change imperatives

Purchasing people, or their colleagues in Materials or Production Control, will recognise these comments: 'Why does our company spend so much time and effort on engineering change?'; 'Surely by now our designers should have got it right!'; 'Someone up there should break their pencils.'

Manufacturing people tend to view product change as some form of evil which should no longer be tolerated. This stems from the disruption change brings to their manufacturing process, and its support processes of production and supply chain management. Yet we cannot let these comments go unchallenged - that is merely an admission of ignorance.

Companies often have good reasons for changing product design, or even introducing altogether new products. No matter how complex these reasons (and in some industries they are complex, indeed), the drivers are almost always the same: companies need to remain competitive in the marketplace, and therefore to reduce the cost of the product. They need to create products which go beyond what is currently available tin the market. To survive, companies must produce products which respond to the ever-increasing demands of their customers - and sometimes they must actually create the customer demand, by introducing new products based on better technology. Product change also enhances product image and reliability.

Finally, looking inward, companies need product change to extend the product life cycle, which in turn (assuming the products are profitable) results in continued market success for the company, and job security for those very employees who continue to doubt the need for the product changes.

Thus we see an overwhelming need for product development, and hence for product change. Yet the widespread antipathy towards the product development process is real, and must be taken into account. Most companies suffer severe disruption to their production and supply chain processes when they try to introduce new products, or even to bring improvements to existing products. The bad feeling colleagues often vent towards the design and development function is often unmerited, but it needs to be managed sensibly.

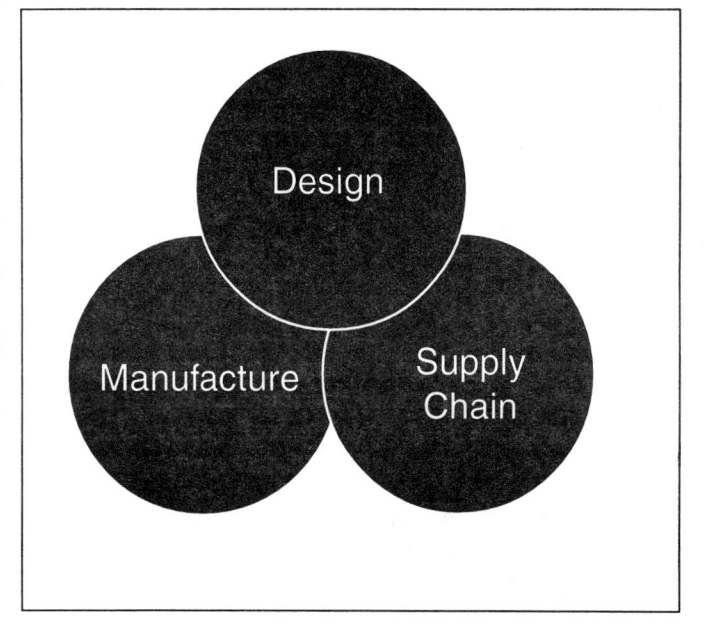

FIGURE 1 Integrated supply chain, manufacture and design processes

Managing the process

Seldom is it a failure of the design team that necessitates a product change. Nor is it their fault when the change causes disruption on the shop floor, or with the company's suppliers. The disruption is usually caused by the lack of a change process that is

- formal
- enforceable
- cross-company
- cross-function

As a result, product change is often poorly communicated; hence we see disruption in every department, as people try to come to grips with a change that seems imposed on them suddenly. The result is usually a fire-fighting flurry of activity to change the bill of materials, provision and procure new parts, assess what to do with the excess inventory generated, expedite delivery of new parts in records times, and so on.

Insufficient control of the product change process usually lurks under the normal lack of communication on product design issues. If people have a chance to absorb a decision, understand its underlying reasons, and prepare for its implementation, they are much more likely to welcome the change when it becomes imperative. Much of today's product change is carried on in small boxes with insufficient links. The effect on the business is ultimately failure to achieve build cost or delivery targets, with a large potential reduction in profits.

The supply chain provides one of the key services to the business, a service just as important as product deign and manufacture.

Without the timely delivery of materials, no manufacturing can take place. If the materials cost more than the company can afford, then it chalks up losses instead of profits. This is all the more reason why the supply chain must become an integrated part of the product development process.

Manufacturing companies traditionally create a division between product design and development activities and the other business processes. You can see it in most companies by the sheer physical location of the R&D teams with relation to the Purchase and Materials departments. Besides physical distance, most companies have irregular communication between these important functions. No wonder it takes so long for a new product to make its stately progress from design to manufacture!

Chase and Aquilanol (1) note that the design process and the resulting specification provide 'the necessary basis for a host of production (supply) related decisions including the purchase of materials.' I would argue with them to the extent that this statement supports the notion of non-integrated design and supply chain processes by insinuating that the supply chain activities are downstream of the production of a specification by the R&D team.

Indeed, Chase and Aquilano take a very sequential approach towards new product introduction, not only with regard to the supply chain but also to the production process itself; they say: 'The first decision in creating a production system is selecting and deigning the product or service to be produced.' They promote a somewhat linear product change process which commences with idea generation, and moves quickly onto product selection as a part of a design process. Their model then moves through preliminary design and then to final design, before assessing production facilities and selecting production processes. Finally, they introduce capacity polarising, production planning, and supplies scheduling as the final part of the process, as shown in Figure 2.

In the modern business environment, I believe it is essential not only to innovate, but to do so efficiently and expeditiously. If companies are to compete on world terms, they must produce their new products faster, and at a lower total cost, than their competitors. This sequential approach Chase and Aquilano advocate will *maximise*, not minimise the time it takes to get a new product to market. PRTM say: (2) 'Best practice companies integrate supply and demand management and new product introduction as part of the new product in production process'.

The cost of linear product introduction

The linear product introduction processes and the resulting lack of integration with the supply chain not only extends the time from design to manufacture, but they also result in a melee of dislocation downstream from R&D. This, in turn, results in an increase in the cost of procuring goods or support services, in my experience, for three important reasons: sub-optimised design, sub-optimised inventory, and fire-fighting excesses.

FIGURE 2 *New product change process - linear model*

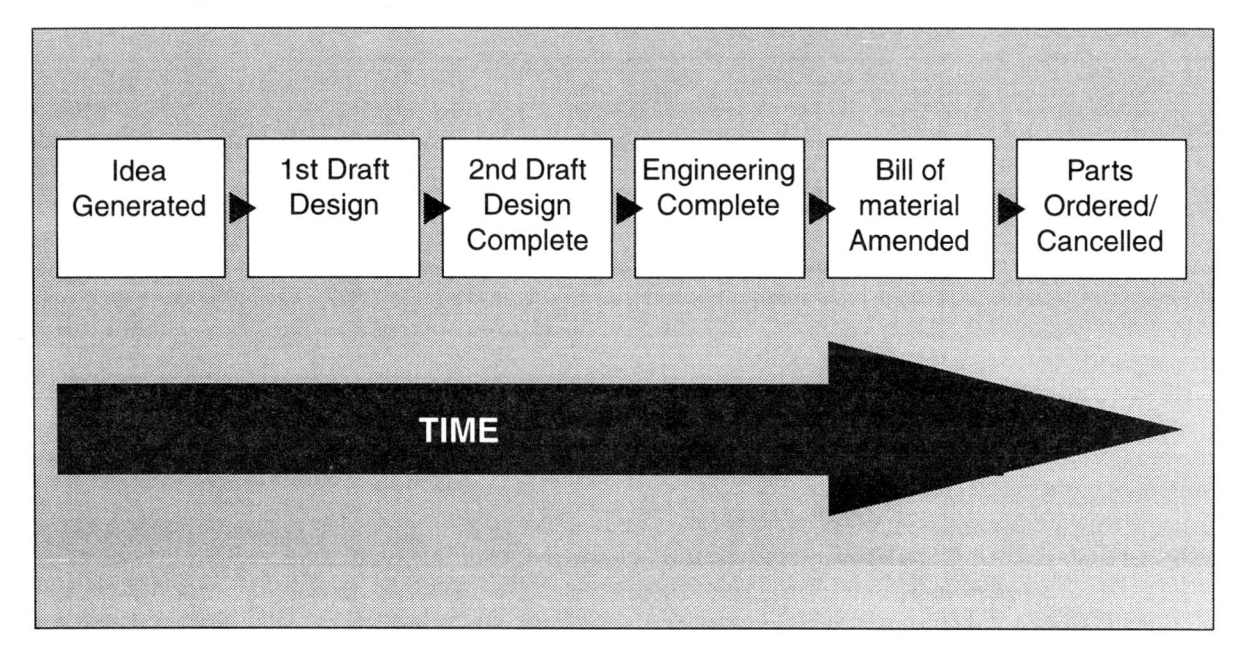

```
[Idea Generated] → [1st Draft Design] → [2nd Draft Design Complete] → [Engineering Complete] → [Bill of material Amended] → [Parts Ordered/Cancelled]

TIME →
```

Design

When purchasing professionals are not involved from an early stage, design if often 'frozen' before any competitive tendering, or even supplier pre-selection activity, which involves the purchasing department. Thus the basic design is likely to use non-standard products, often at high cost, in a way that restricts supplier selection. The know-how that could have saved money or made the product more manufacturable has not been used.

One must be careful, however, not to become totally hung up on going through a competitive tender process for every new design part. Lee and Dobler(3) view the engineer's role as preparing technical specifications for the purpose of going to competitive tender. This ignores other methods of supplier selection and partnership that can improve the overall outcome. Lee and Dobler themselves hint at this when they state: 'If profits are to be maximised, the materials specified by engineering must be both economical to procure and economical to fabricate.' ?But L&D stop a long way short of recommending the closer integration of the Purchasing and R&D teams. Indeed, they fall into the familiar trap of blaming the designers when they say: 'Some opposition to cost reduction exists in the design area'.

Lead times for the supply of non-standard products are often greater than those of standard products, so the overall manufacturing lead tine of a new product can be extended, inadvertently, when the company lacks a process that integrates purchasing and R&D. Compulsory competitive tendering and new supplier selection only extent this lead time further.

I contend that a partnership must exist between designer, buyer and supplier, so the supplier can be involved in the design process under the auspices of the buyer, to provide an input into producing a cost-effective and economical design which can be produced efficiently in the minimum time.

Inventory

The control of the company's inventory plays a major part in profitability. It not only has a direct effect on bottom-line profits, but inventory control also influences the company's cash flows, credit facilities and other measures of success. The linear product change process does not help the company towards it objective to maximise the use of its inventory holdings; too often product change is already approved on a purely technical basis, without taking into account, for example, existing stocks of now superceded parts.

The linear process not only permits but actually *encourages* the designer to design without sensible regard for what suitable parts may already be available from stock or scheduled on an existing purchase order. The result? The designer specifies a new range of parts, which often cost more, and are not available from stock. The cost and lead time for the product change have both been automatically extended, through no individual's fault, but simply as a lack of integration Inventories and R&D people. In a typical example you might find 2000 superceded parts available from existing stocks which were not even considered for the new design. These will either remain in stock until someone finds a requirement for them; or they will never been used at all, in which case they will either be scrapped, sold off at a ridiculously low price, or written off altogether. The company has thus suffered an inventory penalty, but doesn't usually have the mechanism to attribute the cost to the unco-ordinated product change.

Fire-fighting

The third consequence of this linear process is that it results in a wave of fire-fighting activity. Once the design is complete, Marketing is usually advised that they can sell five times when the company can currently produce. Optimism abounds. This leads to downstream attempts to compress supply lead times - often at more cost to the company.

All of this fire-fighting (and resulting blame and finger-pointing) could be avoided if there were a more efficient product change process which involved purchasing and inventories people early in the design process. With their involvement, the company has a chance to use the expertise of approved suppliers early in the process.

In the fire-fighting scenario, the pressure usually falls on departments downstream of R&D; it's no wonder that people in these departments can sometimes feel bitter about product change. Yet one must be careful not to apportion blame too readily. I cannot agree with Carroll(4) that poor specifications and changing designs lead to production delays and interruptions on the shop floor. 'Shortages are caused by ... delays in engineering', he says. I see the problem as cross-functional, manifested by the lack of a product change process which concurrently involves the key representatives of the supply chain.

FIGURE 3 Time versus cost model for product modification

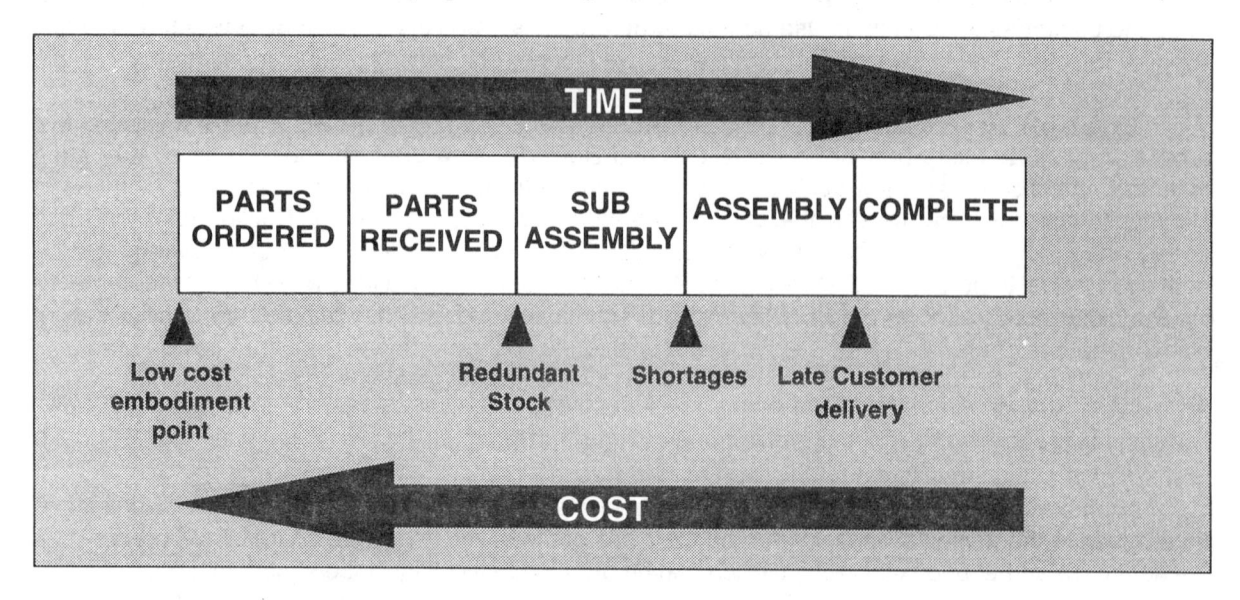

In most fire-fighting firms, the final outcome is either 'success' (the company pulls it off and produces the goods to satisfy its customer - but at what cost?), or 'cockup' (shortages and production delays prevent the business meeting the customer requirements - affecting both its reputation and its balance sheet).

In summary, most companies would eliminate enormous hidden costs if they were able to make a strategic review of their product change processes. This need will be most visible in those companies willing to measure the symptoms of a poorly co-ordinated product change process:
- long lead time to marketplace
- large redundant parts stocks
- frequent shortages of new parts
- long lead times for parts procurement
- fire-fighting and frustration

Having identified that these symptoms exist, a company could use the model in Figure 3 to explore better ways to modify existing products. The model emphasises that the later a modification is made in the production process, the greater the cost impact. The model also gives us an indication of where the symptoms of poorly managed product change will occur in the production cycle. Thus it can be used to provide a 'rough cut' benchmark for most companies. If you introduce modifications after parts have been received to the previous standards, then it is inevitable that you will have redundant stocks. Similarly, if your company suffers from shortages of parts for a modification, then it is odds-on that the modification has been planned for embodiment in assembly or sub-assembly, without proper embodiment planning and due regard to detail part manufacturing lead time.

It may be that your company suffers from many of these symptoms. Generally, the more widespread the symptoms are, the poorer the control of the product change process.

References:

1) Case and Aquilano, Production and Operations Management, 1989
2) PRTM, *Insight,* Vol 6 No.4, 1993
3) Lee and Dohler, *Purchasing and Materials Management*, 1971
4) Carroll, *Practical Production and Inventory Control*, 1966

Quality: in the eye of the beholder, or in the small print?

Geoff Tyler examines the strength of the anti-ISO9000 'backlash' that is supposed to be current

I have always thought it naive - and have said so several times - for buyers to simply add a: 'Thou shalt have BS5750/ISO9000' clause to the purchasing conditions of a contract and assume all will be well.

We are now seeing a backlash against ISO9000 which started among small firms, became well publicised, David and Goliath fashion, by the nationals and is spreading, it seems, to larger companies.

Small-ish firms and their representative organisations are insisting that ISO9000 does not, and was never intended to apply to them. They have a point, as all sides in the row admit.

Mervyn Bass, Managing Director of consultants MRDI, estimates from his own company's experience that 'UK organisations of all sizes must be wasting at least #45M a year in unnecessary management of inflexible and over-complex ISO9000 compliant quality systems. It is ironic that quality, the panacea for sharpening competitive edge in the 80s has, in many cases, turned out to be the root cause of much waste and other management problems.'

Graeme Dell is managing director, chief executive and owner of a thriving engineering company, Cable-flow International Ltd. The company makes cable trunking and installation accessories - of a specialised nature - for installers and industrial users all over Europe. Of his customer list, which reads like an industrial top 100 with a sprinkling of European government departments added, very few even ask whether Cableflow has ISO9000. That is just as well, because it hasn't.

Mr Dell began taking his company through the expensive process, took the consultants on board and so on, but realised part way through that the direction in which they were taking him would increase the administrative burden to no purpose, would cost a small fortune and would actually reduce quality in some areas.

'I fail to see,' he says, 'how one standard can apply to X million companies, all of them different. The standard has a different application to small owner-managed businesses.

'Our kinds of quality control replace bureaucratic regulations and procedures with personal supervision and the care that comes from everyone's feeling an important member of a small dedicated team.'

'Our kinds of quality control replace bureaucratic regulations and procedures with personal supervision and the care that comes from everyone's feeling that they are an important member of a small, dedicated team.'

As I spoke to Mr Dell I was interrupting his work on a design modification a customer had requested and which had to be with the customer, along with pricing details, that same day. He was confident the company could produce it all well inside the deadine. 'If I adhered to the letter of ISO9000' he claimed, 'I would have to have my work internally audited. That would make it impossible to meet the customer's request. One reason why customers as large as the one involved here deal with us is our rapid response and flexibility. And that is as much a part of a company's quality story as, say, having negligible reject rates.'

Cableflow is large among its peers but small to medium-sized in industry as a whole. Mr Dell had the foresight to spot that ISO 9000 would add to his admin burden but not necessarily to his quality standards, but some small firms have gone right through to registration before anything of the sort dawned upon them and on their trade customers.

Andrew Gibb, Compliance Manager with a large company, BET Facilities Management, thinks small companies' approaches may be at fault.

'I suggest many smaller companies experiencing difficulty in wading through the paperwork are being given poor advice.

'Company often start by compiling a manual of everything they do - but ISO9000 is not concerned with everything they do. It does not concern itself with finances, for instance. Purchase order checking is to ensure the order is for exactly what was wanted; it has nothing to do with the pricing. Similarly, the only involvement of personnel departments is in the training record and appraisal measures - employment contracts and all that relate to them are outside the standard's scope.

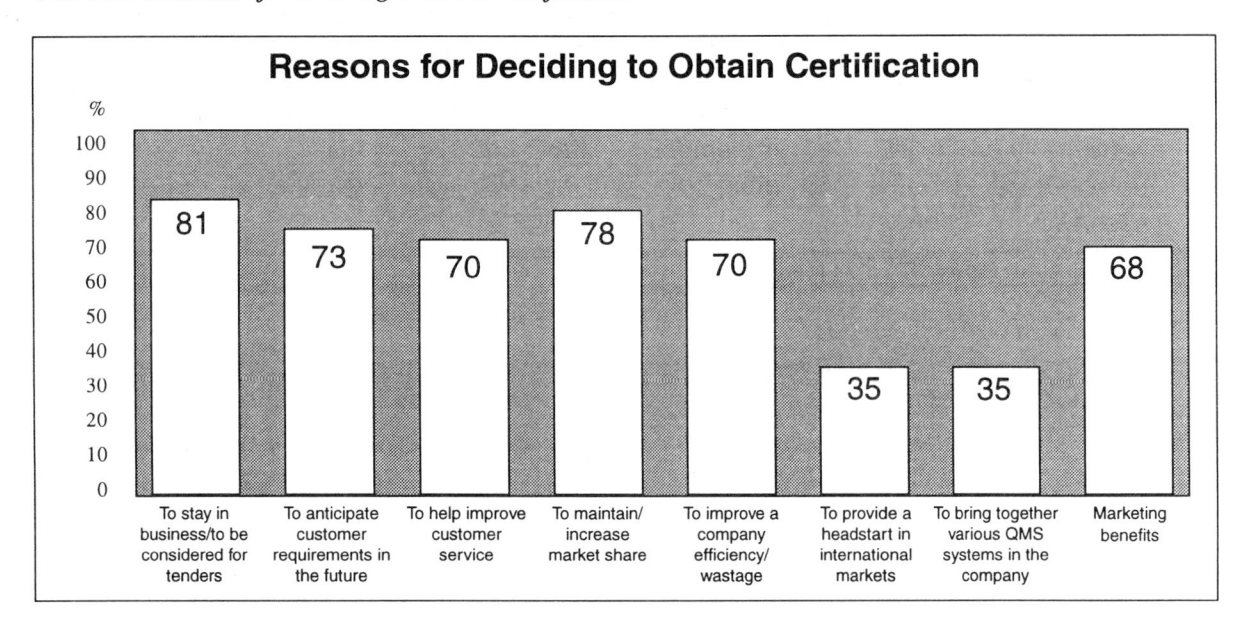

FIGURE 1 Reasons for deciding to obtain certification

Reasons for Deciding to Obtain Certification

Reason	%
To stay in business/to be considered for tenders	81
To anticipate customer requirements in the future	73
To help improve customer service	70
To maintain/increase market share	78
To improve a company efficiency/wastage	70
To provide a headstart in international markets	35
To bring together various QMS systems in the company	35
Marketing benefits	68

'But the advice some consultants are giving over-does the whole project. A company is by no means a small one of course, but I turned away my first consultant for that every reason. We now take a more essential approach which makes it much easier and more effective to implement ISO9000 involving personnel on our 300 or so remote sites.

'Such consultants do their clients, their clients' customers and themselves no long-term service. It may push up the initial consultancy fee and the subsequent audit fees, but in the long term it turns smaller companies away from ISO9000. That is a pity because I believe ISO9000, properly implemented, helps industry - even small companies - see what they are doing and get themselves into shape.

'Rather than starting from the company's activities and making a huge manual of everything, I suggest starting by looking at the standard and what it covers and then working on quality management in only those areas.'

Those areas, too, will be the areas essential to the company's trading position - which is all buyers are concerned with, after all.

Following Gibb's advice, however, does not necessarily involve going through the ISO9000 laundry. These are good management practices aimed at improving quality on a DIY basis. Among companies of all sizes, the overriding reasons for going that stage further into ISO9000 is one of real or perceived external pressures.

A survey by Lloyds Register Quality Assurance Ltd found that wanting to be considered for tenders was the overriding reason why firms of all sizes put themselves in for the standard. It was also the biggest single benefit they felt they had achieved - in contract to the real internal improvement benefits they experienced from quality management systems *per se.* (see charts below)

The Federation of Small Businesses also cites from its members' experience that the most important benefit of the standard is a marketing one.

Linda Campbell, Lloyds Register QA's General Manager, is a critic of the way smaller firms have been blackmailed into ISO9000 by customers' contract terms, which inflexibly insist upon it. She is also conscious of being a member of the consultancy professional Gibb criticises.

'The roll call of culprits is long - purchasers, consultants, certification bodies, trainers, regulators, standards makers, small firms themselves an that old chestnut, hindsight.

'With hindsight I can appreciate that assessing a five-man company to ISO9000 is indeed more difficult than an organisation with 250 employees. That it can be assessed, I am in no doubt, but whether it needs to be assessed is an entirely different matter.'

Linda Campbell refers to the Association of British Certification Bodies and the National Accreditation Council which, with input from firms like Lloyds Register QA, are developing an assessor guide applying to small firms.

The quality industry's initiative is timely because the latest known revisions to ISO9000 are generally being received with disappointment. They, to my knowledge, do little to aid small firms,' says Linda Campbell.

The vociferous Small Business Research Trust has similar views. Its chairman Stan Mendham says of a recent SBRT survey: 'it confirms our view that the formality of the management control procedures imposed by ISO9000 are often at odds with the culture and informality of the personally managed small firm. And informal does not mean inferior. For small businesses, informal can be the better way. From a sample of

FIGURE 2 *Benefits from achieving certification and Benefits for installing QMS*

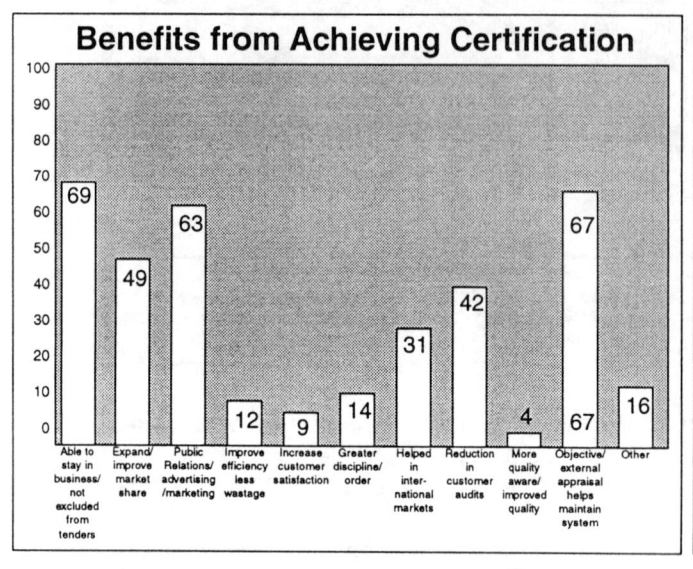

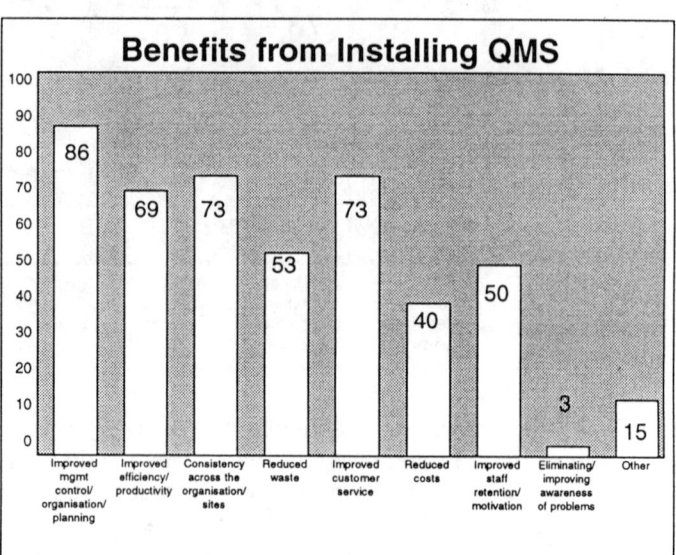

Benefits from Achieving Certification

Category	Value
Able to stay in business/not excluded from tenders	69
Expand/improve market share	49
Public Relations/advertising/marketing	63
Improve efficiency less wastage	12
Increase customer satisfaction	9
Greater discipline/order	14
Helped in international markets	31
Reduction in customer audits	42
More quality aware/improved quality	4
Objective/external appraisal helps maintain system	67
Other	16

Benefits from Installing QMS

Category	Value
Improved mgmt control/organisation/planning	86
Improved efficiency/productivity	69
Consistency across the organisation/sites	73
Reduced waste	53
Improved customer service	73
Reduced costs	40
Improved staff retention/motivation	50
Eliminating/improving awareness of problems	3
Other	15

over 4000 responses, SBRT concludes that for most small firms the cost and administrative burdens of registering to the standard outweigh its perceived benefits.'

SBRT does recognise, however, that ISO9000 can bring operational efficiency and marketing competitive advantages but only, it says, if the barriers to registration are minimised. Measures could include evidence from customers as part of the registration process - ie, whatever they are doing, works!'

So can we take any comfort from ISO9000 among suppliers or not?

The automotive and aerospace industries treated BS5750 with barely disguised contempt when it first appeared. They pointed out, with justification, that their quality assurance measures regarding suppliers already went far beyond what BS5750 required.

That ISO9000 measures only adherence to a given quality level and not the adequacy of that quality level itself is well known, has been well explained in these pages, and I shall dwell upon it not. A Company may still make junk, but it will be consistent junk.

But purchasers do not need ISO9000 to tell them that. Linda Campbell's company has a vested interest in encouraging firms to go for the standard but nevertheless says: 'Before purchasers insist on ISO9000 approval from their suppliers, I'd like to suggest they reconsider their own motives and decide whether it's really necessary. The standard certainly does not insist on the use of ISO approved suppliers. The 'acceptance criteria' for use of suppliers are at the purchaser's own discretion, and the ways are many and varied.'

In fact the BSI's attitude is contained in its guidelines where it says that a company ought not to reject a tender solely because that supplier does not have a quality management system or ISO9000 provided it can provide other acceptable quality assurances.

Linda Campbell believes small firms can also do a lot to help themselves.

'Ask why the purchaser insists on ISO9000 approval. Is there no other means of measuring your suitability? There will, of course, be times when it is a necessary requirement - as a means of complying with an EC Product Directive, for example, but even then, small firms should be aware that approval is rarely mandatory and they should investigate alternative options.'

That attitude is not limited to the small firms area. I approached nine large high street names in the retail industry and found none whose buyers insist on ISO9000 from suppliers. The Debenehams spokesman pointed out that even with a mix of UK and overseas suppliers, they make a point of visiting new suppliers' manufacturing bases, and pit them against the company's own idea of what quality management is all about.

Alan Knight took over B&Q's quality assurance operations some six months ago and inherited a company policy of stating that all suppliers, large, small and indifferent, are expected to acquire ISO9000. That policy is now being revisited, he says, and looks like being dropped gently.

'We realised that a target of all suppliers acquiring ISO9000 was unachievable in practice. Our current thinking is to insist on it only in product ranges where it will help both us and our supplier, and that means, for instance, safety-related products.

'otherwise our inspectors do not need ISO 9000 to tell them they are looking at a supplier who is delivering consistently good quality. We look at the products, not bits of paper.'

RS Components Ltd is Europe's leading stockist of electronic and electrical components, mechanical products and test and measurement instruments. All are stocked for same-day despatch to customers.

RS could be expected to make a great play of ISO 9000 and in a way they do, but not to the point of blind subservience. George Mandaracas, quality conformance group manager, says: 'What we demand of all our suppliers if that they demonstrate to us that they have a quality assurance regime in place and working effectively. That does not mean we insist on their being accredited to ISO9000.

'In cases where ISO9000 has been misapplied, or is misunderstood, the result can be a bureaucratic nightmare. The standard can be a good foundation for the future provided it is used correctly. But firms can apply the spirit of ISO 9000 to their businesses without going through the accreditation process itself and can produce the desired result. Equally, firms which do have accreditation may not necessarily have raised their quality standards as a result.'

MRDL's Mervyn Bass sums it up in his own way. 'The traditional methods developed for producing and managing quality systems are over-complex. In effect firms have a quality system which slows change, showing how they did business yesterday, not how they want to do it tomorrow.'

George Mandaracas advises buyers to emulate the new attitudes among standards authorities when assessing suppliers.

'Standards authorities' emphasis is changing from compliance to improvement, advising on the use of the quality assurance situation the firm has mapped out as the basis for effecting improvements. Then those improvements will themselves be written into the statement and be viewed with regard to yet more improvements as the process continues.

'We ask our suppliers to try to demonstrate to us that they have such quality assurances in place and working effectively. That means our quality engineers need to visit new suppliers and re-visit existing ones from time to time. We make no distinction in that programme between suppliers with or without third party accreditation.'

There are several initiatives appearing now to address the over-costly and complex nature of the quality imposition on firms.

Some consultants have produced packaged deal style quality management measures. Lloyds Register QA has an information pack which laudably summarises what ISO9000 requires on two A4 pages. Den Norske Veritas has a similar pack which includes a questionnaire for firms to complete to obtain a quotation of the cost of the process and a step by step outlines of what that process will cover from initial quality documentation review to the issue and annual renewal of the certificate.

MRDL has what it calls its Minimalist Managing System which, as its name suggests, pares the administrative work to the bone and concentrates only on the key parameters of the quality processes.

Deans Hill Systems has a software package which guides a firm through the requirements of the standard.

None of these products and services, however, require commitment to going for ISO 9000, they are all help-mates for introducing better quality management in its own right. Buyers may well feel that a firm which has taken the trouble to educate and improve itself along such lines, but does not want the cost of going for the standard itself, has acquired an excellent recommendation, subject to the usual confirmation by product quality inspections.

Philippa Collins of Herriot-Watt University specialises in quality management subjects and thinks the fuss about ISO9000 is overdone.

'It tries to formalise what firms should all be doing anyway. The problem is the standard is all about setting things in concrete, and business is all about flexibility. The cost of quality is a measurement few small firms - and a lot of large firms - seldom undertake properly. Rather belatedly it has been realised that many of the hidden costs are the result of poor controls in administrative areas. Their impact on operating costs is something that only a thorough cost of quality strategy can illustrate. One needs to provide proof of the need - the cost of not getting it right first item.'

As a finale, the basic home truth from Linda Campbell: 'At the end of the day, purchasers can demand anything of their suppliers - and quite rightly so. But each requirement adds to costs, so it is in their interests to know why they want it, and whether it represents extra value for money.'

Buying managed value

Clive Bone looks at the implication now that value management can be certified to ISO9000

Purchasers have long required suppliers to have ISO9000 (BS5750) quality certification. In most instances this is an effective measure, but it is not the whole story in terms of quality and value for money. Too often purchasers find that quality certification alone does not prevent late deliveries or ensure high quality of supply.

A new development that could revolutionise quality management is the ISO9000 quality certification of value management reported in *Purchasing and Supply Management*, September 1995. In practice, value management is the systematic and ongoing use of value analysis or value engineering methods on the supplier's part.

Value analysis was first developed in the 1940s by Lawrence Miles, an engineer in the procurement function of America's General Electric Company. His task was to buy bomber engine parts for the war effort, but shortages forced him to find alternative materials and methods. He did this by breaking down the many functions of the engine parts to explore alternative ways to meet their functional requirements.

Value analysis is a systematic mult-disciplinary team-based process. Starting at the 'information stage' the product or service's costs and functions are explored in detail. The team then 'brainstorms' to find alternative methods and materials. These are then evaluated and the best implemented. This yields substantial cost and quality benefits. The Department of Trade and Industry (DTI) booklet *Better value for money from purchasing*, cites savings of 3 to 30 times the cost of applying value analysis. The European Commission's booklet *Value Analysis in the European Community* claims figures of 20 per cent savings.

Because the US Navy had budget for 'engineering' the term value engineering was coined in the 1950s and this name has stuck in the USA and Pacific Rim countries like Japan and Korea. In Europe value engineering tends to mean the use of value analysis at the design stage in construction and engineering. Value analysis spread to Europe and Japan in the early 1960s, and in the 1970s I spend four years in the Post Office Purchasing and Supplies Department Value Analysis Branch.

Inexplicably, interest waned in the UK, but not in Japan. Japan pursued value analysis to the degree that today it underpins *Kaizen* (continuous improvement) and their resultant industrial competitiveness. But Korea caught up with Japan. America's *Purchasing World* in February 1989 reported that the Korean Management Association and the Korean Standards Association were 'vigorously promoting VA/VE discipline and methodology'. But Japan has not stood still. Recently a Toyota executive told Radio 4 that they even use value analysis and value engineering to offset the impact of the rising Yen on exports.

Miles described value analysis as 'an organised creative approach which has as its purpose the efficient identification of unnecessary cost, ie, cost which provides no improvements in quality, use, appearance or customer features.' Value analysis is not about cost cutting, but improved value for money. This is often harden than is realised and for the most part tends to occur on an *ad-hoc* and unsystematic basis.

The advent of quality certification for value management enables purchasers to require suppliers to systematically value analyse their products and their means of production and distribution. Purchasers could advise suppliers that, at a given future date, they should have implemented value management and to demonstrate this by securing quality certification for their system.

This would also subject their ISO9000 based quality system to value analysis scrutiny, giving ISO 9000 a long overdue dynamic shot in the arm. And whilst the scope of value management quality certification could not be less than the existing quality system of the supplier, it could be greater, enabling purchasers to insist that it extends to areas like sales and general administration.

Value analysis methods can also be used for services. Some local council and hospital services have found that value analysis out-performs competitive tendering. Hillingdon Council found this in the case of building maintenance. The regulatory bodies and consumer watchdogs that cover the newly privatised public utilities could also insist on the introduction of value management through quality certification.

Quality certification provides a framework to ensure best value analysis practice is applied on an ongoing basis, and on a scale sufficient for the product range or services in question. Some purchasers may decide that the quality certification of value management is more appropriate than conventional quality certification. this could also prove more cost-effective for the supplier.

Contracts with value incentive clauses would enable the savings to be shared, and this is consistent with the CBI/DTI partnership sourcing initiative. The joint purchaser/supplier use of value analysis is a feature of the Japanese approach to partnership.

The government is taking value management seriously. The DTI supported the 5th European Value Management Conference held in Brighton last year. As President of the Board of Trade, Michael Heseltine saw value management as part of his 'wider message of competitiveness'. HM Treasury is shortly to publish guidance on value management for capital projects. The Construction Industry Research and Information Association will do the same next year. The Lord Chancellor's Office already requires value engineering for the deign and construction of court buildings.

Value analysis, however, is no panacea. It is hard work, an needs to be implemented through a long-term strategy. A value management strategy would typically include:
- commitment of management and staff
- effective teamwork
- adequate training in value methods
- an ongoing schedule of projects
- sound cost accounting
- financial audit to monitor result.

Quality certification requires a senior management steering group to be established to give the programme direction through the setting up of the requisite project teams and facilitating and monitoring results. A value management strategy would include a 12 to 18 month rolling schedule of products/services to be examined, with provision to include or remove projects as the need arises.

Such a programme would facilitate staff empowerment because it is often shop floor staff that have the best ideas for improvement. This in turn would greatly improve the working culture, and is entirely consistent with initiatives such as Investing In People. Of course, autocratic managements might not find value management to their liking. Whilst ISO 9000 based quality assurance can be mechanistic, it is difficult to see how an organisation could have mechanistic teamwork and value management.

A certification body undertaking an audit with a view to awarding a certificate for value management would expect to see teams that include supervisors, technical people, designers, accountants, etc. They will expect documented evidence that all ideas were explored with reasons for rejection. Thus value management has implications for the organisational culture that for some may be too much. In that respect it will separate the sheep from the goats.

It may be the case that some suppliers will be unable to hack value management, just as some cannot hack quality assurance. Purchasers will need to make up their minds on whether to buy from such organisations. In the long run, their product costs will rise for lack of adequate scrutiny. So why subsidise their uncompetitive mindset?

Chapter 8: Contracts and Law

Guarantees within the aerospace business

Graham Grieve describes how warranties and guarantees are passed up the supply chain

The warranties and equipment performance guarantees which are negotiated by buyers are very often an afterthought, or take a low priority over the commercial and financial terms and conditions of business which are agreed with the supplier. In this article I will discuss the wide variety of equipment warranties and guarantees that are commonplace within the aerospace industry, explain how purchasing plays a key role in enlisting supplier commitment to support them and will demonstrate just how critical warranties are to everyone in the business - the suppliers, the aircraft manufacturers and the airline, and that the continuous enhancement of these warranties play a key role in the purchasing strategy.

To better understand the whole logic behind the plethora of warranties that are offered to, and indeed demanded by, the aircraft purchaser, an appreciation of the detailed financial analysis that is always undertaken prior to any aircraft acquisition is required. At its most basic level in the commercial air transport business, an aircraft is merely an asset which an airlines utilises to transport people and often cargo, to make a profit. Exhaustive and detailed analyses of both the cost of operation of a specific aircraft type and its likely in-service revenues are undertaken and it is the airline's goal to fix, or at least cap, all the costs. It will also attempt to remove as much risk as possible from the revenue earning side of the equation, which will ensure the investment in the aircraft does yield the planned financial return. This is sound business practice, and is no different to the risk management policies pursued the world over by prudent companies.

Figure 1 depicts the principal costs and revenues that are analysed in a typical aircraft acquisition.

FIGURE 1 Principal costs and revenues

Costs	Revenues
• Aircraft acquisition price • Crew salaries • Maintenance and repair costs • Service and overhaul intervals • Amount of fuel used • Spare parts inventory • Depreciation of the aircraft over time	• Number of passengers the aircraft can carry • Ticket price for a particular intended route • Despatch reliability of the aircraft • Availability of airport landing rights • The cargo carrying capacity

So, let's look at the cost drivers for which the airline would want specific and unambiguous guarantees from the aircraft manufacturer:
● Aircraft acquisition price from the guarantee point of view, is relatively straightforward, with the affordable price fixed in contract.
● Aircraft a maintenance and repair costs are primarily driven by labour rates and the cost of the replacement parts with are consumed in the process. Maximum standard repair times and replacement breakdown parts costs are guaranteed by the aircraft constructor for all the major equipment on the aircraft including engines, undercarriage, auxiliary power unit, air conditioning system, and so on.
● Service and overhaul intervals are dependant in the main, on the reliability of the equipment that is embodied on the aircraft. Warranties which guarantee the mean time between failures (MTBF) and mean time between removals (MTBR), which are expressed in hours of utilisation, or number of landings for the undercarriage, are given for this equipment.
● The amount of fuel consumed by an aircraft is impacted by both the weight and drag coefficient of the

aircraft as well as the specific fuel consumption of the engines. Guarantees, therefore, are given which assures the weight of the aircraft which is actually delivered as well as the quantity of fuel the engines will burn for a given passenger and freight payload flown over a specific and well defined flight sector.

● The total cost of spare parts the airline must hold in inventory is dependant on a wide range of criteria, and will include the reliability of the equipment fitted to the aircraft, the time it takes to repair items when they are returned to overhaul shops, the unit cost of the spare part, and whether or not the aircraft is permitted to take off with certain parts not functioning. Warranties have to be given on spare parts costs, repair turn-around times, and spare parts availability.

● Depreciation, which governs the aircraft's residual value at specified points in time, can be one of the largest costs that the airline must contend with and plays a crucial part in determining aircraft lease rates for those airlines which choose to lease rather than buy.

The scarcity of capital in world markets to fund the airlines' massive re-equipment programmes combined with financier's experiences in the late 1980s/early 1990s has led to manufacturers supporting financing structures through time-based residual value guarantees. On the revenues side of the airlines business, the airline will seek guarantees from the aircraft manufacturer for:

● The number of passengers and the weight of cargo that the aircraft can transport, which is dependant on the actual weight of the delivered aircraft for the specified engine performance (as well as the number of seats installed in the aircraft!). The aircraft manufacturer guarantees a variety of airframe weights - maximum take-off weight, maximum empty weight, zero fuel weight and maximum landing weight which in turn govern the payload and range of the machine.

● The despatch reliability of the aircraft, whereby the manufacturer will warrant that the aircraft departure rate, when in revenue service, will not be delayed for technical reasons below a certain threshold.

FIGURE 2 - Comprehensive framework of guarantees

Comprehensive framework of guarantees

Maintenance and repair standard times	Spare part costs	Repair turn round times
Service and overhaul intervals	Component reliability MTBF MTBR	Aircraft residual values
Specific fuel consumption	Aircraft weights	Definitive engine performance

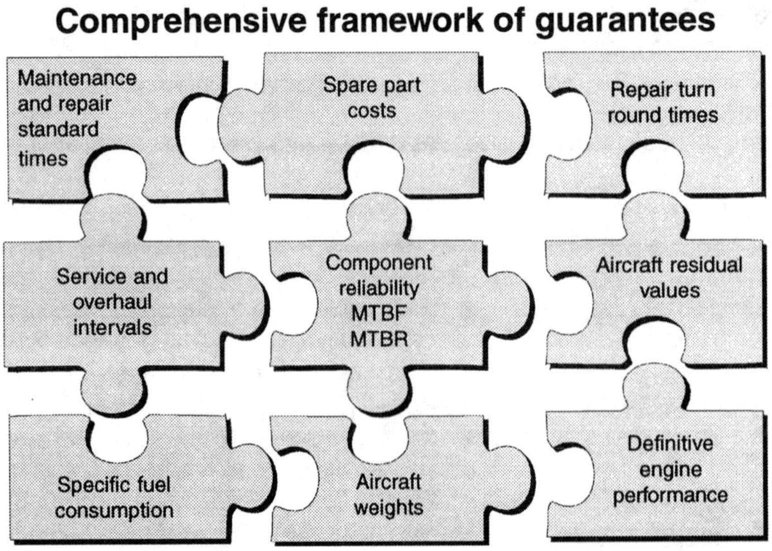

So, all-in-all, the agreement of a comprehensive, all-encompassing package of warranties which are carefully tailored to protect the cost of operating the airline's' fleet as well as ensuring they retain the opportunity to achieve their revenue forecasts, plays a central role in the aircraft selling process and are always meticulously enshrined in watertight contracts.

So, what is the suppliers' role in all of this? Well firstly, for the Avro RJ family of aircraft, 90 per cent of the cost of aircraft production is represented by suppliers' prices. All material, components, equipment systems and pieces of aircraft structure are purchased from external sources, and Avro will obviously endeavour to flow down the warranties that are offered to airlines, where appropriate, back to the supplier community. Accordingly, the equipment suppliers have to warrant all aspects of the operation of their equipment, from its reliability, to repair costs and spare parts availability, its weight, the time it takes to remove and re-install it on the aircraft as well as its functional characteristics. These warranties have to ensure for the design life of the product, and can easily extend to over twenty years.

Within the aviation industry, there is a growing trend in airlines moving to global power-by-the-hour maintenance type arrangements with the aircraft constructors. In essence, in exchange for a fixed hourly fee, the aircraft constructor will supply all the spare parts for the aircraft, repair all unserviceable equipment as it arises and provide appropriate spare parts inventory at the customer's maintenance bases at no additional or supplemental cost.

Obviously, prudent aircraft constructors will ensure that the supplier base totally underwrites the guaranteed figure offered to the airline. This policy of transferring risk to the party who is best placed to manage and minimise it also provides a powerful financial incentive for the supplier to improve the equipment's reliability, repair cost and overhaul intervals which in turn improves the residual value of the aircraft and creates an even more favourable impression with the airline.

So how does the industry ensure that both the aircraft constructors and their suppliers actually perform in accordance with their guarantees? This whole subject, including the range of remedies that are offered, will be the subject of another article.

Strict construction

Peter Marsh explores the practical implications of Sir Michael Latham's recommendations on liability in the construction industry

One of the key areas of the Latham Report deals with the issues relating to defects in the works, especially those which are latent ie only manifest themselves after the end of the defects liability period. His conclusions were that current arrangements are inadequate and his recommendations largely endorsed the views which had already been expressed by the DoE working party. These called for three main changes in the law relating to:
1 joint liability
2 limitation period
3 transfer of client rights

These changes would be restricted to the construction industry and would form part of Construction Industry Act. They would be mandatory and therefore over-ride any contractual terms.

The purpose of this article is first to review each of these as to its merits and practicability from the client viewpoint and then to consider the case for their being applied only within the construction industry and how that industry for this purpose should be defined. It is not proposed to deal with certain related issues which are of significance only as between main contractors and their sub-contracts.

Joint liability

A the law presently stands the general rule is that if two or more persons are independently to blame for the loss which the injured party has suffered, then he may recover the whole of his loss from either of them, regardless of their respective proportions of blame, so long only as their default contributed materially to the total loss. A person is therefore either not liable at all, because his default did not materially contribute to the loss, or he is fully liable.

So if two participants in a project, say the main contractor and the architect are both in breach of their respective contracts with the client the, if the main contractor is 70 per cent responsible and the architect only 30 per cent responsible for the damage which the client has incurred, the client can recover the whole of his damages from either of them.

Of course, the party who is compelled to pay the whole of damages will have a separate claim in contribution against the other, but his usual problem in practice is whether or not that other will have the necessary resources to meet the claim.

Recommendation by Latham

That in construction cases (other than for personal injury), and assuming no joint action and no collusion, a party's liability should be restricted to a fair proportion of the loss related to his share of the blame.

Merits and practicability

The recommendation would not affect the liability of a main contractor for his sub-contractor and down the supply chain. To that extent it is neutral. However the recommendation is disadvantageous to the client in that assuming one party who is responsible to a significant extent for the loss, has in the event no assets with which to meet a claim, then the client will be unable to recover that proportion of the damage he has suffered.

One effect of this would be to reduce the attractions to the client of any method of contracting in which there were a number of contracts placed directly with him. For example a client might well be reluctant to use a form of Construction Management Contract under which there were a multitude of trades contractors with each of whom he had a separate contract. Rather he would favour the type of contracting where there is single point responsibility eg Design and Build or Turnkey and the client would need to take steps to ensure that the contractor would have the resources to meet any claims. But there will be situations in which for other reasons the client would prefer not to take the Design and Build or Turnkey route so that accepting this recommendation could be a restraint on his freedom to choose the otherwise most suitable method of contracting.

Further it seems bound to have the effect that, if the client decides to take legal action, then he will proceed against everyone who could possibly be liable. Construction litigation will therefore become more rather than less complex and expensive and it is difficult to see how the recommendation will assist in reducing adversarialism or the costs of construction. Liability for even a small proportion of the client's overall damages seems likely to remain a deterrent to consultants in becoming involved in suggesting solutions to problems the outcome of which could result in litigation.

For clients, therefore, there seems no reason to support the implementation of the recommendation except as part of an overall package which on balance does provide them with some real benefit.

Limitation period

At present, the statutory period of limitation for actions in contract is six years fromt he date of completion of the contractor's work if the contract is under hand and twelve years if the contract is executed as a deed. In the tort of negligence, other than for personal injury, the limitation period for latent damage is six years from when the date when the cause of action accrued, or three years from when the plaintiff first became aware of the defect, with a long-stop of 15 years from the date of the occurence of the alleged default.

Recommendation by Latham

That there should be a single 10-year period of limitation which should run from the completion of the main contract works so that it applies to all contractors and sub-contractors involved in the project, and applies both to actions for breach of contract and in the tort of negligence, other than personal injury claims.

Merits and practicability

While the recommendation would have the effect of reducing from 12 years to 10 the limitation period when the contract is executed as a deed it is considered that this would be of no practical detriment to a client and that there is a positive advantage in having one single period applying to all contracts in whichever form these are placed. Also the assimilation of the limitation period for actions in negligence to that for actions for breach of contract is a valuable clarification of the present law.

Of more difficulty in practice is when the limitation period should commence if there is more than one main contract or if, as under Construction Management Contract, there is a multitude of Trades Contractors each separately in contract with the client.

The answer would seem to be to follow the French system and for the period to run from the act by which the client declares that he accepts or takes over the Works; in French law *la reception*. It is then for the contract between the client and the contractor to define when the client will issue this act and it would be expected that the client would not do so until all work has been completed on the project, and not just on an individual contract where there was more than one main contractor. With a Construction Management type contract, the client would not therefore issue the act for any trade contractor until all of them had completed their respective work.

It has further been recommended that the same limitation period should apply to all sub-contractors ie there should be one limitation period for the project regardless of when any sub-contractor completed his own work an there would be some benefit to the client in this.

However, one point which does not seem to have been considered is the impact which these proposals would have on the period for defects liability. If there is a single project period for limitation then it is suggested that there should also be a single project period for defects liability which should commence on the client issuing the act taking over the Works as a whole.

Transfer of client's rights

Under the doctrine of privity of contract the general rule is that a contract cannot confer rights on any person not a party to that contract. So the subsequent owner of a building cannot bring an action in contract against a negligent builder or designer. Nor as the law stands following the House of Lords decision in *Murphy v Brentwood District Council*, can the subsequent owner bring an action in the tort of negligence for defects in the building itself or other economic loss which he may have incurred consequent upon such defects. The same applies as regards the original building owner and sub-contractors who are, of course, third parties to the building contract with the main contractor. Such sub-contractors may have design liabilities to the main contractor which the latter does not have under his contract with the client.

This had led to a proliferation of collateral warranties, in order to create contractual rights for the benefit of subsequent owners and for clients against sub-contractors, which are often difficult to negotiate.

Recommendation by Latham

That if any of the works are transferred to a subsequent owner or to a tenant with a full repairing and insuring lease then the client's contractual rights in respect of the repair or reinstatement of the building should automatically be made available to such owner or tenant. This would exclude any right for the subsequent owner or tenant to recover consequential damages for say, loss of rent or loss of profits.

Merits and practicability

Clients in this instance can be divided into two quite separate groups. First there are commercial developers who are building in order to re-sell or let. Secondly there are those who are constructing solely for their own use. For the former group the proposals apparently do not go far enough, since future owners or tenants want the right to recover their consequential losses, and if they cannot obtain these directly then they will continue to insist on on obtaining them through collateral warranties. For the second group such rights are unimportant except to the extent that they may be insisted upon by lenders to the project if the project is being project-financed. However, contracts for most projects of that type will contain significant restrictions on the client's rights to the recovery of consequential losses.

It would appear that in the debates that have followed the publication of the Latham report it is the views of the commercial developers which have dominated the discussions. This has had the unfortunate effect that attention appears to have concentrated on their relatively narrow concerns rather than on the broader issue of the liability of a contractor to a third party. This would include that of a sub-contractor to the client which is of significant importance to the large group of clients who build for their own use, yet does not appear to have been addressed in the recommendations under consideration.

As regards the unresolved debate as to the extent of the liability of a contractor to a third party, then it would seem in principle that if a contractor is to be so liable then the rights of the third party should be no greater than those possessed by the original co-contractant. Specifically:
- whether or not there has been a breach of contract is to be determined exclusively by the terms and purpose of the contract between the two original parties
- any clause limiting or excluding liability, if valid as between the original parties, should be binding on the third party
- any damages payable should be limited to those which were foreseeable at the time of entering into the contract and the foreseability would extend to the extent of the damages and not just to the kind of damage.

In any event, an anticipating the next section, any change to the law of privity of contract is so fundamental that it should not be dealt with solely in the context of construction contracts, but in the much wider context of the law of contract as a whole.

Why only construction?

While it is not unknown in English law for particular legal provisions to be industry-specific, it is unusual when the changes are as significant as the ones proposed. It is considered therefore that for construction to be 'ring-fenced' in these respects there must be the strongest justification.

The reasons put forward for 'ring fencing' can be summarised as:
- construction is, or should be, a team process involving a number of individuals and companies brought together on a one-off basis
- construction work is carried out largely on site, under uncertain conditions which differ from one site to another
- construction defects may not manifest themselves for a long period of time
- limitation periods for the various participants in the construction process may differ widely.

To what extent, however, are these factors unique to the construction industry, which it has been suggested should be defined broadly a building, civil engineering works and process and industrial plants? How do they compare for instance with the design and construction of a ship or an aircraft? There are obviously differences. Construction work is done largely on the client's site, and to a degree each project is a prototype, but there are also similarities. The factors of the need for team work by a number of individuals or companies, of their being brought together for a specific project and of the time it may take for defects to manifest themselves are not significantly different.

It has been commented that French and German law have separate regimes for construction. This is true for French law as regards the liability for defects and limitation periods but not for joint liability nor for actions by subsequent owners. certainly these latter are permitted under French law for breach of the *garantie decennal,* but this is not peculiar to construction. There are similar rules for latent defects in contracts for the sale of goods. In German law the basic distinction is between contracts of sale and those for work, which is a far wider concept than construction and would include for instance the staging of a sporting event.

The further problem is the definition of 'construction'. Broadly the suggested definition given above may not be unreasonable although plant contracts of all types do differ in important respects from those for building. However, more controversially it has been proposed not only that contracts for construction work should be 'ring-fenced' but that this should extend to the whole industry so that suppliers of any materials, components or presumably services would all be subject to the same regime as main contractors. This seems quite extraordinary, and to be devoid of commercial practicality.

Conclusion

The changes proposed are all fundamental to the activities of buying and selling, whether for capital goods or construction works. That there should be changes in the laws governing privity of contract and limitation periods and perhaps concurrent liabilities is agreed. But they should not be restricted to the construction industry, however that is defined. They are all matters basic to the general law, at least that part apply to business transactions, and should be dealt with accordingly.

The Government is reported to be looking at the question of concurrent liabilities in relation to large firms of auditors, who may face very substantial claims on company liquidations when the primary liability lies with the directors of the company who, however, have no assets. It is obviously extremely difficult to deal with liability for one profession alone: if auditors, why not lawyers and architects? If there is evidence to support a change favouring some, then that change should benefit all.

Public sector risk and contract presentation

There is a conflict between safety and value which the public sector needs new tools to resolve, writes Gareth Jones

Public procurement has recently seen an increase in the written word relating to risk. One of the first papers in the field was the Australian Government document of 1992 (reference 1). Recently the Central Unit on Purchasing has produced a document (reference 2) and the Department of Trade and Industry, with a foreword by no lesser person than the Prime Minister, has produced yet another UK version of discourse relating to the topic. Why the discussion and the interest?

I have added a little to this debate through my own research for the University of Ulster (reference 3). My findings do not necessarily reflect the views of my employers, the Department of Transport, or those of my former employers, Central Services in Belfast, but they do relate generally to public procurement both in the UK and in the Republic of Ireland.

The concept of risk in contracting in the public sector is perhaps still too infrequently addressed. Traditional forms of risk-limiting have been secured through organisational size, and the concentration of buying muscle, these being seen as critical in the process of risk reduction. Risk limiting through size has been seen as driving prices down by securing economies of scale and through the ability to carry and maintain rigorous sets of conditions of contract which can be imposed on the supplier. In both these cases there may be a falsehood present.

In terms of large organisations, prices could often be beaten by smaller organisations either through better organisation, better information or the possession of hard-bitten, better buyers who resist price changes more rigorously. Second, having organisational bulk will not automatically attract the good buyer; indeed in the public sector where purchasing may not have the profile it should, concerns may 'pick off' via predatory pricing those who perceive that size along will carry the day. Why, for example, can the UK Celtic countries often beat the English NHS prices when size is against them? How, in my own experience, could the smaller Northern Ireland Health Boards ever have been able to out-perform the larger Belfast Board (the size of all the others put together)? But they could and did! The purchasing index data available to government via the GSI system and in the NHS, the HPSI system, amply justifies this statement.

Conditions of contract too may be useful if a dispute actually gets to court. Before that, the process can be seen as an exercise of raw power aimed at bludgeoning suppliers into submission, or perhaps more accurately, a set of unused tools that rust on the bench. In modern purchasing the bludgeon seems misplaced, or the talk of partnership sourcing has been meaningless to the public sector. If these tools do so rust, it is because the contract actually works and as such there is no need to have recourse to them.

TABLE 1 Use of fixed price contracts for a) goods, b) major non-building projects, c) services

Table 1	(a)%	(b)%	(c)%
Always	18.87	32.65	18.00
Almost Always	52.83	57.14	60.00
More than 50% of Occasions	13.21	6.12	12.00
Less than 50% of Occasions	13.21	4.08	6.00
Very Rarely	1.87	00.00	4.00
Never	00.00	00.00	00.00
Total (no rounding)	99.99%	99.99%	100.00%

If we accept, at least for the point of argument, that there is truth in the scenario that size, and contractual documentation strength, place a limit on risk, the discussion may be as follows. The predominance of the public sector's contracts remain fixed-price in style, and even when allowing for price escalation clauses etc, there must remain doubts that risk is contained.

The fixed-price contract, often in a traditional tender form of bidding pool, is at least partially flawed. The process actually asks bidders to assess all the costs they may face at the outset of the contract and to predict the possible fluctuations in the market. (These markets may be international and involve currency variations at the very least). Clearly in these circumstances, all the risk or a very outstanding proportion of it is passed fairly and firmly onto the suppliers. Is this always wise?

Placing such risk on suppliers when the public service has largely moved (rightly) away from the one-year contracts will affect the price that has to be paid to the supplier. Logically it will move the price upwards. Buyers will be aware that generally sellers will tend to have more information than buyers, in trying to match and predict upward price movements. Where such information asymmetry exists, it will be more problematic for buyers than for sellers. Purchase data will often be historical and sellers may judge from 'now' while buyers are forced to judge from 'then' (generalising of course). This information asymmetry itself may add to buyers' problems and to the difficulty of correctly predicting and managing risk.

In considering the position of fixed-price contracts within the UK and to a lesser extent the Republic of Ireland, what was the balance of usage of fixed price contracting within the jurisdictions from my own research? The data secured is revealing. In Table 1 basic questions were considered and public purchasers in the two Member States were questioned for responses thus:
a) Does your organisation use fixed-price contracting for the purchase of goods?
b) Does your organisation use fixed price contracting for the securing of major non-building projects?
c) Does your organisation used fixed-price contracting for the purchasing of services?
The answers were as in Table 1.

From these responses we can see that the public buyer away from building contracts relies heavily on fixed-price contracts and asks the seller to absorb the major share of risk. It is possible to suggest that this process should be reconsidered in some instances.

What then of organisational size? Do the UK and the Republic of Ireland use their size in public purchasing to create a bludgeon and arm themselves with strong terms and conditions of contract? Again, some response will help. When one considers the UK government's Financial Management Initiative (FMI) and the delegation stance the initiative implies, the results are somewhat surprising; Table 2 relates.

TABLE 2 Response to organisational enquiries

Question	Would you describe the organisation you work in as - **(a)** Centralised **(b)** Decentralised	
Response	**(a)** Centralised	62.45%
	(b) Decentralised	27.27%
	(c) Matrix Structure*	7.27%

*Respondents stated that the structure they experienced at work was a matrix-like structure.

The lowest response rate for arrival at a set of 'centralised' conditions of contract was 79.17 per cent for services. The highest, for goods, was 90 per cent. The framework for bludgeoning is present. Whether the bludgeon is used is, however, a separate question; as is the case relating to whether they secure safety from risk, and at what cost might this security be achieved.

It is interesting at this point to consider government's view of very large projects, which is why the study I undertook specifically excluded building schemes. . The contrast is occasionally staggering and against the current general policy to pass risk to the private sector. Collingridge (Reference 4 at page 82 of his book) notes the following in relation to North Sea Oil: 'One central hypothesis of this book is that behind any example of inflexible technology will be found the very largest organisations, whose close links with Government promote the transfer of the enormous risks involved to the public purse.' Perhaps this difference is explained by, and a measure of, governments' (all governments) sometimes narrow thinking of what purchasing is and can be. The use of North Sea Oil exploration as an example is perhaps old enough not be politically sensitive. One interesting footnote would be to note that the research I understood pre-dated the recent UK government development in respect of the Private Finance Initiative. A degree of further work could well be beneficial in studying risk in respect of the Private Finance Initiative. Ongoing studies will address this field and other related issues.

The development of Terms and Conditions seems also to merit further comment, to judge from my research. Respondents were asked if the terms and conditions they operated has been arrived at centrally across all the three categories (a-c as in Table 1). The figures show the central structure is the source of conditions that organisations operated; possibly due to the high cost of securing such documents. The actual figures are as in Table 3 overleaf.

What of the other forms of contracts such as cost-plus contracts. The style of questioning was the same as for fixed price contracting, but substituting costs-plus for the term previously used. The answers were as in Table 4 overleaf.

These results are not too surprising if fixed price is seen as the risk reducer to the public sector. The trend to see costs-plus increasing in services
(c) over and above the other two selected areas is not so surprising when one considers the figures cover the period when market testing in UK government is so prevalent.

The use of incentive contracts aimed at securing a fixed sharing of risk produced similar results as at Table 5 overleaf.

The incentive contract's small usage in the public sector (outside major building works) is surprising since this mode of contracting is aimed specifically at risk reducing through sharing the potential contracts cost 'overruns' and 'undershoots'.

Three further answers may illuminate the picture. Firstly, 50 per cent of respondents claimed to use compliance with Terms and Conditions of Contract as a baseline for performance measurement of suppliers; this would be seen as working best (or easier) with fixed-price contracts. Quite how this claim sits with the actual performance of a contract may be somewhat less explicable. The second aspect of this question is revealing in that roughly 58 per cent (higher at 68 per cent for major non-build projects) made no assessment of the cost of initiating a contract and of those who had made such an assessment of contract formation costs, 68 pr cent stated the cost factor had not deterred the creation of such a contract. It may be true that contracts may be strategic and *have* to be created; but costs could be avoided by using spot purchases and other purchasing methods (European Union rules permitting!). I am surprised therefore at the 68 per cent figure.

Second, I asked my respondents if, having achieved a contract, any assessment had been made as to the cost of running and maintaining that contract. The answers in the negative across the three type categories ranged from 66-68 per cent. I would suggest that to control risk, some firmer idea of contractual cost would be wise. Also to use cost-plus or incentive-based contracts would apply a scatter gun thinking if buyers were to control the sellers' costs but not their own! Some increased buying rigour would seem to be required. Again, some 62 per cent of buyers stated that if they assessed the costs, they would still proceed with the contract (without question?).

Thirdly, buyers seem happier with renewal contracts as opposed to new contracts. Respondents found them simpler to run, especially away from the major non-build projects. Renewal contracts were seen as neutral in terms of costs incurred as opposed to new contracts. More importantly, buyers perceived at 25 per cent (on average) reduction in bidders for renewal as opposed to initial contracts. This result may carry with it seeds of future difficulty. McAfee and McMillan (Reference 5) for example, base their assessments for incentive contracts upon an Adam Smith type of bidding pool, one which is always present, always responsive and is not contracting or distorted. If renewal contracts reduce numbers of bidder, the bidding pool is perhaps diminishing. The risk may therefore be that by permitting a 'fundamental transformation' in the markets (Reference 6) we move towards monopoly and/or oligopoly and all the risks that carries for buyers. For a country like the UK, whose government's stated aims, elements of the Private Finance Initiative excepted, is based upon competition, the scenario 1 outline is bad news.

TABLE 3 Centrally-dictated terms and conditions

Centrally formed	Agree	Disagree
Purchase of Goods	90%	10%
Purchase of Major Non-build Projects	88.12%	14.88%
Purchase of services	79.17%	20.83%

TABLE 4 Use of cost-plus for a) goods, b) major non-building projects c) services

Table 4	(a)%	(b)%	(c)%
Always	0	0	0
Almost Always	0	0	1.96
More than 50% of Occasions	0	0	5.88
Less than 50% of Occasions	9.62	8.16	9.80
Very Rarely	32.69	36.73	33.33
Never	57.69	55.10	50.95
(no rounding)			

TABLE 5 Use of incentive contracts to share risk, for the same categories as Table 4

Table 5	(a)%	(b)%	(c)%
Always	0	0	0
Almost Always	0	1.96	2
More than 50% of Occasions	0	0	0
Less than 50% of Occasions	0	1.96	2
Very Rarely	12.24	11.76	18
Never	87.76	83.31	78

The UK is not alone, may I suggest, with this difficulty. The European Union and GATT regimes enshrine the competition element in the various codes and directives. Recent EU documentation nominates supplier numbers that should be approached to compete. The recent UK government Efficiency Unit report on the use of external consultants also encapsulates this principle. How is the public sector buyer to achieve his aims with both a diminishing bidding pool and the chance to partnership source circumscribed or severely limited by these self-same codes and directives. A conundrum the UK Central Unit on Purchasing addressed at its Conference in November 1993, with some success in defining the boundaries, but without the freedom of a Honda or Toyota much referred to in purchasing MBA courses and in the lean supply textbooks. The conundrum therefore remains, and I wish to conclude a further study on the private sector's lean supply approach in comparison with the regulated sector's competition style - and which may carry real risks.

Is there any assistance from the brave new world of Europe and the single market? My respondents would suggest this is not the panacea that Cecchini (reference 7) suggested in his report. I am not alone, I realise, in being sceptical about this report. My respondents indicated as shown in tables 6 and 7.

Again, not an encouraging response. I eliminated services from Tables 6 and 7 since the detail was secured around the UK date of implementation of the Services Directive and this may well have distorted the figures. My findings should not shock readers as they are entirely consistent with the thrusts of Professor Andrew Cox's work in Birmingham, which also yields evidence for concern in respect of the competitive performance in Europe.

Professor Cox (reference 8) notes the paucity of actual cross-border trade, which limits competition further; therefore Europe may not be lessening contract risks through application of a European-wide bidding pool. Such a bidding pool is not present, or presents no statistical evidence to prove it is truly there. This question I have put to the Commission during attendance at the European Union's Karolus Seminars; the point was conceded but the statistical base, it would appear, is not being truly addressed by the European Union, outside the work of Professor Cox.

TABLE 6 *Has the single market increased the number of bidders?*

(For goods)	
A more than 50% increase in no. of bidders	(17.07%)
A more than 25% increase in no. of bidders	(9.96%)
A more than 10% increase in no. of bidders	(2.44%)
A more than 5% increase in no. of bidders	(24.39%)
A more than 1% increase in no. of bidders or nil?	(46.34%)
Total (No rounding)	**(100.02%)**

TABLE 7 *Increase in number of bidders for major non-building projects*

(Major non-building projects)	
A more than 50% increase in no. of bidders	(17.65%)
A more than 25% increase in no. of bidders	(14.71%)
A more than 10% increase in no. of bidders	(2.94%)
A more than 5% increase in no. of bidders	(17.65%)
A more than 1% increase in no. of bidders or nil?	(47.06%)
Total (No rounding)	**(100.01%)**

TABLE 8 *European Union input*

Substantially		(3.45%)	
Moderately		(17.24%)	
Minimally		(31.03%)	
Not at all		(48.28%)	
	Total (No rounding)	**(100.00%)**	
Comments	1 "not yet"	2 "expect it to take another 2-3 years"	3 "not so far"

I am a public sector buyer, by history, by training and by current employment. Therefore are my views limited or distorted by such training experience and working culture? In my defence I think not, since I controlled my respondents' results by asking similar questions of suppliers to the public sector.

The responses of suppliers exhibit exactly the same stances and approaches as do the public sector buyers' responses. Incentive contracts seem more popular than amongst buyers but this was the only major difference. Suppliers also had noted very little input from the European Union on competition. Responses were as in Table 8.

On the use of competition, suppliers also exhibited an adherence to the old ways. A UK government forum in July 1994 in relation to market testing for services noted:

'Partnership between the Government and private sector allowed more room for innovation, sharing experiences on best practice and communicating the objectives of potential contractors to civil service staff. The private sector representatives felt that the classic market test with an in-house bid risked being too adversarial, reducing the scope for hanging the way a job was done, and creating problems for relations between staff and potential new employers. There was general agreement that partnership arrangements had an important role to play, but within the context of continuing competition in the selection of the potential partner. The Government's view remains that competition is central to the achievement of best value for money, and that it will be for the departments to decide whether the inclusion of an in-house bid will enhance the quality of the competition in any particular case.'

The firms again are very close to government on the evidence of this quotation. In the UK, government's defence innovation is beginning to break through, notably in the use of incentive contracts in Transport (lane rental) and Defence (target cost incentive contracts) and the UK, Private Finance Initiative offers new hope of fresh approaches for the UK public sector buyer.

In conclusion, where stands public procurement in the UK and Ireland? Largely rooted in old-style power broking, fixed-price contracting and in a restricted GATT/European Union environment based heavily on competition as the leading factor in purchasing thinking. As my Welsh mining ancestors would say, 'the tools are on the bar', meaning we know where such tools are and they are always applied irrespective of effect, with each working shift even when the tools need refurbishing or replacing. I hope that innovation within the regulated sector will allow another Welsh expression to apply in respect of public-sector contribution to the development of purchasing: development through an innovative attitude to contractual risk, possibly using incentive modes of contracting as used by the UK Ministry of Defence and the Department of Transport. The phrase in Welsh is *Dy'n ni wedi g'neud ein siar*. In English: 'We've done our share'. Before that can be stated, extra commitment and further analysis will be needed. I intend to do my share.

References

1 Government of Australia, Department of Administrative Studies - Office of Better Buying, *Commonwealth Procurement Guideline* 8 June 1992

2 CUP Guidance Note No 41 - *Managing Risk and Contingency for Works Projects* August 1993

3 G L Jones - *The Effects of Contractual ?Risk (and related issues) on Purchase Contract Presentation*, University of Ulster

4 David Collingridge - *The Management of Scale* 1992 Pitman

5 R Preston McAfee, John McMillan - *Incentives in Government Contracting.* Ontario Economic Council Research Studies - University of Toronto Press - 1988

6 D Begg, Fischer and R Dornbusch, *Economics* - McGraw Hill 1991

7 P Cecchini - 1992 *The Benefits of a Single World Market,* Windwood House 1988

8 Cox A - Public Procurement in the EC Volume 1: *The Single Market Rules and Enforcement Regime after 1992,* Earlsgate Press, 1993

Gareth L Jones is Departmental Purchasing Adviser at the Department of Transport. The views expressed in this article are not necessarily shared by the Department.

Contractual management of risk

David Pearson looks at different ways in which the public sector can use the contract to control exposure to risk

Gareth Jones very usefully highlighted the ways in which public-sector purchasers seek to manage contractual risk through the contract itself (Public sector risk and contract presentation, *Purchasing & Supply Management*, March 1995). The surveys carried out for that article produced some interesting corroboration of what one has seen as public-sector attitudes to contractual management of risk, and I have been prompted to offer some thoughts of my own by way of supplement and complement to what Gareth has produced.

Fixed pricing as a means of contract control

Gareth's article amply defined the public-sector purchaser's attitude to *fixed prices* generally, but it did not fully bring out the impact of the anomalies that lie hidden behind that facade. There has been a growing trend among purchasing organisations everywhere to seek and even demand fixed prices over increasing periods of time. This has been seen too often not as a means of limiting risk, but of seeking to take the fullest advantage of the buyer's market that has prevailed during the recession. Some government offices have been demanding fixed prices for as much as five years, and it is not uncommon for organisations to expect tenderers to bid on fixed prices over two years.

There is a very real danger that such an approach will not contain risk, but will substantially increase it. At a seminar held last year by a major government purchaser, a supplier asked whether the purchaser thought it was paying more that it needed to by insisting on five-year fixed prices. The supplier's view was that it would comply, because it wanted to be considered for work, but for obvious reasons firms tendering, even in a fiercely competitive marketplace, would build in sufficient cover for their position in order to manage their own risk. From the purchaser's point of view this was acceptable, because the risk was seen to be entirely on the supplier. But is it?

In such a situation the purchaser will pay more in at least years one and two than it really needs to in order to buy the insurance of a fixed price in the subsequent years. There is no guarantee, however, that the purchaser will not also pay more in years three to five than would be necessary for the specified service. So where does the risk *really* lie, and how much of it is the purchaser really carrying? When viewed rationally it is impossible in such circumstances for the purchaser to demonstrate satisfactorily for public audit purposes that it is securing the best value for money.

Although, like Gareth Jones, I am a public-sector buyer by history and by training, I feel a healthy degree of cynicism about some of the fixed price approaches that are adopted by public sector buyers in that they are often seen as the easy way out of potentially complex price negotiations and continuing contract price management. That cynicism was boosted by the response to the question raised at the seminar referred to above that fixed prices for five years were 'Treasury policy'. There were too many in that audience who knew that the Treasury had and has no such policy.

There is, of course, a legitimate attraction for the buyer in fixed prices; price management is simplified by fixed monthly bills, which have only to be checked for accuracy and paid. But, to what do the price and the monthly bills relate? Just as the only certainties in life are death and taxes, the only certainty about contracts for services is that within their term they will change, not once or twice, but constantly. What therefore happens when the purchaser's requirements change during the contract term?

Risk control through contract price management

Services contracts need to contain flexibility for change and provision for change management. The purchaser also wants, however, to maintain close control over the cost to it of the service provision. What is needed, therefore, if a flexible and tightly controlled contract - to many a seemingly insoluble paradox.

In essence, there can be no such thing in services contracting as a fixed price, because there is no such thing as a fixed service. 'Fixed prices' are therefore just a special (and applicable at a particular time) form of variable pricing. The important things to ensure in any variable price arrangement are to:

- make as much as possible a fixed price element, so that the variable elements are minimised
- clearly identify the variable elements and the circumstances that will give rise to their variance
- document these points clearly within the contract and define the process of price management that will be adopted.

Fixed prices used to be seen in public sector purchasing as a form of incentive pricing, but that view does not survive when one is contracting for services. it can be a very useful approach, however, to find some other means of introducing incentives into the variable elements of price with the aim of encouraging effective performance. Such encouragement can also be provided by the existence of damages clauses, but the carrot might sometimes be more effective than the stick. Incentives usually involve some sharing between purchaser and service provider of benefits secured by improved performance of the service. This is an attractive proposition in principle, but the effective implementation of incentive pricing requires the purchaser to have a particularly good understanding of the service provider's business.

- How, for example, would you treat the contribution to costs of assets used by more than one customer of the service provider if each customer is making its own changes to its service needs? Should your costs go up because someone else is using the assets to a lesser extent?
- What about contribution to profit? How is the profitability to the service provider of each customer to be judged? Some customers need a great deal of care and attention; others are more self sufficient, and this can change over time. This is very difficult, if not impossible, to control.
- Who pays for marketing costs? Should a customer, who has gone through a lengthy procurement exercise, pay more, and an old pal of the service provider, who always give it the business, pay nothing?

In many cases incentive pricing arrangements can result in much more work than the returns can reasonably justify, and purchasers should not seek to enter into them without very careful consideration. It is essential to that consideration and to the provision of adequate information for the control of risk that the purchaser should arm himself with a detailed understanding of the service provider's costs; how they relate to the prices, and how they will be affected by contractual change.

How many purchasers readily include in their invitations to tender the questions that will ensure that firms tendering declare the costs base of their tenders? Whenever I raise this question at conference and seminars, I receive a steady stream of responses from delegates demonstrating a total lack of belief in the purchaser's ability to extract this information. At the same time delegates readily subscribe to the principles of partnership sourcing and long-term relationships with their suppliers and service providers. They even talk about 'open book accounting' and the audit of service providers' cost, but what good is that if one does not know at the outset what the costs *ought* to be? Surely what the purchaser is looking for is not an 'actual costs' basis, but one of efficient and competitive costs auditable against a competitively tendered base.

From the viewpoint of risk control, it is essential that the purchaser should establish such a level of knowledge and understanding of service provider's costs, so that

- future changes may be the better controlled and the attendant risks of higher expenditure minimised
- all costs incurred by the purchaser, the prices paid and the payments made under a contract are seen to be fully justified and accompanied by a clear and detailed audit trail.

General management of the contract

Contract price management is one aspect only of the general management of any contract. So one returns to the point raised by Gareth Jones about the use of the contract to control risk, but with one important difference, which is to recognise that the contract comprises two fundamental elements. These are what I term as the 'legal element', which is largely the general or standard conditions of contract, and the 'commercial element', which is the real substance of the contract. Gareth's observations on forms and conditions of contract refer mostly to the legal element, where the concentration is on legal definitions, warranties and what happens when things go wrong. The importance of the commercial element is that it concentrates on the executive aspects of the contract, on what happens day to day, and how the parties will work to ensure that it does not go wrong.

It is not a perfect world, and nothing works faultlessly all the time. Contracts, therefore, raise problems and difficulties will never be avoided totally. It is within the power of both buyer and seller, however, to minimise the failure rate by concentrating their efforts on getting the commercial element of the contract clearly defined, so that day-to-day management of the contract and its performance by both parties can make the greatest contribution to the management of contractual risk. Regrettably, it is this part of the contract arrangements that usually receives the least attention in the contract preparations.

there are some fundamental factors of purchasing, particularly services purchasing, which are not properly appreciated or attended to. The most basic of these is the need for the purchaser to be absolutely sure that it knows what it wants. This is so obvious that it usually does not get mentioned, but that often lies at the root of the problems that purchasers and sellers subsequently encounter. Far too many services contracts are set up without an adequate understanding of what is required, which leads to inadequate specification. If the heart of the contract is inadequate, what price will anyone give on the success of the contract manager in trying to achieve the necessary outcome.

Mention of the contract manager brings me to the second of the fundamentals that are too often passed over. Contract management is generally recognised throughout business and commerce as a specialist skill. No purchasing or selling organisation would seriously consider entering into a major construction contract or a major capital purchase without knowing very clearly who would be the contract manager and how that manager would operate, not just on one side of the contract but for both parties. In the majority of cases the contract manager is identified before the contract is placed and contributes to the pre-contract work. Compare the usual approach to services contracts, which can easily be of major overall value when taken over a three to five year term or longer. The contract manager is usually appointed when the contract has been placed, having had no, or at best very little pre-contract involvement, and will frequently have little real experience of contract management. Consequently, the contract will all too often be inadequate in terms of the contract management structure to which the parties will be required to adhere, and the purchaser's contract manager will be at a disadvantage to his or her opposite number on the service provider's team in terms of experience and training. The level of risk to the purchaser is therefore unacceptably high.

These failings can be overcome, not just be concentrating on the legal element of the contract (although that will make its contribution when all else fails), but also by working very hard at establishing the commercial element of the contract. The questions that have to be asked by any purchaser in preparing that include:

- who does what?
- for whom?
- when and where?
- at what cost and for what price?
- to what quality?
- for how long?
- against what performance measures?
- under what monitoring arrangements?

I know this wood is again very clearly visible, but purchasers of services frequently spend too much time looking at the trees and fail to see it. The trees are all the 'political' issues surrounding the decision to out-source or market test or the compulsion to seek competitive tenders and the opposition often found mounted against it.

In February 1993 at a CIPS conference on Risk and Dispute Management, I presented a paper on 'Optimising Contract Strategy'. In that I referred to the need for purchasers to 'get back to basics'. Unfortunately for me, Prime Minister John Major chose that year's Conservative Party Conference to launch his own ill-fated 'Back to Basics' campaign, which rendered my own choice of phrase inoperable thereafter. Perhaps enough dust has now settled on Mr Major's adoption of my phrase for me to return to it, because it is something that purchasers of services desperately need to remember if they are to simplify the approach to contractual management of risk and start to make it effective.

Risk control through performance measurement

Having awarded the contract, the purchaser has to consider its performance. Is it going to work? Will the service provider perform? Is all the information ready?

Now is the time that the purchaser will start to use the performance indicators, which have been planned and built into the contract. The contract is two-sided, the service provider is contracted to provide a service and, if he does so, the purchaser is contracted to pay for it. The key questions for the purchaser are:

- how do I know whether the service has been provided?
- how do I prove it?
- how do I judge if it is of acceptable quality?
- how much should I pay for it?

The purchaser needs some method, preferably objective, of recording the level and quality of service provided. The acquisition of data on service levels will enable the purchaser to analyse it to determine how closely the service provided matches what is stated in the contract, to identify areas where contract management needs to direct its attention and take corrective action. This is all summed up succinctly by the old management dictum: 'You can't manage what you can't measure!'

Without performance measurement the purchaser cannot manage the contract to optimise value for money and maximise risk control. The purchaser must give serious thought to what aspects of performance it is going to measure. Services vary in their nature and their requirements, so units of measurement have to be selected to match the particular service.

Summary and conclusions

The purchaser of services, be it public-sector or private company, will not be capable of adequate contractual environment that enable it to be in control of the process and not under the control of arrangements laid down by others. Contractual management of risk will be optimised by ensuring that:
- appropriate pricing mechanisms are established to suit the task in hand and not by slavishly following doctrinal approaches usually contained in prescriptive operations manuals
- the contract structure pays proper heed to the executive, commercial aspects, which form the very heart of the contract, and which enable the purchaser to build in measures designed to prevent problems and disputes and minimise the impact of those that cannot be prevented
- the importance of contract management generally is recognised and the status and training of contract managers as an essential resource is given the prominence it richly merits.

Over the last three years, one has been able to detect in both public and private sectors the dawning of recognition of the importance of contract management and the special and wide-ranging skills it demands. In the public sector the CUP has produced its Guidance on Contract Management, but this is only the first small step, and the real impact will await a growing implementation of the principles of good contract management across the purchasing spectrum.

Through association with Grosvenor Consultancy Services Ltd I was able to make a substantial contribution to the CUP Guidance on contract management, and I am indebted also to that association for a number of the other threads of thought in this article.

David Pearson is managing partner of DJP Consultancy, which provides specialist consultancy and training in purchasing and contract management. He is a Fellow of the Chartered Institute of Purchasing and Supply, and chairman of its Legal committee and an Associate of the Chartered Institute of Arbitrators.

So, farewell then, market overt

Everything changes, even the Sale of Goods Act, as Professor Geoffrey Woodroffe reminds us

The sale of Goods Act 1893 has stood the test of time remarkably well. Indeed, for a centenarian, it is still in remarkably good shape with its basic framework intact. Some minor surgery has taken place from time to time, for example in 1973 a statutory attack on exemption clauses was launched by amending section 55, but these controlling provisions were removed within a few years and expanded into the Unfair Contract Terms Act 1977.

Some other small changes were also made in 1973, and in 1954 a number of detailed amendments had been passed. To simplify matter the Sale of Goods Act 2979 was passed. It was only a consolidating statute, ie a statute which was not intended to change the law, merely to re-enact the 1893 Act with the intervening changes. This left us with one piece of legislation to look at rather than the original Act with amendments here and there.

Background to the Act

However, the Act was showing its age and some of the wording revealed its Victorian origins, for example that well-known expression 'merchantable quality' to be found in section 14(2). The judges also expressed some anxiety about the way in which buyers were sometimes able to escape their responsibilities by terminating contracts on the grounds of breach of contract by the sellers, even where the sellers' breaches were relatively unimportant and had no real commercial effect on the buyers' positions. The Law Commission thoroughly examined these matters in their report *Sales and Supply of Goods,* published in 1987. Their conclusions received general support, but the problem was to find Parliamentary time for matters considered by the Government to be of small national importance. An attempt was made in 1990 to introduce these reforms as part of the Consumer Guarantees Bill - a Private Members' Bill supported by the National Consumer Council - but failed at the last ditch because of government objections to other provisions in the Bill. A further - and this time successful - attempt was made in 1994 using the same Private Members' bill route.

The upshot is that the Sale and Supply of Goods Act 1994 received the Royal Assent in the autumn. Before discussing some of the provisions, let me make three main points:
- the Act came into force on 3 January 1994
- the Act is not retrospective: it applies only to contracts made after the Act came into force
- the Act merely amends - not repeals - the 1893 Act.

The essential changes are to be found in the first four pages of the Act in sections 1-4. In addition there are pages of detailed consequential amendments and repeals set out in its three schedules.

there are also special provisions relating to Scotland to be found in section 5 and Schedule 1, bringing Scotland within the Supply of Goods and Services Act 1982 with provisions specially worded to fit Scots law.

Satisfactory quality

The new, end-of-millennium phrase is 'satisfactory quality' and old 'merchantable quality' flits sadly back to its Victorian past. The sub-section imposing this quality obligation on sellers remains section 14(2). However, there is a new definition set out in section 14(2A): '.... goods are of satisfactory quality if they meet the standard that a reasonable person would regard as satisfactory, taking account any description of the goods, the price (if relevant) and all other relevant circumstances'.

The words after the comma are almost identical to those in the old definition, and the earlier words do not in my view make any significant change, but what is new is that section 14(2B) contains a non-exhaustive list of various 'aspects of the quality' - a fitness for all the purposes for which goods of the kind in question are commonly supplied:
- appearance and finish
- freedom from minor defects

- safety
- durability

These amendments are not earth-shattering. For example, the general theme to be found in the above is similar to the wording of the old definition in section 14(6) of the 1979 Act, but there is one distinction which is important in relation to multi-purpose goods, namely, that the new definition requires the goods to be fit for *'all'* their purposes, whereas cases on the old definition made it clear that goods had to be fit for only one of their common purposes. This strengthens the buyer's position against the seller.

The earlier legislation did not set out a list of other aspects; b) to e) above are all new. But cases on the earlier definition had shown that these features were all encompassed by the general definition of 'merchantable quality'. Even so, it is useful for buyers - and this is the main reason for the change - to be able to point a finger at the relevant aspect in the legislation, when discussing a complaint with a supplier, rather than having to rely on judicial statements to be found in the law reports.

Acceptance

Section 2 of the 1994 Act amends sections 34 and 35 of the 1979 Act. It will be remembered that a buyer loses the right to rejection, even though the seller has broken a condition of the contract, where the buyer 'accepts' the goods. There are, and were, three varieties of acceptance set out in section 35:
- the buyer intimates acceptance to the seller, or
- the goods are delivered to the buyer who does something inconsistent with the ownership of the seller, or
- the buyer retains the goods after the lapse of a reasonable time without rejecting them.

It is now clear that in the first two situations, buyers will not be treated as having accepted the goods until they have had a reasonable opportunity of examining them, for example to ascertain whether they are in conformity with the contract.

Here, though, we come across the first of a number of cases where sellers by their terms and conditions of sale may change the rules in their own favour. This comes as no surprise, a s the statutory, commercial code in the Sale of Goods Act is meant to provide a set of rules of thumb which the parties to the contract can alter, if they wish. That is true of this provision. Of course, if sellers attempt to remove the right of a buyer to reject for breach of contract, such clauses are subject to the Unfair Contract Terms Act 1977 and in a business-to-business relationship must be fair and reasonable.

However, the Act specifically provides that the right of examination cannot be removed from a buyer in a consumer contract. This is the first time that the Sale of Goods Act 2979 has included a provision which makes a distinction between consumer and non-consumer contracts. The distinction appears elsewhere, too.

Another improvement for buyers is to be found in section 2 - they are not deemed to have accepted the goods merely because they agree to their repair under an arrangement with the seller or the goods are delivered to someone else under a sub-sale. Hitherto in these situations the buyer was confined to damages, and cold not reject for breach of condition.

Right of partial rejection

There is another amendment to section 35. The problem is this. A buyer accepts part of a consignment and then discovers that the consignment (or the rest of it) does not comply with the contract terms. The buyer wishes to reject the rest of the consignment. Previously, because the buyer had accepted *part* of the goods, he or she was unable to reject the rest (see the previous wording of section 1(4). The buyer is now better off. But, again, observe that the Act permits the contract to provide otherwise where 'a contrary intention appears'. Sellers may therefore change their terms of business to provide that acceptance by a buyer or part of a consignment removes the buyer's right to reject the rest.

Slight breaches

There have been numerous cases where buyers have used a technical breach of contract (a minor and unimportant deviation from specification, for example) as an excuse to terminate a contract, when perhaps the real reason for termination was something unrelated to the seller's breach, such as a fall in market prices: the buyer then wishes to cancel the contract to be able to buy at the new lower prices.

The problem for the courts has been that as the Act states that the terms relating to description, quality, fitness for purpose and sample are all *'conditions,'* once a seller has broken a condition a buyer has a right to treat a contract as at an end because of the seller's breach. The court could go only one of two ways: acknowledge that there had been a breach of condition and therefore permit the buyer to pull out of the contract; or decide that there has been no breach at all, leaving the buyer with no remedy, not even the right to damages. The court could not take a middle route and decide that there had been a minor breach of condition entitling the buyer to claim damages, but not to reject the goods.

The court's dichotomy has now been relieved by section 4 of the 1994 Act. This provides that where 'the breach is so slight that it would be unreasonable for him to reject them', the buyer may not treat the breach as a breach of condition, but may treat it only as a breach of warranty, ie the buyer is confined to damages for the breach. Bearing in mind that it is the seller who is at fault, the Act provides that the seller must show that the breach is a slight one.

But the commercial buyer must bear two points in mind. First, this provision applies only to breaches of the statutory implied terms. Secondly, once again this provision will have no application where 'a contrary intention appears'. This time buyers must look to their own ts and cs, for a well-drafted clause will enable a buyer to terminate a contract for any breach of sections 13-15, whether slight or not. It is, of course, a question of policy for the buyer to reflect on whether such an express provision is appropriate in these days of partnership purchasing.

Finally, in this section, too, we find the distinction made between commercial buyers and consumers. If the buyer is a consumer, it matters not whether the breach is a slight one or not - the buyer may still reject. The thinking behind this exception is that one of the main weapons in the consumer's armoury is his or her right to reject goods for breach of condition; if this right were qualified in any way, the consumer would find it even more difficult to negotiate with sellers when things went wrong. In contrast, commercial buyers are better able to take care of themselves, for example by appropriate terms of business.

Throughout my comments I have been talking about amendments to the 1979 Act. It is important to reiterate that the 1979 Act has not been repealed, merely amended. In discussions with suppliers where things have gone wrong, the buyer will still be referring to the 1979 Act. If buyers wish to be legalistic in appropriate cases they may, of course, refer to the 1979 Act, as amended by the 1994 Act.

Market overt

The second Act which I wish to discuss is the Sale of Goods (Amendment) Act 1994. This is short and sweet - it runs to about a dozen lines. Its essence appears in section one: 'Section 2(1) (relating to the sale of goods in market overt) of the Sale of Goods Act 1979 is hereby repealed.'

What more need I say? This had been the only exception to the *nemo dat* principle which assisted a buyer where goods had been stolen. Its repeal saddens those of us in academic life who have spent decades explaining to law students the background to this Elizabethan rule and its technical application. No longer will we be able to discuss stolen Adam candelabra turning up in the New Caledonian market, for this exception has now been abolished

The upshot is that if your goods are stolen and you later find out where they are, you will be able to recover them. No exception will assist the current 'owner', brimming over with *bona fides* though he or she may be!

Chapter 9: Technology & Communications

The wireless warehouse ... and more

Martin Hiscox outlines the benefits radio frequency communication offers to logistics operations in the shed and on the floor

Anyone who has tripped over the spaghetti of cables dangling from the back of PCs, printers, terminals and modems, will be relieved to hear that 'wire-less' data communications is developing apace, and applications are now in place within organisations in a broad range of business sectors.

Although commercial management has long enjoyed the benefits of wireless computers in the form of batter-powered hand-held and laptop models, Radio Frequency Data Communications (RFDC) has taken the concept one step further by combining portable computing power with the ability to communicate to and from a host computer or network *in real-time*.

RFDC, introduced in the USA in the mid 1980s, links computers by means of radio rather than copper or fibre optic cable, in the same way as a portable telephone. In the UK, the technology has found its niche in warehousing, distribution and manufacturing environments where it forms an increasingly important part of logistics technology solutions.

The range and complexity of applications for RFDC is growing all the time, with typical examples including putaway, picking and shipping industrial and retail warehousing, parts stores control and line feed in manufacturing, and control of containers and vehicles in docks and ports.

These examples are, however, just the tip of the iceberg. The use of RF technology is only limited by the availability of products at the right price and people with the foresight to identify cost justifiable applications, and we are seeing the development of new opportunities all the time.

Real-time role

The growth of RFDC coincides with major changes in the thinking behind materials tracking and control in recent years. Most significant has been the widespread recognition that, with inventory management representing up to 80 per cent of typical operating costs, the fast and efficient flow of materials through the logistics chain is key to business survival. As a result, investment in logistics technology solutions has remained a priority throughout the recession.

Indeed, in our experience, all those involved in the purchase decision, from warehouse supervisor to purchasing manager and the managing director, are keenly aware that, correctly implemented, logistics technology not only revolutionises handling operations, but also opens up new opportunities.

Improved utilisation of resources - both people and equipment - leads to increased productivity, instant inventory information allows stockholding to be reduced, and random stock allocation allows better use of warehouse space. Add to this greater accuracy, reduced paperwork and 'on-tap' management information covering every aspect of the warehouse operation, as provided by RF communications, and the systems quickly justify themselves.

Trends in logistics technology

For most organisation's the implementation of a complete stock/materials management system forms part of a longer term strategy to introduce flexible departmental systems able to support the changing requirements of the business. For this reason, flexibility is now a key factor in the logistics technology market, with conventional warehouses, as well as manufacturing stores operations, looking to adopt systems which can be installed, modified and expanded quickly and less expensively than some bespoke systems.

this can often be achieved by using a modular approach which enables a system to be customised to give the detailed functions, screen presentation formats and management information appropriate to the individual application. In the case of our Dispatcher system, for example, a core program tracks inventory and performs overall management tasks, while operational modules cover every aspect of materials control, from receiving, putaway and picking, to quality control, despatch, management information and data input/output.

Another trend in the logistics technology market today is for companies to move towards integrating the isolated pockets of automation which have often grown up as a result of limited budgets and segregated payback criteria. In this respect, new client/server software, which enables new applications to interface with existing applications within various host computer environments, is enabling organisations with half completed strategies to fill the gaps in both the automation and management information chain.

Equally important has been the introduction of systems which not only improve control of physical material flow, but also management's visibility of real-time operations. This is where RF fits in - communicating data from the shop floor to the host computer and back again in real-time.

RFDC

Most RFDC systems comprise three distinct components: Network Controller or Computer Interface Unit (CIU), Radio Frequency Unit (RFU) and Radio Data Terminals (RDT).

The Network Controller or Computer Interface Unit is effectively the intelligence of the system. It handles messages to and from the host computer, checks message integrity, maintains the host protocol and controls the sending and receiving of messages over the radio link. The CIU in most RFDC systems is capable of supporting one host connection and a number of RFUs. It can also support native host computer protocols which can be useful when configuring a system to interface to an existing application.

The RFU in its simplest form is a modem, a radio frequency transceiver and an antenna system. Designed to convert digital signals from the Network Controller to radio signals, the RFU is generally located to provide optimum radio frequency communication throughout the geographical area. It is linked back to the Network Controller or CIU using current loop cabling (for distances up to 1km). RS232 link, or through Token Ring, or Ethernet networks.

RDTs are available in various formats and are categorised as truck-mounted or hand-held. Today's models incorporate a multi-character display, full keyboard and special function keys, and are designed to withstand hostile industrial conditions.

LIS, which supplies the market-leading LXE range of RFDC equipment, is about to launch a new hand-held RDT product which combines a bar code scanner, full function keyboard and 8 line x 40 column display in a single, ergonomically designed unit.

RDTs can run a proprietary message protocol or, when used in conjunction with the appropriate base station, can emulate some commonly used standard VDUs. In some instances, it is possible to support multiple terminal emulations concurrently. The operator can use this facility to access various software applications on different computers from a single terminal.

Opening the door to RFDC

Technological developments in the computing and communications world have allowed the possibilities of RFDC to expand rapidly in recent years. For example, real-time host computer systems with large, fast access databases and processing power are now available to handle the high number of enquiries produced by an RF system. In the past, none but the largest of computer mainframes could handle the throughput required.

Similarly, computers and terminals capable of handling information processing, presentation and retrieval in the field are now truly mobile. Historically, such devices required mains power or large batteries, and CRTs for displays were generally not portable. In addition, the increasing availability of software packages that permit RDT linkage to the plant or warehouse control system greatly simplifies their integration with existing operations.

Another important development is the ability of an RF system to become an extension of an existing network through the use of network integration techniques, industry standard connections and communications protocols.

LIS is believed to be the first RFDC vendor to offer seamless connectivity to standard Token Ring and Ethernet LANs. The company's LXE RF LAN system architecture can support up to 4000 terminals across multiple facilities, allowing each hard-wired element of the RF system to connect directly onto an Ethernet backbone, for example, and to communicate with multiple applications running on a number of host computers residing on the network. This also eliminates the need for dedicated, often costly, cabling to the RFUs.

RF in demand

With developments such ass these, it is hardly surprising that RFDC systems are now in popular demand for a variety of applications. For example, in semi-mechanised material handling systems where the primary delivery device if the fork lift truck, hand-held and vehicle mounted RDTs have emerged as reliable tools for both inventory and vehicle/driver management. Beyond the basic thrust towards tighter control of inventory, improved use of people is mot often cited as justification of these devices.

The on-line capability of RFDC has also brought the error reduction potential of the computer system right down into the working environment. The elimination of manually written paper systems can dramatically reduce errors caused through writing, verifying and keying information. Typically keying of data will result in one error in every 50 keystrokes. The beauty of an RFDC system is that it can catch each one. In industry, RFDC has become an operational tool for providing timely, accurate data which is so necessary for the implementation of concepts such as Computer Integrated Manufacturing (CIM) and Just-in-Time (JIT).

Automatic identification

RFDC also has an important role to play in complementing and improving the productivity and accuracy gains produced by the use of Automatic Identification, the most common form of which is bar coding. This technology has dramatically expanded over recent years and its acceptance has been achieved for many reasons, including the efficiency gained through productivity improvements, the cost savings resulting from enhanced accuracy, the use of industry standards for the unique identification of products and on-going pressure to improve the quality of customer service.

The use of Auto ID in the factory data collection sector has only recently become widely cost justifiable. The costs of producing environmentally rugged devices has limited applications to all but certain industries that could justify the high level of investment. However, products designed specifically for this sector are now forecast to grow at a faster rate than the established retail sector.

FIGURE 1 Compliance with industry standard LAN architecture and TCP/IP or SNA protocols

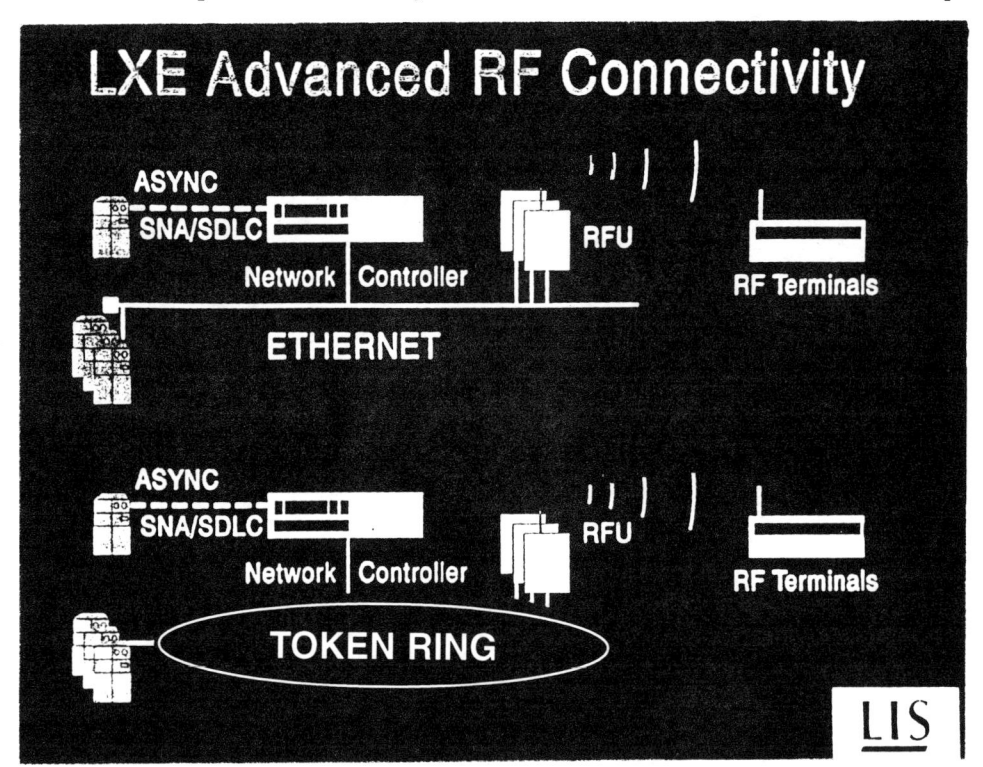

Choosing and using RFDC

Traditionally, the use of advanced logistics technology solutions utilising RFDC has been concentrated in larger facilities, the majority falling between 20,000 and 100,000 sq metres. However, recent advances in technology such as the ability to make use of a company's existing network facilities have allowed more favourable entry level pricing. This has enabled smaller organisations to access the benefits enjoyed by their larger counterparts. Whatever the size of the business, companies investing in RFDC as part of a logistics technology implementation programme can usually expect to see payback within one to three years.

However, selecting RFDC systems, as well as other specialist technologies associated with materials and inventory management, is not a simple purchase, and requires the forming of a business relationship with a supplier. As has been seen in the PC market, the ability to supply product is far from the only consideration when selecting critical system components.

Potential users should satisfy themselves that they are entering a relationship with suppliers which can demonstrate their ability to deliver proven working systems, and their ability to support those systems on an on-going basis. To achieve this, a detailed functional specification and, where appropriate, an RF propagation survey, should form the basis upon which a system can be installed against guaranteed performance criteria and provide a benchmark upon which acceptance can be agreed.

Logistics technology is a dynamic arena within which existing and developing technologies offer companies a dimension to collecting and controlling operation management data previously only dreamt of. The potential for improving efficiency, and thus reducing costs, is vast, and the investment involved in achieving the many benefits that logistics technology can offer should certainly be integrated into any forward-thinking organisation's strategic development plan.

Here's the medium, what's the message?

What is holding back a take-off in electronic trading? Marcia Macleod investigates

There are now approximately 1,000 companies using Electronic Data Interchange (EDI) in the UK - not many, considering the potentially revolutionary effect electronic trading can have on order processing, inventory management, business partnerships and that all-important bottom line.

But no-one should dismiss EDI as a flash in the pan just yet: the barriers which have held up its growth are slowly being overcome, making it easier for even smaller companies to take the EDI plunge.

One of these barriers - perhaps the biggest - has been the investment in both money and time required to implement a successful system. It isn't cheap - but any company which has at least a 386 or 486 PC should be able to become 'EDI capable' ie to send and receive messages - from around £5,000, plus usage charges. (These, however, are said to be less than the cost of physically printing and sending the same information).

'If a potential user is looking at the costs of sending a few invoices a month against the start-up costs for EDI, it may think it's not worth it,' admits Gary Lynch, head of the EDI Association (EDIA) . But, he adds, a number of small companies set implementation of EDI against retaining business - and then it comes cost-justifiable.

The need to retain business by complying with 'requests' from large customers to use EDI is sometimes as much a hindrance as a help. Many smaller companies resent being forced into investing in something they don't see as particularly beneficial. But help is at hand for those attracted to the concept of EDI, but either nervous of taking the first steps or at a loss where to begin.

The EDIA has been granted 87,000 Ecus (£66,000) of EC money to extend its EDI awareness project for small and medium sized enterprises (SMEs) being run with the Chambers of Commerce. The initial project was launched with 100,000 Ecus (£77,000) from TE-DIS, the EC working party set up to further EDI and other technological developments, to establish 20 EDI Awareness Clubs. The clubs, five of which are up and running, benefit from a year's free membership of the EDIA, including a dedicated helpline; an EDI library, including print, audio, video and disk material; an 'introduction to EDI' seminar; and a users' forum in which established EDI users, new and potential users can meet to exchange experiences.

The second phase extends the number of clubs to 30. In addition, the EDIA will set up an SME accreditation and registration scheme to help give users a 'competitive edge'; develop modelling tools to provide guidance to SMEs on costs, benefits etc; produce a directory of EDI software providers and other sources of industry help; and run implementation - as opposed to introductory - courses.

Another initiative comes from UNCTAD, the UN Committee for Trade and Development, which has backed the establishment of trade points worldwide. As delegates at the recent World EDI Congress were told, trade points are aimed at helping SMEs to facilitate international trade - including EDI - in an effort to reduce the US$800bn worth of non-tariff barriers to trade., The British trade point is at Sitpro in London.

Other issues which have been addressed in an effort to progress EDI include security of electronic documents and standards. Security has been looked at by all national and international bodies involved with EDI - the EDIA, the EC, the Edifact Board, etc. Model Interchange Agreements now exist, suggesting criteria and requirements to be included in a contract governing EDI usage between two trading partners; a set of Uniform Rule for EDI, currently being drafted by Unitral, the UN Commission on International Trade Law, will be recommended to governments to provide an internationally harmonised approach to legal aspects of EDI; an the idea of an electronic notary is being examined by relevant bodies within the EC.

The standards issue raised its ugly head again at the World Congress, when delegates heard first, that the EDIA in the US has gone bankrupt, and second, that the Clinton initiative to get US government departments trading electronically was based on the US' Ansi X.12 standard, instead of the UN approved international standard, Edifact. The EDIA failure is said by some to be due to the conflict between the pro-Edifact American EDIA and Ansi X.12 Board.

However, most companies - outside the US, at least - which seriously want to use EDI internationally will use Edifact, even if they may use another standard for domestic trade. Certainly industry user groups are advocating the use of Edifact wherever possible. There are now 42 fully approved Edifact messages, 127 others in various stages, and six Edifact boards worldwide.

Edifice, the ERDI user group for the electronics industry, is just one supporting only Edifact. It has two message sub-groups; one for development, one for assessment - to help develop and test Edifact messages specific to the industry and not yet addressed by the Edifact Board. These include the Delfor, for blanket ordering, and Deljit for call-offs.

Edifice also has sub-groups to deal with communications and technical issues, advising members on protocols and liaising with Vans, for example; business interests; and publicity and promotion. Other industry groups - albeit perhaps not quite as active - exist in many sectors. Rinet, for instance, is a Pan-European user group for the insurance and reinsurance industry; EMEDI, or European Medical EDI, covers the health care sector; and Editex aims to promote EDI in the textile industry.

The freight industry, which lagged behind other sectors after initially pioneering EDI in the early '80s with Dish and Shipnet, is attempting to get the EDI ball rolling again with the co-operation of Ediship, the deep sea EDI user group; Asset for short-sea operators; Lotus, the EDIA transport group, and Edisc, the EDI shippers' council. All are now migrating to the Edifact IFTM freight messages.

The spread of EDI among freight companies is paramount if 'international EDI' - ie electronic trading between countries and continents - is to be effected. And without international EDI, many companies, especially those with overseas branches, subsidiaries or joint ventures, would not be able to benefit fully from electronic trading.

EDI is spreading worldwide - in countries as far afield as Taiwan, Malaysia, Chile, Argentina and Iceland. And while in most cases, EDI begins on a domestic basis, the new entrants, learning from the experience of others, are often targeting shipping and international trade as a prime candidate for the new technology. In Malaysia, for example, one of the first EDI projects to actually get off the ground centres around Port Kelang. Begun in April this year, the Port Kelang Community System enables import and export declarations, duty payments, manifests and free zone declarations to be sent via EDI. It is envisaged that, eventually, PKCS will involve 22 government agencies, 350 freight forwarders, 150 shipping agents, 5 hauliers and 12 banks.

A National EDI project was begun in the early 1990s, and a Malaysian Edifact Committee and an EDI Implementation and Co-ordination Committee formed in 1992. The MEC co-ordinates and implements message standards, and has working groups to deal with Customs, transport, technical assessment, purchasing, finance and insurance, and awareness and education. The EDICC is setting up a single national EDI clearing centre to ensure a planned, harmonised implementation of EDI nationwide, and other industry groups are being set up for the finance community, veterinary services, and textile exporters.

Taiwan - which hosts the 1995 EDI World Congress - has several EDI projects on the go, with government support. Just under US$100m is being spent on a 10-year project to automate all commerce, and ensure all business, however small, uses IT, including EDI. The automation of manufacturing processes is also being encouraged, as is financial EDI (a growth sector in Taiwan) and electronic Customs clearance.

'Taiwan has one of the more developed IT industries in the region', explains Fred Li, chairman of the Taiwan Vanguard Information Group, and a director of the EDI World Institute, based in Montreal. 'But there are technical problems with the Chinese version of EDI. We are trying to solve this locally - especially as there is also a lot of interest in mainland China.' China already has a financial network, Gold, for banks.

Elsewhere in the Pacific, the Philippines has a World Bank grant to start an EDI service, and a Canadian firm is launching a commercial EDI service; Thailand has invited GEIS to launch an EDI van, although there is not too much serious effort to get EDI off the ground, and Mauritius has begun Government-supported EDI activity.

Singapore, Hong Kong and Korea are already well documented: Singapore led the world in creating a national EDI network, and is now insisting that all ships which dock at the island send pre-arrival cargo advice to the port authority and Customs via EDI.

Australia is another world leader in EDI, setting up the EDI Council (Edica) in 1988. there are now 450 corporate members. An Electronic Messaging Association (Emma) was established a year ago to focus on other forms of electronic trading. Shipping was an early industry user of EDI with a national network called Tradegate which now send 13M messages per annum between 2000 user sites - ports, airports, agents, hauliers and shippers. It already links to South Korea's KTNet and Singapore's Tradfenet, and wishes to link to all other world port/airport communities.

There are a number of working parties dealing with a range of other industries - Big (banking and trade finance), accounting, agribusiness, the automotive sector (80-90 per cent of parts are now ordered electronically), chemicals, construction, communications (ie Telecoms Australia), the federal government, HEMMP, which deals with heavy engineering, mining and minerals processing, and the DIY industry, which is now forming an EDI group.

The US, probably the first country in the world to use EDI, is, as mentioned earlier, going through a standards crisis. If Clinton can opt for Ansi X.12 - even while recognising the importance to Government departments of trading electronically with their wide range of overseas suppliers - why should groups like the ISA, the US shipping EDI group, do any differently? Onlookers like Paul Lemme, a consultant helping the ISA and one of the early developers of the AnsiX.12 standard, believes, however, that the US will have to migrate to Edifact. There is,' he says, 'no other standard'.

If the US is an extensive user of EDI, its northern neighbour, Canada, is not far behind. Many Northern American companies - Wal-Mart, Sears etc - cover both countries, so use EDI cross-border.

The Canadian EDI Council has more than 1,000 members and five offices; the federal Government encourages EDI - forcing Government suppliers to trade electronically - and EDI is also growing in the automotive, food, pharmaceutical and retail sectors. It is believed that there are over 6,000 active EDI users in Canada.

EDI is also alive and well in Latin America, Mexico, for instance, has a number of EDI initiatives in progress, spurred by the North American Free Trade Agreement, while Brazil and Argentina have retail companies and some banks - and, in the case of Argentina, a farming group - using, or planning to use, EDI; Columbia has worked on EDI for two years, but is held back by telecommunications problems.

Chile has made the most advances. A full digital telecom network, based on optical fibre networks, and a sophisticated bar coding system made the progression to EDI easier. The Government took a co-ordinated approach to EDI, insisting that the entire country used the same standards, protocols, and so on. Mining, which accounts for 42 per cent of exports, retail, banks, pensions (run by private companies), health care, transport and Customs are all using EDI. Seven banks set up a Van to concentrate on the sector, now trading electronically with England, South Africa and Germany; over 100 mining companies should be using EDI by early 1995; the first medical EDI message was sent in June; and Customs plans for a national EDI clearance system within two years. Government (tax collection, treasury, central bank) and construction will begin trading electronically next year.

Closer to home, continental Europe is catching up with the UK lead in EDI. Holland, Germany and Scandinavia are particularly strong. Denmark, for instance, saw the Copenhagen Telephone Company (KTAS) and IBM Denmark set up DanNet in 1987 as an EDI van, software supplier and consultancy. Major software houses have signed agreements with DanNet to gain EDI expertise and EDI capability for their products.

The EDI Council promotes the use of EDI, now taken up by the freight sector via Translink, which gives an overview of all freight movements; Sony Nordic, for instance, cut its freight cost by 25 per cent through the use of EDI.

The retail sector, health care and plumbing, heating and ventilation are all strong EDI users; ironmongery is about to begin and the textile and clothing industry has also introduced EDI. Banking and insurance are also looking to trade electronically.

Smaller countries such as Iceland and Greece have also launched EDI initiatives - with the Greek Government giving half of 20M drachma funding to help 20 SMEs to start using EDI. Last May the EU provided funding for 100 small business users to start up an EDI system in a five-year project.

Even Central and Eastern Europe are planning to embrace EDI - starting with Customs, which should eliminate Customs checks on virtually every shipment, through the EC Phare project.

If tiny countries with low GDP, a tradition of small business, and/or a recent history of communist rule and suppression of commercial entrepreneurialism can see the benefits and potential of EDI, surely those companies in established industrial countries, such ass Britain, not yet trading electronically, can see the light.

Trading on the Net: corporate fears assuaged

Purchasing, sales, marketing, advertising, recruitment, technical research and virtually any other corporate activity are being widely conducted across the Internet and the information superhighway is coming into such common use that there is now an on-line Internet Business Centre which advises companies on how to use cyberspace to the best advantage. Yet one of the greatest fears of the corporate marketplace is that, apart from employees, there are more than 25M other people also out there in cyberspace who could possibly connect to corporate networks, or even gain unauthorised entry by hacking.

Corporate security is one subject that is always constantly examined, and a newly released paper by Peter Simkin is well worth studying. Mr Simkin is the group vice president of the Firefox Corporation, which has been building secure communications solutions inside the NetWare PC LAN operating system for more than five years, and can provide Internet connect solutions with a high degree of access security and firewalling.

Mr Simkin points out that 'issues of data security, integrity and the prevention of unauthorised access to systems and services is of paramount concern to anyone running a system or network that contains sensitive information. This is nothing new. It happens that the growth of the Internet and its increased use for commercial purposes has highlighted a problem that has not previously been a concern to the Internet's founders and existing users. It has also come about because the Internet is not owned, or run, by any one individual or organisation ... no-one can guarantee the end-to-end data transmission, integrity and security of the information flowing through the Superhighway.'

Mr Simkin believes that the two major concerns facing corporate users on Internet are firstly, how do I provide Internet access, but control the hosts and services accessed by employees? How do I control the applications being used? How do I control what is done with these applications? Secondly, how do I offer services on the Internet and allow external partners to access my services without jeopardising the security or the integrity of my own network and systems?

This extremely useful paper outlines some of these concerns, highlights the shortcomings of some solutions and describes what Firefox is doing to enable the corporate market to offer controlled and manageable access to the Internet.

Peter Simkins points out that security can mean many things to many people, because - in the context of the Internet - much depends on how a company views or uses the Internet, as well as on the Internet applications that a company has in mind. He explains: 'The Internet can be viewed in two ways: as a worldwide network for the carriage of data between end points - and these may be your own offices; or as a value added network where you are using the applications and services provided by the systems within the Internet network. 'This document certainly provides a most concise guide for any organisation seeking to ascertain how best to instal corporate security systems.

Systems growth

Secure Connections to the Internet is another report by the Digital Equipment Company which has been prepared by Dr Brian Neale. He points out: 'Recently, there has been an enormous growth in the number of systems connected to the Internet, typically growing by 100 per cent per year. The corresponding number of potential users is almost impossible to quantify, but has been variously estimated to be in the region of 15-30M ... the relaxation of the previous ban on commercial activities on the Internet (means) the pervasiveness and the ease of Internet facilities have become very attractive to commercial organisations and these are to a large degree responsible for the recent growth. According to one estimate commercial usage of the Internet has grown to more than 50 per cent by mid-1991.'

Each month, the Digital Internet connection currently handles approximately 2M Email messages, as well as providing 20,000 product and service related documents to customers; it also provides access to more than 300,000 files of public domain software as a free service to the Internet.

Digital introduced a World-Wide Web (WWW) server in October 1993 and in the first four months of operation supplied 250,000 pages of information to more than 9,000 external users and the enormous rate of growth in WWW activity seen by Digital - of more than 250 per cent per quarter - is typical of the

Internet as a whole. The higher speeds associated with Internet connections, compared with traditional dial-up connections, and the ability to handle many incoming requests simultaneously have given Digital the opportunity to make several of its new Alpha AXP systems freely available to any Internet user for demonstration or software porting activities, which would not have been practicable using convention dial-up lines.

Digital's development of a secure Internet connection has been driven by the conflicting requirements of this high level of 'public' access and virtually unrestricted access by Digital's employees to Internet resources with maintaining the security and integrity of a large corporate network. Dr Brian Neale adds that 'there are a number of characteristics of the Internet which are derived from its original purpose and which are relevant to any discussion of secure use of the Internet.

'One of these is that the network was designed to facilitate information sharing and for the network designers the availability aspects were probably more important than confidentiality and integrity. In simple terms, if one sends a data packet to the network, there is a very high probability that the Internet's powerful dynamic routing capabilities will ensure that it will be delivered to the destination, whatever destination, whatever the state of the various intermediate links.

'Typically, neither sender nor receiver will know the route the packet, the systems through which it passed, who was potentially able to read it in transit, or whether it was modified, maliciously, or otherwise. The classic example is that of electronic mail (Email), where one can have little confidence in the accuracy of the header information (sender, source address, etc), or the integrity and confidentiality of the actual message content, without additional application-level functionality (typically based on cryptographic techniques).'

Time-lock 'freeze'

Digital Notary software is yet another weapon in the on-going battle to secure corporate computer documents from unauthorised access or tampering. The system has been devised for companies involved in electronic commerce and could be used, for instance, to certify contracts or payments orders.

It is based on a patented cryptographic technology developed by Surety Technologies, working with the American telecommunications industry research laboratory Bellcore, and creates the digital equivalent of a paper audit trail. Corporate users can 'freeze' the contents of any computer document by affixing a secure digital timestamp - without having to reveal the contents to a third party.

The main function of the Digital Notary software is to make an automatic detection when electronic documents have been altered or backdated. This is achieved by the software, which creates a unique digital fingerprint for each document and then records that print with a Digital Notary co-ordinating server, over the Internet, by leased telephone line or by ISDN connection.

Surety Technologies reports an enormous interest in this software from a wide range of security conscious organisations, such as Wall Street companies, which require to automatically certify millions of stock trades as these occur; and from the pharmaceutical industry which believes the Digital Notary software could be used to establish valuable precedence for patent claims.

A single-user version of the software system can be downloaded from Surety's World Wide Web (WWW) server at its Internet address: http://www.surety.com.

A better way of extracting the digits?

ISDN is still thought of by many as the preserve of global corporations with massive data transfer requirements. But as Peter Robson reports, smaller firms can also benefit

Integrated Services Digital Network (ISDN) is one of the fastest growing businesses in the UK, and BT has experienced such an unprecedented take-up of service during the past financial year that ISDN now accounts for 20 per cent of its new business exchange lines. The growth rate for ISDN 2 is an astonishing 147 per cent, the rate for the 'more mature' ISDN 30's growth is 58 per cent, and ISDN 2 traffic to Europe has soared by 236 per cent. This increased usage to Europe has been boosted by the decision of European operators to develop a common ISDN standard, facilitating the integration of pan-European solutions and simplifying the product approvals process.

Increased ISDN usage is spreading throughout the world, as well as Europe, because BT now has connections to 30 countries, including recent launches to South Africa as well as Moscow and new countries tend to opt for European standard. Ray Pritchard, BT's global market manager ISDN, explains: 'This growth can be attributed to the cost and productivity benefits offered by ISDN an the realisation of market-driven applications developed with the customer in mind. BT in particular has focused on its customers' needs, who are increasingly becoming aware of the advantages of switched digital technology. ISDN applications are attractive to all industries and BT does not just sell lines, but addresses markets with tailored solutions.'

ISDN 30 has been regarded as the preferred method for the voice communication required of large companies since 1990 and it is a continuing trend which has been helped both by opening up ISDN 30 to small and medium sized businesses with a six-channel entry and by BT reducing the cost of conducting business internationally on three occasions in the past 18 months. The latest cost savings came into force in April and range from 11 per cent to France, Germany and the Republic of Ireland, to 46 per cent to Israel and the United Arab Emirates, as well as an average of 21 per cent to North America.

Mr Pritchard points out: 'We are meeting our commitment to give customers even better value for money. This latest price cut means BT is driving the use of business applications internationally, positioning ISDN as the most suitable network on which to build the global information superhighway.' For example, he explains that a customer using BT's ISDN 2 service of two channels for a one-hour of video-conferencing between the UK and Frankfurt will now save 11 per cent by paying just £66, instead of the previous rate of £74. Similarly, the cost of transferring a one megabyte computer graphics image from the UK to New York has fallen from £1.26p to 65p to produce a saving of 94 per cent.

BT believes ISDN has at least five major benefits for business users, and these include:

● Fast, secure and high quality communications. For ISDN is an end-to-end digital path which transmits voice, data, text and image digitally. Calls are connected much faster with the information being sent through in seconds with greater quality, reliability and with virtually no transmission errors.

● ISDN is cost effective. BT's ISDN calls are charged on a usage only basis and at the same rates as the UK's current telephone network. ISDN transfers computer files at a fraction of the time it takes across analogue lines, so there are significant savings to be made in time and cost. For example, computer files equivalent to 60 A4 sheets can be transferred by ISDN in just 25 seconds - compared to up to 23 minutes using a modem on the traditional analogue method.

● ISDN's flexibility enables business users to improve communications both within organisations and externally with customers and suppliers. A single ISDN line is sufficient for a business to have the ability to transfer computer files, conduct video-conferencing meetings and fax large documents extremely quickly and cost effectively. ISDN's ability to transmit data, text, image and voice, quickly and clearly provides users with the flexibility to edit and change information at any time. It is especially useful in circumstances when documents must be amended and approved within tight deadlines.

● ISDN boosts work productivity, because it can slash the amount of time and money spent on meetings and conferences, because it allows businesses to use video-conferencing and teleworking. Staff are able to spend more time in the office and less time attending meetings.

● ISDN improves customer service: by viewing, discussing and amending documents on computer screens, ISDN helps to improve customer service by providing clients with faster services and reducing the costs of courier services.

It has been only in the past year that new ISDN applications have attracted so much interest, but there are still just an estimated 55,000 UK users compared with more than 500,000 in Germany and 250,000 in France. One frequently voiced criticism is that BT's #400 installation charge tends to deter new users, especially small-to-medium sized companies, but BT is prepared to provide some impressive case-studies.

OMI LOGISTICS - is a company which provides integrated logistics support, including the production of technical handbooks and illustrations for major defence, aerospace and commercial organisations. Before switching to ISDN, the company sent artwork of text and illustrations by post, fax or courier to colleagues and clients. Now OMI uses ISDN 2 and desktop conferencing which allows instant communication by computers using voice, data, text and image; so potential problems are now resolved instantly, as opposed to hours - or even days - when hard copies of artwork had to be exchanged.

AUTOGLASS- is the UK's largest automotive glass replacement company, and is also an ISDN user. The company operates a nationwide freephone service for customers, so first-class communications are of paramount importance. Autoglass is currently using ISDN 2 to provide immediate data transfer between its nationwide network of branches and is accessed only when required, so costs can be kept to a minimum. The number of telephone calls made for everyday business has been reduced, and more effective financial management has been achieved by facilitating automation of data collection and distribution between branches.

NATIONAL POWER - operates power-stations throughout England and Wales, and a great deal of time and money was spent on travel to different destinations for meetings. After ISDN 2, dial-up desktop video-conferencing units were installed at several sites, meetings were able to be arranged more quickly and cost-efficiently without the need for staff to make long journeys.

Chapter 10: Staff Development

Purchasing leadership and competence development

Jon Hughes and Ian Billson outline the application of competence analysis as a strategic tool for the development of purchasing staff

The aim of this article is to guide the reader through some key features of strategic competence development, an approach that concentrates on establishing precise links between business needs, broad areas for purchasing performance improvement and the requirements for staff assessment, recruitment and development. It will, we hope, enable you to consider 'competency gaps' in your own organisation while challenging your current purchasing approaches in this area. We believe that competence development is an area where the prime business deliverables from purchasing and supplier management, such as margins improvement, year-on-year cost reduction, enhanced innovation, value delivery and complexity reduction, overlap with forward purchasing plans design to restructure supplier relationships and other long-term capabilities. Tools such as competence analysis help challenge the more traditional thinking which so often dominates the purchasing area.

Purchasing leadership is characterised by the building of fundamentally different ways of working with suppliers, developing a strong external focus on sourcing strategies that fully support business needs, creating internal platforms for change through the development application of reliable purchasing processes and ensuring appropriate collaboration with internal customers, clients and cross-functional groups. At ADR International purchasing Consultants we argue that a commitment to these goals reflects the full use of the purchasing resource, and enables firms to achieve either business or competitive advantage in the private sector, or enhanced value for money and service delivery in the public sector.

Improving organisational, team and business performance

Looking back through the last three to five years' issues of *Purchasing & Supply Management,* one cannot help but be struck by the significant changes that are occurring in the field. Many long-established beliefs, practices, working processes, tools and techniques are increasingly being challenged and questioned - by both purchasing functional heads as well as top executives. ADR is aware from its clients in major organisations across Europe, North America and the Asia Pacific Region that leading companies have finally woken up to the full potential for improving organisational, team and business performance dramatically through turning the spotlight on to purchasing and supplier management. Certainly, this has often produced interesting reactions on the part of purchasing staff - sometimes they see it as an opportunity to be grasped (one client referred to it as 'like walking in the sunshine'); more frequently as a challenge to be confronted and accommodated; and occasionally as a somewhat threatening and uncomfortable realisation that the function must now deliver greater contribution and in a way that is capable of being measured and tracked within specified business requirements.

Progressive organisations are demonstrating that whenever senior executives pay real attention to purchasing, it leads to fundamental changes in the way in which the function operates. As we have described in an earlier article in conjunction with Mark Ralf at SmithKline Beecham (see references), such change management programmes have to be planned and developed carefully, with structured and reliable implementation of proven, world class methods and tools. And they need to be fully supported by training and development, not just for full-time purchasing professionals, but for the considerable number of staff who have substantial contact with suppliers, and who are frequently found in departments such as marketing, R&D, engineering, operations, human resources and so on.

Not surprisingly, this has led companies to review systematically the types and possibilities of purchasing organisation that exist, the capabilities that are required, and the staff competencies needed.

Unfortunately, much purchasing thinking and practice has tended to adopt a somewhat simplistic approach with tendency to be stronger in concept than in successful operational implementation. Furthermore, it has at times been inclined to focus on purchasing skills and behaviour in isolation from the reality of the business contest in which many supplier relationships are operating. This is perhaps one of the reasons why there is now a reassessment of the scope and extent of partnership practices, particularly at a time of rapid price increases in many commodities and market sectors.

A core proposition of the approach advocated in this article is that if any organisation is to derive maximum benefit from its commitment and resources dedicated to staff training and development, then it should be integrated within a systematic framework as part of a structured approach, and one which majors on practical delivery of defined and valued business requirements.

FIGURE 1 Competence development process

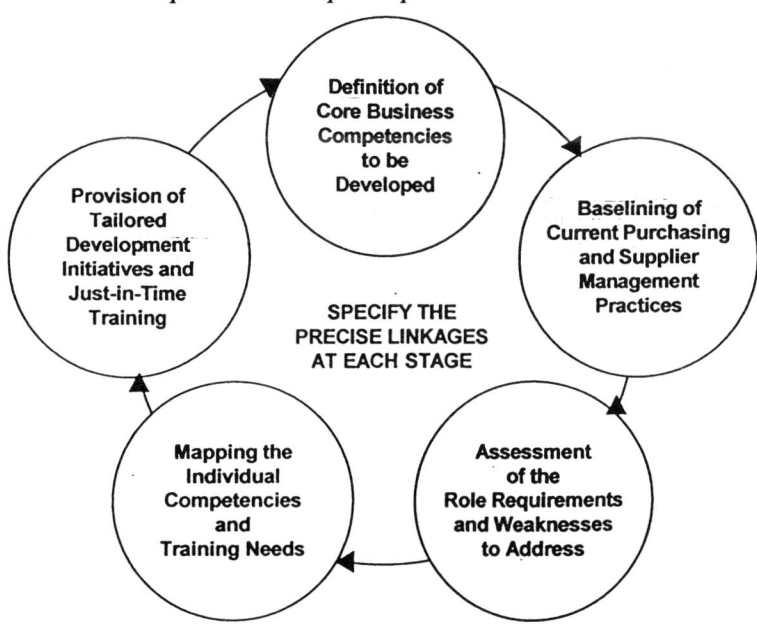

Linking business requirements and purchasing development needs

In the early 1980s, we became aware of some of the pioneering work being done on the structure of managerial competence by Richard Boyatzis at Harvard University. Over the last decade, this approach has risen in prominence and is one of the intellectual drivers behind much of the thinking that is now apparent in the Management Charter Initiative (MCI) in the UK and the implementation of educational and qualifications restructuring being driven through by the National Council for Vocational Qualifications (NCVQ). However, before appraising the current status of these approaches, we would like to summarise our five-stage process that effectively links business requirements and purchasing development needs. As you can see from Figure 1, it is an integrated, interlocking approach which assumes that it becomes a continuous business process with regular evaluation, review and updating. Let's look at each of the stages in turn:

The first stage requires a definition of the core business competencies that need to be developed. Examples of these might include speed to market, exclusive access to innovation, superior customer service, quality of manufacturing response, supply chain integration with customers or the need to achieve lowest cost production in a specific sector. There are many examples of organisations which have pursued such an approach as part of restructuring, corporate renewal, process redesign or post acquisition integration strategies. A number of these have received attention in the public domain such as Seagrams, Sainsbury's, British Airways, Anglian Water, Chase Manhattan Bank, Glaxo, the Civil Service, Mobil Oil, Rover Group, the National Health Service, the Automobile Association and Kodak.

Having mapped out the core business competencies, the net stage is to structure and complete a baselining of current purchasing and supplier management practices. The greatest benefit is achieved when this is done in the context of the explicit business competencies that need to be developed. Invariably, it highlights significant gaps in current purchasing effectiveness.

Having created a profile of business competencies and purchasing practice, the next stage is to assess the new or emerging requirements for purchasing teams and, inevitably, this usually exposes a number of prime weaknesses in expertise and individual competence that need to be addressed in the training and development plan.

The fourth part of the process is a systematic mapping of these individual competencies an training needs. The tricky bit is to keep on making explicit the linkages between business requirements, the purchasing improvement themes that will doubtless have been detected, and individual competencies for development. As a way of illustrating what we mean by these linkages, Figure 2 provides an example from a company that is focused on achieving lowest cost production status in its sector. This business requirement led to an analysis of a number of 'improvement themes' such as the need to develop a stronger regime of cost management, plan more effectively for cost reduction, strengthen strategic supplier management and enhance cross-functional team processes. In turn, a series of individual competencies were profiled and incorporated into a two-year coaching and action learning programme.

The final stage, therefore, is to design, resource and deliver tailored training and development across all of those functional groups who are involved in sourcing and supplier management. In particular, we advocate that modern methods of training delivery, for example videos, audio cassette packages and computer-based multi-media, become an integral part of such delivery programmes to provider 'Just-in-Time' training. this is particularly important for the larger, multi-site and multi-country firms.

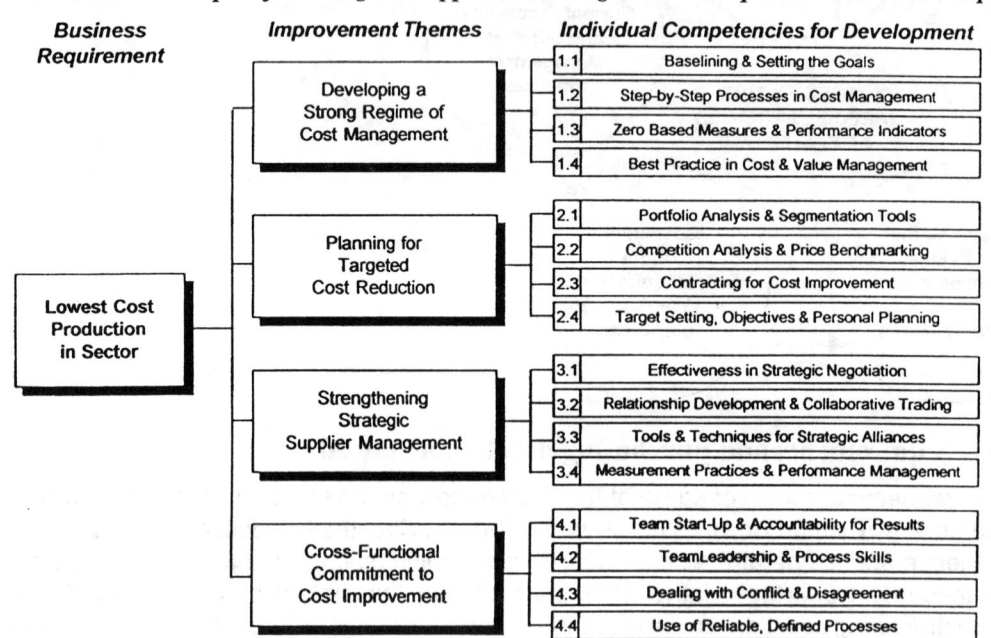

FIGURE 2 - Example of an integrated approach linking business requirements and development needs

Business Requirement	Improvement Themes	Individual Competencies for Development
Lowest Cost Production in Sector	Developing a Strong Regime of Cost Management	1.1 Baselining & Setting the Goals 1.2 Step-by-Step Processes in Cost Management 1.3 Zero Based Measures & Performance Indicators 1.4 Best Practice in Cost & Value Management
	Planning for Targeted Cost Reduction	2.1 Portfolio Analysis & Segmentation Tools 2.2 Competition Analysis & Price Benchmarking 2.3 Contracting for Cost Improvement 2.4 Target Setting, Objectives & Personal Planning
	Strengthening Strategic Supplier Management	3.1 Effectiveness in Strategic Negotiation 3.2 Relationship Development & Collaborative Trading 3.3 Tools & Techniques for Strategic Alliances 3.4 Measurement Practices & Performance Management
	Cross-Functional Commitment to Cost Improvement	4.1 Team Start-Up & Accountability for Results 4.2 TeamLeadership & Process Skills 4.3 Dealing with Conflict & Disagreement 4.4 Use of Reliable, Defined Processes

Focusing on competence rather than knowledge

The approach to competence development described within this article, and particularly the emphasis on the need for explicit linkages between defined business requirements and investment in planned purchasing training, is in line with the guidelines on best practice that have emerged in recent years from bodies such as the Institute of Personnel Development, the MCI, the NCVQ and the Purchasing and Supply Lead Body. Before looking at the main learning that has come from such approaches, it is worthwhile summarising and describing their development.

The MCI was formally launched in July 1988 in response to serious and justifiable concerns over the quality of management in the UK. In turn, MCI had also been inspired by a series of depressing and condemnatory research findings on the state of prevailing business practice in the mid to late 1980s. In the words of one of these influential reports, there were some clear common denominators; 'an abysmal lack of management development' and a 'real need to improve the quality, quantity, relevance and accessibility of management education and training'. Unfortunately, while there has certainly been some progress over the last five or six years, this commentary still applies to a number of organisations and educational providers today. And, dare we say it, to more than a few departments headed by purchasing managers, directors and vice presidents!'

FIGURE 3 ADR competency profiling and purchasing planning

Functional Competence		Business Requirement →
5 Expert / 4 Advanced / 3 Proficient	**Over Qualified** ◆ Purchasing is out of touch with business needs. ◆ Competent - but in the wrong areas. ◆ Characterised by poor morale & staff turnover.	**Business Leadership** ◆ Purchasing is a strength of the business. ◆ In-depth functional competence. ◆ Characterised by reliable application of best practice.
2 Developing / 1 Basic	**Low Priority** ◆ Purchasing is not an important function. ◆ No need for in-depth training. ◆ Characterised by a low level contribution.	**Prime Opportunity** ◆ Purchasing is an under-developed process. ◆ Real need for competence development. ◆ Characterised by internal customer dissatisfaction.
	0 Not Required / 1 Nice to Know / 2 Relevant	3 Important / 4 / 5 Crucial

Originally funded by the Government, MCI was the collective brain-child of the Confederation of British Industry, the British Institute of Management and a group of major employers such as Shell, IBM and BP. During the past few years, a growing number of organisations from many different sectors, public and private, have signed up to the competency approach under the MI banner. Indeed, considerable resources have been invested in the development of competency models, particularly at the managerial level. So, what have been the main features of the approach that has contributed to its success? MCI, as a Government-sponsored and quite high profile body, successfully brought together many practitioners, providers and professional bodies. This led to the launch of some much needed research, and a challenging review of past approaches and appraisal of new directions. In particular, an emphasis was placed on locating, describing and communicating best practice, together with a major push on the development of standards designed to overcome many of the historic weaknesses associated with management training in the UK.

The last five years have certainly seen the emergence of nationally agreed and properly determined standards of occupational and managerial competence, ie statements of what someone in a job is expected to be able to do, with an indication of the minimum standards to which they should be doing it. As Will Reid of the PSLB has cogently stated, the competence approach has one not inconsiderable advantage over many of the more theoretical or academic perspectives on training and development: by definition it concentrates on someone's ability actually to do a job of work, an to show that they can do it.

As a result, a distinctive feature of many MCI-endorsed competence based training programmes has been an emphasis on the establishment of standards, together with clear assessments and, on some occasions, formal accreditation processes. For example, since the MCI is also the Lead Body for Management and Supervisory Development, it published middle and first line management standards in 1990, supervisory management standard in 1992, and senior management standards in 1994. These have helped guide the redesign of many vocational qualifications and in-house management development programmes. In turn, they are impacting thinking about the most appropriate means of designing and delivering training for purchasing managers, up to and including the highest levels.

Aligning vocational qualifications and competence

Contemporaneously with the criticisms that were levelled at British management and the emergence of the MCI approach, it was becoming apparent that other elements of the UK's vocational and educational system, and particularly those relating to foundation training and professional qualifications, were equally failing to address the needs of employers adequately. As a result, in 1986 the Government established the NCVQ to oversee, co-ordinate and regulate the overhaul and establishment of a more coherent framework of vocational education and training. In particular, the emerging framework was composed of new national vocational qualifications (NVQs) based on nationally agreed standards of competence that ranged, in defined levels, from the straightforward, routine and predictable through to more demanding and complex professional activities of higher level jobs. In the purchasing context, this covers roles from logistics and expediting, through to buying and purchasing management.

An excellent summary of the intricacies involved in the establishment o the NCVQ approach can be found in a series of *Purchasing & Supply Management* articles published by Will Reid of the PSLB and Andrew Erridge of the university of Ulster.

A cautious welcome to competence

In the past, with a few notable exceptions, many educational, vocational, training and development programmes lacked any fundamental in-depth research or analysis of the working requirements of businesses, managers and their staff. Not surprisingly, therefore, many of these programmes were inappropriately targeted and just did not produce staff with the range of modern competencies needed by employers. Without any doubt, the MCI and NCVQ approach has been a step in the right direction and has received a cautious welcome from many companies. Inevitably, however, there are still a number of concerns and disappointments:

● Despite the apparently self-evident attraction of the competence approach, insufficient progress has been made in moving beyond the definition of basic and lower-level competencies required during initial training and entry into the professions. This is certainly true in the context of purchasing where there is an urgent need to focus on the new skills and capabilities required for those organisations wishing to attain purchasing leadership.

Despite the fanfare of MCI and NCVQ, there are still insufficient examples of where competence-led approaches have helped to underpin business strategy, directly contributed to improved operational performance and delivered demonstrable business benefits. Again, this is partly because the main focus has been on the lower level staff rather than key decision makers.

● There has been a somewhat bureaucratic proliferation of Lead Bodies. For example the setting of standards in some areas has gone through the protracted processes of consultation and committee work. Inevitably, this has diluted the quality of output, some of which have been too vague, overly prescriptive or smacking of a somewhat academic exercise.

● A particular concern has been raised that many of the standards set are biased towards recognition of historical competence, and as such are not sufficiently focused on future development needs. In particular, with so many major changes taking place in purchasing and supplier management, it is essential that competencies are defined to meet future rather than past or just current needs. Training and development programmes incorporating the competence approach should endeavour to ensure that they match the changing needs of evolving businesses and organisations.

● Competence definitions have to be made as explicit as possible; this often means that they have to be couched in terms of specific practices and observable behaviour. Rigorous derivation of these competence descriptions and skill languages is essential. As some Lead Bodies have found, the more you try to generalise these descriptions into generic competence profiles, the more you lose that specificity.

● Equally, the other side of the coin is that the more any organisation defines purchasing competence in the context of its own business needs, organisational culture and customer requirements, the less likely its scheme will be relevant to other companies. Hence it is not surprising that some of the world's leading businesses are now developing their own competence approaches and have no intention of sharing them with their potential competitors. Indeed, a well structured and effectively implemented purchasing competence development approach is one of the potential sources of competitive advantage.

Future directions in competence and development

It has already been mentioned that there is considerable research evidence to support the widely held view that employee development remains relatively poorly implemented in the UK. Despite the increased focus that has come about as a result of initiatives such as MCI and NCVQ, and the sterling work done by the Chartered Institute of Purchasing & Supply, most organisations still have far to go.

Clearly, if employee development is crucial to the effective implementation of organisational and business strategies, then the precise relationship and links of development to the performance of a business is highly relevant. Unfortunately, one of the constraining features in the past has been insufficient evidence of a clear relationship between training and development initiatives and improvements in business performance. ADR believes that much more work has to be done to map out precise links between business requirements, purchasing improvement themes and individual development needs.

Our experience across sectors and countries has confirmed that the starting point for effective employee development has to be a vigorous definition of the role of purchasing in meeting customer, business and operational needs. Unfortunately, as many readers of this article will be only too painfully aware, there are almost as many definitions as individuals who claim to practise them. For example, one of our own clients has summed it up quite well: 'Everyone seems to be in favour of strategic purchasing, just as they appear to be in favour of virtue.' However, notwithstanding such a comment, there are a number of tools and techniques that can be applied to ensure that appropriate connections are made between purchasing roles and individual/team development.

An entry point into this process is a conscious decision to measure where you are in business terms, where you want to be, identifying how training can bridge the gap, and evaluating the range of options and training methods available to gauge which ones will be the most effective and efficient to the needs of your business and purchasing team. For example, as you can see in Figure 3, you can make an assessment of the prime business requirements and map these against the current levels of purchasing functional expertise. The central question, then, is into which of the four categories your team falls. While this can sometimes be a painful exercise, it is the first stage to realigning your training and development approaches so that they are really in line with the direction that you need to travel.

FIGURE 4 Example of assessing competence in 'contracting for cost improvement

Basic	Developing	Proficient	Advanced	Expert
Can place standard orders and use simple terms and conditions	Understands the rules of contract and can deal with straightforward cost related issues	Wide knowledge of contractual matters and able to draft appropriate clauses on cost improvement	Significant expertise in target costing and use of principled pricing mechanism	Capable of leading complex contractual negotiations at executive level to achieve year-on-year cost improvement

Finally, and again it can be 'bad for the ego but good for the soul', there has to be a realistic assessment of the gap between an individual's current competence and the highest levels of expertise. In Figure 4, we have illustrated a scale that ADR has developed and used successfully for a number of years, which is the profiling of competence on a five-point scale that accommodates specific definition of purchasing thinking, practice and behaviour.

As we said in our earlier article on SmithKline Beecham, it is rare indeed for companies to invest the resources required for transformation of the purchasing process into a real strength of the business. However, it is encouraging to note the rapid acceleration in the number of purchasing managers who have started to give serious attention to the competence gaps, not just in their purchasing teams but elsewhere in their businesses.

While competence development can be a demanding journey, the ultimate benefits are potentially huge, since the quality, calibre, focus and motivation of purchasing staff is the greatest single differentiator of the 'leaders from the followers'. We wish fellow travellers the best of fortune in their journeys.

References:
Boyatzis, R, *The Competent Manager: A Model for Effective Performance*, Wiley 1982Constable, J & McCormack, R, *The Making of British Managers,* British Institute of Management & Confederation of British Industry, 1987
Handy, C, *The Making of Managers*, Manpower Services Commission, National Economic Development Office & British Institute of Management, 1987
Reid, W, *National Standards of Competence in Purchasing and Supply,* Purchasing & Supply Management, May 1991
Erridge, A, Competence in the Workplace - *Setting the Standards for Purchasing*, Purchasing & Supply Management, December 1992
Ralf, M, & Hughes, J, *Re-Engineering through Training: Transforming the Purchasing Process,* Purchasing & Supply Management, March 1994.
John Hughes and Ian Billson are Directors of ADR International Purchasing Consultants. They would welcome contact with other organisations applying leading edge tools in purchasing development. Telephone 01344 303078, fax 01344 303071.

Communications and training

Purchasing must work out how to communicate with five distinct groups of people, writes Stephen Cannon

A previous article looked at the importance of communication and training as a means of improving managements' perception of both the function and the activity.

These perceptions are important if the purchasing and contracts activity (that is, how purchasing and contracts work is done, and what is done) is to be integrated with the overall strategy of an organisation and if the function (the department which does the purchasing and contracting work as its full-time activity) is to play a role in the development of that strategy.

this article continues with the theme of using communication and training as a means of obtaining acceptance of the function and the activity amongst the five client groups (see Figure 1).

Top management

Reasons why top management needs both training and communication in purchasing and contracting matters include the following:

● External suppliers are one of five forces identified by Professor Michael Porter which can seriously constrain the way in which the organisation operates in the marketplace, and even if suppliers are not a limiting force, relationships with them can still be of interest/importance to top management. There is thus an obvious requirement for an input from purchasing and contracting expertise to the organisation's corporate strategy.
● Not infrequently, top management contract directly (and often informally) for their own requirements with suppliers. Good examples are contracts for consultancy work. A better awareness of purchasing and contracting techniques might yield benefits when such purchases are made.
● It is top management which will decide the future of the function and the extent to which it will continue to exist. If the role of the function is not valued, the function is likely to be at risk.
● Top management decides the budgets and approve the expenditure of the organisation. The first of these will affect the running of the function, the second will affect what the organisation spends.

When formulating the organisation's strategy, top management needs to take into account the changes in the markets from which the organisation procures its needs. Information is needed about these markets and how they are likely to change. This should be provided by the purchasing and contracts function and the need to gather and supply it imposes upon that function the requirement to think strategically and therefore long-term. In progressive organisations, this will pose no problem. However, in those organisations where the function is rated poorly or the activity is not seen as core, the function's management will have two problems:
1 How to rise above the day-to-day in order to think long-term and strategically
2 What to communicate to top management.

Each purchasing and contracts function should have a research group ;whose duties should include a review of the possible procurement futures facing the organisation and the range of strategies to deal with them. Various tools exist for doing this, such as gap analysis and scenario planning. These studies should be an ongoing and programmed activity involving the buyer and the internal customer. The future supply position of each critical material and service to the organisation should be examined once a year; firstly on a two-to-three-year basis and then on a longer-term basis. It should not be forgotten that what is critical can change quite abruptly, and contingency plans might also be needed for other seemingly less important supplies (see Figure 2).

Access to top management

Having obtained the information, the senior management of the function will need to pass it up the tree.

It would be interesting to know how often and in how many organisations procurement strategy is discussed at board level and the extent to which it is considered when formulating strategic plans. Where this already occurs, the function has a direct access, perhaps board level representation, along which it can pass its communication.

If access does not exist, then the senior management of the function will need to find ways of gaining it. It will be necessary to use enlightened opportunism, that is to grasp any opportunity for communication and training even if this involves unorthodox routes. How this can be done will depend on the structure and culture of the organisation. The senior management of the function should set aside time to think creatively about this problem, perhaps using problem-solving tools such as the various forms of fishbone analysis, force fields analysis and brainstorming.

Reports of strategic significance should raise the perceptions of top management with respect to the function. it will move the function from a 'do-er' to a 'thinker/planner' type. However, it is also important not to neglect the need to report at regular intervals on the 'do-er' activities. Achieved target-added value and improved levels of service should be reported up the organisational tree. These sort of day-to-day reports are the only way top management has of seeing whether this important part of the organisation is on course to meet its objectives. Such reports will be in competition with reports from other functions, so they should be styled to capture attention.

Top management training

There is a need for some training in techniques if top management involves itself in actual purchasing and contracting work. This is obviously easier said than done, particularly in organisations where the function is poorly rated. Training in the basics is likely to be unwelcome, partly because no top management will admit that it needs such training and partly because it will not have the time for it. The method of delivery is likely to be as important as the content. Once more, this will be less of a problem if the function is adequately represented. For less fortunate practitioners, enlightened opportunism is the only recourse open to them.

The internal customer

It is, of course, essential that the internal customer understands and values the service which the function offers. There is usually agreement about what is to be bought and when it should be done. However, who should do it, how it should be done and where it should be done are matters about which it is dangerous simply to assume there is agreement. So, good communication and training are not just a means of improving the relationship between individuals nor a way of ensuring that, where appropriate, the internal customer can purchase effectively on the organisation's behalf; they are a way of ensuring that the function is not undervalued, a feature which is likely eventually to put the function itself at risk.

The starting point therefore has to be the need for the internal customer to have a good appreciation of what the purchasing and contracting activity is, and what the purchasing and contracts function can do. Indeed, without this appreciation, the negotiation of a co-operative contract (which has been discussed in a previous article) will not be very fruitful. This will improve on the search for targeted added value and the setting of service levels and thus on overall performance (see Figure 3).

Joint team building sessions

Joint team-building sessions away from the office provide an opportunity for the function to sell itself. The agenda could include informal but prepared presentations of the role of the function to the internal customer. The latter could then be invited to provide their viewpoint. Such joint team-building sessions offer a safe environment for an exchange of views, provided that any negative feelings have been previously dissipated, perhaps earlier in the session. A formal presentation outsider such sessions is a less satisfactory means for the function to communicate as it will have all the disadvantages of self-justification / propaganda unless a good relationship already exists.

In general, such team-building sessions work best if held away from the workplace, with an agreement that interruptions are not permissible. It also helps if the session is run by somebody who does not come from either the department of the internal customer or the function; in fact it can be advantageous if that person comes from outside the organisation. Team-building sessions can also provide the opportunity for the internal customer and the function jointly to explore the concepts of targeted added value and service levels. This should be helpful when the concepts are new to either or both parties and it could be at these sessions that the basis of a successful co-operative contract is established.

Joint team-building sessions should not be seen as a one-off. A day or two every 12 or 18 months could well be a useful way of checking that all is well.

It is also important to monitor regularly the receptions of senior people in the internal customer department. Occasional audits to check the degree of satisfaction with the function are a means of providing this sort of information and, of course, the buyer assigned to the internal customer should be monitoring continuously the attitudes of the people with whom he/she deals. This sort of monitoring can be built into the co-operative contract and form part of the review of service levels.

Internal customer training

Training should cover the information and skills which the internal customer needs for all the procurement which has been assigned to them. It might include training in computer systems which deal with low-value ordering, or in terms and conditions, ways of inviting tenders (if appropriate), convenient payment systems such as credit card and cheque book etc. This training should be carried out by the members of the purchasing and contracts function and not by outsider experts. It is important that the function cultivates expertise in such training amongst staff. By undertaking the training, the function will enhance its status as the centre of excellence in purchasing and contracting matters.

The internal customer also needs to know what support the buyer requires when it is the buyer's responsibility to purchase/contract. This might concern specifications, the layout of schedules, special conditions and requirements and a timetable.

For collaborative purchasing, the training is more like an exchange of information about who is going to do what, what is going to be done, how, when and why. The exchange of this sort of information can eventually be proceduralised, but if it becomes too much of a routine, the collaborative relationship could suffer owing to a lack of personal contact. Such procedures should be reviewed from time to time, and any failures explored and corrected.

The purchasing and contracts practitioner

Buyers possess the skills needed to undertake their duties, but without continuous updating they are likely to fall behind in a field which is in a state of continuous improvement. it is here that external courses come into play, but such courses are only part of the training which buyers need.

Ambassadorial role

The buyer is the ambassador of the function and he/she needs interpersonal skills which will enable him/her to perform well in this role. As a minimum, these will include the skills involved in training and in making presentations, in public speaking as well as such skills as active listening and the reading of body language, the heightening of personal awareness using such techniques as Belbin questionnaires and theories such as transactional analysis etc. If inadequately equipped, the representation is likely to be poor whether within or without the organisation, and the perspectives of the function and the activity will be coloured accordingly (see Figure 4).

Although such training is included in the requirements for professional qualifications, it has a short shelf-life, and it should be regularly reinforced.

Some specific training

Of course, buyers must also be IT-literate. This requires not only knowing how to use the packages which one finds in almost every office nowadays but also familiarity with computerised procurement systems. it should be the responsibility of the research group to identify what procurement systems are available and to screen these in order to find the most suitable candidates for the organisation. The buyers (and the internal customers if they are eventually going to use it) should be involved in any further selection, and they will require training in whatever system is finally chosen. If the system involves a process for low-value ordering which is to be used by the internal customer, as it should be, the buyer will train/support the customer.

In order to provide a high-quality service to internal customers, purchasing and contracts practitioners should be capable of providing a range of expertise and advice. For example, a buyer should be well versed in the legal aspects of his work. Details of individual cases are not necessary, but an understanding of the principles is important. The object of any training here is to make the buyer a good initial substitute for a lawyer, capable of identifying when he/she needs to refer to that profession for guidance.

Refresher/repeat training in such topics as the legal systems of England/Scotland, contract law, TUPE, European Procurement Law (for the public sector and utilities etc) will be required.

The practitioner should also be trained in marketing techniques, particularly those for influencing purchasers, as well as skills such as reading a profit and loss account, a balance sheet, cashflow statements, and the use of discounted cashflow statements and other appraisal methods.

With respect to technology, buyers are often left to pick up a knowledge of the technology of the product/services which they buy. There is often little in the way of formal training, although such training could easily be part of a mutual exchange of training and communication with the organisation's suppliers and contractors (see below).

Staff development

Each purchasing and contracts practitioner will require an individually tailored package of training which should be supplemented by staff development measures. These are likely to be increasingly necessary for the retention of capable staff as organisations adopt flatter structures which will deny the career progression hitherto associated with taller, pyramidal structures. Individuals will be forced to find job satisfaction other than by promotional moves (see Figure 5).

Organisations might pay dearly in the future if they disregard their staff's aspirations. The current surplus of applicants for vacant positions is unlikely to last indefinitely, particularly when demographic factors such as the declining number of young people are taken into account. Sound, regular training and development programmes could be one way of satisfying their aspirations. In the context of purchasing and contracts, it is for senior management to accept responsibility for putting such programmes into place, deciding with each buyer the pace of the training and development as well as the most appropriate mode.

while manager managers might feel they do this, their actions are often prompted by activities such as the annual personnel appraisal.

Expenditure on training within British industry is significantly less than in its main trading competitors and there is no reason to assume that training in purchasing and contracts work is more favoured than any other type of training. It is important to be proactive about staff development, especially during the present era of continuous organisational change.

External suppliers and contractors

External suppliers and contractors are usually not high on the function's list of people requiring purchasing and contracts training. it is normally expected that they will pick up how the organisation does its procurement in the same way as the buyers are expected to learn about the technology associated with the products/services which they buy. Eventually, this might be true, but a programme of agreed training/communication, which could take the form of an information exchange is an improvement on this *laissez-faire* approach (see Figure 6).

For major suppliers and contractors, this would require that each organisation trains the other in depth about itself, describing all aspects of the organisation including its culture, its structure, its strategy, policies, plans, marketing, products and production processes. This form of information exchange is essential to the development of partnership arrangements and can only be a benefit, irrespective of whether or not a full partnership arrangement develops.

The information exchange should ideally involve a range of personnel at various levels including top management from both organisations.

Initiation by the function

It is preferable that they are initiated and organised by the purchasing and contracts function. This would bring the function and the activity which it performs into focus with other departments within the parent organisation, and it has the obvious advantage of putting the function at the van of any partnership arrangement which might eventually develop.

Not all procurement relationships are suitable for partnering, and even where partnering is a possibility, staff changes owing to natural wastage, redundancy etc can still make regular exchange training useful.

For important but not necessarily major suppliers, such a detailed information exchange might not be suitable. The organisation should still be prepared to describe itself to its suppliers and contractors, and they should be encouraged to reciprocate.

The internal suppliers

The purchasing and contracts function is also an internal customer of many other service functions within the organisation.

These departments often supply their service with no clear understanding of whey they are supplying it and the use to which it will be put.

A better understanding of the activities of the function could improve the delivery of the service. It could also be helpful in motivating staff within the internal suppliers by giving them a sense of purpose and an enhanced relationship with the customer.

In organisations adopting matrix-type structures, this sort of contact might not be necessary. In many other organisations, where such structures are not employed, training/communication in the form of an information exchange with internal suppliers could be beneficial. Preferably, it should be organised by the staff who supply and receive the service.

It is necessary to ascertain the extent of each internal supplier's knowledge of the function and the activity and then to design a specific training/communication package. Internal suppliers will not in general need detailed knowledge. The objective is not to convert them into purchasing and contracts experts, but to provide them with an understanding of what the function needs from them, why it needs it, and when.

Conclusion

This article has looked at the communication and training needs of five groups associated to a greater or lesser degree with the purchasing and contracts function.

It has suggested some areas of communication and training and some ways in which they can be delivered:
- to improve the quality of the performance of the function
- to improve the interpersonal relationships
- to disseminate a message about the contribution of the function and the activity.

It has obviously not been possible to be specific, as so much depends on the individual organisation, its culture and structure.

Communication and training are important aspects of the function and they could be central to any improvement in its status. No purchasing and contracts practitioner should neglect them.

Communications and training: Part 2

Purchasing must work out how to communicate with five distinct groups of people, writes Stephen Cannon

A previous article looked at the importance of communication and training as a means of improving managements' perception of both the function and the activity.

These perceptions are important if the purchasing and contracts activity (that is, how purchasing and contracts work is done, and what is done) is to be integrated with the overall strategy of an organisation and if the function (the department which does the purchasing and contracting work as its full-time activity) is to play a role in the development of that strategy.

this article continues with the theme of using communication and training as a means of obtaining acceptance of the function and the activity amongst the five client groups (see Figure 1).

Top management

Reasons why top management needs both training and communication in purchasing and contracting matters include the following:

- External suppliers are one of five forces identified by Professor Michael Porter which can seriously constrain the way in which the organisation operates in the marketplace, and even if suppliers are not a limiting force, relationships with them can still be of interest/importance to top management. There is thus an obvious requirement for an input from purchasing and contracting expertise to the organisation's corporate strategy.
- Not infrequently, top management contract directly (and often informally) for their own requirements with suppliers. Good examples are contracts for consultancy work. A better awareness of purchasing and contracting techniques might yield benefits when such purchases are made.
- It is top management which will decide the future of the function and the extent to which it will continue to exist. If the role of the function is not valued, the function is likely to be at risk.
- Top management decides the budgets and approve the expenditure of the organisation. The first of these will affect the running of the function, the second will affect what the organisation spends.

FIGURE 1 Client groups for communication and training

CLIENT GROUPS FOR COMMUNICATION AND TRAINING

- TOP MANAGEMENT
- INTERNAL CUSTOMERS
- PURCHASING AND CONTRACTS PRACTITIONERS
- EXTERNAL SUPPLIERS AND CONTRACTORS
- INTERNAL SUPPLIERS TO THE FUNCTION

When formulating the organisation's strategy, top management needs to take into account the changes in the markets from which the organisation procures its needs. Information is needed about these markets and how they are likely to change. This should be provided by the purchasing and contracts function and the need to gather and supply it imposes upon that function the requirement to think strategically and therefore long-term. In progressive organisations, this will pose no problem. However, in those organisations where the function is rated poorly or the activity is not seen as core, the function's management will have two problems:

1 How to rise above the day-to-day in order to think long-term and strategically
2 What to communicate to top management.

Each purchasing and contracts function should have a research group ;whose duties should include a review of the possible procurement futures facing the organisation and the range of strategies to deal with them. Various tools exist for doing this, such as gap analysis and scenario planning. These studies should be an ongoing and programmed activity involving the buyer and the internal customer. The future supply position of each critical material and service to the organisation should be examined once a year; firstly on a two-to-three-year basis and then on a longer-term basis. It should not be forgotten that what is critical can change quite abruptly, and contingency plans might also be needed for other seemingly less important supplies (see Figure 2).

FIGURE 2   Key Points

KEY POINTS

- PROCUREMENT IMPACTS ON CORPORATE STRATEGY
- FUNCTION'S INPUT CAN IMPROVE STRATEGY
- ACCESS TO TOP MANAGEMENT CAN BE A PROBLEM

Access to top management

Having obtained the information, the senior management of the function will need to pass it up the tree.

It would be interesting to know how often and in how many organisations procurement strategy is discussed at board level and the extent to which it is considered when formulating strategic plans. Where this already occurs, the function has a direct access, perhaps board level representation, along which it can pass its communication.

If access does not exist, then the senior management of the function will need to find ways of gaining it. It will be necessary to use enlightened opportunism, that is to grasp any opportunity for communication and training even if this involves unorthodox routes. How this can be done will depend on the structure and culture of the organisation. The senior management of the function should set aside time to think creatively about this problem, perhaps using problem-solving tools such as the various forms of fishbone analysis, force fields analysis and brainstorming.

Reports of strategic significance should raise the perceptions of top management with respect to the function. it will move the function from a 'do-er' to a 'thinker/planner' type. However, it is also important not to neglect the need to report at regular intervals on the 'do-er' activities. Achieved target-added value and improved levels of service should be reported up the organisational tree. These sort of day-to-day reports are the only way top management has of seeing whether this important part of the organisation is on course to meet its objectives. Such reports will be in competition with reports from other functions, so they should be styled to capture attention.

Top management training

There is a need for some training in techniques if top management involves itself in actual purchasing and contracting work. This is obviously easier said than done, particularly in organisations where the function is poorly rated. Training in the basics is likely to be unwelcome, partly because no top management will admit that it needs such training and partly because it will not have the time for it. The method of delivery is likely to be as important as the content. Once more, this will be less of a problem if the function is adequately represented. For less fortunate practitioners, enlightened opportunism is the only recourse open to them.

The internal customer

It is, of course, essential that the internal customer understands and values the service which the function offers. There is usually agreement about what is to be bought and when it should be done. However, who should do it, how it should be done and where it should be done are matters about which it is dangerous simply to assume there is agreement. So, good communication and training are not just a means of improving the relationship between individuals nor a way of ensuring that, where appropriate, the internal customer can purchase effectively on the organisation's behalf; they are a way of ensuring that the function is not undervalued, a feature which is likely eventually to put the function itself at risk.

The starting point therefore has to be the need for the internal customer to have a good appreciation of what the purchasing and contracting activity is, and what the purchasing and contracts function can do. Indeed, without this appreciation, the negotiation of a co-operative contract (which has been discussed in a previous article) will not be very fruitful. This will improve on the search for targeted added value and the setting of service levels and thus on overall performance (see Figure 3).

Joint team building sessions

Joint team-building sessions away from the office provide an opportunity for the function to sell itself. The agenda could include informal but prepared presentations of the role of the function to the internal customer. The latter could then be invited to provide their viewpoint. Such joint team-building sessions offer a safe environment for an exchange of views, provided that any negative feelings have been previously dissipated, perhaps earlier in the session. A formal presentation outsider such sessions is a less satisfactory means for the function to communicate as it will have all the disadvantages of self-justification / propaganda unless a good relationship already exists.

FIGURE 3 Joint Team Building Sessions

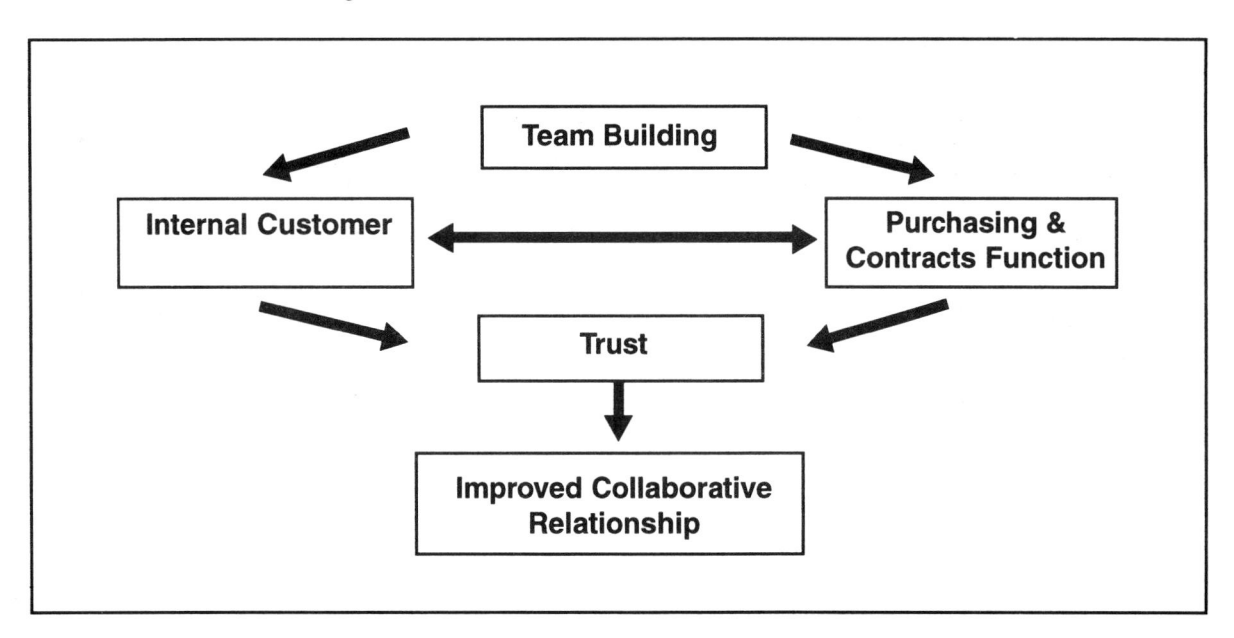

In general, such team-building sessions work best if held away from the workplace, with an agreement that interruptions are not permissible. It also helps if the session is run by somebody who does not come from either the department of the internal customer or the function; in fact it can be advantageous if that person comes from outside the organisation. Team-building sessions can also provide the opportunity for the internal customer and the function jointly to explore the concepts of targeted added value and service levels. This should be helpful when the concepts are new to either or both parties and it could be at these sessions that the basis of a successful co-operative contract is established.

Joint team-building sessions should not be seen as a one-off. A day or two every 12 or 18 months could well be a useful way of checking that all is well.

It is also important to monitor regularly the receptions of senior people in the internal customer department. Occasional audits to check the degree of satisfaction with the function are a means of providing this sort of information and, of course, the buyer assigned to the internal customer should be monitoring continuously the attitudes of the people with whom he/she deals. This sort of monitoring can be built into the co-operative contract and form part of the review of service levels.

Internal customer training

Training should cover the information and skills which the internal customer needs for all the procurement which has been assigned to them. It might include training in computer systems which deal with low-value ordering, or in terms and conditions, ways of inviting tenders (if appropriate), convenient payment systems such as credit card and cheque book etc. This training should be carried out by the members of the purchasing and contracts function and not by outsider experts. It is important that the function cultivates expertise in such training amongst staff. By undertaking the training, the function will enhance its status as the centre of excellence in purchasing and contracting matters.

The internal customer also needs to know what support the buyer requires when it is the buyer's responsibility to purchase/contract. This might concern specifications, the layout of schedules, special conditions and requirements and a timetable.

For collaborative purchasing, the training is more like an exchange of information about who is going to do what, what is going to be done, how, when and why. The exchange of this sort of information can eventually be procedurised, but if it becomes too much of a routine, the collaborative relationship could suffer owing to a lack of personal contact. Such procedures should be reviewed from time to time, and any failures explored and corrected.

FIGURE 4 (upper) and FIGURE 5

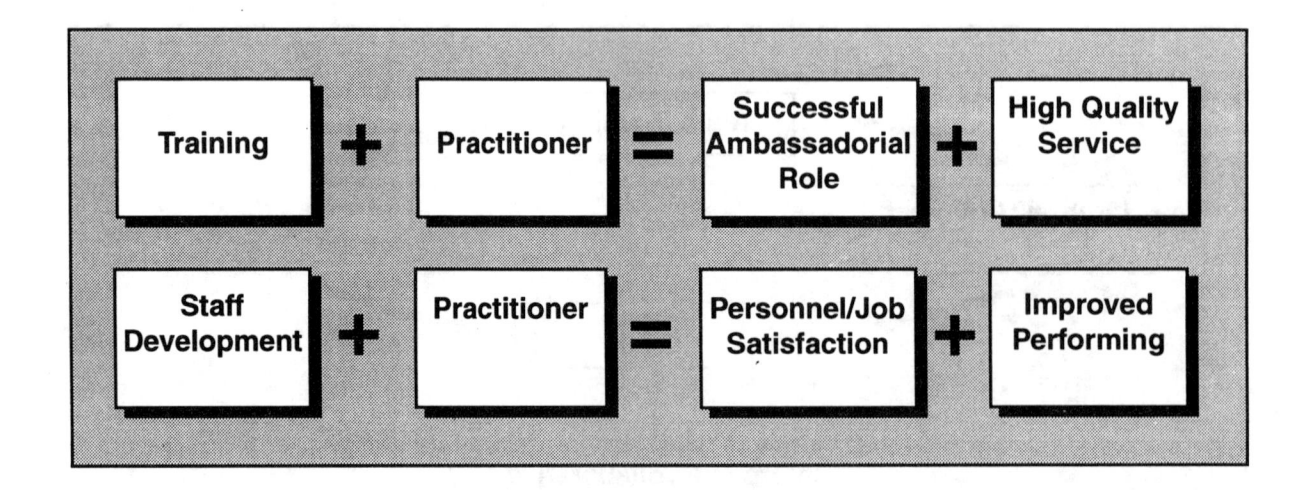

Training + Practitioner = Successful Ambassadorial Role + High Quality Service

Staff Development + Practitioner = Personnel/Job Satisfaction + Improved Performing

The purchasing and contracts practitioner

Buyers possess the skills needed to undertake their duties, but without continuous updating they are likely to fall behind in a field which is in a state of continuous improvement. it is here that external courses come into play, but such courses are only part of the training which buyers need.

Ambassadorial role

The buyer is the ambassador of the function and he/she needs interpersonal skills which will enable him/her to perform well in this role. As a minimum, these will include the skills involved in training and in making presentations, in public speaking as well as such skills as active listening and the reading of body language, the heightening of personal awareness using such techniques as Belbin questionnaires and theories such as transactional analysis etc. If inadequately equipped, the representation is likely to be poor whether within or without the organisation, and the perspectives of the function and the activity will be coloured accordingly (see Figure 4).

Although such training is included in the requirements for professional qualifications, it has a short shelf-life, and it should be regularly reinforced.

Some specific training

Of course, buyers must also be IT-literate. This requires not only knowing how to use the packages which one finds in almost every office nowadays but also familiarity with computerised procurement systems. it should be the responsibility of the research group to identify what procurement systems are available and to screen these in order to find the most suitable candidates for the organisation. The buyers (and the internal customers if they are eventually going to use it) should be involved in any further selection, and they will require training in whatever system is finally chosen. If the system involves a process for low-value ordering which is to be used by the internal customer, as it should be, the buyer will train/support the customer.

In order to provide a high-quality service to internal customers, purchasing and contracts practitioners should be capable of providing a range of expertise and advice. For example, a buyer should be well versed in the legal aspects of his work. Details of individual cases are not necessary, but an understanding of the principles is important. The object of any training here is to make the buyer a good initial substitute for a lawyer, capable of identifying when he/she needs to refer to that profession for guidance. Refresher/repeat training in such topics as the legal systems of England/Scotland, contract law, TUPE, European Procurement Law (for the public sector and utilities etc) will be required.

The practitioner should also be trained in marketing techniques, particularly those for influencing purchasers, as well as skills such as reading a profit and loss account, a balance sheet, cashflow statements, and the use of discounted cashflow statements and other appraisal methods.

With respect to technology, buyers are often left to pick up a knowledge of the technology of the product/services which they buy. There is often little in the way of formal training, although such training could easily be part of a mutual exchange of training and communication with the organisation's suppliers and contractors (see below).

Staff development

Each purchasing and contracts practitioner will require an individually tailored package of training which should be supplemented by staff development measures. These are likely to be increasingly necessary for the retention of capable staff as organisations adopt flatter structures which will deny the career progression hitherto associated with taller, pyramidal structures. Individuals will be forced to find job satisfaction other than by promotional moves (see Figure 5).

Organisations might pay dearly in the future if they disregard their staff's aspirations. The current surplus of applicants for vacant positions is unlikely to last indefinitely, particularly when demographic factors such as the declining number of young people are taken into account. Sound, regular training and development programmes could be one way of satisfying their aspirations. In the context of purchasing and contracts, it is for senior management to accept responsibility for putting such programmes into place, deciding with each buyer the pace of the training and development as well as the most appropriate mode.

While manager managers might feel they do this, their actions are often prompted by activities such as the annual personnel appraisal.

Expenditure on training within British industry is significantly less than in its main trading competitors and there is no reason to assume that training in purchasing and contracts work is more favoured than any other type of training. It is important to be proactive about staff development, especially during the present era of continuous organisational change.

External suppliers and contractors

External suppliers and contractors are usually not high on the function's list of people requiring purchasing and contracts training. it is normally expected that they will pick up how the organisation does its procurement in the same way as the buyers are expected to learn about the technology associated with the products/services which they buy. Eventually, this might be true, but a programme of agreed training/communication, which could take the form of an information exchange is an improvement on this *laissez-faire* approach (see Figure 6).

For major suppliers and contractors, this would require that each organisation trains the other in depth about itself, describing all aspects of the organisation including its culture, its structure, its strategy, policies, plans, marketing, products and production processes. This form of information exchange is essential to the development of partnership arrangements and can only be a benefit, irrespective of whether or not a full partnership arrangement develops.

The information exchange should ideally involve a range of personnel at various levels including top management from both organisations.

FIGURE 6 Mutual Training

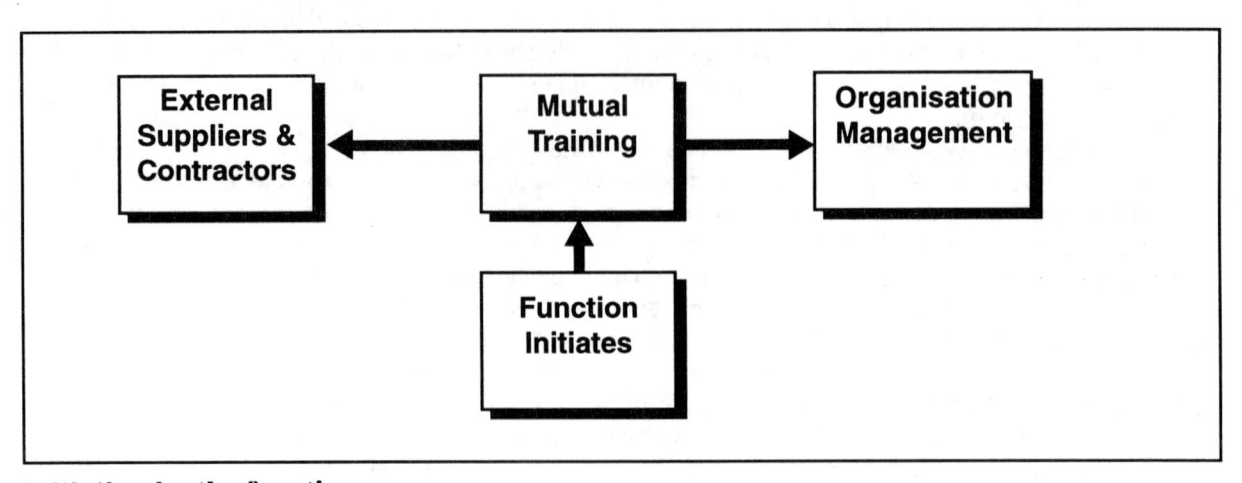

Initiation by the function

It is preferable that they are initiated and organised by the purchasing and contracts function. This would bring the function and the activity which it performs into focus with other departments within the parent organisation, and it has the obvious advantage of putting the function at the van of any partnership arrangement which might eventually develop.

Not all procurement relationships are suitable for partnering, and even where partnering is a possibility, staff changes owing to natural wastage, redundancy etc can still make regular exchange training useful.

For important but not necessarily major suppliers, such a detailed information exchange might not be suitable. The organisation should still be prepared to describe itself to its suppliers and contractors, and they should be encouraged to reciprocate.

The internal suppliers

The purchasing and contracts function is also an internal customer of many other service functions within the organisation.

These departments often supply their service with no clear understanding of whey they are supplying it and the use to which it will be put.

A better understanding of the activities of the function could improve the delivery of the service. It could also be helpful in motivating staff within the internal suppliers by giving them a sense of purpose and an enhanced relationship with the customer.

In organisations adopting matrix-type structures, this sort of contact might not be necessary. In many other organisations, where such structures are not employed, training/communication in the form of an information exchange with internal suppliers could be beneficial. Preferably, it should be organised by the staff who supply and receive the service.

It is necessary to ascertain the extent of each internal supplier's knowledge of the function and the activity and then to design a specific training/communication package. Internal suppliers will not in general need detailed knowledge. The objective is not to convert them into purchasing and contracts experts, but to provide them with an understanding of what the function needs from them, why it needs it, and when.

Conclusion

This article has looked at the communication and training needs of five groups associated to a greater or lesser degree with the purchasing and contracts function.

It has suggested some areas of communication and training and some ways in which they can be delivered:

- to improve the quality of the performance of the function
- to improve the interpersonal relationships
- to disseminate a message about the contribution of the function and the activity.

It has obviously not been possible to be specific, as so much depends on the individual organisation, its culture and structure.

Communication and training are important aspects of the function and they could be central to any improvement in its status. No purchasing and contracts practitioner should neglect them.

Can you create your own world class supply chain?

Peter Hines describes the supply chain development programme under way at the University of Wales

The essence of business is creating competitive advantage. Such advantage can come in a number of ways; for example, low-cost production or market differentiation. Almost without exception, when competitive advantage is discussed it is done with regard to a company and its direct competitors. However, is this the most appropriate scale of analysis, and indeed is competitive advantage merely a manifestation of internal excellence?

A number of articles and books produced in the last five years point to a rather different opinion. In the works of eminent professors such as David Farmer, Martin Christopher, Richard Lamming, Douglas Macbeth and Daniel Jones, a note appears, one concerned with competitive advantage through the effective networking of companies. For instance professor Jones has claimed that in future it will not be individual companies competing in the marketplace, but 'value streams', in other words supply chains. This new philosophy, although expressed in differing terminology, is common among these five leading authorities, but what agenda should the enlightened company or purchasing/logistics executive follow in order to become the new architects of competitive advantage for themselves and their value streams alike?

There is no simple answer to this question, partly because to date there has been insufficient research by practitioners, academics and consultants into this subject area, but it is possible to give some clues as to what these new value streams should look like and how they may operate. The following key characteristics may not be atypical:

1 An awareness of a shared vision of what the complete value stream seeks to achieve, with a focus by all the individual companies on the demands and interests of the ultimate consumers of the products or services produced.

2 A dynamic transparency between the firms, so that each can proactively assist any of the others, as well as reacting rapidly to others' changing needs and circumstances.

3 A focus on the total effectiveness of the whole supply system rather than an introverted improvement of individual parts of the great whole.

4 A range of new tools and techniques will be employed not just within or between pairs of companies, but right along the value-adding chain, from raw material supplier to the ultimate point of consumption (and indeed beyond to point of recycling and reuse).

5 A shared strategy that ensures that improvements are continuous and are particularly focused where existing weaknesses and constraints exist, rather than on the parts that currently enjoy the best resources. As such, improvements are likely to be carried out not only within a single organisation but also as part of inter-company cross-functional teams within a range of other value stream partners.

This focus on the whole value stream is designed to provide advantage to all its members, and may well become the key improvement paradigm of the late 1990s and beyond. However, it may be useful to return to the question of how enlightened executives may learn how to create competitive advantage for the value stream in which they operate.

Although there is no one answer, nor one single article or text to read, an involvement with a group of leading edge academics and like-minded companies may well provide the required answers. In this respect a consortium has been formed by three of the UK's leading academic centres of excellence in the area of purchasing and logistics, namely Cardiff Business School, the University of Bath and the

University of Glamorgan. These three partners have been brought together as each offers a range of complementary and overlapping skills that can synergistically allow the issues of the late 1990s to be addressed in an holistic manner.

Towards the end of 1993 the three institutions jointly launched a three-year programme of practical customer focused research called the *Supply Chain Development Programme.* The programme is co-directed by Professor Daniel Jones and Peter Hines (Cardiff), Professor Richard Lamming (Bath) and Professor David Jessop (Glamorgan). It has been designed to offer sponsoring companies some of the answers to the important strategic and operational questions and issues that they will be faced with into the next century. In so doing, the research programme addresses what companies and organisations need to know in order to form their strategies and operational programmes. The research is therefore designed to be outside the traditional ivory towers and to focus on the participating companies together with other exemplar companies from around the world. The focus is as much on providing practical implementation routes as on understanding and extrapolating best practice.

The research work has four concurrent stages as shown in Figure 1 described below.

Stage 1: Requirement definition

This stage is designed to gain an understanding of the key issues and areas where companies can be assisted, particularly over the medium to long term. A discussion of the particular benefits to an individual organisation is undertaken. These discussions provide the research team with a clear focus for the programme based on the needs and requirements of the world class organisations of the future. Through a process known a Quality Function Deployment (QFD), these requirements are combined with the views of the research team to provide an agenda for research. This process was undertaken in the autumn of 1993 with the interest areas of the 12 sponsors combined into a programme of action research.

FIGURE 1 - Supply chain development programme: research methodology

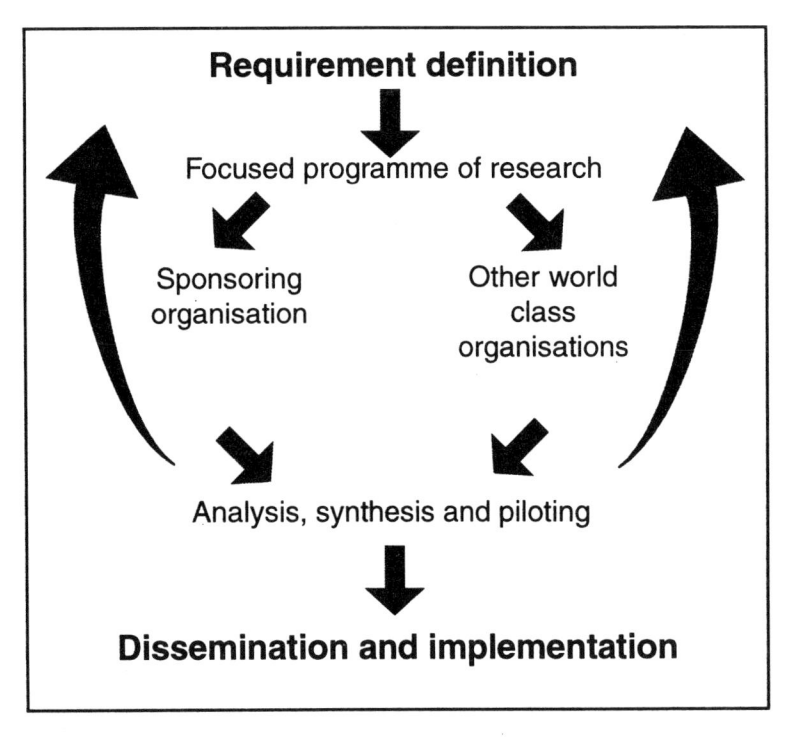

Requirement definition
↓
Focused programme of research
↙ ↘
Sponsoring organisation / Other world class organisations
↘ ↙
Analysis, synthesis and piloting
↓
Dissemination and implementation

Stage 2: Focused programme of research

The requirement definition highlighted five major areas that the sponsors wished to see addressed. At a meeting last September, individual outline research projects were suggested that would address each of these areas. Each project was designed to run from between six months and two years, depending on their complexity and whether the work was carried forward to an implementation stage. Over the course of the three years between six and eight projects will be undertaken. Although five research projects were suggested at first, the assembled sponsored were asked to prioritise the three that they would like to see addressed immediately. Due to the close synergy between the needs and requirements of the sponsors, all 12 firms were unanimous in choosing three initial projects: Supply Chain Reponsiveness, Supplier Development, and Communications Between Organisations.

The **Supply Chain Responsiveness** project in many ways reflects the essence of the whole programmes of research. Supply chain responsiveness is the ability of the various companies in the delivery process, through a shared strategy, to be able to react to the demands of their customers in a timely and effective manner, particularly in terms of requirements for existing and new products. The project is designed to address three key interrelated supply chain issues:

- how to reduce agreed lead times and eliminate late deliveries
- how to reduce planned time to market and introduce appropriate controls to avoid overruns
- how to increase last-minute supplier flexibility.

The second project, **Supplier Development**, is concerned with both enabling supply chain responsiveness to occur and providing the mechanisms to facilitate both evolutionary and revolutionary improvements up and down the supply chain. Supplier (or customer) development can be defined as a process where one partner in a relationship modifies or influences the behaviour of another partner with a view to mutual benefit. The project is deigned to address four key issues within the participants' companies:

- how and why should supplier development be undertaken
- how to build partnerships in more than just name
- how to eliminate waste from the entire supply chain
- how to build synergistic inter-enterprise systems.

Given that businesses operate within a larger network of suppliers, buyers, intermediaries and competitors, the sources of competitive advantage lie partly within a given organisation and partly in the larger business network. Thus, sources of efficiency and effectiveness need to be exploited through integration of activities in the larger network. As a result the **Communications Between Organisations** project is designed to understand firstly, what communications are necessary and, secondly, to investigate the best tools to undertake this communication. It therefore endeavours to get past the rhetoric of IT and EDI in particular and by revisiting the strategic requirements for information exchange to define the most useful human and technological methods.

Stage 3: Analysis, synthesis and piloting

Once the field research work has been undertaken with both the sponsoring companies and other world class organisations the data needs analysing and synthesising into working methods that can usefully employed by participants in their respective journeys to excellence. In doing this it is useful to undertake piloting work with one or more of the sponsors. This allows these firms to gain priority access to the resulting models but also provides the other participants with an opportunity to learn from a practical implementation programme. This subsequently allows these firms to gain useful insights that can substantially reduce their learning curves when they come to implement such strategies and tools for themselves.

Stage 4: Dissemination and implementation

The fourth stage that runs concurrently with the first three is a series of regular workshop involving the sponsoring companies and the combined research team. These meetings allow for the active dissemination and implementation of a range of strategies, tools and techniques to companies that can then be diffused to a wider audience within these firms. These workshops are used to report on the latest research, pilot implementation programmes, other research carried out by the three universities as well as significant advances made by other academics or companies outside the group. In addition the events provide an important networking opportunity between leading practitioners and academics for discussion, debate and exchange of information to the benefit of all.

As mentioned above, the Supply Chain Development Programme was launched in the autumn of 1993 and is already producing some interesting results as well as forming the agenda for change in the world in which the modern purchasing and logistics professional lives. As such, the existing sponsors are increasingly learning from the programme and each other. In creating this programme, the 12 participants were invited to join on the basis of their pre-eminent positions within their own industrial sectors. It was the firm intention of the research directors only to involve those that were already regarded as well above average and who understood the necessity to become world class through a continual improvement culture. In addition, all the firms that have joined the programme have a firm commitment to the sharing of knowledge both with the researchers and the other participants. The existing membership profile is dominated by the grocery chain, the automotive chain and the electronics chain, with participants coming from:

> Bass Brewers
> Birds Eye Walls
> Britvic Soft Drinks
> Calsonic Llanelli Radiators
> Clarks International
> IBM UK
> Lever Brothers
> Northern Telecom (Europe)
> Pedigree Petfoods
> Tesco Stores
> Unipart Group
> Van den Bergh Food

To date the work has been going very well and although the programme has been kept on a low profile outside the group; there have already been several requests to join the group from interested companies and organisations. This possible growth path was discussed with the existing participants, who decided that their group was already large enough, but suggested that a second group might be formed that could benefit from the activities of the first, and vice versa. As a result a similar second group was launched on 1 January 1995 consisting of no more than 15 corporate members. A number of members have already been assigned and potential members identified based on informal approaches and the networks of existing members and the research directors. However, in order to develop a balance, particularly outside the more well-researched industries, a small number of places were made available for innovative firms wishing to set the agenda for the next decade, and gain access to the benefits of an interactive and highly customer-focused research programme.

Best practice around the supply chain

Keith Smith describes the experience of helping to set up a Best Practice Club for logisticians

Part of the remit of the Centre for Logistics at Newcastle Business School is to support and promote the development of best practice in the supply chain. One of the most productive ways we have found of doing this is to set up and run a Logistics Best Practice Club for a group of firms in the North of England. There was already a natural precursor on which to model ourselves because the Business School had for four years run a manufacturing best practice club which had proved very successful indeed. There were also a number of similar clubs around the country which focused on the supply chain.

Being a historian by training, I often think that it is just as instructive to learn about the origins of an organisation, how it was put together, what problems were encountered on the way, as to examine it now. With the Logistics Best Practice Club, we are still in the early stages. So, perhaps it would be relevant to ask how we went about setting it up. What interest was there? What were companies' expectations? and how successful is it now?

Obviously, first of all, some background research took place in which we examined existing clubs, talked to organisers and had a look at their programmes of activity to see what exactly made them tick, and what their underlying approach was. Did they focus on the firms themselves, or were they more wide-ranging, picking up on various themes and inviting expert external speakers to their meetings? Some certainly were like that. But that begs the question: is there then much difference between their regular meetings and those of a professional institute? The experience of the manufacturing club was that firms learn most from each other rather than from any outside party. In fact one can perhaps see a model of progression in which, say 10 years ago, to get a wider view of the world, a firm would employ a consultant. Five years ago, the emphasis shifted somewhat to partnerships with academics via such vehicles as the Teaching Company Scheme. But now active learning from other companies is 'flavour of the month'. It seemed natural, therefore, to set up such a club in the North of England.

But, how were we to proceed? Who were to be the members? Luckily, at the Centre for Logistics, we have a very strong network of external contacts, so our first move was a presentation of our ideas to our Industry Advisory Board, which consists of senior practising logistics managers. This enabled u to get a small, strong core membership of two or three companies with which we were familiar, and which were willing to work with us. Secondly, we approached members of the manufacturing club to see if any of their logistics colleagues wanted to join a more focused club concerned solely with supply chain matters. Again, this threw up another two or three companies which were already converts to the idea, and therefore ideal founder members. After that it was a case of cold-calling on companies which we thought would give the club breadth as well ad depth; companies across a range of industries covering all channels - manufacturing, distribution, retail and service - and companies of all sizes. Frankly, we were amazed how positive the feedback was in this exercise. Virtually every company expressed an interest, and the only apparent reason for not taking things further was an inability to give the required commitment.

Having gathered a group of companies which were interested in the idea of learning from one another, convinced of the possibility of transferring best practice in the supply chain, the next step was to reach some consensus on what it was that the companies actually wanted to do, bearing in mind that we were there just to facilitate things. A first meeting was therefore called for interested parties, and I arranged for a colleague who runs the manufacturing best practice club to make a presentation on what its companies had achieved over the last four years, what had been the approach, and how the club was actually run. In the event it was agreed in discussion afterwards that our format should follow virtually the same pattern - a #150 annual fee, regular monthly meetings an the venue to be a different member company's premises each month.

However, surprisingly difficult to achieve was some consensus on the objectives of the club, an the detailed mechanics of how it would work. I had thought that the companies would be interested in the 'big issues', and therefore to get the ball rolling I proposed that we concentrate on three main themes in the first year - people, partnership and information technology. it turned out though that everyone had their own idea as to what they saw as issues they wanted the club to deal with; some were at a strategic level, some at a tactical level, and some quite definitely at a day-to-day operational level. Everyone also had their own ideas as to how the club should be run, when it should meet, who should be involved and so on! After a short round table at one of our first full meetings it was agreed that I should circulate a questionnaire in order to get an overview, and try to come up with an agreed statement on the way forward. After completing some background information, the respondents to the questionnaire were simply asked:

- Are you willing to become an active member of the club?
- When would you be willing to share the strengths and weaknesses of your own operation with other group members?
- Do you have any serious problems about meeting once per month at four o'clock on a Wednesday?
- Are you willing to pay #150 a year membership fee, entitling your company to have two representatives at every meeting?
- Will you be able to influence your MD or other senior management to participate when relevant?
- Are there any companies/organisations you feel strongly should be members?

They were then asked to comment freely on how they thought the club should develop, and any other issues they would like to raise.

At this stage 10 firms indicated they would like to be active members. This represented a really good nucleus with a reasonable spread of activity - heavy manufacturing, retail/road distribution, pharmaceuticals, food retail, infrastructure/service, household products, manufacturing, logistics, service and manufacturing. However, most were large companies, and one smaller company commented that 'it is intimidating and also at times self-defeating where members have the in-house support of HRM, Logistics, production etc when the members from smaller companies carry out these roles themselves. A good mix of company size and sector would help to generate meaningful discussion'. Well put - and something we decided to act on.

Only one company jibbed at the #150 a year fee (to cover running costs, admin time and catering where necessary) and, as you would expect, everyone had different ideas as to when meetings should take place, but we decided to tick to the proposed time which was generally regarded as OK.

Everyone thought that they could get other members of their management team to participate when relevant, and this was important because the manufacturing club was finding that the key decision makers in the company were unable or unwilling to see the importance or relevance of some of the findings their members wished to implement.

Other points made were:

'I think that the club should develop around a set of key goals where we can make improvements for the good of our respective companies and the industry as a whole. The way forward on this, I think, is to establish a number of key logistics areas to concentrate upon. To determine this, I think each club member should introduce 10 or so, through a questionnaire ... a definite and focused effort is required by all members, otherwise the club will fail ...'.

'Best practice is essentially an interchange of views, policies and strategies. It may even cover the intuitive elements of successful management. Whatever we call it, there is a strong element of benchmarking in the interchange. A structured agenda is, I feel, a distinct need for this kind of meeting..'.

'I fully support the idea of an active group of like individuals who wish to discuss the logistics issues that we face in business today. I have no doubt of the potential benefits to be gained from open and frank discussion, even if the companies on the surface are significantly different in terms of product, size or market. In addition the benefits from creating close links to university resources should not be underplayed ... recognising that some issues may be specific to particular market sector or business types, selection of suitable topics may prove limiting in time. However, I am sure the common ground within the topics already raised offers ample opportunity for discussion over the coming year'.

Lastly, one company participant stated: 'I would prefer to start with an open mind, and not be constrained t the start.'

I think it is worth emphasising that if something like this is to be a success, then this sort of process - which sometimes seems like going 'round the houses' - is inevitable.

Everybody has to be happy that they have had their say, that they have contributed to the direction that is being taken, and that they feel comfortable with what is happening. Further discussions led us to follow through one point, and issue the second, and for the time being, last questionnaire. The purpose of this was to get members to note what they regarded as priority issues and also where they had had both good and bad experiences, for right from the start, everyone had indicated that it was a key task of the club to look at problem areas for individual members and to try to bring to bear the combined experience, knowledge and enthusiasm of the club as a whole, to indicate a way forward.

The questionnaire was divided into four area: people, partnership, IT and other - and some subject headings were suggested under each area. But it was really left to respondents to indicate their own issues. All they were asked to do was:
1 Indicate areas of interest: Good experience? Bad experience? would like to know more.
2 Use spaces to insert their own headings
3 Indicate some priority, by circling their top five areas of interest.

What came out of all this was very interesting. The top 10 issues weighted to include the results of question 1 as well as question 3 in descending order of importance were:
Shared delivery services
Bar coding
Motivation of staff
Payment systems
Partnerships with suppliers
EDI/POS
Partnerships with customers
Global positioning systems
NVQs and employment issues
Europallets and pallet control systems

So, a complete mix of all theme areas, containing both strategic and operational elements.

What was finally agreed was that we should proceed with 'getting to know you' meetings at each member company, for obviously it was important for this process to take place in order to enable the club to gel. If this was to be a true *active learning* group then we needed to know all about the member companies, their background, mission statements, priorities, problems - in effect what made them tick. But at the same time, at each meeting, the member company was to take two issues of his own choosing from the above list, talk about his own experiences in those area, good or bad, and open up a round-table discussion on them.

This format - four o'clock meeting, buffet, welcome, introduction to the company, tour and round-table discussion - will, I am sure, serve us well for the rest of the year. All the meetings have now been timetabled, and everyone is really keen to press on with the programme. At the end of the year we can then review where we are, and change the emphasis as we see fit. But by that time we will all have some knowledge of each others' operations, and a perception of each others' strengths and weaknesses. We will be able to make a more balanced judgement of what our priorities should be.

Incidentally, whilst all this was going on, we were not idle. 'Getting to know you' meetings were taking place, at which there were discussions centering around the three big themes with which we had started. it may be worth giving a flavour of the first of these.

After a short introduction, tour of the site and review of current operations, the future direction of the company was suggested. This was particularly interesting and fluid because an MBO was being organised, and this in fact made the round table discussion very pertinent, because the host was for that reason anxious to introduce best practice into his supply chain operation as soon as possible.

In terms of IT, the company recognised that it was behind the times, but felt that this presented plenty of opportunities for making real progress in terms of increased efficiency and provision of better and more tailored services for customers. Barcoding of its containers was certainly one issue it wanted to examine as well as in-cab keyboard entry of traffic details. An interesting parallel was drawn here with a process-manufacturing member which used keypad entry for noting the details and paths of its basic raw material. This led on to a discussion of what it was that customers might want; and it was agreed that in this day and age there was no reason why real-time tracking of products and containers could not take place. Customers could then start to take account of stocks in transit when planning their production or through-put schedules, what some of the more sophisticated operators call 'virtual stock'. In this particular company, it was felt that one of the constraints which had held it back was the big-company mentality which meant common standards and systems and a reliance on mainframe solutions when perhaps what was really needed was local hardware and software at a much cheaper price. The key suggested by a few members was having a common database and allowing everyone access to a common set of information (and trying to overcome any problems of confidentiality on the way); but it was the link with the customer which was highlighted as being so important.

Inevitably at this point, the meeting went on to consider the issue of partnership. Who in the supply chain should be forming partnerships, how should they do it? What did the various parties want out of such an arrangement? Different levels of relationship were discussed and analysed. Examples were quoted, and the power play involved felt to be significant. After all, someone has to initiate a partnership and most examples involve the control of the supply chain relationship by one party. At a more basic level, it was important to ask how many companies actually knew what their customers wanted - in detail. Probably for this to happen you needed multi-level linkages between the parties. It was more important that operational people should be talking and sharing information than that buyers and national account managers should be meeting occasionally. A huge subject area was opened up, one which we will obviously be exploring further.

The last theme - people: how to manage and motivate them, was important to the company not only because of the changes which had taken place but also because it was at a critical point of change. The current situation was that manning levels had been reduced and multi-skilling introduced, but staff were on a very low basic wage, which they needed to top up by heavy overtime working. There we also still too many levels of management and supervision, and more than one union on site. If the MBO were to succeed, what was the way forward?

Member of the Best Practice Club proved to have varying experiences of methods of award, promotion and motivation. One company making health and beauty care products very successfully locally was now outperforming many of its US sister plants. Underpinning these creditable levels of performance was, of course, the workforce. There was no union and no consultation, but there was plenty of communication. And there was a flat structure in place, lots of incentives, good rewards (the company always made sure, for instance, that it was in the top quartile where basic levels of pay were concerned), and a positive culture. Other comparisons were made. But the interesting question is, of course, how transferable many of these solutions are. This led to much discussion.

To conclude, the format of the meeting meant that the three key issues we had started with were batted around at both a strategic and operational level. The group was small enough to gel almost immediately, and the discussion was very free flowing. There was a reluctance perhaps to cut the meeting short, but on the other hand a recognition that there was much to be taken forward to other meetings!

So, although an article like this can give only a flavour of our North of England Logistics Best Practice Club, I really do believe that its time has come. Members do have a lot to learn from each other. We have already, in it short life, proved that best practice within the supply chain is transferable (a proposition, incidentally, which many senior managers seem to doubt); and the people in the club are clearly enjoying themselves. There is a real sense of excitement in company-to-company learning which rubs off on everyone involved. What more could you ask?